ellsworth mason

MASON ON LIBRARY BUILDINGS

the scarecrow press, inc., metuchen, n.j., & london, 1980

Library of Congress Cataloging in Publication Data

Mason, Ellsworth.
  Mason on library buildings.

  Includes index.
  1. Library buildings. 2. Library architecture.
I. Title. II. Title: On library buildings.
Z679.M22   022'.3   80-12029
ISBN 0-8108-1291-6

This book is dedicated to a very fine librarian

and even better wife, Joan Shinew Mason,

and a remarkably interesting young man,

my son Sean,

with love and pride

and forgiveness for ten thousand interruptions.

TABLE OF CONTENTS

"A university library, a great up-to-date library, is a very complex product of architecture and engineering, and I have read with astonishment the list of industries, represented by thirty-two sub-contractors and twenty suppliers, which have contributed to make this edifice what it is. When one considers the rate at which *necessary* books must be acquired by a university library . . . one begins to understand something of the forethought, skill and industry that must go to the design and construction of the building to house the books so that the needs of readers and of staff may be met, and the books themselves cared for properly."

T. S. Eliot's address at the
opening of the Sheffield
University Library in 1959

PREFACE

The problem is simple to state and impossible to encompass. There are more than half a million details in the plans for a library building of a hundred thousand square feet. The aim of planning the building is to make sure that every detail is: (1) the best of the possible alternatives to serve its unique purpose; (2) the final choice from plans that have shifted constantly for a year; (3) the detail intended by the planners and no last minute ad-hoc change; and (4) that it is directly related to the functional requirements of the library operation. The multiplicity of details alone makes for error and mis-communication, and the entire process is infinitely complicated by the fact that during the long period of planning, various members of the architect's staff develop the plans, each lacking the detailed information developed through his predecessor's experience. In addition, while architects' plans are developing, four different teams of specialists in structural, mechanical, and electrical engineering and plumbing are developing in separate offices, often in different cities, plans which must coordinate with each other and with the architectural plans.

This multifarious process is clearly chaos-prone to a high degree, and to achieve even approximate success takes a great deal of effort and more knowledge than I have ever seen brought to bear on a single building. Over the past twenty years, in planning and consulting on more than a hundred and twenty buildings, I have seen the major forces that make for a good planning situation come together right only eight times.

The observations that follow are reports back from the field by one who has been there, seen the range of mistakes that have been made, and the range of excellence achieved, and has studied for a long time the spectrum of dynamics in the planning process from shovel-carrier to architect's office, to understand what makes things go well or badly.

Despite our descent into practical details of planning, I hope to convey in some measure some of the exhilaration of building, and the soaring revelation that accompanies great architectural spaces. Years ago Jonathan King, then vice-president of Educational Facilities Laboratories, said that he liked my ability to write interestingly about things generally considered to be cultural plagues. I hope he was right, because the combination of shortage of funds and intensification of library costs makes serious thinking about every detail in a library building planned today critically necessary.

The Council on Library Resources asked what kind of a book this was to be. I replied that it was not like an integrated novel, but more like a collection of related short stories. We already have a good simple book on how to plan libraries by Ralph Ellsworth and a monumental treatise on library planning, encyclopedic in extent, by Keyes Metcalf. There has been in addition a range of writing on separate practical aspects of library buildings for the past thirty years. On the average it is not very good and much of it is painfully amateurish. Writing about library buildings after your first experience with one is a little like writing about Love after your first experience with sex.

What I miss in almost all the literature is depth and sophistication of understanding of the subject treated. This is a critical lack, because an understanding of the building in depth, even while it evolves in skeletal form in floor plans, is the essence of successful library planning. In all the literature I miss treatment of the planning process as humanly experienced by the planner, as something that living people do, rather than a performance according to an instruction sheet.

The intention of this book is to share with readers a wide range of experience in library planning and construction that runs a gamut through elementary, secondary, high and prep schools, community colleges, four-year colleges, urban and emerging universities, large established research universities, and private research libraries. In addition to the facts presented, my observations attempt in a variety of ways to lead readers to an understanding of how a building emerges, the kinds of complexities involved in the process of planning, and to equip them with tools to perceive more deeply when they look at library buildings.

Experiences in human terms are presented to show the kinds of shaping forces, often unexpected but generally controllable through skill, that intrude on processes that ought to proceed logically and smoothly. Much of this information is given in the footnotes, tucked away at the ends of chapters for those who prefer uninterrupted reading. Their rangy style owes a great deal to the footnotes in Bernard DeVoto's remarkable trilogy on the exploration and settlement of our country, especially to those of *Across the Wide Missouri,* one of the richest and wisest history books ever written.

If along the way I seem to neglect the literature on library buildings, let me state that I have soaked in it for a very long time. I simply have not found much of it worth sopping up, especially in literature of the past six years. We are still in a state of decline in professional standards that began in the mid-'60s. Putting aside for the moment the matter of literacy, the number of writers who combine sound knowledge with disciplined thinking and sensitively accurate observation is minuscule.

This book emerges primarily from experience with academic libraries, but its general concerns are applicable to other kinds of libraries. It presents American practice in library building planning. I have seized the occasion to present three significant Canadian libraries, out of deep admiration for Canadian librarianship and the methods the Canadians are developing, from which we can learn. Architectural practice in Canada, which has produced at least three cities whose architectural design far outstrips anything we have except Chicago, is massively ignored by the American architectural press, centered in that unreal city, New York.

A lifetime is not long enough to acknowledge all those who have helped me become this book, since in forty years of librarianship I have never asked for help from my betters without receiving it. Specific acknowledgements are made in footnotes to the separate chapters. Here I must acknowledge the aid of the Educational Facilities Laboratories and the Hofstra University Research Fund which financed trips to the Sedgewick Library (at the University of British Columbia), the Countway Library (at Harvard), and the Rockefeller Library (at Brown). A generous travel grant from the Council on Library Resources enabled me to review the Dalhousie University Library, the University of Toronto Library, and once again (ten years after) the Countway.

I give thanks to the help rendered by:

Herman Liebert, Kenneth Nesheim, and John Ottemiller on the Beinecke Library.

David Jonah and Charles Churchwell at Brown University.

Ralph Esterquest and Foster Palmer at the Countway.

Louis Vagianos, Mrs. Dorothy Cook, and Alan MacDonald at Dalhousie.

Robert Blackburn and M. J. McCahill at the University of Toronto Library.

Basil Stuart-Stubbs and Ture Erickson at the University of British Columbia.

I owe specific debts of learning to Ralph Ellsworth, Ruth Weinstock, Danforth Toan, Eugene Mackey, Theodore Wofford, Dolores Miller, John Kraehenbuehl, and George Rainer, which I gratefully acknowledge here. Any enterprise that emerges from interaction with remarkable people like these should be worthwhile.

I give special thanks to Lyn Sheehy and to Sonia Jacobs, my two fine assistants, who typed this manuscript over a long stretch of time and saved me from many crudities and errors.

E. M.
Boulder
1978

PART I

LIBRARY BUILDING PROBLEMS

A Brief Overview of Library Building Planning
Writing the Library Building Program
Library Lighting
Air-Handling Systems in Libraries
Interior Design in Libraries

CHAPTER 1

A BRIEF OVERVIEW OF LIBRARY BUILDING PLANNING*

Many academic libraries have been built in the past 25 years, but only a handful of them are very good. The architect is sometimes the source of failure, but more often the client has demanded unreasonable results from a poverty budget or has imposed an impossible timetable on the planning. Most bad library buildings result from the inability of the client, through ignorance and bad planning procedures, to state clearly to the architect what he wants in a building and why he wants it, and to conduct negotiations to their conclusion in successful plans. Even today it is astonishing how poorly understood are the elements of good library planning, despite well-documented examples of totally good planning methods that have led to good library buildings.[1]

The Planning Committee

The first step in planning a library building, and one of the most important, is the appointment of a local planning committee and the establishment of proper organizational procedures for negotiating on plans with the architects. If a power struggle develops within this committee, decisions are thrown back to the architects. Architects cannot produce a good library building, whose problems are complex and sensitive, without constant, informed review of their planning by the clients. The role of each member of the committee must therefore be carefully spelled out in writing to the entire committee.

The librarian is a key member of the committee because so much of the planning involves library technicalities, which are extremely complex and sophisticated at present. Without a strong librarian, it is impossible to achieve a totally successful library building. He should be released from half of his administrative load by additions to his staff while planning the building. The librarian's special function should be to project, with his staff, the building implications inherent in future operations and to work more closely with the library building consultant than other committee members can. He should draft the library building program for review by the committee. Most important, he must be the one responsible for the exacting, detailed review of each set of plans and variations in plans that go on for more than a year.

If the librarian is weak or unable to learn with the guidance of a library building consultant the new skills and ideas required to manage the planning details, the committee must use the consultant for this crucially important function. In such a situation, the consultant must be involved much more constantly in the planning than otherwise would be necessary.

The head of the campus planning office should represent on the committee a specialized knowledge of design and construction and campus planning problems, but he should not be allowed to control the design

---

*Footnotes to this chapter begin on page 10.

of the building. He should represent the campus administration, who should receive from him a constant flow of information through frequent formal reports. No member of the higher administration or the board of trustees should be on the committee, since their position would lend undue weight to their reactions. However, the chairman of the planning committee should participate in all meetings of the administration or the trustees that discuss the library building. Decisions thought unimportant at such meetings have undone many a library building.[2]

The faculty members of this committee must have a proven interest in the library's welfare and be of high standing among their faculty peers. They should form a two-way information channel, to discuss with the faculty and report back to the committee, throughout the planning. They should concern themselves particularly with those aspects of the building which are pertinent to student and faculty use.

When the administration has appointed a strong committee, defined in writing each member's function, and issued instructions for periodic reporting, the committee should be empowered as the *only* body on campus to negotiate plans with the architects. Impatient pleas to the administration from any source, however reasonable they seem, must be referred to the committee as the center for negotiations, since the administration cannot possibly be informed enough to make unilateral decisions. All local differences must be settled locally and through the committee. More buildings are damaged, and some in a major way, by architects who have access to the administration behind the committee's back than by any other factor.[3]

The Consultant

Immediately after this committee is formed, a library building consultant should be appointed. He should serve as a guide in planning and a constant reviewer of planning documents throughout the planning process. It is a waste of money to hire him for only a few days, because the problems which occur constantly during the development of drawings are shifting, remarkably varied, and totally unpredictable. Merely to detect them requires a background of experience which cannot be developed on campus even under the best condtitions.

The consultant will charge about $250 per day, plus expenses (in 1978). If he is good, he will save the institution ten times his total fee in actual savings on the final cost of the building. In addition, he will speed the planning process, ease the way for the architect to achieve his peak performance, and maximize the usefulness of the building, with consequent savings in the cost of running the library when it is completed. A library building consultant must be hired by the client, even if the architect has hired his own, since he must represent the client's interests in negotiations with the architect.

The consultant should be brought on campus as soon as possible. He will need a day or two to get the feeling of the physical plant and the educational dynamics and trend of the institution. He will discuss possibilities of site, outline the proper sequence of planning steps, indicate sources of information, discuss the future of the entire library system, predict implications of nonbook media, including the computer, for the local situation, suggest library buildings to be inspected, suggest architects for consideration, describe what negotiations with the architect involve, and warn against pitfalls. In general he will focus in the minds of the committee a vague and chaotic situation and start it along the preliminary steps that must be taken before the building program can be written.

The consultant should be intimately involved in developing and reviewing the program. He should review every version of preliminary plans, well into working drawings, and review final working drawings. Much consultation can be done by mail or by phone, but the consultant should be present at every meeting in which the weight of his experience and expertise is needed to establish confidence in the proceedings of the planning committee. It is especially important for him to participate in meetings with the architects at which the general concept of the building is presented and at subsequent meetings until the direction of planning is definitely set. Subsequent to construction bid drawings, he should be consulted on the special problems involved in planning stack bid documents, and, if he has aesthetic skills, should be used to review presentations of the interior design as they develop.

Sources of Information

As soon as possible, the committee should begin to read significant literature on library buildings. The literature of this field is vast, repetitive, and extremely uneven in quality. Fortunately, a few key books on planning academic libraries provide an excellent foundation for neophytes. The most important is Keyes D. Metcalf's *Planning Academic and Research Library Buildings* (New York, McGraw-Hill, 1965), a massive and extremely thorough treatise on every conceivable building problem, which should be studied and kept at hand for reference during the entire planning process. This book contains a useful annotated bibliography. A much shorter and simpler introduction to the subject is Ralph E. Ellsworth's *Planning the College and University Library Building* (Boulder, Colo., Pruitt Press, 1968). By far the best collection of articles on specialized aspects of library building is Hal B. Schell, ed., *Reader on the Library Building* (Englewood, Colo., Microcard Editions Books, 1975).

The Educational Facilities Laboratories in New York City are a source of information about new problems in library buildings, especially those involving the use of nonbook media, and can recommend consultants for most aspects of library planning. The Library Administration Division of the American Library Association in Chicago maintains a collection of library building programs and library floor plans, available on interlibrary loan, and a list of library building consultants with a summary of buildings on which they have consulted.

Study of Library Buildings

All information about three-dimensional facilities requires solidification by observation: after reading about library buildings the next step is to visit a number of libraries at similar colleges or universities. They should be selected carefully with advice; a study of bad buildings wastes time and is confusing. The librarian and at least two members of the planning committee should visit together, so that future reference to these libraries will have a common basis of understanding.

This study visit should aim at observing meticulously all aspects of the library and gathering information about sizes, shapes and brands of furniture and equipment, and the names of consultants, architects, or other good specialists. Traffic patterns and acoustics should be observed, and the function of each of the library elements carefully analyzed. Much of the best information about the virtues and shortcomings of the building will come from the library's department heads. In addition to a study of details, the committee should pay special attention to the site, the building's exterior and interior design, its lighting, and its temperature comfort level.

By this time, the committee will have a good deal of information about architects who have designed successful libraries—and the architect should be chosen on no other basis. At least two of his libraries must be visited and studied before he is hired. It must be understood that an architect is not one man but a firm, with various levels of talent on its staff. The university must make sure that the staff that has planned successful libraries in the past, or a strong core of it, will be used on its job. Frequently this is not the case.

Basic Decisions

The architect can advise on the site location, but he should not begin thinking about the nature of the building until the library building program is completely finished and handed to him in a dozen mimeographed copies. Before the program can be started, the administration must make the following series of basic decisions, which must be firm, realistic, and stated in writing: (1) the time period, stated in years, for which the library is intended to serve, *after* it is open; (2) The maximum student enrollment, broken into significant segments, during that time period; (3) the percentage of that enrollment which the library plans to seat at one time; and (4) the maximum book collection to be housed during the life of the building. These statistics must not be drawn out of a hat but should be developed responsibly with the aid of those on campus who are most informed about these various factors.

The budget is *not* a basic decision that should be made in advance. The library building program should emerge intelligently from the quantities stated above and must estimate accurately the net area required. This can be converted by formula to gross area. It then will be apparent how much the building is likely to cost; and the budget can be set. Obviously, no loaves-and-fishes act can produce money when not enough exists, but intelligent basic decisions can now be made about revising the library planning, whereas they cannot be made before the program is developed.

If the size of the building is reduced, accurate estimates will indicate how many years its space will last and provisions for expansion or alternate arrangements made. Recent experience indicates that most libraries will have storage facilities for less-used books within the next ten years. It is therefore extremely important to plan the library building large enough to house a collection of a critical mass to provide a high enough response to users when they look for books to keep them returning to the library.

Writing the Program

The library building program should emerge from an outline of the building elements to be included in the library that has been worked out with the library building consultant. Ideally, first drafts of the specifications of the units should be written locally, revised by the consultant, reviewed locally, and then fully outfitted with detailed lists of furniture and equipment and accurate square footage estimates for each unit by the consultant. The process of writing the program for a building of 200,000 square feet will take about three or four months, and no less than three months for smaller academic libraries.

Problem Areas

Three areas of the building are particularly difficult to plan—the main floor, the technical processes areas, and special collections areas. The main floor requires a larger area than can be conveniently massed with the rest of the building's requirements because so much of the library's operation must be close to the main card catalog. One solution is to have a large main floor which becomes a platform for a tower of considerably smaller dimensions. The platform may consist of one to three stories depending on the size of the project. On a sloping site the main floor may be cantilevered, producing a design which is both artistic and functional.

Ideally, the technical processes should be close to the card catalog, their basic tool, but competition for space can drive them from such proximity to some other part of the library building even when they are properly located to begin with. If the technical processes are removed from proximity to the catalog, they may as well move out of the library building, and the future of technical processes may involve placing them in a separate building, much cheaper to construct than library square footage and planned for easy and cheap expansion.

No totally satisfactory rare book library, or special collections department in a general library, has yet been built. The problems of ultraviolet-light control from windows and fluorescent lights, temperature and humidity control, air filtration, fire prevention, the hazards of electrical and water systems, and exhibition cases have never been satisfactorily solved in one library. The way is open for any library willing to undertake the study required to solve these problems before planning the first totally successful special collections facility.

Subject Organization

Library organizational arrangements based on subject specialties are capable of a wide range of solutions, especially in larger universities. The solutions, which must answer sensitively actual needs of the instructional program, vary with each institution, but a few generalizations can be made from recent experiences with these problems. The practice of establishing separate subject areas for the humanities, social sciences, and sciences within a central library has largely been discontinued because of numerous difficulties found to exist in systems presently established. Separate departmental libraries within buildings occupied by the corresponding faculty have given way, with the overlapping of disciplines, to the combination of similar disciplines into divisional libraries or larger group libraries. Physical facilities for both departmental and divisional libraries, when part of office-classroom buildings, have been badly planned, almost without exception, because their planning has been largely in uninformed hands, more concerned with faculty office and classroom problems. There is at present a heavy trend to dissolve subject branch libraries and undergraduate libraries into the central library, because of staff shortages in universities.

Mechanical Systems

Security can be obtained by guards at exits controlled by turnstiles, a system not aesthetically pleasing and not entirely effective, but better than nothing. In recent years, libraries have installed electronic detecting systems at exits. Such systems should be investigated before the building is planned, since conduits have to be poured into the structure at fixed locations to provide for them.

Interior communications by loudspeaker systems are an anathema in libraries. Interconnected internal telephones and chime-signals or radio-signal devices to summon individuals to telephones are preferred.

Vertical movement of books should be supplied by key-summoned staff elevators wherever the building requires them. Enough should be supplied to avoid long staff waiting. Mechanical book-conveyor systems from the stacks and mechanical book return systems to the stacks have long been used. Book lifts of the dumbwaiter type should not be used, because they require double loading of books in and out of the lift. Lifts sized to hold only book trucks can be used when economy dictates.

Fire authorities sometimes urge installation of sprinkler systems throughout the library for fire prevention. Since water is more destructive to books than fire and students set off sprinkler heads for fun, this provision should be resisted in favor of a heat- or smoke-sensing or ion detection system. These should be wired directly to the campus security office or the local fire department so that response to a fire is immediate. The first five minutes in a fire are crucial in determining its intensity.

Lighting in most library buildings is bad because few architects understand the basic principles of good lighting. Electrical engineers themselves are often not well informed about illumination engineering, which is no longer taught in most engineering schools. Consequently, the university must inform itself, by empirical evidence, about the kind of lighting fixtures that produce well-diffused, good *quality* lighting.

Temperature discomfort in buildings is common, and a careful study must be made of temperature zones planned for the building and the location of temperature controls during the drawing stage. Recently, with budgetary shortages, there has been a tendency to economize on heating, ventilation and air conditioning systems, and some of the results have been disastrous. It therefore is necessary to plan these systems at this time with greater care than ever before, while at the same time refraining from overbuilding them. An engineering consultant who specializes in ventilation systems should be used to review drawings of the entire system before plans are let out for bid.

Since the future will require more use of electrical machines for media, electronic calculators, and computer consoles, a premium is placed on providing the building with the greatest possible electrical flexibility. It should be possible, with a minimum of alteration, to tap electricity anywhere on the peripheral walls of a floor. Under-floor ducts should be poured into the building on six-foot centers in at least one direction wherever changes in electrical demand are expected. It should be possible to run cables and lines from floor to floor through vertical ducts, and one outlet should lead out of the building to connect with remote central production units.

Planning Standards

Seating: 20 per cent of the maximum student body at one time for resident campuses; 10 per cent for commuting institutions.

Shelving: 250 books per standard double-face section of 7 shelves. One double-face section will average 18 sq. ft. in stacks on 4′6″ centers.

Ceilings: 8′ minimum, 8′6″ preferable. Over 9′6″ should be avoided except for special effects.

Lighting: 70 footcandles of *good quality* light for all reading and work areas. Intensities below 50 footcandles drive students away.

Air conditioning: 75°F temperature, 35 per cent humidity in general; 70°F, 50 per cent humidity in rare-book areas.

Filtration: 85 per cent effective filtration of dust. In polluted atmospheres, activated charcoal filters must be added to extend the life of book paper. Ninety-five per cent filtration of dust plus activated charcoal filters for rare books.

Floor load: 150 pounds per square foot live load throughout. A load of 125 pounds is possible, but it limits where heavy units such as map cases can be located.

Column spacing: If stacks fall between columns, they require clear space that is a multiple of 3 ft. (for the stacks) *plus* 6 in. (4 in. for two end uprights and 2 in. to allow for irregularities in pouring).

Timetable

Haste is the worst enemy of successful buildings, and the following is a reasonable timetable for the planning of a library:

Reading literature—1 month.

Visiting libraries—1 month.

Writing the program—3 months.

Developing final preliminary drawings—6 to 7 months.

Developing working drawings—5 to 8 months, depending on size.

Calling bids—1 month.

Contracting and setting up machinery—1 month.

This is a total of 17 to 21 months from the beginning of planning to the time of breaking ground. It will take about a year and a half to build a library of 150,000 to 200,000 square feet, 2½ years for 500,000 square feet, 5 years for a million square feet.

Costs

While the distribution of costs varies greatly, some rule-of-thumb generalizations about library building costs can be made. In a university library, assuming no cost for the site, the following can be used as a general distribution of the total *project* budget:

Building costs	72%
Furniture and equipment, including stacks	15%
Architects fees	5% of project costs 7% of building costs
Administrative costs (legal, surveying, consultants, supervision)	2%
Contingency	6%

The *building* costs can be broken down as follows:

Structural (not including walls unless load bearing)	18%

Mechanical:

Electrical	11%
HVAC	17%
Plumbing	5%

Total mechanical costs 33%

Other (outer walls, interior walls and
finishes, windows, doors, etc.)   49%

These estimates are for high-quality construction and equipment, good lighting, and a well-designed interior.

Library costs in 1978 tended to run from $50 to $60 per square foot for the building, without furniture and equipment, depending on the extent of the building's provision for energy conservation (thermopane, heat recovery systems, etc.).

It is possible to hold costs down by using simple materials and inexpensive finishes. Usually, the lighting is skimped in an attempt to reduce the costs of libraries, cheap furniture is bought, and the interior design of the building is dispensed with. These sacrifices in the feeling of the building's interior inhibit use of the library and its collections by the students and faculty, a staggering waste of a very large investment as well as contrary to the central intention of a learning institution.

The largest factors that vary building costs are the intensity of bidding competition among contractors, which can send prices up or down unpredictably, and the costs of labor delays during construction. If it is necessary to finish a building by a specified date, it can cost ten per cent more than contracted costs in premium wages for overtime, standby labor, etc., to finish the building on time. Penalty clauses in contracts are nearly impossible to invoke successfully, and in the case of time pressures, it often pays to contract with a company other than the low bidder if its performance record indicates that it will deliver the building on time.

Construction Management

In recent years, the practice of using construction management firms during the planning and construction process has developed as a way of insuring the lowest possible costs for the building's requirements. Such a firm, if good, can save far more than its costs in the price of the building. In a period of rapidly soaring construction costs, such as that of 1968 to 1973, they can greatly help to phase construction in order to shorten the total planning-construction time. If a client is willing to make judgments on their recommendations, and take full advantage of their management skills while accepting higher costs for elements of the building that are architecturally important, they can contribute significantly to a building's quality and cost control, and greatly improve its schedule of completion.

Notes

1. This chapter is a revision of an article entitled "The Library Building," published in Asa S. Knowles, ed., *Handbook of College and University Administration.* New York, McGraw-Hill, 1965. 2 v. See pp. 4–19 to 4–27 of v. 2—Academic. It is republished here by permission of the McGraw-Hill Book Company.

2. In planning the Hofstra University Library the trustees decided, thinking it a small change, to substitute brick facing for a facing of preformed concrete panels that exposed fine pebbles quarried on Long Island's north shore. In planning the Dalhousie University Library (discussed below), the trustees changed the facing from Indiana limestone to Nova Scotia field stone to give their good local people some business. Both decisions were made when the design of the building was virtually complete. It took six months of strenuous effort to turn around the Hofstra decision, and the Dalhousie decision, when discovered by the Librarian, was beyond reversal.

3. Most of the disabilities of the Northwestern University Library are due to this condition.

CHAPTER 2

WRITING THE LIBRARY BUILDING PROGRAM*

(When the first version of this article was written in 1966 I complained at length about the fumbling, uninformed procedures of library building planners, who at that time tended to be optimistic amateurs looking to the architect for answers that they should have given him.[1] Since then the importance of writing programs has been solidly established, and enough good programs have been widely used as examples to insure that, at least for academic libraries, programs are nearly always better than adequate.

However, it is still generally true that no one on the planning team has had experience in planning libraries, and few have had any building planning experience. The tendency now is to totally underestimate the enormous demands on the planners if a good building is to be achieved. It is hard to convince neophytes of the remarkable amount of thought and imagination required to write a good program, and the endless amount of detailed communication, with the architect and a range of other specialists, necessary to produce good building plans. By the time plans are finished, every detail in them is laden with thought to the extent that few of them can be changed without repercussions echoing through a whole range of other details that have to be adjusted to fit the change.

Today, it still is as true as when I first was hurled, terrified and naked, into the process of planning a library building, that by the time plans are completed those most intimately involved with the planning have accumulated about the amount of knowledge they should have had before they began. To bridge this information gap someone deeply experienced in libraries and library planning must be involved in the process. As a Long Island library director said to me when he was well into the planning of his building, before he began he didn't think a consultant would be of any use, although his architect was required to hire one, but now he didn't know how you could possibly do without one.

In the past ten years, the data for planning the size of library buildings have shifted radically. Now the pool of candidates, rather than limitations of physical facilities, determines the projected size of the student body. Bursting budgets have curbed the continual expansion of acquisitions. At the same time, information accumulated about the actual use of specific kinds of materials and individual items in collections indicates that our former projections of the size of collections required, especially in serials, were too large.

Requirements for technical processes space, underestimated and quickly overrun in every sizeable library built in the 1960s, have been reduced by lower acquisitions and by computer access to cataloging data for books and serials. Computer Output Microfilm catalogs have reduced pressures for space at the main card catalog. Computerized circulation systems, though the most erroneous ever devised by man or beast, save room formerly occupied by charge-cards. On the other hand, space for on-line access to bibliographical data must now be planned.

---

*Footnotes to this chapter begin on p. 19.

Some new conditions have eased the planning of buildings. Specific counts of student use have indicated that the percentage of student FTE for which seating was projected in the past was generally too high. The entire field of non-book media, wild and woolly and completely brainless in the 1960s, has sloughed off most of its idiots and become practical and useful. At the same time, greater experience with space requirements for materials and machines and special users makes it easier to predict space for it.

One wholesome development in the past five years has been the reduction of time-pressures in writing the program and planning buildings. When construction costs were escalating one per cent each month, administrators wanted plans immediately. Now that architects are hungry and less busy, they can complete plans in a shorter time. At the same time, construction costs throughout most of this country have stabilized, though they still escalate slowly. Since, in my twenty years experience, unrealistic time schedules for planning have been the greatest destroyer of buildings, this is all to the good.)

* * * *

Most library buildings before the end of World War II emerged from the tradition that turned the project almost completely over to the control of the architect, who was to build a monumental building. Even in the late 1950s, in the planning of an addition, the Director of the University of Connecticut Library was ordered by the President not to inflict himself on the architect. Library planning did not begin to establish a firm base until a brand new kind of structure,[2] that emphasized function instead of appearance, rose to suggest that interior function, rather than exterior shape, was the most important requirement for a library and that beauty was really compatible with usefulness.[3]

At the same time in history, the complexity of a range of new technical factors in buildings (from new building materials to remarkably complicated air-tempering systems), broke architects loose from the fact that they could any longer work with the total knowledge that they used to command in planning a building.[4] In the 1960s, their most frequent complaint to me was about the extreme difficulty of getting a clear statement from their client of what he wanted in the building and why he wanted it. Fifty years after its pronouncement, Sullivan's "Form follows function" more or less dominated the tradition in American architecture from the mid 1950s until about 1970, at which point it again began to disintegrate into self-indulgent "artistic" expression.[5]

Architecture is a highly demanding profession. It requires a demanding training in its education, and architects work under very demanding conditions. It is one of the few professions left that has maintained its original integrity and dedication to applying its skills productively, rather than using them to gouge a better deal out of the public.[6] Architects are highly literate, imaginative people, and a delight for academicians to work with. Because they are highly persuasive, they are sometimes put in a commanding position in planning the building, rather than made one part of a planning negotiation.[7]

Aside from the fact that architects have only one of the two essential bodies of knowledge that must interact fruitfully to produce a good library building, my experience with more than eighty architects and long study of conditions within their operations convinces me that left to feed on himself the architect is likely to spin out of his innards a sticky web that will entrap the user rather than help him. The architect has his own problems, and the dynamics of his office constitute a very important reason for writing a program that tells him meticulously what is wanted in the building and why it is wanted.

First of all, the architect is a businessman; he has to make money to live. He runs an expensive operation, and cannot work exclusively on one project until it is finished, before he takes up the next one. At any one time he is working on many jobs. Every client pushes to have his job done fast, so the architect lives by rotating his attention among the clients, working on one job periodically, in turn with the others he has on the line.

This pressure makes for two dislocations. The best men in the firm work only occasionally on your plans. Although these are the men you will see in your negotiations, most of the work is done much lower down the ladder. At peaks of great pressure students from schools of architecture are hired to work part-time on plans even in highly reputable architects' offices. (One version of the plans for the Colorado College Library I conjectured had been drawn by the doorman.)[8] Secondly, the gaps in time between the spurts of working on a set of plans make for discontinuity in the architect's mind. That is why flaws carefully discussed and agreed upon in one set of plans are not corrected in the next set. Within the broad limits of professional conscience, the architect will do your job as rapidly and as easily as possible. One more factor complicates the planning in the architect's office. Despite the evidence of their neat meticulous drawings, architects are not orderly thinkers, like good librarians. Their temperament is essentially artistic,[9] and such grubby things as counting, to make sure that there are still seats for the programmed 200 students, do not come naturally to them.[10]

Since the process of planning in the architect's office is considerably less than totally controlled, the process of negotiating with architects involves detecting when they fall short of reasonable solutions and insisting on better ones. In order to be able to negotiate, the architect must be told precisely what is required in the building, and the librarian must understand, himself, what he wants. For these reasons the program is written.

A building program is a multi-headed document. It tells the architect what he should try to achieve. No one is likely to get everything he wants, but the program is his basic position in negotiating with the architect. Although its demands should be reasonable, it should not compromise; the time for compromise is later.

The program provides meticulous notes from the librarian to himself. When the 10,000 details have faded from his mind during the two-year period of planning and building, the program will remind him of what he originally intended, and how he conceived of various segments of the building. He should save his backing papers—the calculation sheets and the preliminary drafts of the program—because he will sometimes have to pursue his thoughts back that far to clarify a decision a year and a half later.

The program is a reference handbook for the architects to use throughout their planning. The easier it is to use, the more they will use it. It should, therefore, contain such reference elements as a table of contents, an index, summary lists of space requirements, and other useful summaries. It is easier to use if each separate library unit begins on a new page so that breaks between units are clear. A program is also a checklist, like one used to assemble equipment for a camping trip, to make sure that nothing is left behind at the last moment, when all looks complete. Finally, if it is at all good, the program will be a public relations document, since it will be borrowed by other schools that are planning libraries. It should be typed in meticulous graphic form, and mimeographed in a generous number of copies.[11]

I have referred to the process of working out building plans as a negotiation, which implies that there should be valid teams on both sides of the table, and I take it as axiomatic that it is not possible to develop satisfactory plans for a library building unless 1) there is a good librarian on the spot, thoroughly familiar with the dynamics of the present operation; 2) there are clear-cut administrative decisions on such matters as maximum student body for the period the new building is to serve, etc.; and 3) the librarian is in a central position on the university's team in the negotiations. If the librarian is weak and does not understand the library's needs, or if the architect is allowed access to someone behind the librarian's back to circumvent him (such as the president or business manager, who cannot possibly know what is going on), negotiation will be impossible.

The first requirement for the program, therefore, is a good librarian who has been given free reign to write it, within reason and subject to responsible elements in his community. What do we do if there is no good librarian on the spot? Who, then, will write the program? Some architects will do it, but my view of the negotiations in building planning insists on an interaction of counterbalancing skills, and in this case, the program should be written by a library building consultant, briefed fully on the dynamics of the institution, and allowed to get from the library staff and the librarian something of the feel of the operation.[12]

Ideally, the program should be written by the librarian, constantly consulting with his staff, because only if he has struggled with the thought involved in projecting imaginatively the dynamics of the operation for the period the building is intended to serve can he review with full understanding and sensitivity the plans as they develop. Most poor buildings fail because the dominant voice in the planning has not been able to see what movements, what materials, what equipment and furnishings, what kinds of feeling are required in each unit of the library building.

The purpose of the program is to define the library building for the architect as interacting separate units of the library operation in intellectual packages that the architect can comprehend and manipulate. Each unit must be specified in terms of square footage, and in terms of relationships to each other. This information enables the architect to mass the building by knowing which units must be grouped together on a common floor and which allow leeway in their placement.[13] Without this information (and buildings are sometimes planned without it), he cannot intelligently determine how many floors the building should have, or what the overall size should be. The program must further make the architect understand what will go on in each unit, since the internal arrangement of each depends centrally on human movements, which govern the arrangement of the equipment. If the program states clearly and intelligently 1) what units must be included in the library, 2) how large each one should be, and which must be grouped together, and 3) what will go on in each, the initial planning of the building is substantially complete. The subsequent problems involve getting the architect to respond to the program, which now provides the librarian with a basis of carefully developed thought that clarifies what he must require of the architect, and for what reasons.[14]

Let me emphasize what the program should *not* do. It should not usurp the proper function of the architect. It should not, for instance, tell him how many floors the building should have. If there is a height limitation above ground, for zoning or other reasons, if the building must be low or high, the architect should be so informed in the program, but he should be the one to propose how many floors the building should have; then the proposal can be discussed. Confusing oneself with the architect is analogous to confusing oneself with God, and that is the essence of *hubris* in the Greek tragedies, which leads only to destruction.

The architect will do his job as well as possible, within the limits of time pressures and professional consciousness. If something appears to be a given condition, he is not likely to think about it as thoroughly or as creatively as if the condition is flexible, and he may be discouraged from doing exactly what you are paying him a great deal of money to do—give you his version of what he thinks you should have in a building to meet the requirements you have presented him.

In addition, his past experience may have given the architect a low opinion of academicians as planners.[15] If he finds the client telling him what only he has the knowledge to tell the client, he will tend to treat him as an inferior in the negotiation process. This can lead to great difficulties. If the program indicates clearly what is required and why it is required in the building, if it shows that the client has addressed his problems intelligently, but with clear understanding of his own limitations, the architect is likely to respond well. It therefore is extremely important for the client not to play architect (which always is as incredibly naive as faculty playing librarians) at any time in the planning process, and very especially in the program.

It should not be necessary to give this warning, but there is something about the entire building process that leads normally sane people to mad and pretentious actions far beyond their field of competence. Twice have I seen a building, completely laid out by the client in an uninformed and unimaginative way, being pushed on the architect before he had been told what the client wanted and had a chance to think about it at all. In this direction madness lies.

Assuming, therefore, that the librarian knows what he is doing, and that he understands what he does not know, the program should do three central things: it should describe the dynamics of the institution that shape the library operation; it should pinpoint respectfully for the architect some elements of the building that need special attention; and it should specify each unit of the building.

The dynamics should be defined by a brief history of the institution, and a statement of its projections for the visible future. This statement should be short, and rigidly selected for the purpose of making the architect understand what will go on in the library in the future. Longwindedness is the enemy here; a five-page history of Old State U., replete with details of athletic triumphs, is more likely to confuse the explanation than clarify it, but there is nothing like a hired captive audience to bring out the divine afflatus in people, as some programs show. This statement should be pithy, succinctly written, and focused sharply on the library and its needs.

Study of library buildings similar to the one being planned should precede the planning, and the more buildings studied the more noticeable will be the fact that the same mistakes in libraries are repeated by architects. These tend to be period clichés. At one time they were Greek columns throughout, monumental stairways, and forty-foot ceilings. In the 1960s they were lighting, ventilation, and over-use of glass. At present building failures still tend to be lighting (which is getting worse), ventilation (which is getting worse), and a whole range of inhuman, illogical practices forced on buildings by the energy shortage strained through puny minds. We may end up building dungeons. It is highly appropriate, and necessary, after inspecting a number of buildings, to call the architect's attention in the program to problems commonly left unsolved in buildings, and ask him to pay particular attention to them.[16]

The Specification of the Library Areas is the most important part of the library program. It should arrange the units to be provided in the library building in groups, to encourage the architect to think of those within each group as related to each other. There is no absolute rule for these groups. I like to use seven categories: Introduction to the Library, Special Service Areas, Special User Facilities, Books and Readers, Administration, Technical Processes, and Miscellaneous.

I. Introduction to the Library—those units that should be located just inside the main entrance, plus the keys to the library materials, the general reference materials and services that students will use in preliminary exploration of the library's resources. There is a good deal of movement and noise connected with these preliminary explorations, and the student is likely to move from one unit to another before he proceeds to the stacks or to a seating area. Consequently, they should be thought about as a network of sensitive relationships. This section of the program includes the Vestibule, the Lobby and Control area, the Circulation desk and office, the Card catalog, the Reference and Bibliography area, the Periodical Index and abstracts area, and the Reference office.

II. Special Service Areas—include Reserve Books, Periodicals Reading Room, Audio-Visual, Special Collections, Government Documents, and Subject departments such as Education, Music, etc. These are small libraries that contain their own staff, materials collection, equipment for using them, and reader accommodations.

III. Special User Facilities—include New Books, Photoduplication department, Group Study Rooms, Smoking lounges and studies, Typing rooms, Seminar rooms, and the Library Instruction room.

IV. Books and Readers—include Graduate carrels, Faculty studies, General Seating, and General Shelving. These facilities relate readers of various kinds to the general stack collection.

V. Administration—includes the director, associate and assistant directors, their reception and secretarial area, an area for their business machines and records, and a conference room. Unless they have separate operations and equipment of their own, this is where the budget specialist, the systems analyst, and the collections development specialist should be located to encourage the most fruitful interaction between the administration and these specialists. Though this area should be easily available to the faculty and staff, it is far less important in the daily operations than the service areas and should yield to them if it is not possible to get everything desired on the main floor.

VI. Technical Processes—include the Order department, Catalog department, Serials department, Preparations department, and any other satellites of any of the technical services.

VII. Miscellaneous—includes convenience facilities such as Staff lounge and toilets, Custodial Rooms, Public Toilets, Elevators, Bookdrops, Exhibition walls and cases.[17]

So much for the grouping of library units. How does the librarian projecting plans ambitiously beyond his present building, decide which units he will program for his library? The easiest way is to study existing programs designed for successful building somewhere in the range of the size and nature of the one he is planning.[18] Study of such programs, added to the experience of visiting several library buildings, plus consultation with the librarian's faculty and staff, and some imaginative projection of what the new library could do that the old building cannot should complete the list of units to be included in it.

Let me emphasize here the necessity for local consultation and exploration before the program is finally written. It should go through a number of versions—three or four—before it is final. Each should be mimeographed and distributed widely to the staff and faculty for comments. Good ideas come from unexpected sources. Some of the best we received in developing the program for the Colorado College library came from a young woman, barely twenty-two years old, who had just begun to work as a circulation subprofessional assistant. She had almost no experience with libraries, but had imagination and the ability to visualize in reacting to the program. Some of her vision is embodied three-dimensionally and functionally in that building.

Comments invited from the faculty should be carefully evaluated. Along with the book-lined seminar room they may recall from Old State U., with its never-failing stock of books (like loaves and fishes), will come information about how the present operation fails to meet the needs of the institution, and some brand new points of view about the library. Ideas that make sense can be used, others forgotten, and the faculty will feel much more receptive to the new building for having been consulted. Their ultimate reaction to it will depend not on whether their suggestions have been accepted, but on its bookstock, its esthetic feeling, and its ease of use.

It can be extremely useful, if possible, to collect a massive response from students. In planning the University of British Columbia undergraduate library building, an exhaustive questionnaire of their preferences, which received enthusiastic response, was run in the student newspaper. The information collected participated heavily in determining the nature of that building. Lacking a massive response, a range of student reactions should be gathered by whatever means are available. These evaluations, again, must be carefully evaluated.

Three statistics underlie the writing of Specifications of the Library Areas: the total number of student seats to be provided, the total staff to be accommodated, and the total number of books to be shelved in the new building, at peak capacity for the period of time it is intended to serve.[19] The number of students seated will be a portion of the largest student body that the institution plans to enroll during this period. A firm statement on this basic fact must come from the top administration. Until 1970, college libraries tried to provide seats for one-third of their FTE or more. Since that time specific counts in more than thirty small residential liberal arts colleges have shown that (aside from exam study time) eleven per cent of student

FTE at maximum seating (which generally is only one hour in a semester) is typical in these colleges. Consequently, unless there is evidence of a drastic variation from this figure, library buildings should plan to seat twenty per cent of the student FTE.

The tendency in universities is much less uniform because their library systems are much more varied and complex, involving a division between undergraduate libraries, graduate libraries, and divisional libraries. Most students use more than one library. The problem requires analysis of the numbers projected for those segments of the student population that will use each building in the library system most heavily. Such a projection is difficult in the present state of education, when undergraduate and graduate level needs for books overlap, and when subject disciplines themselves are becoming far less definable than they have been in the past. Nevertheless, from experience decisions have to be made, on the basis of enrollment projections, of the maximum number of students that the new library building will seat. The total seating in a university library system with a sizeable residential population should be about 20 per cent of student FTE, but the percentage accommodated in the separate libraries, based on the estimated student FTE that concentrates on its specialty, will vary widely from Law, which will probably be the highest percentage, to Geology or Chemistry, if subject libraries are that finely defined. Total seating for an academic library with a largely commuting population should be about 10 per cent of FTE.

The total shelving requirement can be arrived at by assuming an ambitious aim, computing how many volumes must be added on the average per year for the projected period of the building's use to attain this figure, and extrapolating from this yearly average the peak number to be added in any one year. The reverse method is to project from current acquisitions the annual acquisitions, year by year, through the period the building is intended to serve. The total of these figures, added to the present collection, will indicate the ultimate size of the collection for which you must build.

The projection of stack capacity for a new building must take into consideration new factors, such as access to lending networks, greater ease in obtaining locations of books in other libraries, cooperative retention of serial titles, and the very real fact that we all will be using remote storage facilities, on campus or within the area, in the future. Studying the actual use of individual books in the collection, through analysis of computer circulation records or otherwise, will make us feel more confident about selective storage. However, despite our enthusiasm for economy, we should make sure that the collection capacity of every element in the library, in specialized collections or the general collection, is large enough to house that size collection that forms the critical mass which encourages use by responding to sixty or seventy per cent of the needs of the user, on the spot and at the time that he tries to find books.

The ultimate staff for the building must be projected on the basis of the peak acquisitions (which should emerge from projections of collection capacity) and from the number of service points required by the building (keeping in mind that in larger libraries these are shrinking continually), analyzed in terms of the projected volume of use for each of them. Random sampling of current use at service points will give a basis for projections; however, if new service points are to be developed, an educated guess based on information from other libraries must be made. New library buildings characteristically have generated a fifty per cent increase in use within two years after opening.

Staff projections must be made not in terms of FTE or of permanent staff, but in terms of work stations. If three students will work in an area at the same time as the permanent staff, additional stations must be provided for them. There is at present a trend to use more part-time staff and more students than were formerly used, and many libraries have developed highly effective cadres of volunteer workers, all of whom must be taken into account in projecting staff for each area.

These three basic statistics—total seating, total shelving, and staff work stations— are applied to each of the units in the program to determine the furniture and equipment that must be supplied and to estimate their square footage requirements. At this point in the program it is extremely important to understand the human movements of each unit—the likely traffic patterns, and how much noise will result from them. The necessary and desirable relationships between units must be described. The program states which other areas each must be near, and which areas it would be helpful to be near. Beyond that, nothing should be said about arrangements. The program should not require the documents area to be in the basement if there is no cogent reason why it must be there. The architect's job in arranging good floor layouts is difficult enough without depriving him through personal whim of what flexibility is possible.

The building being planned is not built for now, but for the ultimate future, and not for one staff, but for any staff. Arrangements that fit personal preferences either must be reasonable arrangements in light of standard library practices, or ones that can be easily changed.[20]

The next to last step in planning each unit involves detailing precisely what furnishings and equipment are required for its function, staff, seating, and shelving. These must be included in the program, because they explain to the architect why you need the square footage requested. As soon as he gets beyond schematic drawings into floor plans, he must be required to lay out the furniture and equipment. Until this is done, it is impossible to know whether the space assigned to each unit is adequate or of the proper shape. Without a definition of furnishings and equipment, the librarian is completely lost in reviewing the separate spaces in a floor layout.[21]

The final step in specifying library areas is to determine whether each unit has special requirements in terms of mechanical elements—special ventilating, lighting, or noise problems, special fire hazards, special protection of any kind. A statement of what is required must be included in the specification of each unit.

At this point, the librarian has been extended to his limit. I have assumed along the way that a good deal of guidance in working out the steps detailed above will have been given by an experienced library building consultant, and the estimation of square footage requirements should be turned over to him. It is possible to use gross formulas for estimating shelving, seating, and furnishings, and Keyes Metcalf's book supplies a number of them.[22] However, any formula must be used with a great deal of discretion and altered to fit different requirements of different conditions.[23]

The librarian-programmer's final step is to tidy up the program, compile summaries of seating, shelving, and area requirements, make an index and table of contents, and send it for mimeographing. It is a happy day that sees it finished.

Writing the program is a long, arduous, time-consuming, soul-searching process which takes about three months to complete, assuming that the existing library operation is in reasonably good condition and that the new building will house no more than a million volumes. Larger, and more expansive and more complex university libraries can take a year or more to program. During this entire time, the mills of the mind will be grinding problems of library buildings consciously or unconsciously most of the time. Seventh and eighth thoughts about these problems are infinitely better than first thoughts, and the mind should be given time to digest and regurgitate them. Half the librarian's usual work load should be turned over to someone else; if it isn't, either the program or the librarian will suffer greatly. But properly done, the production of a good library building program can be the librarian's greatest intellectual achievement.[24]

Notes

1. This chapter began as a speech delivered on May 16, 1966 in a workshop on Academic Library Buildings conducted by Keyes Metcalf at the Graduate School of Library Science, Drexel Institute of Technology. It was published, revised, as an article in *Library Journal*, 1 December 1966, pp. 5838–5844, which was reprinted in Hal B. Schell, editor, *Reader on the Library Building* (Englewood, Colo., Microcard Editions Books, 1975), pp. 111–118. The present version, augmented and considerably rewritten, is published by permission of *Library Journal*.

2. New, that is, for libraries, although the loft type of modular structure was old-hat for factories and many other kinds of more humble buildings. There is still haziness in many minds about what a modular building is. Aside from complicated definitions which are still thrown around, in practical terms a modular building is one in which floors above the lowest level are held up by a series of columns, rather than by fixed, load-bearing walls.

Total modularity requires complete regularity in the pattern and strength of columns, lightly built (so-called "screen") exterior walls, and quickly erected, easily removable interior walls. The main contribution of this kind of structure is the minimization of rigidity formerly imposed on buildings by fixed, load-bearing interior walls and load-bearing exterior walls, thus making it infinitely easier to change the interior compartmentalization into rooms. The advantages for libraries, which in the 1950s and '60s underwent radical changes of physical requirements, are obvious.

The advantages of the modular system are best pointed up in my experience by the St. Lawrence University library, which was built as a partially modular building, the strength and pattern of supporting columns being varied to accommodate the initial load of the building as originally laid-out. When an addition and floor revision was needed, it proved impossible to locate bookstacks where they should go in the area originally occupied by the entrance-circulation area, because the floor could not support the weight of bookstacks.

3. In 1966, John Johansen designed for Clark University Library a fixed-function building, an atavism so blatant that it was supportable only by the self-indulgent ego of the "artist." Described by the architect as a building "of the electronics age," it is actually one of the best examples of eighteenth-century mentality in existence. Johansen's secondary description, "an accretion of shells as barnacles attaching themselves to a rock," is more accurate.

4. In 1969, while I was working in my office with two young architects on a proposed addition to Southern Illinois University Library, Walter Kilham of O'Connor and Kilham dropped in for a courtesy visit. The young men from the firm of "Geddes Brecher Qualls Cunningham: Architects" (look, Mom, no commas) were of the latest: Kilham in his late seventies was still an engaging and remarkable man. In a discussion among us at lunch, Kilham recalled his first job as an architect working for a well-known name in what can only be described as his atelier.

The master was located in a balcony, from which he looked down on a large room in which three or four separate teams were working on different designs. Occasionally as a check, and immediately when he discerned they were having difficulty, the master would descend to one of the teams and with a few skillful strokes straighten out their difficulty, then re-ascend to the balcony. Those *were* the days of simple architecture.

5. In the present condition of architecture there is no dominant tradition, or even a small group of commanding traditions. Radical strains of ideas, most of them rehashed from 19th century art, pull the field in all kinds of directions. What emerge most strongly, if hazily, are an overt disdain for the restrictions of function, and a tendency toward self-expression by the architect. As never before there is a high premium on examining the most recent work of any architect you consider *before you hire him*.

6. Until 1970, Librarianship, too, was one of the professions still holding out against the general decline of standards in the professions. It is hard to believe and painful to see how fast our standards as a profession have declined, especially in the past four years and very especially in academic librarianship, which has become (generally speaking) self-deceived and self-seeking to a high degree.

7. Examples of the architect in command: The library planning committee at Northwestern University was so badly split within itself that fruitful planning was made extremely difficult. In addition, the designer of the building, a man who performs brilliantly when subjected to precisely understood requirements and competent review of his productions, was the brother-in-law of the Vice-Chancellor to whom the library reported. There consequently was no way to establish a clear negotiating position with the architect. The result is a building that is very difficult to use, and in its stack layout a throwback to the 1890s.

The main library building at Yeshiva University had already been designed and let for bid, found too expensive, and partially redesigned before I was hired as consultant in 1965. Up to that point, the plans had been developed by the architects, Armand P. Bartos and Associates, with review only by the university's attorney!!!! I discovered that I

had been hired only to keep the library director, a scholar and non-librarian, from complaining about this situation. To the very end this project was solidly in the hands of the architects. The result is modern monumental sculpture which succeeded the tradition of monumental decoration. The exterior is a rather interesting irregular straight-line form, the interior is total disaster, with the main floor having three different levels, spilt levels between stacks and seating, rampant open airwells, etc.—a totally ignorant library building.

8. This version of plans that had been developing well brought in a corridor measuring 6' x 8', off of which opened *six* doors. Stacks that had formerly protected rows of peripheral carrels were shoved flush against the exterior walls, with the carrels at their entrance ends. Walls that had separated the reading area from rare book stacks had been removed, providing a nice intimate theft condition.

9. In 1967 I participated in a two-day conference with a group that included Walter Netsch, chief designer of Skidmore, Ownings and Merrill, Chicago. On the afternoon of the first day, he began to doodle among his meticulous, very pithy notes. For the next day and a half, the doodles became increasingly varied, and sophisticated, (as his mind moved deeper toward the subconscious, I assumed), incorporating color as well as complex designs of repeated basic shapes. At my request he generously sent me his pad sheets, the most powerful evidence I have seen of the incessant urge toward esthetic design of the architect's mind. Here are two examples:

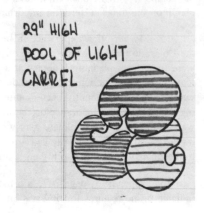

10. Two examples of many—One version of the Colorado College Library plans, on which furniture and equipment were laid out, cut the programmed book capacity of 300,000 volumes, which had been maintained up to that point, to 180,000. In one version of the Colorado State University library plans, by moving a line on one side of a floor, the architect eliminated fifteen group study rooms. In neither case did the architect inform his client that a change had been made; it was caught by the client.

11. We distributed more than 250 copies of the program for the Hofstra University Library before the stencil ran out.

12. I have helped plan half a dozen libraries where the librarian was inadequate to the task. The problem then is to keep some uninformed localite from filling the power gap. These include the faculty chairman of the library committee, the president or vice-president, the business manager, and the plant-director. In only two cases was it necessary for me to institute the program sheets for review by the librarians. In all normal cases, the sheets should be written initially by the librarian, questioned critically by the consultant, revised by the librarian, and re-reviewed by the con-

sultant. When satisfied that it is complete and accurate, he will then estimate a square footage requirement for the area represented on the program sheet.

13. The best evidence of the importance of area estimates I know is in a letter to me dated 11 November 1967 from Eugene Mackey, of Murphy and Mackey, regarding his conception of the plans for the Fieldston School Library, in which he says "as you can see, from your program I could proceed with a set of overlapping squares (or logical groupings) corresponding to program areas . . . to facilitate carrying in my eye . . . the sense of size and shape . . . while speculating on images of space arrangements . . . and the consequences . . . without stopping to measure and draw precisely. I have found this approach extremely useful and economical . . . and possible only with a well-developed program." (Ellipses are the writer's).

The illustration on page 23 shows Mackey's worksheet of space-squares developed for the Fieldston School Library.

14. At the Beinecke Library, Yale University, and the Hamilton College Library I encountered the view that written building programs inhibit the architect's creativity. This would only be true if the client considered the program to be absolute, and required exact conformity to its every detail. Actually, in the development of plans, considerable variations from the program sizes and quantities can occur. As areas begin to be laid out with furniture and equipment and the human movements that will occur in the area become clear, the changes that should be made become apparent. But without the program statement, the client is unable to understand what dimension of change is being made, and lacks the perspective that comes from having thought out carefully what he wanted in the first place. Both the Beinecke and Hamilton buildings suffered in important ways by not having developed a written program.

15. My very first experience in building planning, with the Chicago office of Skidmore, Owings and Merrill on the Colorado College Library, was terrifying partly because of the past experience of that very talented firm. They were fresh from planning a library at a college where the librarian, a displaced faculty member, was almost nonexistent. Their last experience in Colorado Springs had been with the planning of the Air Force Academy complex, in which they had apparently been dealing with a small army of idiots prevented only by their own confusion from imposing their cumulated ignorance on the architects. They were not about to listen to a client. We stood fast when they were wrong, because we knew why we had asked for what was in the program, and after about three months of beating us over the head, they looked around and decided that we were a new order of client. From then on the problems in the plans were solved with great skill and that building still is one of the best small college libraries in the country.

16. Appendix I, page 247, is a list of buildings that can be visited with profit, with critical annotations of each to indicate prime features for observation.

17. Appendix II, page 263, contains a complete demonstration model program for a library building.

18. The size of many academic buildings completed in the last fifteen years is contained in the following useful articles:

D. Joleen Bock, "Two-year Academic Library Buildings," *Library Journal,* 1 December 1971, pp. 3986–3989.

_____. "Two-year College Learning Resources Center Buildings" [three articles with the same title], in *Library Journal* for 1 December 1972, pp. 3871–3873; 1 December 1973, pp. 3529–3531; and 1 December 1976, pp. 2452–2455.

Jerrold Orne, "The Renaissance of Academic Library Building 1967–1971," *Library Journal,* 1 December 1971, pp. 3947–3967.

_____. "Academic Library Building in _____," *Library Journal* for 1 December 1972, pp. 3849–3855; 1 December 1973, pp. 3511–3516; 1 December 1974, pp. 3099–3104; 1 December 1975, pp. 2207–2210; 1 December 1976, pp. 2435–2439.

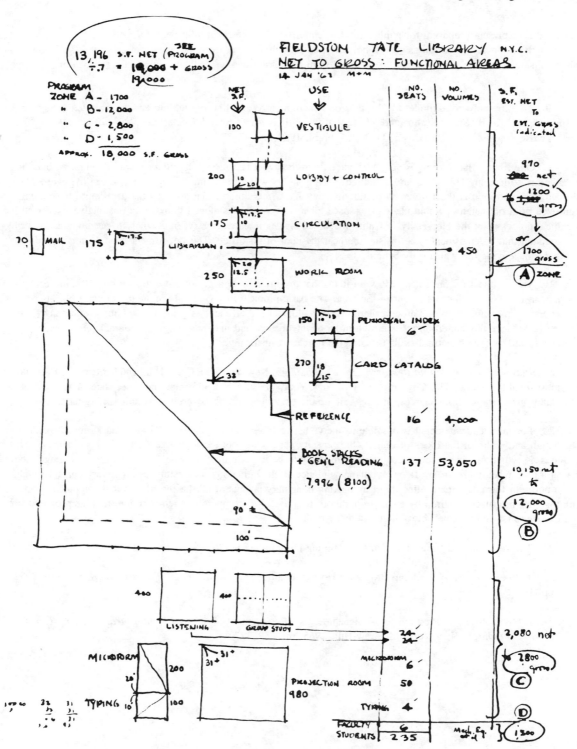

Eugene Mackey's space-squares worksheet.

Dr. Orne is at present preparing for publication this entire body of information in book form.

Programs for library buildings can be borrowed on interlibrary loan from the American Library Association, which has a considerable collection of them, or obtained from the library that wrote them, on interlibrary loan or in Xerox copies.

19. An extremely good model for the data on which the size of a library building can be projected is Section VI, "Appendices," in B. Stuart-Stubbs and W. J. Watson, *University of British Columbia, The Library; a Plan for Future Services*. Revised Edition, Vancouver, U.B.C. Library, 1969, pp. 37–58.

20. One library that I know is very idiosyncratic in its layout because of the illogical way its librarian liked to arrange his collection. This librarian has retired, leaving in his wake a building that no one else can live with. The shift in administration at the University of Illinois, Chicago Circle library, that reversed the decision to have a computerized print-out catalog, found inadequate space for a conventional catalog. I think of an obstructive fixed wall in technical processes at the University of California, Los Angeles research library, built solely to accommodate a drinking fountain that a department head insisted be near the door of his office. This department head soon departed for another job, leaving the wall firmly behind.

21. The architect is concerned only with items that occupy floor space, not those that sit on tables or desks, and the human movements that will occur in the area. The basic problem in laying out the area is to place objects so that the necessary movements to and around them can be as logical and efficient as possible, without wasting any floor space. To achieve this condition takes a high order of intelligence and understanding, considerable conversation with the client, and high architectural skills to solve the problem esthetically.

22. *Planning Academic and Research Library Buildings*, New York, McGraw-Hill, 1965. Metcalf's formulas are the most reliable I know. The City University of New York, the state of California, and other states have established area allowance lists for library areas, but they all are circumscribed by the governmental unit issuing them.

23. For instance, whether it is possible to shelve ten or fifteen books per square foot in stack areas depends on the length and width of the block of ranges, the capacity per square foot increasing as the dimensions increase. This requires a prediction of how long book ranges are likely to be in each area, or what their most effective length should be, at a time when there are no floor layouts as guidance at all. In making area estimates for library units, I rough them out with formulas, then refine them by making imaginary layouts of all the furnishings and equipment, and adding together the space required by each. In addition, it is useful to compare the actual square footage provided for a similar area in a comparable library that is already built.

24. The following writings on the library building program are worth reading:

Ernest J. Reece, "Library Building Programs: How to Draft Them," *College and Research Libraries*, July 1952, pp. 198–211.

Keyes D. Metcalf, "The Program for Assignable Space Requirements," in his *Planning Academic and Research Library Buildings*, New York, McGraw-Hill, 1965, pp. 259–277.

CHAPTER 3

LIBRARY LIGHTING*

(This chapter was born at Colorado College out of deep despair, like a Phoenix rising from its ashes, as we watched a master of the art of illumination, armed only with a portable GE light meter, redeem a lighting proposal that even those as ignorant as I was knew from the mock-up fixtures was terrible. On May 16, 1966, it became a paper at the workshop on Academic Library Buildings conducted by Keyes Metcalf at the Graduate School of Library Science, Drexel Institute of Technology. It was published in revised form as an article entitled "Lighting and Ventilation" in *Library Journal*, 15 January 1967, pp. 201–206, which was reprinted in Hal B. Schell, editor, *Reader on the Library Building* (Englewood, Colo., Microcard Editions Books, 1975), pp. 235–241. Part of it was included in a drastic revision entitled "Lighting and Mechanical Progress in Universities" in the University Library Buildings issue of *Library Trends*, October 1969, pp. 246–261. Since then it has participated in papers at three or four meetings on library building problems, the latest at the annual meeting of the American Library Association, June 19, 1977, at the Library Administration Division Buildings and Equipment Section program. The shreds of the two original articles that remain in the present radically revised and greatly augmented version are published by permission of *Library Journal* and *Library Trends*.)

* * * *

The problems connected with library lighting are simple if we consider lighting merely as preventive medicine, that the function of lighting is to keep us from going blind, or at least to keep our vision from seriously deteriorating. It takes remarkable abuse to impair vision. We can prowl around in darkest midnight without much strain, stretch our book out on the grass against the afternoon sunlight (about 15,000 footcandles in Colorado) without impairing vision. So far as we know, the eyeball cannot be impaired by bad lighting. In fact, in the current state of our culture we have a much greater chance of going deaf than becoming blind. But light and lighting are more than preventive medicine.

Listen to a prominent art critic, Aline Saarinen: "Light is a magic element. The great builders of the past used it masterfully to manipulate mood. The Egyptians cut the Temple at Deir el Bahri from rocks on the west bank of the Nile so the morning sun would stain it an awesome purplish-bloody red. The Byzantine architects covered their domes with glistening mosaics, so light would reflect dizzingly and dazzlingly back and forth, obscuring form with mystery. The Gothic builders filtered light through colored glass, to set it dappling and dancing on the gray stone. And the baroque masters, in their churches, focused the sun like a spotlight to heighten the drama of their designs, and in their palaces, let it in against a wall of mirrors, to flood the room with brilliance."[1]

---

*Footnotes to this chapter begin on p. 36.

Saarinen is talking about sunlight, which is of much greater intensity than the lighting of buildings, but I bring her into this discussion early because designing in any field is an art and is therefore highly dependent on the esthetic sensitivity of the designer. Lighting design is generally in the hands of engineers, and my lifelong observation of this profession, with a few remarkable exceptions, convinces me that the qualities of mind that make good engineers minimize the imagination, and in general they have less sensitive perceptions than most professional people.

Mastery of computation alone cannot make a lighting designer. Any specified illumination level in a given space of a given shape is relatively easy to achieve, but it generally does not produce good lighting design. The key to lighting design is quality of illumination, and to achieve quality it is necessary to be sensitive to a range of complex considerations, such as:

1. The quantity of illumination required for the given task.

2. Control of the conditions that cause direct glare and reflected glare.

3. Esthetic enhancement of the colors in the space.

4. Enhancement of the architectural details of the space.

5. The efficiency of the lighting system, with regard to energy consumption.

The designer must also consider other major impacts of lighting. Light sources are the most prominently visible factors in a building, and they greatly influence its esthetic success or failure. They can also be used in numbers of ways to control people's psychological responses. Light sources can focus attention on a location, by moving light or by high-contrast brightness. They can lead us in a given direction by the use of rows of lights. They can make us feel comfortable, even relaxed, in soft light, such as indirect light, or can make us leave an area through harsh glare, which is used deliberately for the purpose of causing high turnover in cafeterias. Unfortunately, it is also used unintentionally in many libraries, and achieves the same effect. For these reasons, among others, the lighting designer must think about lighting in a far more complex and esthetic way than is involved in a simple consideration of reading intensity. Lighting design requires highly informed technologists with highly developed esthetic sensibilities, but it nearly always is in the hands of mechanics. This is the basic fact of life, and until it changes, poor lighting design will be as commonplace as it is today.

What can librarians contribute to the planning of library lighting, we who are totally ignorant of the technicalities of lighting, babes in the woods as it were, surrounded by voracious beasts called illumination consultants, who charge very high prices to design very bad lighting for us? First, we must understand the physiological problem of seeing.[2] In the presence of glare, which is caused by concentrations of light intense enough to cause discomfort, the pupil of the eye contracts. When it contracts, less light from the object being observed and its background gets into the eye, and it becomes harder to see. The problem is to reduce glare to a level at which the eye can see maximally at a given intensity.

It is possible, under the best conditions, to achieve good reading light at comparatively low intensities. Just recently, I was early in reaching our Director's office for a meeting with our campus planning officers. The Director, obviously, was not in, since his office was pitch black. In a few minutes, he called out to me, and not only was he in, he was composing a letter in that blackness, beside a west-facing morning window away from the sun side of the building. I bounded up the stairs like a wounded deer after my light meter to gather data for this chapter, and found him writing in nineteen footcandles of light. His paper was easily readable, since the light was totally glare-free, but his office felt like the depths of a Neanderthal cave. When the rest of our meeting arrived and his lights were turned on, it felt normal and human.

In 1964 I moved into a house where I discovered the best lighting for studying architectural plans that I have encountered, beneath a chandelier above our dining-room table. It was a five-lamp incandescent fixture (a multiple light source), with the bulbs pointed upward (semi-indirect light), each covered with a frosted globe (glare-free diffusion). The fixture was about three feet above table top and three feet below an eight-foot-high ceiling. The room was 12' by 12'. The walls and ceiling were painted off-white. Above table height, the walls were comparatively unbroken, except for a few small paintings and one arched entryway. In a sense, this is the closest we can come in a cube to the illumination engineer's experimental white-painted internal sphere, the best of all possible lighting environments. Noting the remarkable lighting, I tested it with my light meter. It measured twenty-six footcandles at table height. Therefore, if you can split up your library into walled rooms 12' by 12', with an eight-foot ceiling, painted off-white, with a similar fixture, you can have excellent reading light at twenty-six footcandles intensity.

This condition cannot be repeated in large open spaces, which lack numbers of vertical reflecting surfaces like the walls of our dining room, but this example shows two centrally important factors that make for good quality in lighting: (1) the absence of glare, either direct or reflected glare, and (2) the endless reflection of tiny points of light from multiple surfaces, creating an extremely complex interreflection of light rays within a room. Interreflection is extremely important, since the best reading conditions result when light strikes the task to be read from as many directions as possible.

For any library the following types of illumination, ranked from best to worst in quality, can be provided:

1. Luminous ceilings—the entire ceiling covered by light. These must be completely shielded by a good quality lens.[3]

2. Indirect light—all of the light from fixtures reflected from the ceiling.

3. Semi-indirect light—more than 50 per cent of the light from fixtures reflected from the ceiling, the rest directed downward.

4. General diffused light—directed entirely downward from a system of fixtures that diffuse light well. (The system most commonly used in libraries.)

5. Semi-direct light—more than 50 per cent of the light from the fixtures directed downward, the rest reflected from the ceiling.

6. Direct light—from fixtures that concentrate the areas of light that strike the task. These include downlights and local lamps.

These systems become more expensive as the quality increases, and none of them automatically guarantees good quality light. They all can be of poor quality unless good principles of quality are applied in their design.

To achieve quality in lighting, it is necessary to control glare inherent in the light sources. The glare problem became more serious with the advent of fluorescent tubes, which are more intensely bright over a longer span of space than frosted globe incandescent bulbs. Less glare is caused by incandescent lighting, but its heat load is so much greater than that of comparable fluorescent lighting that its use is impractical in an air-conditioned building, since the cost of the additional tonnage required of the cooling system is great. Fluorescent lighting will be with us for a long time, and we must solve its problems.

Glare is of two different kinds. Direct glare is caused by intense light that comes directly from the light source to the eye. It is most irritating at an angle of 45° to the eye, the spot on the ceiling about eight-feet in front of a person sitting at a desk, with a nine-foot-high ceiling. If glare can be controlled to an acceptable brightness at this angle, the problem of direct glare is solved.

However, we still have to cope with the second kind of glare, reflected glare, caused by light sources immediately overhead reflected by the reading task. Coated book paper, which libraries have in abundance, acts as a mirror and will reflect streaks that nearly obliterate the letters on the page when held at certain angles. This very clear term *reflected glare* has recently fallen into disuse, having been replaced by the term "veiling reflectances," a more elegant and sophisticated term, but far less clear than its predecessor. I therefore continue to use the term "reflected glare."

Direct glare causes the pupil of the eye to contract, restricting the amount of light that can enter. Reflected glare in addition reduces the contrast on the reading task between the black print and its white background. Both effects intensify the difficulty of reading. While no fixture can completely eliminate either direct or reflected glare (even the ceiling in indirect lighting can produce both types of glare), it is possible to reduce glare so that it is not an irritant. To do so is the central problem in selecting lighting fixtures.

It is impossible to control reflected glare without interposing a layer of translucent glass or plastic between the light source and the reading task. It cannot be controlled by any open-bottom or louvered fixtures. Among these are downlights—incandescent bulbs contained in round or square metal tubes—which for many reasons are among the worst enemies of libraries, but architects love them. A good librarian should lay down his life to keep them out of all reading areas. If a translucent lens fixture is used, it must have two properties. It must obscure the appearance of the fluorescent tubes as nearly as possible. If the tubes show through clearly, that is, can be seen through the lens clearly, they will produce nearly as much reflected glare as an open-bottom fixture. In addition, the lens must have the quality of diffusing the light from its sources over a broad area, to maximize the interreflection of light in the area.

If the light fixture meets these qualifications, i.e., its lens controls tube show-through, and diffuses well the light that emerges from it, reflected glare will be controlled. However, use of the lens creates another problem, produced by the surface brightness of the lens, which must be minimized in order to control direct glare. Low brightness depends on both the materials and the construction of the lens. The four kinds of materials we are likely to encounter these days are glass, acrylic plastic, opalescent plastic, and multi-layer plastic.

Glass, however treated, and despite earnest representations of the Corning Glass Company, is useless in controlling direct glare except for good quality opalescent glass, which is fairly thick, heavily whitetinted, and quite expensive. Its cost makes it unlikely to be a competitor in bids these impoverished days. Experiments in bonding a coating to glass lenses have so far failed. Acrylic plastic lenses are either rolled or molded. Both are processes of creating diffusing properties in the lens. It can be categorically stated that no rolled plastic lens is satisfactory. All of them have extremely bad tube show-through, and none of them diffuses light well. Injection molded acrylic lenses with an inside surface composed of tiny conical or octagonal prisms provide good lenses. However, they vary greatly in quality, and they have to be compared in a way that will be described later.

Opalescent plastic lenses in general control both direct and reflected glare but they, too, vary greatly in quality. Their effectiveness also depends on their dimensions. They are best in 2′ by 4′ fixtures, still acceptable in 3′ by 3′ fixtures, but tend to get overbright in 4′ by 4′ fixtures, since the solid mass containing light gets so large that it can become an irritant.[4] Opalescent lenses have the additional virtue of masking the stroboscopic effect of fluorescent tubes, which irritates some people.

In 1967, at the LAD Library Equipment Institute in St. Louis, Professor H. Richard Blackwell of Ohio State University made impressive claims, which had been presented earlier in a series of technical papers, for the supremacy of multi-layer polarized lenses in achieving quality lighting.[5] He was also, incidentally, advocating intensities in the range of 110 to 150 footcandles for library lighting. Since that time there have been a number of installations of polarized lenses in libraries, and on the whole they have achieved good lighting. However, Blackwell's contentions have been attacked by other illuminating engineers, and it is clear that polarized lenses are not the Utopia that Blackwell claimed.[6]

In the first place, they are extremely expensive. While consulting from 1973 to 1975 on the addition to the Ohio State University Library, in Blackwell's back yard, I asked why they weren't using him as lighting consultant. Their plant department and university architect replied that although they had great respect for the knowledge of their expert, he had not been able to recommend a lighting fixture in a price range they could even begin to consider on other buildings.

In the second place, the most efficient polarized lenses cut efficiency, that is, the percentage of the total light produced that emerges from the fixture, to 50 per cent, as against 70 to 72 per cent efficiency for good alternatives with acrylic lenses. This makes the building more costly to light and more expensive to cool.

In the third place, at this point in time, polarized lenses vary greatly in effectiveness. The polarization of light produces two different kinds of polarized light, one of which is not yet coped with by any commercially available lens.[7] The polarized fixtures in the Stanford University Undergraduate Library, though of reasonably good quality, contain a noticeable amount of direct glare. Last year, in consulting for the architects on a large addition to Texas A. & M. University, we considered three different polarized lenses, only one of which was effective in controlling direct and indirect glare.

There has been some use in libraries of plastic diffusing lenses of a flat translucent kind above eggcrate louvers and while this reduces the efficiency of the fixture, it solves the problem of surface brightness, since the louvers effectively conceal the lenses from the eye. Two-way parawedge louvers, which have a 45° cut-off for the light, effectively control the surface brightness of even large or total areas of ceiling, but they produce an uncomfortable effect, since there is absolutely no light visible on the ceiling or upper walls of the room, and it feels strange. These are open-bottom louvers, and must be used in combination with a translucent lens to control reflected glare if they are to be acceptable.

I have spent this much space on lighting fixture lenses because they are critically important in achieving good quality lighting; however, they cannot do the job alone. They must be part of a properly designed lighting fixture, and it is important among other things that the tube be located 4½″ to 5″ from the lens surface, to prevent tube show-through and control surface brightness.

In addition, the quality of lighting depends on the management of contrast ratios between the reading task and large areas in the environment that differ in intensity from it. Large dark areas should not be less than one-third the brightness of the reading task. This fact demands light colored surfaces on all reading tables and carrels, only slightly darker than a book page. The tendency to use wood tops on tables violates this basic requirement in lighting.[8] In addition, large bright areas in the environment should not exceed ten times the brightness of the reading task.

In addition, the reflectance of all surfaces and objects in the library must be carefully planned. Glare from plastic table tops, or from waxed vinyl floors can be highly distressing to the reader. All plastic reading surfaces must be of matte finish plastic, and the use of carpeting, if you can afford it, automatically upgrades the quality of lighting in any room. Surrounding ceilings should have 80 per cent reflectance, and all furniture and floors 30 per cent reflectance.

Three more principles of quality lighting relate to the surrounding areas in the building: (1) If the fixtures are placed in a coffer of a waffle-ceiling, a large percentage of them will be out of the line of sight in any direction. This greatly minimizes the problem of controlling direct and reflected glare; (2) the greater the percentage of the ceiling that is covered with light, the better the quality of light;[9] (3) if you are limited in the number of fixtures that can be placed in an area, locating them toward the periphery of the ceiling of the area improves the quality of light.[10]

I have said that there is considerable variety in the effectiveness of all the kinds of light lenses that can achieve good quality light. How can anyone tell the good ones from the bad ones? This critical point brings us to a discussion of the state of the art of illumination. Five years ago I began an article in *Library Trends* with the following words, which need no modification now, "Illumination practice is presently at a low ebb. Illumination engineering has been dropped as a separate course from the engineering curriculum, teachers of illumination are nearly a departed breed, and the expertise available to architects lies in the commercial engineering firms."[11] These engineers, through lack of training and the general demands on them for display lighting, which has no concern with quality, are on the whole quite ignorant of ways to achieve quality in illumination.

The flabby condition of the field is indicated by the fact that in the 120 buildings I have consulted on over the past twenty years, only once has the electrical engineering firm proposed a good quality lighting fixture for the library on the first presentation. Only occasionally have the fixtures proposed been as good as mediocre, and frequently they were as horrifyingly bad as only perverted genius could make them. At the Colorado College Library in Colorado Springs, my first experience of any kind with buildings, the world-eminent firm of Skidmore, Owings and Merrill proposed three fixtures for the library that were progressively worse each time. We finally told them to go home, and that we would tell them what kind of a fixture to use. The fixture in that building provides the best library lighting I have encountered.

How does one reach this enviable position of knowing that the architect's fixture is wrong, and proceeding to pick a good one as a substitute? We had on our faculty, by remarkable coincidence, John O. Kraehenbuehl, who had taken early retirement from the University of Illinois College of Engineering and was known throughout the land (as I later discovered) as the preeminent expert on achieving quality in illumination. If you can't depend on the architects, who tend to think of lighting fixtures as spots of luminous paint, the obvious procedure is to hire a good illumination consultant.

This is very difficult to do. By working hard at it, I have found three over the past twenty years. One is fifteen years retired, now stubbornly retired. The second is dead. The third, now retired ten years, still consults occasionally. In desperation, I have reviewed the installations of about twenty others, who, after a careful explanation of what I needed, have been recommended as men centrally concerned with the quality of light. None of these experts (many of them with very big reputations in their field) knows anything about quality lighting. Talking to these men about quality is like talking to the Russians about democracy; they simply lack a basic understanding of the concept. So if we scrape dry in the most obvious location, let's turn to the library building consultant. To the best of my knowledge we draw a complete blank here in expertise that can either identify good fixtures as alternatives to those proposed by engineers, or can review fixtures proposed.

There is only one other source of aid—the librarian. That is the state of the art. The fact is horrifying and hard to believe, but true. Placed in such a situation, everyone will say "Who, me?? Little old me, who would have flunked out of vo-tech even if I studied macrame???" Let me point out that my principal formal education was in English literature, and I can assure you that illumination is one of the subjects not touched upon in James Joyce's *Ulysses*. Of the three libraries where I was librarian-planner, in the first we had Kraehenbuehl, who made us aware of the basic problem of lighting and chose our fixture. In the second, three years later, I knew at once how bad the proposed fixture was and located a second consultant, after talking to him for three hours to be sure he was concerned with quality. The thinking about lighting on our project immediately rose several quantum jumps. By reviewing a range of fixtures we were able to select a very good one, and even to improve its lens. In the third library, which we are still working on at the University of Colorado, I found the fixture we are using after the electrical engineers failed us.

This was the result of sheer grinding experience in viewing lighting fixtures in more than five hundred library buildings and thousands of other buildings. First, we have to study the basics of lighting in a simple forty-page pamphlet published in 1948 entitled *American Standard Guide for School Lighting*.[12] Then we begin to look intensively at fixtures to accumulate a wide range of experience viewing them. The chances are very high that the one proposed for any library building will be of bad quality. Fortunately, lighting fixtures are in every building, and anyone can quickly gain a lot of experience.

In viewing, it is necessary to feel physically, in the eye muscles and retina, whether the fixture produces irritation, a feeling of harshness, or whether it is reasonably comfortable. The harshest fixtures provide bare, exposed tubes. These are generally used in supermarkets, which are very brightly lit with incredibly bad quality light. Bare tubes produce the highest footcandle readings at the lowest price, but they make the pupil of the eye contract so that only part of the light reaches the retina.[13] Most convention buildings and a large percentage of public meeting rooms use what I consider to be lighting's public enemy number one, downlights. Most of them have open bottoms. They should be viewed by looking directly up into them from below, which is what the book read below them will do. *All* open-bottom fixtures, in which no shield is interposed between the light source and the task, have intolerable reflected glare. They can be made acceptable only by adding translucent plastic diffusers below the light source.

Fluorescent fixtures in broken strips should be viewed from the long direction, and from the side, in both cases at a 45° angle, the angle at which direct glare is most intense. If they irritate, if the surfaces of the lenses are overbright, if they have open bottom louvers without lenses, they should be rejected. Fixtures in a continuous strip should be viewed some distance from its end and from the side, again at the 45° angle. Make up rhymes to remember things:

> If it's open below,
> Say no.
>
> If the lens is too bright
> It's something to fight.
>
> If the glare is severe
> Pitch it out on its ear.

People can learn to detect direct glare if they are at all visually perceptive, and with practice be able to distinguish fixtures which are acceptable from fixtures that are not acceptable. I have done so.

It is necessary to become a bodily measuring instrument because all fixtures for a library should be approved only after reviewing a mock-up of them. They must be hung at the same height they will have in the finished building, and must have the same lens to be specified in your bids. They must have exactly the same tubes, the same color tubes, and the same number of tubes that will be used in the building. There should be at least four of them hung, in two rows of two, the same distance apart they will occupy in the building. They must be viewed at night, to keep exterior light from skewing the observation.

Anyone who has practiced well, can tell whether they contain glare. If they have bad show-through, that is, if the light from the tube shows in intense streaks on the lens, they can produce nearly as bad reflected glare as bare tubes, and will not diffuse the light well enough to produce good interreflection. It is especially useful to hang different fixtures together at the same time for review.

Bid documents must specify by manufacturer and model number all fixtures that have been considered acceptable after review. Many bid situations allow bidders to substitute "or equal" fixtures for those specified. If this is allowed, specifications should require bidders to submit four samples of the "or equal" fixtures, exactly as they are to be supplied, *at the time bids are accepted*. The new fixtures should be put through exactly the same process of review as described above, and hung beside the specified fixtures, so the difference between them can be seen.

If the fixture proposed by the electrical engineer fails the test, which is par for the course, what should be done? Asking the same engineers to propose another fixture is useless. If they don't recognize quality the first time, they will strike it only by chance any other time, and no one has enough time or lives to play Russian roulette. In that case, it is useful to know which manufacturers are really concerned with quality in lighting. Among others Daybright, Lighting Products Inc., Peerless, Lightolier, the Holophane Corporation, and the Miller Company are such manufacturers. We are using a very good quality highly efficient Lighting Products Inc. fixture in the University of Colorado Library addition. Good fixtures can be found among the offerings of such companies. Mock-ups of those considered must be reviewed, since all manufacturers produce both good quality and bad quality fixtures.

Good quality fixtures used only in limited numbers present a shadow problem. In present day libraries which use freestanding carrels with baffles, bookshelves, and often side-baffles, lighting that casts shadows makes readers feel they are in a cell. Shadows can be dispelled by using a large number of light sources, rather than a few, high-powered sources. Blackwell (see note 9) has shown that the quality of lighting improves as the portion of the ceiling covered with light increases. In the case of a luminous ceiling there are no shadows at all.

Shadow patterns can be predicted in low-budget libraries if a lighting layout review is held with the architects and electrical engineers, an extremely important practice that has fallen into almost total disuse. This review requires a set of lighting layout (so-called "reflected ceiling") drawings printed on paper transparent enough so that you can see the furniture layout drawings which must be placed beneath them. This overview can avoid some of the most common faults in library arrangements, such as dimly lit reading areas on walls that run at right angles to the lighting strips.

These strips should come to within one foot of the wall, but since fixtures come in multiples of four feet, if the ceiling dimension will not accommodate an extra fixture, it is left out. In some cases where carrels are located along the wall, it is necessary to place a separate lighting strip, at right angles to those illuminating the interior of the ceiling, directly above the carrels to provide adequate reading light.[14] The same observation will indicate whether interior lighting strips, always spaced on symmetrical centers across the entire ceiling, help or hinder rows of carrels. The symmetry should yield to the needs of the carrels.

This overview can avoid mistakes, such as a single lighting fixture that is cut in half (and therefore must be omitted) by a partition wall. If desks are placed against a wall in small graduate or faculty studies, the overview will show whether the single lighting fixture the space will accommodate is in the right place—so located that the center line of the long direction of its lens coincides with the outer edge of the desk. Close analysis of the size of interior rooms can predict how intense the interreflection of light within the room will be. If it is high the number of fixtures in the room can be reduced. In larger rooms, which may have too few fixtures, it is possible to predict that arranging them toward the periphery of the ceiling, rather than on parallel equal centers, will improve the quality of lighting. These considerations show the importance not only of the lighting review, but of having a detailed furniture layout developed very early in coordination with the floor plans.

Variations in the type of fluorescent tubes used in fixtures can have profound effects on the appearance of the furniture and equipment in the library. A proper selection is important if the building has an interior design. Tubes are designated as cool white, deluxe cool white, warm white, deluxe warm white, daylight white, white, and soft white/natural. Each has a different effect on different ranges of colors and on the appearance of people in rooms lit by them. It is important in choosing a tube to know what effects they will produce.[15] Then it is equally important to make sure that plant maintenance replaces burned out tubes with exactly the same kind.

During the 1960s there was much talk about the desirability of using colored light in certain areas of libraries. I know of only one attempt to do so, by the use of sheets of thin colored plastic above fluorescent fixtures that have a strong uplight component. My chapter on the Sedgewick Undergraduate Library at the University of British Columbia discusses the results of this experiment, but two things must be observed at this point. First, any use of colored light rather than white light immediately reduces the contrast on the task between printed or written letters and their white background. Increasing that contrast and eliminating all the conditions that reduce it is a central problem in producing good quality illumination. Second, extremely sensitive consideration must be given to the effect of the color on every texture, color, and shape in the furniture and equipment below it.

The noise of ballasts in fluorescent fixtures can be annoying to library readers. My chapter on air-handling suggests that a low background noise should be designed into the air-handling system to mask ballast noises. In addition every possible precaution should be taken to minimize ballast noises in lighting fixtures. This is an acute problem in very high-output fluorescent tubes, such as power-groove, or in mercury vapor or metal halide fixtures. It is possible to locate ballasts remote from the fixtures, where the noise will not matter, instead of inside them, but this is expensive. Specifications for the fixtures should call for select ballasts with a sound rating of A.

There are special lighting problems for some specialized areas of the library. Except in the general stacks of large research collections, where it is virtually certain that the stacks will never be moved, or in tier-built stacks which are once again creeping up on libraries, stack lighting should not be planned solely to light the stacks. If stack areas are replaced by reading areas, good quality lighting should be available to accommodate readers. In addition, it should be possible to change the width of stack ranges without tearing out the existing lighting. To accommodate these changes, lighting should not be centered on the stack aisles, and lighting planned for stack areas should be the same as that for general reading areas.

Although it is not possible to achieve this condition for all stacks throughout the building, since they are not all oriented in the same direction, lighting strips should run at right angles to stack ranges, because it provides more even lighting within the stack aisles than lighting centered on the aisles.[16]

There have been systems of lighting attached directly to stack units, which move with them if their location is changed. All of these systems except one that I have seen give inadequate and uneven light over the span of the seven shelves in the stacks. The successful system in the Sedgewick Undergraduate Library at the University of British Columbia mounts bare tubes on top of the stack canopies, concealing them with a slight upturn of the canopy edges. With a nine-foot ceiling painted white above, this provides superlative quality indirect lighting at about forty footcandles on the lowest stack shelves.

If the location of stacks is predictably fixed forever (give or take a few days), or if tier-built stacks are used, it is reasonable to consider stack lighting fixtures centered on the stack aisle. There are two fixtures specifically designed for this purpose by Columbia Lighting and by the Leslie Wax Co. These fixtures can be provided with two-way parabolic baffles that provide a 39° cutoff of the light as it emerges from the sides of the fixtures. Both of them have "batwing" light distribution curves, which distribute most of the light down at an acute angle on both sides and very little directly below the fixture. These fixtures provide reasonably even intensity of light to all seven shelves, including the lowest. However, they are expensive, and they contain open-bottom louvers, which makes them highly unsatisfactory for reading areas in the event that the stacks are ever replaced by readers. In the University of Colorado library addition, we use in our tier-built stacks single-tube Lighting Products Incorporated fixtures with a wrap-around prismatic plastic diffusing lens that provides very good stack lighting centered on the stack aisles.

Rare Book stacks and reading rooms require special lighting to avoid the destructive effects of ultra-violet light, produced by fluorescent fixtures. As museum specialists have long ago realized, ultra-violet light destroys paper, dyes, leather and vegetable substances—which pretty well cover the range of materials of which books are made.[17] The best way to avoid these problems is to provide rare book areas, both stacks and reading rooms, with incandescent lighting. If this is not possible, ultra-violet light can be controlled by the use of UF II or UF III plexiglass (made by Rohm & Haas) as panels below fluorescent tubes, or as flexible sleeves that completely encompass the tubes. This material absorbs most of the ultra-violet light produced by the tubes.

These panels can also be used to glaze the tops of flat exhibition cases, but since they scratch rather easily they should be protected by a sheet of plate glass laid on top of them.[18]

An alternative method is the use of Fadex fluorescent tubes, made by Verd-a-Ray Lighting Products, which contain a coating that absorbs ultra-violet light. It is extremely important to use one of these alternatives in rare book stacks, since the fixtures are so close to the books that they can inflict severe damage to colors of leather bindings, especially greens and blues, in a very short time.[19] All fixtures with ballasts used in rare book areas should have fused ballasts, because normal ballasts can become hot enough when they burn out to melt their insulation, which drips on anything below it and occasionally drips liquid hot enough to cause fires.

Exhibition cases pose special lighting problems that are extremely difficult to resolve. Ideally, the lights should be in the case to dissipate the reflections, especially pronounced in flat cases, inherent in their glass enclosures. However, if fixtures are enclosed, the cases must be air-conditioned to avoid heat rise. This can cause great damage to vellum substances and certain kinds of paper, especially if they are transferred from stacks where 50 per cent humidity has been maintained. For cases without air-conditioning, the fixtures must be mounted outside the cases, which must have glass tops, and high enough above them so that the heat produced has no effect on the books exhibited.

Microform reading areas and audio-visual areas have special requirements for lighting. They must combine general lighting high enough to make the areas feel reasonably pleasant, while providing local areas of low overhead intensity so that images on rear-projection screens will not bleach out under the lighting. The problem is complicated by the fact that directly beside the reading or viewing machines must be local lighting adequate for taking notes. In my experience, the problems of proper lighting for these areas and properly designed furniture to accommodate the diverse requirements of the equipment have never been completely resolved.

Standards for lighting intensity are established periodically for different kinds of activities, including libraries, by the Illuminating Engineering Society, which is largely composed of those illumination engineers I have described in such discouraging terms. Among them are a group of research-minded illumineers who really are concerned with quality in lighting, and who have worked for a long time trying to devise statistical methods of measuring the properties of fixtures that will enable us to predict from the technical data those fixtures that produce quality lighting. Over the past fifteen years they have devised the Scissors Curve graph and the Equal-Area Equal-Glare Effect diagram to predict the impact of direct glare, and Equivalent Sphere Illumination to describe intensity of good quality lighting. None of these methods seems to help illumination engineers select from the technical data fixtures that produce good quality lighting. Each step in the progression has moved further away from the empirical lay observer.

The change in the I.E.S. (Illuminating Engineering Society) standards between the fourth and fifth edition of the *I.E.S. Lighting Handbook,* the bible of the profession, is a shift from a logical absurdity in the fourth edition to sheer madness in the fifth, published in 1972.[20] Recommended intensities for various kinds of library areas and tasks in the former were stated in footcandles, which have very little significance if the lighting is riddled with glare. However, footcandles can be measured by an easily available light meter, and if the light is of good quality they are highly significant.

The fifth edition recommends standards of intensity for some areas in the library in measurable footcandles, but for the most critical areas, such as reading areas, card catalog areas, and important work areas, it states intensities in Equivalent Sphere Illumination. Equivalent Sphere Illumination can be computed from other technical data (which, I have contended, do not help predict the quality of lighting) but it *cannot* be measured, so it is impossible to know whether it is attained. This is a standard? More like Catch-22, the kind of systematized insanity that runs throughout the intellectual world and does not impress the general population.

The question of lighting intensity is treated at length, and with important historical considerations, in Keyes Metcalf's book.[21] I quite agree with his unstated opinion, inferred from the details he presents, that we are subjected to conditioning at the hands of the lighting industry that has led in the past to demands for ever higher intensities. In a country where home lighting is nonexistent or, at the most, one footcandle, five footcandles is intense. In a country where supermarket lighting is a hundred and twenty footcandles, seventy-five is not intense. Except for the energy crisis, where this would have ended short of burning our eyeballs to cinders I could not predict. But at the present time, it means that low lighting intensities in libraries do not feel good to mid-twentieth century Americans. This fact has led to the simple-minded insistence on very high lighting intensities, far above a hundred footcandles in some libraries, with no concern at all to achieve good quality in the light. Not only is too high intensity of no use; if the quality of light is bad, *the higher the intensity the worse the light is.*

I indicated earlier that low intensities are adequate for reading, and further indicated that a much larger range of visual and psychological and esthetic considerations must go into the determination of proper intensities in a library. With the very best quality, which is indirect lighting, thirty-five to forty footcandles is sufficient. However, since this is the most expensive kind of lighting, we are not likely to encounter it in our lifetime, and will almost certainly be coping with general diffused lighting which poses very large glare problems. With this kind of lighting, we are lucky to achieve even reasonably good quality in lighting. Under these conditions 55 to 70 footcandles is needed to provide adequate illumination for the entire range of factors in a library that depend on illumination intensity for their success.

With budget and energy shortages, will we be allowed to provide enough intensity? The illumination needs of the future will be exactly what they are now—good quality lighting of the intensities described. But the present energy crisis reminds us of the fact that most of the world has been without very much illumination of any kind for most of the history of mankind. Only luxury areas such as Western Europe and North America have advanced much beyond a candle-tip.[22] On the evening of England's declaration of war with Germany at the beginning of World War I, the British Foreign Secretary Earl Grey, looking out of his windows said, "The lights are going out all over Europe." Sixty years later they are going out all over the world.

I join Keyes Metcalf in complaining that lighting intensities in the past have tended to be much too high. In the future they will be much too low. Two years ago at the "Farewell to Alexandria" conference in Chicago, I predicted that library buildings in the future will tend to be far less pleasant and comfortable than they are now.[23] Future libraries will probably contain no incandescent lighting at all, because of its high cost of maintenance and heat loads. Buildings will tend to have low general lighting, instead of reading intensity lighting, thirty footcandles or less, supplemented by lamps at tables and work stations. Williams College library presently has this condition, and both the feeling of the building and the heat load on the reader's head from metal lamp shades (which act as little radiators) are quite bad.

Libraries will tend to have unlit stacks, which are unpleasant in feeling, with time switches at ranges to keep them dark most of the time. There will be much greater use of high-intensity light sources such as mercury vapor, metal halide, and sodium vapor lamps, which have much higher intensities per watt than fluorescent, are much less pleasant and present nearly insuperable glare problems.

Illumination of the future, through the sheer pragmatics of cost and energy pressures, will tend to fall into the hands of mechanics and cost accountants, who manipulate data and have no professional concern about human values. The kinds of lighting systems used are likely to be determined by computations on a comprehensive basis of the total wattage demand and total net BTUs produced as heat load by the configuration as a whole. This condition will be one more fraud perpetrated on mankind by technology and its handmaiden, statistics, both of which move us continually further from real needs, but this seems to be the tendency of our times. This condition leaves those of us who will plan library buildings the happy choice between the reek of tallow candles and the smoke of tapers on the one hand and the twilight glare of the future on the other.[24]

Notes

1. For this quotation and most of the substance of the next two pages I am indebted to an unpublished brochure entitled *Lighting Design Notes,* used for teaching by Professor Emeritus George R. Peirce of the Electrical Engineering Department of the University of Illinois College of Engineering. I am indebted to Professor Peirce for a whole range of refinements in my knowledge of lighting problems, the result of conversations with him in Urbana and working with him on the Fieldston School Library. Quite obviously, he should not be blamed for anything I may have taken wrong, and as usual my opinions are my own.

2. I acknowledge my deep and pervasive debt to Professor John O. Kraehenbuehl, Sr., Double Emeritus, from the College of Engineering, Electrical Engineering Department, University of Illinois, and later from the Colorado College. Dante would call him "The Master of those who know." He is in my experience the most remarkable illumination engineer concerned with quality in lighting. A figure nearly legendary among his peers in his time, most of whom are gone and are not being replaced, his remarkable expertise was not used in construction at the University of Illinois, not even in the section for the Electrical Engineering Department in the new College of Engineering building. Neither was Professor Peirce's. Such is the loss of knowledge among plenty in all universities.

Professor Kraehenbuehl and I were colleagues at Colorado College for more than two years before I discovered an article by him in a collection of essays on library buildings, one of his special interests. He taught me soundly the basics of quality in lighting, and has repeatedly untangled confusions in my knowledge of it. Without him my special interest in library lighting would never have developed and this chapter would never have been written.

3. Ceilings which contain shielding, in which the entire ceiling surface is covered with light, should not be confused with ceilings composed of bare fluorescent tubes hung above a grid of open-bottom louvers. These are the equivalent of bare exposed tubes, so far as reflected glare is concerned. Instead of providing the best illumination these ceilings provide high-glare illumination.

4. See R. C. Hopkinson and R. C. Bradley, "A Study of Glare from Very Large Sources," *Illuminating Engineering,* May 1960, pp. 288–294.

5. "Lighting the Library—Standards for Illumination," in Library Equipment Institute. 2nd, St. Louis, 1964. *The Library Environment; Aspects of Interior Planning.* Chicago, American Library Association, 1965, pp. 23–31. See also these more technical articles by Blackwell: "Development and Use of a Quantitative Method for Specification of Interior Illumination Levels on the Basis of Performance Data," *Illuminating Engineering,* June 1959, pp. 317–353; "A General Quantitative Method for Evaluating the Visual Significance of Reflected Glare, Utilizing Visual Performance

Data," *Illuminating Engineering,* April 1963, pp. 161–216; "A Recommended Engineering Application of the Method for Evaluating the Visual Significance of Reflected Glare," *Illuminating Engineering,* April 1963, pp. 217–235.

6. See C. L. Crouch and J. E. Kaufman, "Practical Application of Polarization and Light Control for Reduction of Reflected Glare," *Illuminating Engineering,* April 1963, pp. 277–291.

7. See Kenneth E. Fairbanks, "Polarization in Lighting," unpublished paper presented at the Symposium on Polarized Lighting, 4th National Lighting Exposition, March 4, 1963; and his "Task Brightness and the Control of Reflected Glare," unpublished paper presented at the 1963 East Central Regional Illumination Engineering Society Conference, Wheeling, West Virginia. Both papers are in my files.

8. Architects and interior designers prefer wood for reading surfaces to supply richness of tone and grain. Ironically, the quality of woods now available except at exorbitant prices are unable to provide richness of tone and grain. It is possible to persuade designers that equally good appearance can be obtained by providing furniture with a wooden frame around the edge of a matte formica top of an appropriate light color. We were able to do this at Hofstra University and the University of Colorado.

9. See Blackwell's Library Equipment Institute paper cited above, especially p. 28.

10. See Foster K. Sampson, *Contrast Rendition in School Lighting,* New York, Educational Facilities Laboratories, 1970, a book well worth reading for its discussion of the basics of quality lighting, as well as this particular point.

11. "Lighting and Mechanical Progress in Universities," *Library Trends,* October 1969, pp. 246–261.

12. Published New York, Illuminating Engineering Society, 1948 (their publication number A23.1-1948). There is a later edition of this title published in 1962 (number A23.1-1962) and a counterpart title, *School Lighting,* published in 1970 (number A23.1-R1970). The editions after 1948 are less useful, one more example of the erosion of solidity in most fields of knowledge since the end of World War II.

13. By now the idea should be clear that footcandle readings are meaningless unless the lighting measured is of good quality. With great irony, in the present energy crisis I find the plant maintenance crew in numbers of colleges and universities removing the shields from lighting fixtures to get more light out of the fixtures, even when no other changes in the lighting arrangement are made. They indeed get more footcandles to measure, but at the same time anyone exposed to the fixture has constricted eye pupils, and *he* gets less light. In addition, the diffusing properties of the fixtures are greatly impaired and interreflection of light in the room drops enormously. *Sic crescit stultitia!* (Loose translation, "Fools may take over the world").

14. The periphery of the second floor of the Bowdoin College library, where carrels were planned (and located when I was there), is almost devoid of light, and therefore unusable for a kind of seating extremely important for a liberal arts college library. Not only does the lighting system of the interior ceiling stop short of coming to the walls, the carrels are lit with downlights spaced with no regard to the possible spacing of carrels. The result is a peripheral dungeon, marring what is otherwise a pretty good building.

15. A chart of these effects appears in a pamphlet entitled *EDL Quick Reference* (NECA Electrical Design Guidelines). Washington, D.C., National Electrical Contractors Association, 1972. The Association's address is 7315 Wisconsin Ave., Washington, D.C., 20014.

16. Charles Gosnell's otherwise good article entitled "Lighting of Library Buildings" in the *Encyclopedia of Library and Information Science,* New York, Marcel Dekker, 1975, volume 16, pp. 170–184 contains one prodigious error. He "proves" by a diagram on page 181, as well as by argument, that lighting at right angles to stacks provides

greater intensity on the backs of books than lighting centered on stack aisles. This is totally wrong. As I have indicated, lighting at right angles provides *more even* lighting on the seven shelves, but the following example of the same fixture used in identical strips at right angles to the stacks and on stack centers will suffice to show what happens to intensity:

Measured at Texas A. & M. University library on 3 June 1976, their stacks on 4½ centers:

at right angles — 30 to 45 footcandles at 30″ height,
15 footcandles off book backs.

on stack centers — 60 to 75 footcandles.
30 footcandles off book backs.

17. For information on ultra-violet light deterioration see: Robert L. Feller, "The Deteriorating Effect of Light on Museum Objects," Technical Supplement no. 3, to *Museum News,* volume 42, no. 10, June 1946; Laurence S. Harrison, *Report on the Deteriorating Effects of Modern Light Sources.* New York, The Metropolitan Museum of Art, n.d.; and "Light" in Francis W. Dolloff and Roy L. Perkinson, *How to Care for Works of Art on Paper.* Boston, Museum of Fine Arts, 1971, pp. 17–20.

18. Six flat exhibition cases custom-designed for the Hofstra University Library used this combination of glazing.

19. Ultra-violet light can be a hazard even in rooms with windows facing north and even with all the lights turned off, through reflection of light rays off particles in the air. A simple test for ultra-violet light hazard is to enclose a sheet of blue construction paper in a book with half the sheet hanging out. After three or four days the difference in color between the exposed portion and the covered portion will show how much bleaching has been caused by ultra-violet light. If it is severe, steps should be taken to control it.

20. Illuminating Engineering Society, *I.E.S. Lighting Handbook* edited by John E. Kaufman and Jack F. Christensen. 5th edition. New York, Illuminating Engineering Society, 1972.

21. *Planning Academic and Research Library Buildings.* New York, McGraw-Hill Book Co., 1965, pp. 175–188.

22. A few incidents may remind us how recent the general availability of electric lighting really is. In 1923, less than fifty-five years ago, one of my most vivid childhood memories is watching a lineman (who was bringing in electric lines) go up a pole with climbing spurs before the ground had been thoroughly tamped down around the foot of the pole, while it was still held upright by three steel pikes bracing it against the ground. This happened in a Connecticut village adjacent to a city of one hundred thousand people. In 1933, less than forty-five years ago, the advent of kerosene mantle lamps was a great technological advance in another village adjacent to the same city. In the same year I recall how greatly enlivening it was to a party, replete with fiddles and folk-dancing (yes, kiddies, some New Englanders danced), when one rear wheel of a Ford Model-T was jacked up, and the tire removed to convert the rim to a pulley. This drove a portable electric generator which fed a rectangular string of unfrosted bulbs. I recall how romantic were the dim lights glowing in the dark.

It was only thirty years ago that electricity reached a large part of our farm population in this country, and even today lightly populated areas of the Rocky Mountain West do not have electricity.

23. Daniel Gore, editor, *Farewell to Alexandria; Solutions to Space, Growth, and Performance Problems of Libraries.* Westport, Conn./London, 1976, pp. 22–33. The title is somewhat inflated; I did not hear many solutions.

24. In addition to works specifically cited, the following pamphlet can be consulted, with profit, if caution is used: Illuminating Engineering Society. Subcommittee on Library Lighting. *Recommended Practice of Library Lighting.* New York, Illuminating Engineering Society, 1973.

CHAPTER 4

AIR-HANDLING SYSTEMS IN LIBRARIES*

(Although we can logically expect mechanical properties in library buildings to change much more rapidly than architectural or structural properties, since 1966 when this chapter had its beginning there have been no startling developments in air-handling systems for buildings.[1] There have been experiments with water-cooled lighting troffers and water-cooled vertical blinds for the purpose of removing the heat that originates at these points, and with the use of heat from lighting systems to produce thermo-electric cooling. These experiments have produced no practical results. At present, there is growing use of variable-volume temperature control.

Future emphasis in this field is likely to be diverted to producing alternative sources of heat and cooling from solar energy (though the experts say that practical application of solar energy to any significant degree is twenty to thirty years away), and to finding ingenious ways, probably deleterious to the feeling of the library building, to minimize or eliminate chilling from air-handling systems. In the meantime, there are stubborn problems inherent in the systems we have to use now and in the near future.)

* * * *

A good ventilation system is as important as good lighting in affecting the student's reaction to a library, and, as in the case of lighting, good quality in the air distribution is more important than temperature settings. The design requirements for a good quality air-handling system are basically simple. Air must be pumped in sufficient volume to keep the air fresh for the occupancy planned for an area, and at a velocity sufficient to temper the air for the size of the room. Care must be taken to assure that penetration of the air-stream is sufficient to mix with air already in the room, but that its terminal velocity is below the level that disturbs people. Achievement of this condition in smaller rooms is bread and butter routine to a good engineer.[2]

Handling of air in large open spaces which are characteristic of modern libraries is more difficult. Air must flow evenly around the periphery, and at the same time in the middle of the open space. Many spaces are too large to respond to a single temperature or humidity control; therefore they are divided into invisible zones, each of which has its own set of controls. The division, of course, is fictitious, since the air from one zone, with its temperature and humidity already provided, meets air in the open space coming from other zones, and must be compatible with it if hot and cold spots are to be avoided. Uniformity of temperature and humidity in such areas, though theoretically easy to achieve, is in my experience a rare accomplishment.[3]

Handling of air in very small rooms, such as faculty studies, is even more difficult. The attachment of

---

*Footnotes to this chapter begin on p. 46.

an addition to an older building confronts, where the two buildings join, the air conditioned by two different (probably vastly different) systems, and equalization of air pressure must be achieved in both areas unless a gale is to sweep from one to the other.[4] Add to these complexities the fact that the knowledge of the engineer is subject to adjustment or veto by the architect who hires him, and that installation of mechanical system components must be reconciled with the space demanded by a whole range of other technical and functional elements. Then stir in the fact that at all times the mechanical engineer is generally developing his technical drawings on a set of plans one or two versions behind the current floor plans, and must periodically change them by leaps to catch up with the new space conditions. Then mix in thoroughly the obstinacy of all temperature control systems and the immutability of human perversity, which insists on gathering in the same department sixteen people who prefer sixteen different temperatures, and you begin to understand why, of all aspects of a library building, the air-handling system receives the most constant complaints. The right combination of factors is so difficult to achieve that I have never seen a building that is uniformly comfortable in temperature at all seasons of the year. Those that are uniformly comfortable at some seasons are rare enough.

The greatest comfort difficulties are encountered during the interim seasons, or in climates where great differences in temperature occur within the same day. To achieve any pre-set temperature all the time it is necessary to have both heat and cooling available constantly. Whenever the outside temperature changes enough to make internal temperatures vary from the thermostat setting, the air in the ventilation system must be either heated or cooled, depending on the direction of the outside change. Most buildings are run, for budget reasons, on the crude basis of banking the fires at the end of May, and turning off the cooling system at the end of September. As a result, it is impossible to heat the air on cold days during summer, or to cool it on hot days during the winter. In Spring and Fall, when temperatures flip randomly, the comfort dislocations in a building can be extreme.

The control of air temperatures is very difficult for a number of reasons, all due to space limitations in the building. In the first place, the ventilation system, in any turnover of air, that is, when it has circulated throughout the building and returned to the air intake fans again, should spill out of the building through adjustable vanes about 25 per cent of the air, picking up a new 25 per cent at the ventilation fans to freshen the recirculated air.[5] New air enters the system at a temperature different from that of the tempered air returning from the building to be recirculated. The two airs mix before they reach the heating or cooling coils on their way to air diffusers throughout the building. They have a tendency to stratify, with the warmer air riding on top of the cooler air. It is extremely important to homogenize the temperatures before they reach the tempering coils. If this is not done, the same amount of heat or cold is applied to the two strata of air, raising the temperature of one, for example, from 50° to 60° and of the other from 70° to 80°. In this case 60° air would come out of some diffusers in the building and 80° air out of others, neither temperature suitable.

By providing a properly designed mixing chamber it is possible to homogenize air of different temperatures, but this takes space, and engineers constantly complain that architects never provide adequate mixing chambers. If this is the case, and my experience convinces me that it is, the entire ventilation system is to a certain extent disabled from the start.

The second problem in temperature control involves the ducts, great hollow metal shafts that conduct air from the fans vertically up through the floors, and horizontally out along floors to the air diffusers that distribute air out into the rooms. Ducts require an enormous amount of space, and there is never enough space to accommodate easily all that are needed. Horizontal ducts are concealed in ceiling cavities hung below the structural ceiling, and must compete for limited space with the plumbing and lighting of the building. Indeed, one of the marks of a skillful mechanical engineer is how much duct work he can get into a ceiling.

The easiest way to distribute air is vertically through one large continuous duct with a smaller horizontal duct for each floor, from which are fed individual air diffusers. This duct system is essentially one great, irregularly shaped box, with holes around the outer edge. With only a slight degree of sophistication, this kind of a system can feed any unit of space that needs only a single temperature control, such as a large unbroken bookstack and reading area up to a certain size, about 10,000 square feet. If within that area one room, such as a seminar room, is enclosed, it must have a separate temperature control to provide satisfactory air conditioning. Response to that control requires a separate re-heat coil within the duct system, which requires a larger duct-box. Given six rooms on the same floor, the competition for space to locate ducts can be extreme, and the cost of controls noticeable. Consequently, the engineer has a tendency to place too large or too complex an area on a single temperature control. As a result, somewhere in the zone the control breaks down. To a considerable degree this accounts for hot and cold spots as you walk through the building.

An additional complication in designing temperature control springs from the fact that in any area, the system must be designed to handle its peak occupancy. A room for twenty-eight readers must have a system sufficient to cool the room when twenty-eight bodies are radiating heat in it, by moving a volume of cooled air through the room. The volume of air can be varied within limits and the temperature dropped within limits to absorb the increased heat load that results from more people entering the room, but it is never flexible enough to accommodate just a few readers in the room. For the few it is always too cold. This is why many supermarkets and movie theaters are freezing cold except when they are jammed with people.

I have said enough to indicate the magnitude of the problems involved in controlling the temperature of internal spaces. A different problem arises at the outer walls, caused by the fact that a body sitting close to them (a typical arrangement in contemporary library buildings) will radiate heat to the outer wall if it is cooler than the air circulating in the room, especially if the walls are glass. This heat loss makes the reader feel cold, even though the air surrounding him may be comfortable in temperature. To counterbalance this effect, the entire perimeter of the building must have a supplementary heating system to produce a heat rise along the wall, a vigorous heat rise if the wall is glass. In drier climates where heat transfer is inhibited, forced-air floor ducts supply adequate heat. In a wet climate fin-tube heaters, fan-coil units, or induction units are preferable. These systems take the tempered air within the room and heat it further, sending it up the wall by heat rise or by air movement.

Fin-tube units depend on the natural rise of air passing over heated fins to produce upward movement. They produce no noise. A fan moves the air through fan-coil units, which have two or three speed settings. At high speed, fan-coil units produce far too much noise for comfort in a library. This problem can be eliminated by listening to sample units in the planning stage, discarding the noisy ones and specifying models that can produce the required air-tempering capacity at *medium* speed. Induction units force air under high pressure into a chamber from which it escapes through nozzles, thereby inducing a movement of the room air upward over the tempering units. At peak capacity the passage of high pressure air through the nozzles produces an annoying whistle. Again, the solution lies in choosing models that can temper the air adequately at less than peak capacity.

Fin-tube units do not supply enough heat rise to provide comfort in very cold weather in any building I have observed. They should not be used in wet climates unless the outer walls are unusually heavily insulated. They should be avoided like the plague at all exterior window walls, where ironically they are used most often. Not only do they fall radically short of supplying enough heat, they induce convection currents at the window wall in cold weather that are extremely drafty.[6] The periphery can also be tempered by the use of electric baseboard heaters. If used, they must be located far enough from the normal position of feet at peripheral seating so that they will not be uncomfortably warm.

Air is generally diffused in an area through overhead diffusers, which provide even distribution of air at comparatively low volume. They require a dropped ceiling to conceal the feeder ducts. In some simple systems, it is possible to fasten diffusers directly to exposed horizontal distribution ducts, but it is more difficult in such systems to equalize the volume of air coming from each diffuser. Where dropped ceilings are not used, for reasons of function or economy, lateral diffusers are used to blow air across the room at relatively high volumes. These diffusers can be both noisy and uncomfortable. They can throw air up to thirty feet and it is not possible to get uniform comfort the whole length of this distance. When used in stacks, lateral diffusers must throw air either above stack heights, which does less to temper the lower part of the area occupied by people, or through the stack aisles. Attempts to throw air against the sides of stacks (I have seen some) are doomed to failure, since the books act as a wall that prevents the spread of air.

Since 1960 a rival diffusing system has been available in air-supply ceilings. These depend entirely on dropped ceilings, with acoustical tiles that contain holes or slots, or with slotted spines that support the tiles. The inlet duct terminates at a point in the ceiling nicely calculated to provide equalized pressure in the entire cavity. The air then descends into the room through the holes in the ceiling. Tiles perforated with one-eighth inch round holes should be avoided, since they become clogged with dust, which inhibits air passage and can be balanced only by pasting patches of paper to the tiles. For appearance this should be done on the cavity side, which requires re-entering the ceiling. The slots in tiles or in the splines on which the ceiling hangs are adjustable, and are preferable.

This kind of a ceiling must be made completely air-tight. It therefore is unsuitable if the ceiling contains much ductwork, piping or conduit, which requires frequent repair, since it is impossible to maintain air-tightness if the ceiling has to be opened often. An air-supply ceiling prevents use of the ceiling cavity as an air return, as is often done to remove 30–50 per cent of the heat generated by inset light fixtures before it gets into a room.

Air-supply ceilings are just as difficult to balance as are overhead or lateral diffuser systems. However, they are comparable in cost, and they have the advantage of being able to supply a very large volume of air with minimal noise. They should be considered for high heat-generating rooms, such as computer rooms and photoduplication rooms. The penetration of the air stream into the room and its terminal velocity must be very carefully calculated for human comfort. Overhead radiant heating systems are available which use running hot water or electric coils as a source. The former is installed above the outer bay areas in the library at Towson State College, Maryland. The risk of water damage through leaks will make anyone hesitate ever to place stacks under them.[7] All radiant heating systems have the disadvantages that the feeling of heat radiating from overhead is oppressive, and that the ceiling area occupied by the heating coils cannot also contain the cooling system. Infra-red radiant heating is occasionally mentioned in construction literature, which heaven forbid! It is intensely uncomfortable when radiating, and only crudely controllable.

Combinations of air-diffusion and return with light fixtures have been used in some libraries. There is an advantage in using the heat of the fixture as a supplement to the general heat source in winter, and in preventing heat from coming into the room in the summer, but the great sophistication required to take advantage of either of these factors economically has prevented any such system from providing completely good ventilation conditions, in my experience. This system has the considerable disadvantage of distributing dust heavily over the lenses of the lighting fixtures, which greatly impairs their efficiency and appearance.

All of these systems result in uneven temperatures in every library I have been in. When the client complains about this condition and seeks redress he finds that architects tend to blame the mechanical engineers and the plant maintenance crew, engineers tend to blame plant maintenance, and plant maintenance tends to blame the architect and the engineer. Whoever is to blame, it usually is true that the best condition of an air-tempering system falls short of being completely satisfactory, and the worst condition makes the building unliveable.

Most air conditioned buildings are not completely air conditioned; to be so requires humidity removal equipment to dry excessively wet air. Such an "unnecessary" expenditure made shudders run through plant department officers ten years before the present budget crunch, so they never planned humidity removal for libraries. Yet it is needed in most of the United States.

At seventy per cent relative humidity or higher, the growth of molds (so omnipresent they may inherit the earth) is greatly encouraged. They destroy paper and a whole range of vegetable and animal substances we use for bindings. High humidity can build up the moisture content so high that I once saw the sizing on a cloth binding inside of a dust wrapper turned to liquid.[8] Consequently, humidity removal should be included in air-handling systems in wet climates.

On the other hand, in dry climates like Colorado, where relative humidity sometimes registers ten per cent or lower in summer, systems are not provided with humidification units designed to maintain a constant rate of humidity, though humidity is added in an unsophisticated way during the winter when the heating systems are running. Humidity should be maintained at all times, since for every ten per cent rise in humidity, the folding strength of paper (whose failure wears out books) doubles. If humidity is added during winter, there is a problem of dripping on the coldest part of the outer wall, which is usually metal window frames, and humidity will have to be adjusted below this drip point. At any time of year, it should not be above forty per cent for human comfort.

The only way to tell the humidity content of buildings, a crude way, is by the feel of your skin, because most buildings lack humidity recorders. Although humidistats are readily available, and recording humidity indicators available at a higher price, they are seldom used in buildings. This fact indicates how unimportant the humidity factor is considered in providing comfortable conditions for people. Consequently, if the building is provided with humidity control, no one, including the installers, the engineers and plant maintenance, can tell whether it is working right without testing it by a portable sling hygrometer. There is no visible basis, as there is for temperature, for correcting humidity disorders. Obviously, buildings should be provided with humidity recorders.

Efforts to achieve balance in the air-handling system, so that air volume and temperatures are comfortable everywhere, always seem endlessly agonizing to the staff, and highly unnecessary in a technological society. Engineers play at balancing for more than a year after the building opens, adjusting dampers, reviving temperature controls, changing settings, checking drafts. There are two generally used kinds of temperature controls—electrical and pneumatic—and one can even install for about $300,000 a remarkably sophisticated central control system where changes in any zone can be made from a central source, where constant readings of conditions in the zones appear on dials. All of these controls require prolonged delicate adjustment and constant maintenance.

No matter what the system, balancing an air-handling system and maintaining the balance within reason after an approximate balance has been achieved is a matter of trial and error comparable to "air-conditioning" a living room by raising and lowering the windows. Nothing demonstrates more dramatically the fraudulent promises of a great range of contemporary technology than air-handling systems, which contrast the enormity of the extremely expensive equipment and devices provided with the meagerness of the results obtained. From watching this process in numbers of libraries, some of which have had disastrous experiences, I am convinced that balancing is beyond the capacities of the engineer-installers (who tend to skimp it) and the do-it-yourself-if-you-have-time attempts of local plant maintenance. There are specialized companies who contract to balance air-handling systems, after the building is finished, and one should be hired to check the installation of the air-handling system and balance it completely.[9]

Filtration of outside air that enters air-handling systems is more important for libraries than for most buildings since noxious gases and the chemicals carried by dust are highly deleterious to book papers and bindings. It therefore requires much greater attention than is usually given to it in planning library buildings. There are three basic kinds of filter systems in general use, two of which remove dust from the air and one of which removes gases.

A good filtration system for libraries would include a stationary or rolling pad prefilter rated at about 16 per cent efficiency, backed by high efficiency bag filter strainers rated at about 85 per cent efficiency. Bag filters come in various efficiencies, from 40 to 95 per cent, and too low efficiency is usually provided for libraries. Even worse, only very low efficiency pad filters have been provided in many cases in my experience. Both these filters work by placing barriers in the way of the dust and keeping it from entering the building.

Electrostatic filters work by passing air over a grid of electrically charged wires, which attract and hold the dust. These have to be washed at frequent intervals, and the most sensible kind are self-washing at periodic intervals. If these are used, great care must be taken to provide unusual traps for the drainage system for the wash water, because the air flow tends to dry out the traps, opening the pipe directly into the sewage system, and sewage odors will be distributed throughout the building. Electrostatic filters should be backed by after-filters to catch the particles that elude the magnetic action of the grid.

Activated charcoal filters should be used with one of the two basic dust filters. When air is passed through activated charcoal, the charcoal absorbs the gases in the air. With chemical pollutants infesting our entire nation, every passing day makes the use of these filters, especially in industrial urban areas, more important.

For all of these filtration systems, there is a very high premium on maintaining them or changing filters strictly in accordance with the manufacturer's instructions. Economy in these matters will undo the benefits the filtration is designed to provide.

All of these systems will be improved if the building's air intakes are mounted high on the building, to avoid the accumulations of dust that are heaviest at street level. If the air-handling system is adjusted so that there is a slight positive pressure on the inside of the building, this will keep dust from infiltrating the building through minute cracks that are omnipresent, especially around windows, doors, and all other penetrations of the outside walls.

Special areas of the library will require special treatment. Rare book rooms should have their own air-handling system independent of the general system for the library, to avoid interruptions in the general system and to provide more refined filtration. The rooms must have the fullest filtration available to protect their collections—prefilters, 95 per cent high efficiency bag strainers, and activated charcoal filters. With modern technology, it is possible to think about preserving materials forever.

Computer rooms have a very low tolerance of humidity and temperature variations, which warp the data contained on their tapes and interfere with the handling of IBM cards. Special machines designed for computer rooms, variously sized for different capacity rooms, can be used for rare book stacks and reading rooms. Their ability to control variations in humidity and temperature closely are ideally suited to the requirements of rare book areas, and if separate machines are used for the rare book stacks and for reading areas and offices, it is possible to keep the stacks cooler and more humid than humans are able to endure with comfort.[10]

Noise in air-handling systems can work for or against the library. It is highly desirable to maintain a comfortably low background noise in the air escaping from diffusers (which can be achieved by design) in order to mask the ballast noise of fluorescent lighting fixtures and low-toned conversation. On the other hand, it is extremely important for the library to avoid noises of the movement of air in the ducts, and the architect's attention should be drawn clearly to this requirement in the building program. Many libraries have duct noises.

I have indicated the importance of hiring an outside engineering consulting firm with a specialty in air-handling to review the work of the mechanical engineers supplied by the architect. The argument that the architect has his own engineer is specious. Engineering is a profession that, in the commercial world, has declined more than most, and some of the most irresponsible work I have seen in buildings (and in twenty years I have seen a great deal) has been in the mechanical systems. The client needs to have working for him a firm that makes its money by correcting and improving the work of others. Just hiring such a firm will greatly improve the performance of the architect's engineers.

This consultant will contract to review for a fixed sum the work of the mechanical engineers. Two stages of review are held at different times in the development of plans. There should be a preliminary review when the mechanical engineers have a single-line heating, ventilating and air-conditioning system to propose for approval, complete with the proposed zoning. At this same time, the outline specifications of the mechanical system should be reviewed. There should be a final review of the documents at the completion of working drawings, and long enough before the bid date so that changes in the drawings can be made as necessary. There will be changes. One of the great contributions a librarian can make to his building is to have money planned in the building budget to hire such a reviewing firm.

The librarian can make other important contributions to the air-handling system in his building. In the beginning, he can absorb with his local technicians the requirements of a high quality system as discussed above, and insert in the library building program at appropriate points what is required. He can query how these requirements are to be provided for early in the preliminary plans. He can question whether they have been provided in the design of each of the library areas and have further discussion of them. Most important, he can make sure that a final review of the plans is made with the help of his local technicians, before they are totally completed. This review should call together the architects and mechanical engineers to go over the entire set of drawings, and the following questions should be asked:

1. What are the control zones, and are they of a size and shape to be comfortably controlled by a single thermostat? Will they join contiguous zones to provide uniform comfort? Will separate rooms within each zone be comfortable for their occupancy on the general zone temperature setting?

2. Where are the thermostats located? Some will probably be in locations that common sense tells you are wrong—on a sun-struck wall (the engineer not noting how the sun will enter). Some may be on a different floor from the zone itself; ask if this is a good arrangement. Almost certainly, the architects and the mechanical engineers will have difficulty interpreting their own drawings, because it is hard to set down clearly the intentions for installation in graphic form. But they will grope out the answer if you ask simple and pertinent questions, and may improve the drawings as they do so.

3. For every separate room, is there both an inlet and an outlet sufficient to carry the volume of air planned? Especially in very small rooms like faculty studies, the outlet is often omitted, since it is extremely difficult to locate the outlet in such rooms in a location that provides proper ventilation. If no smoking is permitted in the study, outlets can be provided under or through the door.

4. For each separate room that generates odors, such as toilets and smoking rooms, is the outlet connected to a separate exhaust system which goes directly outside and prevents recirculation of the air? Smoking rooms especially become stale and sour unless they are directly exhausted to the outside. The fans that pump air in this separate system should be deliberately oversized to do their job properly. In my experience, all too frequently the fans provided are not strong enough to keep the air fresh.

When we finished a long two-hour review of the mechanical plans for the Colorado College Library (I knew nothing except what the building needed) one member of the crew said in amusement to the engineer in charge, "You can get down from the witness stand." But in the process we had improved the temperature control in one large zone and in three separate rooms.

A good quality air-handling system is not inexpensive. What is the future of such planning in light of the budget shortages hanging from every tree in the grove of academe? What will be the impact of energy conservation? Almost, but not quite everything, will work to produce less satisfactory systems. There will be complete elimination of air-conditioning (cooling), as was done in the state of Colorado by one governor's edict three years ago. The first library built after the edict went into effect, the Auraria Learning Resources Center in Denver, got up to 138° the first summer it was open.[11]

There will be more exposed ceilings in buildings, and although overhead diffusers can be hung from exposed ducts, the tendency is to use more lateral grills, which are less satisfactory. There will be savings on all kinds of building components. There is a tendency to reduce lighting intensity by lowering wattage, and this will decrease the size of the cooling systems required, which is to the good. But there is also a tendency to use much cheaper air-handling systems.[12]

This is often done by turning from a centralized tempering system for the building to air-handling units on each floor. While these units can be used successfully, since they are being used to save money, cheaper equipment is also used to save more, and this can be disastrous. The use of mechanical rooms on floors adjacent to work areas or seating areas requires the best possible sound insulation in all their contiguous walls and in their door, or the functions located near them will be severely handicapped.

We can expect filtration systems and humidification systems to be skimped or almost completely eliminated. Other surprises are undoubtedly in store for us, such as the underground bunker with foot-treadle air pumps. Not all of the developments to date have been bad, and we can hope for the emergence of a cheaper, common-sensical, simpler, reasonably effective system. This will occur if the most intelligent people involved in all aspects of the planning on both sides of the negotiation prevail. But it will take a lot of work and goodwill.[13]

Notes

1. This chapter began as a speech delivered on May 16, 1966 in a workshop on Academic Library Buildings conducted by Keyes Metcalf at the Graduate School of Library Science, Drexel Institute of Technology. It was published, revised, as an article entitled "Lighting and Ventilation" in *Library Journal*, 15 January 1967, pp. 201–206, which was reprinted in Hal B. Schell, editor, *Reader on the Library Building* (Englewood, Colo., Microcard Editions Books, 1975), pp. 235–241. Part of it was incorporated in revised form in my "Lighting and Mechanical Progress in Universities" in the University Library Buildings issue of *Library Trends,* October 1969, pp. 246–261. The present version, considerably augmented and rewritten, is published by permission of *Library Journal* and *Library Trends.*

2. I acknowledge the pervasive debt in these pages to my long-time friend, George F. Rainer, formerly CM2c, now M.M.E., P.E., who began thirty-three years ago teaching me German on Eniwetok atoll in the Central Pacific during World War II, and twenty years later taught me a great deal of what I know about air-handling systems. His review, gratis, of the mechanical drawings and specifications for the Hofstra University Library showed me clearly the importance of using outside air-handling engineers to review library technical drawings, a practice seldom followed in library planning.

Since he approaches this subject from the practice of a professional engineer and I approach it through sheer, multiple, empirical experiences in walking, sitting and dwelling in libraries, we respectfully disagree on some of the facts of this chapter. I did, however, remove the paragraph he labeled "FICTION" when he reviewed its first version.

3. On the other hand, there were problems in achieving comfortable temperatures in the smaller areas in the Colorado College Library. One corner of the main floor, with window walls, was a refrigerator in summer, but the large open areas were comfortable. I remember one Spring morning in 1962, enchanting to a neophyte, when we had a smoke bomb test for air balance in the one very large open space in that library before the building was finished. This atrium area opens two stories to a series of skylights twenty-four feet above floor level. It is thirty-five feet wide by sixty feet long, a lovely area which has now been put to ingenious additional uses not originally planned.

Air is fed into this area from the peripheral diffusers on two floors overflowing into the atrium from all four sides, supplemented by thirty-two lateral diffusers feeding directly into the atrium on two floors, a complicated combination. The smoke bomb was released in the ducts leading to these upper two floors, and it was a lovely feeling to watch the smoke floating gently out from all sources to meet almost exactly in the middle of the atrium airwell.

4. The Government Documents Department is located just inside the old library building of the University of Colorado where it joins the new addition through a seven-foot doorway. Their reference desk was planned to intercept users right at the entrance point, but before a new air-handling system was installed in the old building to provide sufficient counter-pressure, the force of the wind sweeping in through that door made it impossible to staff that desk.

5. Economy measures now tend to cut the air turnover to 15%, but this is not enough.

6. The ineffectiveness of fin-tube heating systems is best seen in Chicago. Chicago's extreme temperatures in summer and winter make it highly inadvisable to use glass walls, but it has more glass wall buildings than any other major city in the country, thanks to Mies van der Rohe. The University of Illinois at Chicago Circle library is more than half glass-walled. (The basic design for this building, was submitted with all that glass wall by the same architects as the first proposal for the Colorado College library building, despite the statement in the first sentence of the program warning about the intensity of the Colorado sun and the necessity for sun control.) The fin-tubes at these glass walls fall so short of proper heating that it feels cold three feet inside the window wall on a reasonably cold day. The Illinois Institute of Technology library is completely glass-walled with fin-tube heating at the periphery. In this building, seven feet from the window walls is uncomfortable on a cold day.

7. The planning of the Towson State College Library was controlled by a hard-headed president and the architect, neither of whom knew much about designing libraries. While a modular building and reasonably functional, it incorporated some horrendous mistakes. The overhead hot-water radiant heat was one, although the consultant on the building (hired to keep the librarian quiet, and completely ignored) recommended a very good double-duct forced air system. The main entrance to the building, which is long and narrow, is on the long end. Most unusual, the size of the librarian's office, despite her repeated protests, is about five times what was required, making it a safari to reach her door. My evaluation of the library on a Middle States Association evaluation visit severely criticized the building, at a time during the construction when its defects could have been remedied. The president, when he heard these criticisms, foamed and fulminated. What else he did I do not know, but my remarks about the building were not included in the final report submitted to the College by the Association.

8. On Long Island in the summer relative humidity sometimes reaches one hundred per cent, occasionally reaches ninety-five per cent and hangs there for a week. This sounds like the ideal element for fish, but people live through it, though not in comfort. Books live through it for a while, though not unimpaired. During our first summer in Garden City we were horrified to find mold spots on the books in our basement den. We immediately bought a dehumidification machine, which removes moisture from the air by forcing it over cooling coils. This machine would remove five or six quarts of water a day from the air in a room twenty by fifteen feet, with an eight foot ceiling. In the Hofstra University Library, which had chilling but not dehumidification units, the humidity would gradually build up to the point where the Associate Director's office door could not be closed from early July until the heat was turned on in October.

9. The worst case of dislocation I have ever encountered occurred at the Rockefeller Library at Brown University. A member of the university staff had been serving as Clerk of the Works, the man who matches drawings and specifi-

cations meticulously with construction performance at all stages of its progress. A good one is worth his weight in OPEC oil stock certificates. This man was completely diverted from this supervision by the intrusion of other severe demands on his time about three months before the building was finished, and the first summer in that library was hell-hot for the staff.

When the Director finally convinced the University to hire a firm to review and balance the system, they found that nearly half of the peripheral air-tempering units did not work, that access panels to certain motors in the system had not been provided (and when they opened the ceiling and found the motors they were unwired), that cross-wiring made parts of the system supply heat when the room conditions called for cooling and the like.

At the Hofstra University Library, we suspected that two ducts were either not connected to the system or were completely blocked by a corpse, with no way to improve the situation except by prohibitively expensive tearing out of parts of the building.

10. Before the energy kick, settings for 75° summer and winter were recommended for people. Lowering below 75° in the cooling cycle is very expensive. Humidity settings of 40 per cent for people were usual. Nowadays, we do what we can get away with, or what we are beaten into doing.

There is good reason to set rare book stacks below 70°. I have been in that of the Syracuse University old library building when it was 68°. We have reason to believe that the cooler books are kept the longer they last. Settings in rare book stacks should therefore be as low as human activities in them will permit. Humidity should be held constantly at 50 per cent, and there should be an alarm to ring in the local security office if humidity gets above 65° (as it will through malfunctioning or water leaks).

11. This building won a 1976 Chicago Architectural Award (on the basis of plans and photos) and had a glowing, nay, effusive, article of praise in the December 1976 *American Libraries,* an ignorant so-called journal. Among other things lauded by *AL* was its skillful handling of sun—it *only* gets up to 138°!!! The building is a turkey—nearly completely glass-faced, under Colorado sun, squat and ill-proportioned, with a facial grid taken directly from factories, and totally unprepossessing on the inside. There was almost no librarian input in its planning.

12. Most of the highly sophisticated and expensive air-handling systems I have seen in libraries have been under-used because the level of knowledge necessary to run them was lacking in the local plant department. The Hofstra University Library had a $900,000 air-handling system which included a three-pipe fan-coil peripheral heating system that could provide even temperature at any time of year, if both cooling and heating were available all year long, which was not the case. The plant officer in charge of this system was the product of maintaining boilers on tugboats. Since the air-handling system costs about twenty per cent of the total building cost, operating it at about thirty per cent of its potential is a fantastic waste of money.

13. The following article on air-handling systems is worth reading: Ian Grad and Alfred Greenberg, "Air Conditioning for Books and People," *Architectural Record,* June 1957, pp. 231–234.

CHAPTER 5

INTERIOR DESIGN IN LIBRARIES*

(Since 1966 when this chapter had its beginning there has been greater acceptance of the importance of interior design in libraries than there was at that time.[1] The old, bland, light maple furniture that, as a friend of mine remarked, "feels like yogurt" has yielded to a variety of substitutes, and we now tend on the whole to get too dark in the dominant color tones. Libraries should have bright and joyful and inviting interiors, but going in this direction has led to some gimmicky, shrieking interiors as forbidding in their way as the worst of the old interiors. The rare quality, as is true of all esthetic experiences, is good taste.[2] Good interior design is therefore still uncommon.

Since 1966 there has been a student reaction against carrels, which at that time were so popular that they tended to dominate a library in a way as sterile as the old long tables. In recent years, as I surveyed libraries, I have consistently found carrels available in large numbers but very lightly used at all times of day and night and on all days of the week. In the past five years lounge chairs have come to be preferred as seating for study, even when a variety of alternative kinds of seating are available nearby.

Very recently, tier-built stacks have begun to return to libraries, and these can present formidable problems of appearance unless they receive treatment to upgrade their appearance.)[3]

* * * *

The interior design is the most important single element in generating the use of any library dedicated to serving undergraduates. Graduate and professional students are more highly motivated and less addicted to the luxuries of feeling, for they take the vow of poverty (if not chastity and obedience) with their entrance exams. If a library feels good to be in, it will be used even though the air conditioning freezes, and the lighting obscures, and the bookstock dwindles, and the staff offends. Though the architect lead the student through labyrinthine ways, yet will he follow if it feels good to be there.

If I am right in this contention, it is a national failure that so many library interiors are poor in feeling. They have no interior design, in the sense of objects brought together in a visual relationship. Most libraries have poor and uncoordinated colors and flat or aggresively ugly design, the ill-feeling heirs to a long tradition of bad interiors in libraries. Good taste is one of the rarest of human qualities, and its presence on library planning committees is not assured.[4] Consequently a whole range of interiors that are meretricious or simply bad are approved because those controlling the planning do not know any better. In the present budget shortages, thoughts of sybaritic things such as carpeting (the best acoustical property by far that can be used in a library) raise hackles throughout the land. If anything in the library has to go by

---

*Footnotes to this chapter begin on p. 58.

the board through lack of funds, it is the interior, thereby condemning the library to diminished use for its entire lifetime.

One high school library in Illinois that promised to be exciting and remarkably ambitious turned its interior design over to the purchasing agent, not wishing to spend money on the "fancy frills" (their term) an interior designer would provide.[5] The purchasing agent is to good interior design as the real estate agent is to orderly zoning. Ask him to buy furniture that is indestructible at the lowest possible price, and he does it well. Ask him to buy a good looking chair costing four dollars more than the monstrosity he is foisting off on his college and he quivers. And yet, many interiors are left to the mercies of the purchasing agent.[6] In this direction madness lies.

Having decided to save money on the interior, some libraries still are intelligent enough not to trust the sensibilities of the purchasing agent; they instead choose the second enemy of good interior design, the library supply house furniture expert. He will do a great deal of work for his client, will cater to his whims, will give him advice, within the range of furniture made by his company, and it will cost nothing, except the purchase of his furniture. This generally is well-made furniture and across the board it is poorly designed. The best of the lot is still not good, and without well-designed furniture a well-designed interior is impossible. That many libraries are dominated by library supply house furniture is the second reason why our interiors are bad.

In addition to human obstacles there are three large factors over which the interior designer has no control and which erect sizeable barriers to achieving good interior design. First is the shapes of rooms within the building itself. I have several times seen buildings designed by establishing the outside perimeter and slicing it up into rooms with a ruler, with no perceptible attempt to make the sizes required by the functions within the building determine its outer shape. If a room is ill-proportioned, it is extremely difficult to make it attractive.[7] Second are the lighting fixtures, which, especially at night, dominate the view in a building of any size. If the fixtures are very large (such as 4' x 4'), they have an enormous impact which combats the interior design. Fixtures can be so multiple that the ceiling becomes extremely busy and distracting. Strip fixtures can run in the wrong direction to enhance the furniture and equipment below it. If color over which the interior designer has no control is injected into the lighting system, as discussed in my chapter on the Sedgewick Undergraduate Library at the University of British Columbia, it can rend and rack the interior designer's color combination. The emergence of fluorescent as the dominant type of lighting made the interior designer's job much harder.

The third massive element in libraries which no interior designer can escape is the bookstacks. Their design, nature, height and width, the length of ranges and mass of stack blocks are all powerful physical facts in many library areas, and the designer must cope with filling the spaces left around them gracefully. He generally can influence only their color.

Stacks can be stripped of their raw metal bulk by the use of canopies on top and end panels made of fine grained wood stained to enhance the other interior furniture and equipment around them.[8] It is even possible to redeem totally the fearsome mass of a triple-tier-built stack seventy-five feet wide by one hundred and sixty feet long that flanks a reading area, as we have done in the University of Colorado Library addition.[9]

The Colorado College Library architects designed label holders to be mounted flat on the stack end panels to hold 4" x 6" labels (a size we considered readable at a far greater distance than 3" x 5"). Since two were required on each panel, they designed a single holder strip that ran completely across the end-panel, with the two ends grooved to hold the labels and the center grooved to hold a colored plastic chip. The color chip, which was changed every eight ranges, added a very pleasant touch to the appearance of the stacks. However, even treated at their best, to incorporate stacks harmoniously within the total interior design of a library is one of the most formidable tasks facing the interior designer.

In addition to coping with these problems, five centrally important elements must be considered in the interior design of each unit in the library: (1) The character of the building, the feeling it achieves visually outside and inside, which should enclose an interior in harmony with it. No Louis XIV interiors in a building of modern design, to give a stark example. But more positively, the feeling of the interior design should reflect the building itself. (2) The function of the library unit. If it is a reference room, the feeling must be different, for a number of reasons, from that of a smoking lounge. (3) The dynamics of the unit's use, especially the typical movements of readers and staff in the room. The predominant traffic patterns will dictate to a certain degree the feeling of the furniture to be placed in a given spot. (4) The needs of the readers in the unit (for smoking or non-smoking, standing, sitting, reading, talking, *etc.*) will dictate what furniture and equipment must be included. (5) Finally, and most important of all, the relationship of every object to every other object in the room, and to the surrounding walls, ceilings and floors, in terms of position, shape, color, and texture, must be arranged so that the whole produces a feeling of pleasantness appropriate to the circumstances of the room. In a well-wrought interior design, every detail is heavily laden with thought, and it is impossible for example, to change a kind of chair used extensively in the building without considering carefully the effect of the substitution on everything else related to the chairs.

It should be apparent that a major talent is required in an interior designer. As with hiring a library architect, before a designer is hired he must be tested by examining at least two of his completed jobs and talking to his clients. The designer should be hired early in the building's planning and involved with the architect before preliminary plans are completed. It is possible to achieve major advantages for the interior design without interfering with the library's function or the architect's concept of the building if interaction with the interior designer can be arranged at this point. It is not always possible to do so. The architect will want his interior designer, if his firm has one, to do the interiors, on the theory that a designer automatically is superior by virtue of being part of an architect's firm. This theory is false; some of them are not very good. I find that the interior designers in architects' firms are subordinated to the architects in a way that is not true of an independent interior designer. Nevertheless, there are distinctive advantages in coordination in having the designer in house.

If an independent designer is hired, he should be accustomed to working with larger buildings, since the vision required to design a library is considerably different from that required for house interiors. He must be congenial to the architects and acceptable to them if he is to enter fruitfully into the total design operation. He will contract for a defined fee to do the interior design.

The process of working with an interior designer goes through the following stages:

1. *Layout*. If the program has specified in detail the furniture and equipment required for each library unit and the architectural drawings have been managed well, there will be available a set of furniture layouts drawn by the architect. The designer will work with the program and with the architect's furniture layout drawings, but will re-layout the furniture and equipment, probably on a larger scale than the architect has used. There will be some changes in arrangement reflecting the interior designer's esthetic sensibility, and there will be some surprises. Some areas will really not accommodate all the furniture the architects have indicated will fit in it, because a wall is not long enough, or heating elements are in the way, or doors must open, and the like. The designer's layout will reflect the human needs of the area far more sensitively than the architect's. When this is reviewed and approved by the client, a firm count of each separate item of furniture and equipment can be made.

2. *Budget*. When the itemized count is in hand, the designer will set up categorical budgets for major items—chairs, lounge chairs, tables—with an estimated unit price for each, and approximate budgets for other items. At this point, the designer has begun to reach out into the market to get rough estimates from

a range of suppliers on kinds of items that may be considered in the interior design. At this point, he will tell the client whether or not the budget is fat, sick or in crisis. If not enough money is available, decisions must be made on what will be left out if bids indeed reflect estimated prices, and in what priority they will be added to the purchase list if money is left over. Decisions can be made on reallocating the budget, allowing more money for better quality tables by using less expensive chairs for example. When a budget has been firmly approved by the client, the designer will proceed to selection.

3. *Furniture and equipment selection.* This procedure involves gradually narrowing, by the process of weeding out, the range of choices available for items that, used together, will produce the kind of feeling that reflects the five governing considerations I have discussed. This process, of course, is worked out within the framework of utility—that is, we select the furniture that has been detailed, unit by unit, in the program. We select a desirable shaped and sized filing case not because we want an object of that size in the room, but because we need a filing case there. As the interior design develops, the quantities stated in the program will undoubtedly change somewhat. As the units begin to shape into living spaces, some furniture will probably be added or dropped for a variety of reasons. Some of the reasons will reflect the esthetic balance between the items, as it becomes apparent what they will feel like when located in proximity to each other in a given arrangement.

During this procedure, it is extremely important to see in three dimensions all of the furniture and equipment items being considered for the library. It is impossible ever to get an accurate idea of what a piece of furniture will really look like from a picture of it, even in color. In every detail of planning a building, whether reviewing architectural or interior details, three-dimensional experience is absolutely essential.[10]

4. *Textures, colors, surfaces.* When the shapes of objects have been defined reasonably well, but probably before final selection, an elaborate exploration of the nature and color of reading surfaces, walls, carpeting, doors, stacks, washroom tiles, and any other large surface areas still amenable to the designer's influence will be considered, both separately and together.[11] The choice of upholstery materials for seating and their colors will enter into this consideration. Obviously, if the interior designer has been coordinating with the architect in the development of the building, some of this thinking will have already occurred.

This phase is sometimes referred to as "color coordination," which is a crude term to describe the complicated range of considerations of textures, colors, and surface locations that must combine harmoniously to enhance each other in a good interior design. If it is not possible to hire an interior designer for the entire job, hiring one for just this portion of the planning will make a noticeable contribution to the appearance of the interior.

In reviewing this stage of the interior planning it is important to make sure that there is enough basic variation of colors, located in the right places in the building, to avoid monotony, but that the scattering effect produced by too many colors has been avoided. This scattering can take place either in separate areas if they are large or in the building as a whole. The relationship of colors and textures throughout the building must be such that there is always a feeling of consonance, that we are still in the same building.

5. *Custom designed furniture.* At about this point, if part of the furniture is to be custom-designed, the development of requirements in such items as circulation desks and inspection desks will take place. There is widespread belief that custom-designed furniture is more expensive than ready-made furniture. This belief is completely wrong. At the Colorado College Library, a lovely custom-designed carrel manufactured by Steelcase was bid a little below the cost of a similar, esthetically inferior carrel than offered by Steelcase.

The Hofstra University Library's architects had an in-house furniture designer as part of their interior design department. As a result, we used custom designs for three different tables, two different carrels, and the card catalog cases, as well as some large service desks. Every item of custom-designed furniture was considerably cheaper than similar quality counterparts from ready-made furniture companies.[12]

The problem in custom-designed furniture is not the price, which in units of six or more is always comparable or cheaper than similar quality ready-made units. The problem lies in finding a designer who is sensitive enough and aware enough of the character of the building to design esthetically superior furniture for your particular needs. Such talent is rare.[13] In addition, this rare talent must be imbedded in someone who understands thoroughly the physical strains placed on all kinds of furniture and sound ways of constructing furniture to make the pieces sturdy.

This combination of sensibility and knowledge is only occasionally encountered, and I have seen a range of custom designs that were either esthetically bad, esthetically good and structurally bad, or both esthetically and structurally bad.

6. *Major review presentation.* When the long series of decisions affecting the details of the interior have been made, with agreement along the way, a total review of the interior design is required to see everything in an overview and once more reconsider everything that has been agreed upon. This review should consider both esthetics and cost.

The interior designer will prepare for the client a series of panel boards, containing for all the major areas chips and swatches of materials to be used, color samples, material samples of wood, tile, etc., and layout drawings with each piece on it number coded to designate a specific combination of factors—such as a Breuer skid chair with a blue naugahyde upholstered seat and a cane back. This will be differentiated from the same chair with a red naugahyde upholstered seat.

Area by area, the entire library should be reviewed to make sure that the total combination within the area achieves good interior design. Furniture wood and fabrics can be laid on top of rug samples and against colored chips of stack end-panels to observe their effect on each other. This review will probably take all day and much discussion, during which some changes will be made. The total scheme must be reviewed in a comprehensive manner to make sure that the scattering of color and furniture produced by too large a variety is avoided. If the client has participated in the design development with perception up to this stage (and not with glazed eyes and confusion), this review will be extremely rewarding, as the totality of the accomplishment of the interior design is envisioned.

At this review a complete price list should be presented, with every item in the interior design marked with the designer's most mature estimate of what the unit cost will be in bids for the quantities contained in the building. These prices, which now are as close to actuality as expertise can get, should be scrutinized carefully to make sure that any unusually expensive items that may have been overlooked are removed. In every good interior designer's heart lurks a love of luxury, and even when budgets are tight they tend to feel unsatisfied unless they have slipped in one or two extravagant items that may be beautiful indeed, but have no place in fiscally responsible planning.[14] The argument that is generally made—"It's within the budget"—should be rejected by the statement that we don't want to pay that much for it.

7. *Bid documents.* There are two parts to the documentation for bidding. Both should be prepared by the interior designer. The specifications in writing contain three sections. The first swears that you will obey all laws, treat labor and all humanity fairly, love your wife and family, and observe every stupid regulation OSHA can invent.[15] The second is a description of general qualities of construction and materials that must be observed in the furniture to be supplied. The third section is the specifications of furniture and equipment required, a description in specific terms for each distinctive item in the interior design. The bid-

ders will be asked to state their bid in unit prices for each item, and the general conditions of the specifications must provide for a time period during which the number of units specified in the bids can be increased or reduced at that unit price. How many items can be bought will not be known until bids are
submitted, and quantities may have to be varied.

The specifications of furniture and equipment can be arranged in different ways. The best I have seen
were the specifications for the Colorado College Library, which listed for each area in the library full specifications for each item within the area. This method requires repetition of the exact specification for the
same desk when it is repeated in the building, and requires the bidder to count through the specifications to
determine how many units he is bidding on. But it makes blindingly clear what is to go in each area, and
places a unit price beside each item, so if it is necessary to cut budget, this can be done on the basis of the
importance of areas.

A more usual way, because it is easier to do, is to list only once each item in the building, with the
number of units required. This makes the designer responsible for the count of items, and the librarian
must check his count before bids are let. It is difficult to believe until you have tried it how hard it is to
get an accurate count from plans of a complex building of the chairs, for example, of which there are four
different kinds upholstered in four different colors.

Another way of arranging items, which makes no sense to a librarian and is accident prone, is to arrange items and count by the supplier who will originate the items. No matter how the items are arranged
in the specifications, it is advisable to contract for items to be set in the exact place in the building indicated for them by code number. Otherwise they are likely to be dumped unassembled on your loading dock
by a truck driver following his orders, or delivered to another part of the university where anything can
happen to them.[16]

Accompanying the specifications will be a set of furniture layout plans with each item in it bearing a
code number which correlates exactly with an item in the specifications designated by that number. This
layout must be checked carefully by the librarian before bidding, to make sure that colors of upholstery are
located exactly where they should be and are designated correctly. It is useful to color each item according
to the upholstery it requires so it will be easy to check arrival and proper location of items shipped, and so
that at a later date furniture can be kept in the order planned by the interior designer when the building is
in use.

Three kinds of complications can enter the bidding process, depending on the rationality of your organization's purchasing policies. In an attempt to get active competition and the lowest possible prices,
specifications are sometimes written in generic form, which tries to guarantee the quality and design desired but does not specify items by manufacturer and model number. Although the client must have in
mind the kind of items he wants, if anything like an interior design is intended, this method assures certain
disaster.

Another method requires specifications to designate for each item three competitive pieces from three
different manufacturers at approximately the same estimated price. I long believed that this was impossible
to do, since any one of three chairs, for instance, would have to relate to any one of four different tables
and to any one of three of all the other items in an area for the interior design to exist at all. However,
with the creep of furniture designs, which apparently are very hard to patent, items that look very much
alike in competitive price ranges are available. We achieved a very good interior design for the addition to
the University of Colorado Library on this basis, required by the State.

Another method requires multiple bidders, even when only one manufacturer and model is specified
for each item. There is no difficulty getting four or five bids on such specifications from different suppliers
or from different agents of the same manufacturer from around the country. In the same way, it is easy to

get a spread of competitive bids for custom-designed furniture from custom design companies and from companies like Risom or Remington Rand, whose stock in trade is ready-made.

8. *Follow-up performance*. There are two terminal functions that should be performed by the interior designer after bids are let. First is the review of working drawings submitted for approval by all manufacturers of anything that is custom-designed or requires modification of standard units. The specifications of furniture and equipment will include the interior designer's drawings for each piece, but these are skeletal drawings that control proportions, dimensions, and appearance, but do not designate methods of construction. The supplier is required by the specifications to return working drawings complete in every detail and designating exactly how the piece will be made. It is important to have the interior designer review these drawings to make sure that the appearance of the piece is exactly what was intended, and to check solidity of construction. Working drawings can be approved by the client, but doing so is accident prone.[17]

The interior designer's final assignment is to follow up after all furniture and equipment items have been delivered to make sure everything is exactly as specified in type of item, color, quantities. He will arrange for the repair or replacement of all damaged items, and make sure that anything in the interior design that is fastened to the building such as signs, plaques, carpeting, has been installed properly. In the case of carpeting, proper initial installation is critically important for long wear, and it often is installed very haphazardly.[18]

Attention should be called to some highly undesirable styles in interior design which should be avoided like the Boyconnell Flux:

Sombre. This is an attempt to achieve the tradition of the conservative nineteenth-century English gentleman's style, strained through the eyes of a twentieth-century provincial. This style is very low toned and very low keyed, contains nothing exciting in shape and nothing light in color. Its total effect is to drag down the appearance of the library.[19]

Sunday Supplement. This is an attempt to suggest the 25th century, to appear really with it in outer space. Shapes are overdramatic, colors used overbright, materials call attention to themselves and good taste is quite in abeyance. We recall the wife who is having her conservative ancestral English mansion re-papered with chrome plating in Evelyn Waugh's *A Handful of Dust*.

Schrecklich. (This German word conveys precisely the combination of horrifying with the scream that ensues.) This style leans to the point of groaning on dramatic colors that are violently intense, spread over large areas of walls and floors, and disagreeable in tone. The Education Library at Harvard University is the shoutingest example of this style that I know, and it shouldn't happen to a dog house.

Four items of major impact on the interior design—chairs, tables, walls and carpeting—require some detailed practical consideration.

There will be more chairs in a library than any other single item. They will therefore influence to a considerable degree the feeling of the entire building, and must be chosen and designed with the greatest care. For side chairs, choices involve wood frames or metal frames, wood or plastic backs and seats, with or without arms, with plastic or fabric upholstery, on the seat or on the back as well.

To a considerable extent, the choice will be restricted by the budget. Plastic chairs with metal legs are the cheapest, and now are sturdy, well designed and quite colorful. Wood chairs, especially in such wood as teak or walnut are the most expensive, especially if fabric upholstered. There is a place for more expensive side chairs—special collections rooms, for example—but on the whole, chairs should be selected to meet the requirements, visually and functionally, at the most reasonable price.

A variety of chairs is needed, partly because one chair will not feel comfortable to all readers, and partly to vary the feeling of the building in different areas. Three different side chairs, two of which are versions of each other, will provide enough variety. It is often possible to get the same chair with arms and without arms. Chairs with arms cost a little more, but they are popular with readers. If arm chairs are used at tables the arms must slide easily under the table that will be used, even after the table has sunk a little into the carpeting. The two must be tested together.

I plead for some arm chairs at tables, and for upholstery at least on chair seats to ease those long hours that so compact even padded flesh. Naugahyde and similar plastic materials make colorful seat covers. In hot weather they tend to sweat, as they condense evaporation from the body. So do shell plastic seats, but both wear like iron. Fabric materials provide a much wider range of color and texture in seats but will soil and wear out faster. If plastic fabrics, such as woven nylon, are used the weave must be tight. Loose weaves are picked at by readers with pencils, and by their nature they wear out faster than tight weaves. Nylon threads have a tendency to absorb dirt through their open ends, and it cannot be removed. Therefore, if brilliant colors, such as bright yellow, are used a constant maintenance program is required for them or they will become impossible to clean. Bright fabrics of a solid color can be kept immaculate if they are wiped lightly once a week with cleaning fluid tinted with a dye the identical color of the fabric. All fabrics should be Scotchguarded, a process of spraying fabric to make the threads cling together for longer wear.

All chairs should be equipped with glides to suit the surface on which they rest; they are different for carpeting and tile. Chairs must be sturdily built to absorb the violent energy that young people discharge so casually. In less used areas, such as staff lounges or library offices, sturdiness is of much less importance. A hard-nosed purchasing agent can be helpful in testing the chair construction and he should demand a sample of every furniture item before signing a contract for their purchase, preferably before the interior design is final.

Lounge chairs should be used in general reading areas as liberally as can be afforded, up to thirty per cent of the seating. They should also be used in smoking lounges and other relaxation areas. They present the same problems of choices as do side chairs.

Other seating includes sofas, stools and stacking chairs. Long sofas lend themselves to sleeping, belly-sprawling, or sexual activities depending on the occupancy of the room, so two-seaters should be used. Rarely are sofas seated to capacity, so they must be used sparingly. Backless stools are used in certain areas to encourage readers not to linger—low ones at periodical index tables and high ones at card catalog tables. Hard seats are recommended. A few low stools in front of a mirror in the women's rest rooms will be much appreciated. Low stools scattered throughout open stacks will be used. Stacking chairs should be used only for temporary seating for lectures. There is no point in using them as permanent chairs anywhere.

Tables are extremely important in libraries. I grew up in a reserve room that had long tables for thirty students, with a center rail running down the entire length. How vividly I remember those tortured hours during which one of the thirty steadily tapped the center rail with his foot, but which one I knew not. For such reasons, we abandoned multiple seating, and there was a trend toward single-seaters in libraries, as well as in plumbing. For about ten years single carrels threatened to take over the world, but experience with them proved the value of multiple seating, and of as much variety in seating groups as possible.

Tables for four and for six are needed in a library. The larger should be used in reference rooms, map rooms, and other spread areas not crowded with readers, and tables for four should be mixed throughout all reading areas, especially where large numbers of books are shelved. The reader can never predict when he will find on the shelves eight books that he must survey briefly, and spread to do so. Sometimes the reader wants to sit on a particular day at an area that feels more luxurious than the 2' x 3' space provided by single seating. These needs require tables.

On the other hand, seating for more than six should not be used. I recommend 3' x 8' tables with three chairs on each side for seating. They provide less than the 2' x 3' space for each reader at multiple-seating tables that is clung to like Mother by some librarians (they should choose larger tables), but after carefully observing the acceptance of 3' x 8' tables for six in Hofstra's periodicals reading room for nine years, I became convinced that they have their use in libraries. In group study rooms, where students want to be close rather than separated, 3' x 6' tables with two chairs on each side and one at each end are more than adequate for six. Needless to say, if two tables for four are placed touching each other, they form in effect a table for eight, and this should be avoided by allowing at least two feet between tables juxtaposed laterally. Yeshiva University Library uses tables to seat four and six that are 3' wide, with readers seated on one side only.

Tables as long as 8' pose problems of construction if made of wood. It is possible to carry this length on a metal frame without difficulty, but to support it with wood requires either a fifth center leg, which makes the table difficult to move, or center bracing. Reading tables should never have a deep apron to knock against. Their legs should be located to avoid interfering with readers at places where they logically will sit at the table. All tables should be equipped with adjustable glides to suit the surface on which they will rest, and the glides should be adjusted after the tables are in place.

The surfaces of tables are the largest horizontal reflecting surfaces in the building other than the floor, so it is extremely important for good lighting that they be light colored. If plastic laminate tops are used the bottom side of the table top must also be covered with plastic laminate to prevent warping. Some furniture designers do not seem to know this. If the surface is of satin finish, its high gloss will produce bad glare. It should be of matte finish which prevents glare and helps diffuse the light.

Do light plastic tops invite defacement? At the Colorado College library, all tables and carrels used a putty-grey suede formica top, which under fluorescent light looked white. The students at that college lived in a permissive atmosphere and were self-indulgent in many ways. They abused furniture in other buildings. Four years after opening I checked with the plant director to see what their experience had been. He reported that although there was some occasional writing on the surfaces it was easily removed with Bon Ami, and the custodian responsible for the building said that if the choice were left to him, he would choose this kind of surface. From such a source, there could be no higher recommendation. Light plastic laminate has been treated well by users at Hofstra and the University of Colorado also.

In small conference rooms for librarians to use with students a 2' x 3' table is suitable. At the card catalog, stand-up tables for consulting drawers of cards should be 3' wide to be graceful. The same stand-up table can be used in reference areas to hold multiple large dictionaries. If stacking tables are used in the staff lounge, this area can be cleared to provide reception space. None of these tables poses special problems other than selecting a suitable design.

Walls are often painted off-white, to serve as a background against which to play colors in the foreground. If they are painted a color, it must be analyzed for its effect on every item that will be seen against that color, even at a distance. Glass walls provide as background whatever can be seen through them in the daytime. If this is greensward, there is not much problem; if it is other buildings nearby, the only real solution is covering them with drapery or louverdrapes. At night, for all practical purposes glass walls are black, and consideration must be given to this fact in designing colors that stand in front of them.

Carpeting will affect everything around it, because its color will be reflected in the light that rebounds from it as far as the ceiling. Its color will influence the atmosphere of the entire area it underlies. Therefore, it must be selected with great sensitivity, and its reflectance kept in the range of 10%. While some variation of color should be used in a building of any size, striped carpeting has been used in libraries, and is very distracting. Too often, carpeting is overbusy in its variation. Carpeting can be a destructive element if its color is unpleasant and constantly fighting against everything above it. Good taste must dictate its selection.

It will take from four to six months to work through the various stages of developing an interior design, during which the client will learn a great deal. However, it cannot be overemphasized how important it is to have someone with good taste as the reviewer working with the interior designer. Without such a positive check, it is impossible to know the quality of what is presented for review. Too often, the planning team just accepts what is handed to it, and this can be downright foolish.

Notes

1. This chapter began as a speech delivered on May 16, 1966 in a workshop on Academic Library Buildings conducted by Keyes Metcalf at the Graduate School of Library Science, Drexel Institute of Technology. It was published in revised form as an article entitled ''A Well-Wrought Interior Design,'' in *Library Journal* for 15 February 1967, pp. 743–747. This article was reprinted in Ralph D. Thomson's *Organizing the School Media Program*. (Salt Lake, University of Utah Division of Continuing Education, 1973), pp. V-5 to V-9, and in Hal B. Schell, editor, *Reader on the Library Building* (Englewood, Colo., Microcard Editions Books, 1975), pp. 160–165. It is reprinted here, heavily revised and greatly augmented, by permission of *Library Journal*.

2. I thank the fate that brought me early in my planning experience at Colorado College to work with Dolores Miller, then the interior designer on the staff of the Chicago office of Skidmore, Owings and Merrill. Of that highly talented architectural team, hers was the greatest talent. Since that time, in her capacity as owner and principal of her own firm (presently Miller, Krusinski Associates, Chicago), I have worked with her on four other interior designs, most recently on the addition to the University of Colorado Library. On her training and experience as an architect, Mrs. Miller brings to bear superlative taste, and a wider range of knowledge of furniture items, shapes, textures, colors and price ranges than any other designer I know.

3. For instance, in parts of the new addition to the Ohio State University Library, still under construction, and the entire new central stack in the University of Colorado Library addition.

4. I point out the results of this lack on the planning team in my chapter on the Sedgewick Undergraduate Library, University of British Columbia.

5. Ridgewood High School, Norridge, Illinois. The interior is poor. The ambitious scope of this library, ''twice as big as a football field'' they boasted, and half dedicated to media, was not matched by the demands of the curriculum on the students. When I was there, although a large number of students had been assigned to the library for that morning hour, very few of them were at work, and the instructors prowling the floors like lion tamers were barely able to contain the bedlam short of frenzy.

6. Even worse than the purchasing agent is the plant director, although only once in my experience has he been able to control the interior. Most plant directors are perceptive enough to know they can't handle such an assignment. However, at Lincoln University in Pennsylvania in 1972, after two years of planning, a new president arrived on the scene and to save about $20,000 abandoned a very fine interior design, completed through documents ready to let for bid, and put the plant director in charge of the interior. The results are sad to see.

7. Designers sometimes retrieve such situations. One smoking lounge in the Colorado College library turned out to be ten feet wide by twenty-four feet long with an eight and a half foot ceiling. This was turned into a reasonably pleasant space by painting the end walls two different tones of the side wall colors, which miraculously obscured the fact of the room's length. There is one library at the University of Denver whose very fine interior design redeems a building whose exterior falls flat on its face.

8. We must not confuse wood end-panels with end-panels of plastic-impregnated wood. If wood is to be used for appearance, full advantage must be taken of its grain. When wood is impregnated with plastic, this unholy coupling flattens the appearance of grain and leaves only the color of the plastic-mixed wood. In such cases it is far better to go to a plastic laminate for a cover. This is true of any use of wood in furniture or walls in a building.

However, properly handled and located around the building wood can be a brilliant addition in small touches to the feeling of the interior. On the main floor of the Colorado College Library, the only place we could afford this treatment, the stacks and a large wall directly behind the circulation desk (which, together, pretty well dominate the feeling of that floor) are of a handsomely grained quarter-sawn English oak, rubbed with Watco oil. The result (which has deteriorated through lack of maintenance) was beauty to warm the heart.

9. The tier-built stacks at the University of Colorado have light tan oak end-panels in a pleasant grain throughout. Use of a matching wood to cover ducts within the stacks masks nearly entirely the raw, industrial feeling usually produced by tier-builts. The use of wood commands only a small premium over alternative treatments, since panels are veneer. If this treatment of wood is used in this way throughout a building whose properties will be supplied by different crafts or bidders, it is possible for a designer to reserve in the stock of a supplier a single flitch large enough to supply the wood veneer to all bidders, who are required by specifications to apply for that flitch. This is the only way possible to have matching wood throughout an entire building.

10. The accuracy of this observation can be easily tested by carrying around a Remington Rand furniture catalog when you visit libraries. The best instance I know of the importance of three-dimensional experience occurred when we were choosing the color for our vertical louverdrapes at the Hofstra University Library in 1966. Sitting in my old office we chose from the sample chips the color we considered to be most appropriate to the building and its interior design. We then went to the new building and held up that color chip at the windows, which were bronze tinted, and were startled to find that under the conditions it was to be hung it showed a bilious yellow. We then, on the spot, chose a different color from the samples. Anyone who has studied painting knows how radically the appearance of a color can change with changes in its background color. It is extremely important to test colors by seeing them against their background color; in the library this will probably be walls or carpeting.

11. Imagination and good taste can find a large range of locations where special touches will enhance the feeling of the building. I discuss window lettering and the use of supergraphic strips in my chapter on the Sedgewick Undergraduate Library at the University of British Columbia. The washrooms in the Hofstra University Library have a three-inch-wide band of colored tile (orange for men, blue for women), that separates the upper part of the wall from the lower. This provides a nice touch in an area that usually is sterile.

12. The supplier, from the Keller Furniture Manufacturing Co., Oneonta, N.Y., was not only satisfied with his profit, but told me that in larger volume he could even lower his prices. He later offered in his literature these same tables and carrels as stock items. One great advantage of custom designing is that pieces can be reviewed before the production run, and alterations made in them at that time to accommodate needs that may have become clear after the original design was completed.

13. Not only is Hofstra's furniture quite good, it lends a distinctive flavor to the interior that reflects the strong character of the building. My wife and I, who are of different sexes (the right sexes—she female, I male), both agree that this feeling is masculine. Masculine enough to set the swamp-libbers shrieking if they had any sensibility.

On the other hand a prominent woman's college missed the boat when they had the chance of designing specifically feminine furniture for the new Wells College Library and did not. As they surveyed the old library the architects observed that girls assumed a pattern of unconventional positions—curled in chairs like cats, "seated" on their shoulders with their feet up against the wall, and the like—that seemed to fit their anatomy. Although they talked about designing furniture specifically for these kinds of sitting, they did not do so.

14. One reason for the president's rejection of the entire completed (and paid for) interior design for the Lincoln University Library, which presented a reasonably priced interior, was his discovery that for the Librarian's office had been specified a desk estimated at $500, which no one had caught in the review.

15. The federal Occupational Safety and Health Authority seems to be burgeoning with mongolian idiots whose sole function is to issue regulations that have the effect of law without undergoing the reconciliation of interests involved in legislation, governing safety conditions throughout the land. The land varies. The mentality of OSHA does not. At Otterbein College, a small liberal arts college faced with the financial pressures that haunt such institutions, a cost survey indicated that compliance with OSHA safety regulations, to prevent accidents of which they had no record in a long history, had raised their tuition costs almost $200.

In Boulder, Colorado, where no teacup in recorded history has ever shaken from a shelf, we were required to bolt to the floor all the stacks that had been planned as freestanding, for the exigencies of a major research library, to cope with earthquake conditions characteristic of the San Andreas Fault. Indeed, OSHA's model was the accident at California State University at Northridge, in the San Fernando Valley. Undoubtedly these bolts will hold the stacks (but not the books) to the floor in case the earth reverses itself on its axis. Meanwhile, back at reality, six months after move-in we had to tear up and move a hundred and twenty stack sections in the reference area which were bolted to the floor through carpeting!

16. I remember the Saturday afternoon I was called from home to open up the new Colorado College Library to receive a shipment of some important custom-designed furniture made by Woodworking Corporation of America. The contract called for them to be installed in place in the building. They were in flat wooden cartons, obviously unassembled, but the driver had instructions only to deliver them to the library. Only by refusing delivery, which caused the driver to phone back to Chicago, was an arrangement made for the driver himself to assemble this furniture and install it in place.

17. We really goofed at the University of Colorado on the design of new card catalog cases to be added to a large number of existing cases. In an attempt to improve the appearance of a diverse group of nondescript catalogs, we decided to pay a small premium to use better wood and better design in the cases which would be seen first as one entered the reference area. The interior designer produced a good design, and drawings were accepted by bidders.

To save money, our Office of Planning had not hired the designer to review working drawings, since they had a new young man with experience in furniture manufacturing methods. The successful bidder, for peculiar reasons, decided that the interior designer's drawings did not indicate what we really wanted, and submitted alternative drawings to our Office of Planning. I was at a Midwinter ALA meeting at the time, and our new young man approved drawings for a radically different appearing card catalog case. I caught up with this goof when they were delivered, but when I instituted action to return them, found that we had no ground whatsoever for doing so. The cases that resulted do nothing to enhance the appearance of our reference room.

18. I once heard a man on Long Island, a hotbed of union abuse, who had been hired from the local union hall as a qualified carpet mechanic at fifteen dollars an hour, complain loudly that he had never done this work before, and no one was telling him how to do it. That installation had bubbles in the carpeting all over the place that were finally rectified by the determined follow-up of the interior designer.

19. My chapter on the University of Toronto Library discusses an example of this kind of interior style. Another recent example is the Clarke Art Institute Library, Williamstown, Massachusetts, which does its best to become a richly caparisoned mortuary.

PART II

LIBRARY BUILDING REVIEWS

The Beinecke Library at Yale
The Rockefeller Library at Brown University
The Countway Library of Medicine
The Dalhousie University Library
The Robarts Library at the University of Toronto
The Sedgewick Undergraduate Library
   at the University of British Columbia

CHAPTER 6

THE BEINECKE LIBRARY AT YALE

The Beinecke Library in its setting.

At left, Berkeley College. Upper left, the Sterling Memorial Library. Upper right, the Law School. Extreme right, the Corinthian columns of University Commons. The cenotaph, the memorial flagpole, and the opening of the sunken court of the Beinecke Library are clearly visible. Photo: Ezra Stoller © 1963 ESTO

The glass book-vault, viewed from the mezzanine level of the cap. This level, which contains all of the exhibition cases except the very long cases below, is used for receptions. The small exhibition case, the shape of the marble facing panels and their frames, and the lighting coffers can be seen. Photo: Ezra Stoller © 1963 ESTO

The reading room, showing the lighting louvers, the feeling of the furniture, and through the far window wall, the Noguchi sculptures in the sunken court. The diagonal at the upper right is the underside of the stairway to this level. Photo: Ezra Stoller © 1963 ESTO

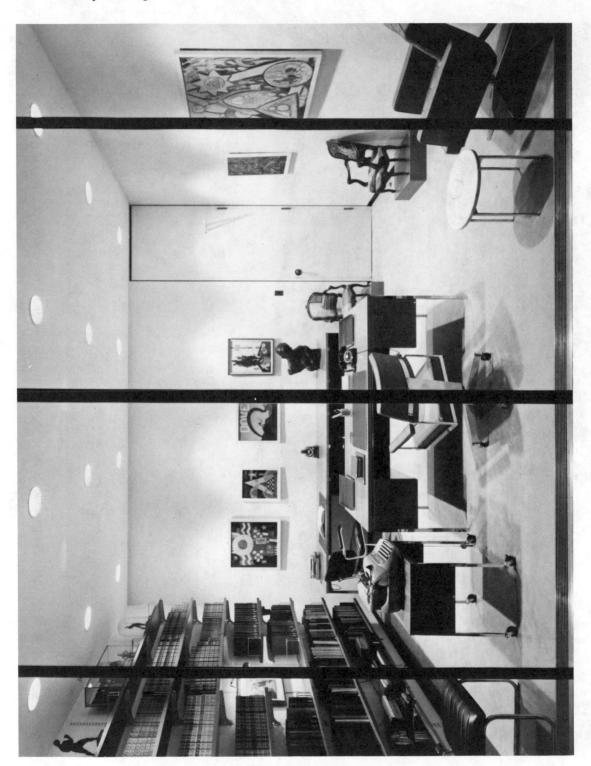

A curator's office, shot through the glass wall of the sunken court. Photo: Ezra Stoller © ESTO

The Vierendeel Truss Under Construction.

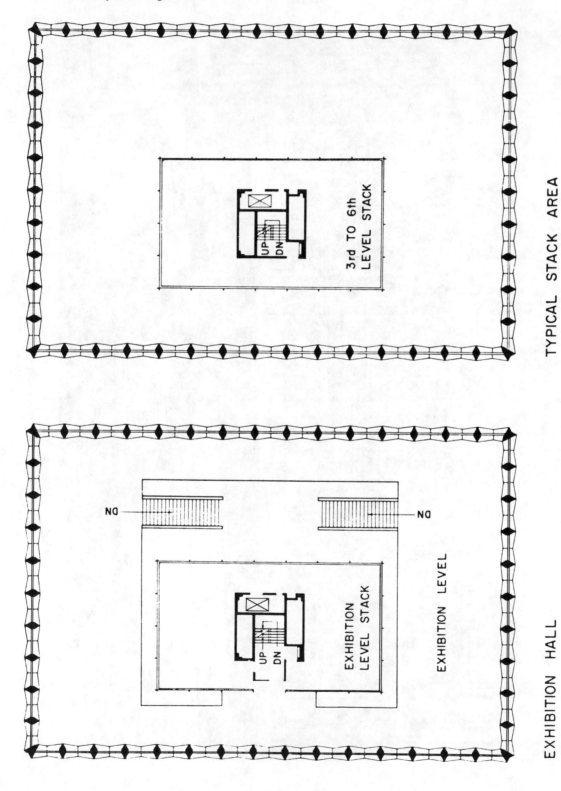

TYPICAL STACK AREA

3rd TO 6th
LEVEL STACK

EXHIBITION HALL

EXHIBITION
LEVEL STACK

EXHIBITION LEVEL

Floor plans of the Beinecke Library cap, showing the dimensions of the glass book-vault.

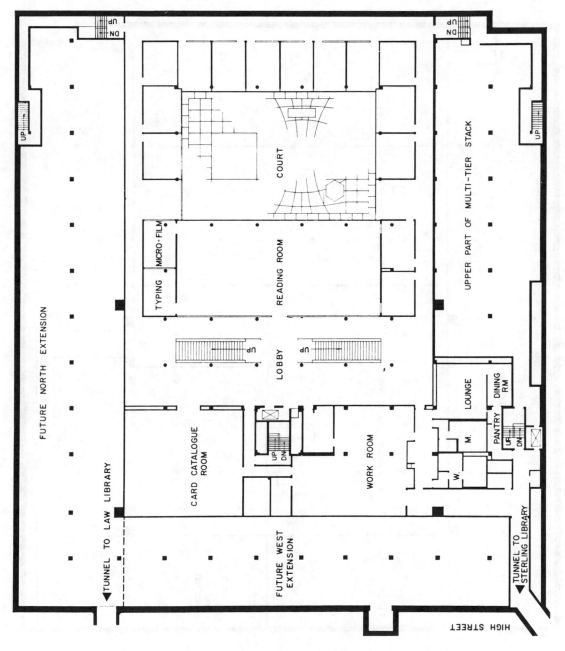

Floor plan of the library floor. The Circulation desk is located directly in front of the work room.

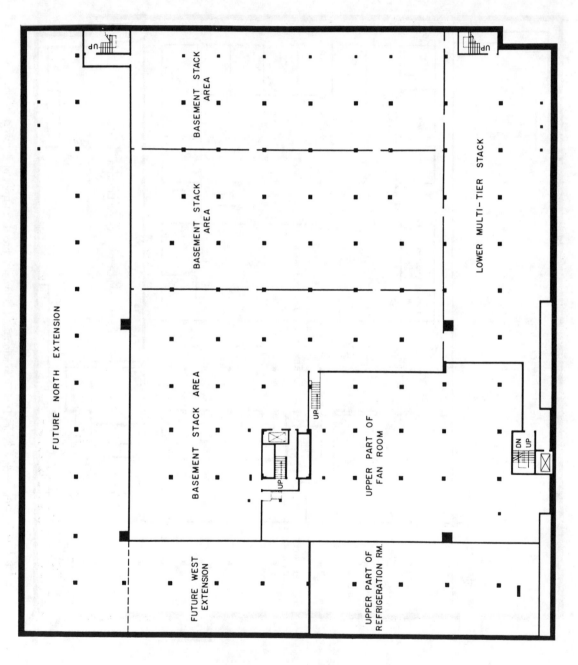

Floor plan of the stack area.

THE BEINECKE LIBRARY AT YALE*

(In 1952, when I returned to librarianship from a successful interlude spent completing a doctorate and teaching college literature, it occurred to me that I should put my literary experience to use by publishing articles on librarianship. When I asked myself what area I knew well enough to write about, the hollow answer returned: "None!" This answer should return to more librarians these days! The next twelve years served to fill up the void.

This review of the Beinecke Rare Book and Manuscript Library was the first article of any substance I ever published in librarianship, but it was an article in which everything came together right. Except for the war years, I had spent from 1934 to 1948 at Yale as a social science and, later, literature student, and as staff member of the library when it still was one of the four greatest university libraries in the world. I knew the university's educational needs and the library's potential and tradition.

I had perceived vaguely, in an immature way, the remarkable growth of Yale's rare book collection under Chauncey Brewster Tinker, great teacher and lecturer and even greater bookman (who by 1946 had replaced every rare book he'd inherited as Curator with a better copy), and the range of spectacular satellite collections that had settled at Yale in the late twenties and thirties. I was fresh from working with a branch of Skidmore, Owings and Merrill on the Colorado College Library, and was acquainted with the stylistic preferences and working methods that pervade all offices of that firm. Through the Yale library staff, I had full and prolonged access to floor plans, and to the job captain from Skidmore, Owings and Merrill who had been in charge of the architectural planning. Through a very close friend, a member of the firm, I had access to the engineer from the eminent engineering consulting firm of Jaros, Baum and Bolles who had been in charge of the mechanical planning. From all of these sources came valuable information about the background and details of the emergence of this library building. Together, these factors generated an unusually large body of information to work from.

The article had a slight impact on the operation of the Beinecke. My complaint about the obscuring of two superbly grained burl olive table tops by the dimness of the overhead light led to an increase in the light intensity somewhat. Now, with the energy shortage, the lights have been dimmed again. The hopes I expressed of engaging undergraduate interest in rare books through the Beinecke's fine exhibition facilities have been fulfilled by a vigorous exhibition program correlated with the university's intellectual events. The hazard of leakage through the plaza above the rare book stacks that I discussed has turned out to be real, and leaks have resulted.

My expectations that the building would lure the donation of collections to Yale have been fulfilled to a startling degree. The Beinecke has emerged into public view as the most glamorous rare book building in the world, fulfilling the aspirations of the Beinecke family. Since its opening, the richness and importance of its collections have more than doubled through gifts, and its command on the resources of the university has grown. In meager times, it continues to thrive.

My article made no impact whatsoever on one of its primary aims—to encourage fellow consultants to write similar critical reviews of buildings with which they had no connection (though it has generated an

---

*Footnotes to this chapter begin on p. 84.

article in Germany). In 1964 I was able to persuade Keyes Metcalf to travel from Boulder to Colorado Springs to survey carefully the Colorado College library, half promising to write a review of it; but he ultimately declined because the consultant on the building was a friend of his.

Since 1964, when this article was written, there have been only two attempts, to my knowledge, at reviews of academic libraries, both of them enthusiastic puffs instead of critical reviews and neither well informed. Recently *American Libraries* has launched a series of feature articles on library buildings in the worst tradition of yellow journalism, these days turned to fool's gold. They result from snow jobs on ignorant little journalists whose eyes pop right out on their cheeks at the dramatic wonders claimed by the snake-oil salesmen. They not only are bad, they are dangerous, convincing librarians with no experience in planning that very bad buildings are good.

In the course of time and exposure to a large range of architectural literature, I have come to realize how truly rare are critical reviews of buildings of any kind that combine both a functional and esthetic approach. The next six chapters are among that handful of reviews. In each I have tried to emphasize a different aspect of library buildings of general interest to library planners, so that the cumulative effect of the group as a whole would be broadly informative.

The Beinecke planning is surrounded by a variety of choice anecdotes, best narrated by Fritz Liebert, that cannot logically be included in the text. I have recorded a few of them in the footnotes, to preserve their art, though I am unable to vouch for their substance. The original article was not accompanied by illustrations since *College and Research Libraries* did not run photographs at that time. This defect has been remedied in this chapter.)

*   *   *   *

We would be morally offended to read the review of a book by the author himself, but we accept without question the account of a new library building by the librarian who planned it, the very person totally unequipped to give it any objective review.[1] For he has moved out of a rat's nest into spacious quarters, which would seem grand no matter what they were, he is under heavy pressure from his university to feature this prime piece of public relations, there often is a kindly donor pleased as punch in the background, and the building itself is the librarian's baby. Consequently, the effervescent flow of bland reviews of buildings (just run through an architectural issue of *LJ*), all of which say that they incorporate in the highest possible degree all of the successful elements, described in clichés, of the totally good building.

The simple fact is that a limited number of good academic library buildings have been built since World War II, and many of them are defective in important aspects, such as lighting. This article aspires to inaugurate a series of objective reviews of the most important recent academic library buildings, which should be written by consultants completely unconnected with them.[2] The purpose of such articles should be to delineate the character of each building sensitively, pro and con, and conclude what we can learn from it about planning and construction.

The Planning

The Beinecke library was not planned under the best of circumstances. It had an open-ended budget, with no firm upper limit of expenditure stated to the architects.[3] This is a situation tailored for Skidmore, Owings, and Merrill, whose New York office is noted for expensive architecture, and it is exactly the same kind of financial situation that called forth the architectural extravagances of Yale's Sterling Memorial Library in the early '30s, while Rome burned. It led directly to some of this building's flaws, and better results could have been achieved by setting a large but firm budget.

In the second place, the librarian of the Beinecke library had not been appointed when the planning began, and was not appointed for about six months thereafter. This placed Herman Liebert, the logical (and later successful) candidate and the man who knew the dynamics of the operation, in a tangential position, whereas he should have been in a more central position of strength and authority from the beginning.

In the third place, there was no detailed program for the building. The Beinecke library was a radical departure for Yale in that it fused, for the first time, its special collections, each of which has its own curator, with the rare book room. Yet the components of this building were not defined in detail and the dynamics of the operation it would house were not completely delineated in a written program before the project was handed to the architects. As a result, the present dynamics of the Beinecke library have, to a certain extent, been determined by Skidmore, Owings and Merrill, which is not entirely to the good, as will be seen.

Finally, the University should have used a library building consultant, and a lighting consultant in the planning. John Ottemiller was central in the university's negotiations with the architects, and there is no question that he was responsible for some fine things in the building. But in negotiating with an architectural firm with an unshakeable reputation for dictating to its clients, a library building consultant of broad experience would have helped considerably, and he certainly would have insisted on a written program.[4]

The lighting shortcomings in this building, where they occur, are naive and predictable. Yale had on the faculty of its school of drama one of the greatest experts on lighting in the country, Stanley McCandless, but he was not consulted on the lighting plans of this building, or of any of the recent Yale buildings.[5]

The Site

The Beinecke library was built on the southwest corner of Hewitt Quadrangle, on the last piece of uncommitted ground at the center of the University. On the northwest corner of the quadrangle, with its back to Beinecke, is a small, heavy, windowless imitation Greek temple built of white marble blocks, now considerably weathered. On the far side of the building are large bronze doors. Both the marble and the bronze carried over to the Beinecke library.[6]

Just east of this building is the University Commons, a massive rectangular structure that flanks the entire north side of the quadrangle with a portico behind a dozen huge Corinthian columns, whose acanthus leaves on their capitals are discreetly covered with chicken wire to avert the pigeon scat (the wire is not visible from the south entrance of Beinecke).

On the northeast corner is Memorial Hall, a rotunda whose copper dome, heavily green with sulfation, looms high over the quadrangle. Running south at right angles from Memorial is Yale's largest auditorium, Woolsey Hall, a limestone building pierced on the face opposite Beinecke with five huge Romanesque windows. On the southeast corner of the quadrangle is Woodbridge Hall, the administration center, a smaller, squat, two-story limestone building.

Across the street south of the Beinecke library is Berkeley College, a residential college in cottage Gothic style, of light brown fieldstone, whose five stories incorporate feeble attempts at buttresses, parapets, and leaded windows, to conform to academic respectability in the early '30s. Across the street west of Beinecke is a façade of the law school, whose light brown fieldstone lower level is topped by a red brick inset wall pierced, between buttresses, with elaborately ornate Gothic windows that culminate above in a series of knobbed shafts and two gingerbready Gothic towers at the ends of the building.

And across the street on the diagonal to the southwest, is Sterling Memorial Library, whose window-slotted, buttressed stack rises thirteen stories to a series of medieval towers (the nearest topped by a weathercock), and whose awesome Gothic mass could be ignored only with peril.

Commons and Woolsey Hall, which dominate the quadrangle, are strong buildings, with a feeling of quiet dignity enhanced by the names of great World War I battles incised in the frieze, a fifteen-foot-high cenotaph to that war's dead in front of the portico, and a forty-foot memorial flagpole of painted bronze. Into these grounds an interloper dared not enter lightly. The 200' by 350' sunken quadrangle between the buildings was paved entirely with cobblestones, roundly cursed in slippery weather by generations of students, since this is one of the main walkways between dormitories and classrooms (see p. 65).

For an architect who works in a modern style, the site could not have been more incongruous, but the most obvious thing about the building at first glance is that it has coped with the site problem brilliantly, and Hewitt Quadrangle has never looked so good. The building had to be oriented north-south, and the size of its cap (that portion visible above the quadrangle, which is less than half of the building) has been held to the right proportions to balance nicely the other buildings in the quadrangle, both in its height and its facade.

The use of marble facings and the simplicity of its form provide enough suggestion of the classical style to make it consonant with the buildings on the quadrangle, while the sharply cut, grey granite frames around the marble, which rise to a pointed boss where the frames meet, provide strong jagged lines across the face of the building and at its corners that relate it to the surrounding Gothic. In addition, the provision of a sunken court has added interest to the quadrangle, which has been raised to sidewalk level and paved entirely to the edge of every building with the same warm grey granite used in the Beinecke facing frames. As a result the whole quadrangle is brought together in an unusual way.[7] And there is no question that the building sustains the memorial tone of the quadrangle.

The Exhibition Cap

As indicated, the architects were restricted by the existing quadrangle in how large a building they could mass at this location, and the Beinecke library runs to something like 112,000 square feet.[8] They also faced the problem of excluding sun from the building, to protect fine books. This is difficult to do if any windows are used at all, but the mass of a building is exaggerated if it lacks windows. In addition, they had to provide for preservation of the books delicate temperature and humidity controls, which are extremely difficult to maintain in a building with exposed walls. Both the window and control problems could best be solved by burying the library, and this they did; the library proper is entirely under ground.

The architects planned a second building, the cap, above the library, connected to the library by stairways. This is not a library at all but a grand and elaborate exhibition case faced with marble, with a glass wall on the main level, inset far enough so that the sun never gets in, and a fifty-foot ceiling. This is the part of the building visible above ground. It does its job in a remarkably impressive way, as is shown by the usual photographs of the interior of the cap (see p. 66). Entering from the east through a revolving door, which is required at times, we are confronted with a 35' × 60' glass-enclosed vault that rises six stories in the center of the building on tier-built stacks until it touches and helps to support the roof. Facing outward in a hollow square of stacks on all six levels, on all four sides of the vault, is a major part of Yale's rare book collection, an admirable sight.

The books are lighted on each level by small incandescent lights on the ceiling edge of the glass wall, shielded from the public so that the lighted books command attention. The surrounding area is lit by down-lights mounted in the ceiling forty feet above the mezzanine level, and these are kept deliberately low so that, in contrast with its gentle gloom, the vault is more spectacularly dramatic. Down on the main floor, paved in granite, where daylight enters through the glass wall, very long flat exhibition cases flank the vault on the north and south.

Ten feet above the main floor the vault can be approached from a mezzanine level separated from it by a three-foot gap. At the head of the north and south stairs on the mezzanine level stand large upright bookcases, brilliantly lit, with a curved glass front. From the entrances on the main floor, they give the illusion of books out in the open—real rare books—which gave me a great feeling of warmth when I first entered the building.

Against the east and west mezzanine walls a row of nine specially designed bronze exhibition cases (which will be discussed later) display some of the greatest rarities in manuscript and print of the eastern and western world. The bright light of the cases divides the dark air (Dante's phrase, and Joyce's), and strikes through their glass backs to the marble facings framed in granite, which at a distance of four feet are quite magnificent.

These panels are of white Montclair Danby marble with a soft drift of gray running through it in diagonal streaks, a beautiful stone cut with rare craftmanship. The panels are hexagonalized, the lines pulling out slightly to a point from what would otherwise be a square face, measuring eight feet eight inches from point to point, in both directions. These are framed in warm grey granite crosses, which taper from the boss to the end of the arms, raise to a high point at the boss, and are cut on a sharp angle from the center to the edge of the arm.[9] Measuring eight feet eight inches in both directions, they are so arranged that each panel is held in place by two arms of each of four crosses. Up close, this arrangement is most impressive. When the sun strikes the panels from the outside, this marble glows a warm brown-yellow, and the grey streaks dark brown. This effect is most spectacular at a distance, from the main floor.

The mezzanine also contains two large bronze cases specially designed to exhibit permanently the Gutenberg Bible and an elephant folio Audubon. On the north and south ends are carpeted lounge areas with chairs and divans, and an eight-foot diameter single-pedestal table of Italian burl olive, its dark beauty completely lost in the dim light.[10] The ceiling is coffered, with a dark spot in the center (which is actually its light) and a dark relief around the edge through which the ventilation is supplied. But the ceiling and the seating areas are not very noticeable. The central glass vault dominates in the center, with the exhibition cases against the walls as satellites, and behind these cases the grandeur of the marble facings and granite frames.

This entire building, as I have stated, is an exhibition case, magnificent in a style that would have pleased Lorenzo, brilliantly original, and most striking outside and in.[11] The architects have reason to be pleased with their creation. It is by no means clear, however, that the University entirely approves of it, because by its very nature it sets major policy not completely in accord with the academic and library community and the general tone of the Yale campus. It is a showcase, a prime piece of public relations, a bijou in a bowl, to be visited by the curious and the idle whether or not they are interested in books or things of the mind. In short, a kind of bibliographical zoo, with the prime animals on show, no matter how tired they may get, and no matter how their keepers may fret.

Against this should be stated that the excellent and commodious long exhibition cases on the main floor are designed for exhibitions to coordinate with the instruction of courses in the undergraduate schools, that there is some hope that a few of the throngs who come to peer will be touched, and that the impressive style of the entire building may well lead collectors to choose this library to house their treasures. While this building leaves many unhappy, the architect's concept of the exhibition cap and the buried library is clearly defensible.

The Library

While the exhibition cap measures 88' by 131' at its outer walls, the library proper measures 188' by 160' and is comprised of two high-ceilinged stories, flanked on the south side by a three-tier stack.[12] It is therefore much more than twice as large as the building above, its mass skillfully concealed by burying it.

Unfortunately, it is connected to the upper building in a way that makes it impossible to control incoming traffic (and sightseers are not invited down here). The stairs begin about eight feet inside of the north and south entrances and at just a slight angle to them, so they have a tendency to draw people down, and through glass doors about halfway between a twenty-seven-foot-long circulation desk (often manned by one attendant) and the reading room. It is possible to emerge from the stairway fifteen feet from the desk, take a quick turn to the left or right, and be shielded from view by the staircase to go meddling down the corridor to the curators' offices, which are full of treasures. While I am sure that people inspecting Yale's Saarinen hockey rink also cause difficulties, this arrangement is especially distasteful to bibliophiles, who insist that rare book libraries are for scholars, and rare book librarians should not have to pop up and down as inspectors. It is impossible to keep the casual or the curious from coming down to this level, a problem which could have been avoided if the building had been programmed.

This floor, carpeted in a pleasant textured apricot color, is divided into two areas by the lobby at the foot of the stairs. To the west are a card catalog room, the processing room (behind the circulation desk), and a utilitarian cluster composed of a coathanger-corridor, rest rooms, lounge, and kitchen.

The card catalog room is pleasantly panelled in teak, with teak bookshelves on the walls holding the reference collection. The catalogs are teak, with ebonized drawer faces and bronze drawer pulls and bases. The wall edges and bookcase sections are set off by dark inset relief strips, a hallmark of SOM. The feeling is one of dignified, handsome, luxurious simplicity. The eight-and-a-half foot ceiling is mounted with downlights, which at this height are unpleasant and offend the eye in certain locations at the tables. They are hot, even with the air conditioning, and only supply thirty to fifty foot-candles of illumination.

This room connects, through a small corridor, with the technical processing room, which lies behind the circulation desk, and is a commodious but unpleasant room. There is a generous amount of shelving on the walls, room for a dozen standard desks, four large tables, a sink, wall-built bars, and the like, but this area of 1,650 square feet, completely internal and unrelieved in any way, is the only part of this floor left uncarpeted (except the small kitchen and rest rooms). This parsimony in a palace not only deprives the room of a pleasant feeling of comfort, but the light tile floor also compounds the eye-blinding glare of the lighting, which is very intense but of very poor quality. The glare from the ceiling and floor reverberates from white walls behind the stacks, which, for the most part, are not filled with books.

Built into the corner of this room, immediately behind the circulation desk, is the assistant librarian's office, which involves the same difficulties of feeling, for similar reasons, as the processing room. But they are not so intense because the room is smaller, and the librarian who occupies it keeps the lighting at its lowest intensity, supplemented with a desk lamp (though the overhead lights can produce 120 footcandles). On the east wall is a huge white enamel panel filled with impressive dials, which indicate by flashing red lights undue changes in humidity and temperature in all zones of the library, the opening of doors, and fire hazards. A much more complex and sensitive panel board in the mechanical area downstairs, which records the conditions in every zone of the library, is the basis for action by the maintenance crew.[13]

The other half of this floor, to the east of the lobby stairs, is composed of the reading room and the curators' offices, which look out from a hollow square through glass walls into the sculpture court. The reading room is completely successful in feeling. Thirty-six by seventy-eight feet, its size is disguised by the glass walls that enclose it on both of the long sides. It is carpeted, and contains a dozen four-by-six reading tables, each equipped with adjustable book stands over which are laid two flexible cloth tube weights filled with lead shot, the most practical device ever devised to keep a book open. The tables are handsome in teak. The surrounding chairs (Thonet, designed by Marcel Breuer), covered in black naugahyde with chrome frames, match them well.[14] On the end walls are six 30″ by 72″ tables with slanted tops, with a single chair at each. At both ends of the central seating are low, marble-topped bookcases 26′ long, which are quite handsome, if not much used.

The lighting in this room is as excellent as that in the processing room is bad, and a comparison of the two throws a great deal of evidence on what makes for good quality in lighting. Except for the extreme edges of the room, which are mounted (I can't say lit) with downlights, this room has a luminous ceiling, which is to say that it is almost completely covered with light. Illumination is provided by a combination of fluorescent and incandescent lights above a milk-plastic sheet diffuser, and while milk-plastic diffusers of considerable area are offensive to the eye, these are supported by an egg-crate louver composed of 6″ squares 4″ deep, made of teak, which is quite handsome and puts the plastic out of sight. The lighting in this room is about 120 footcandles, but is of very high quality, and habitués of the room informed me that it does not tire the eyes during an all-day session. Beyond the inner glass wall is the sculpture court, and a more pleasant and useful reading room would be hard to find (see p. 67).[15] Its one defect is that the feeling is achieved partly at the expense of the security of the materials used in the room.

After proper identification at the circulation desk, the reader is instructed to put coat and briefcase, everything except his immediate working materials, in the coatroom-corridor near the desk. The book is then brought from the stacks for him by a page. He is directed to use it in the reading room, whose entrance is straight across from the circulation desk, at a distance of twenty feet, but in the far corner of the room he is seventy feet away from the circulation librarian. The use of pens is prohibited, but this is a difficult restriction to enforce at this distance. If the reader is bent on mutilation and feels inhibited by the glass walls, and the glass panels that connect the room with the librarian's office and conference room on the south wall, he can go into the small typing and microfilm reading rooms that open off the north end of the reading room and slash in a corner completely protected by a solid wall.

The typing room and microfilm reading room each contain five stations. A means has not yet been devised for holding typing copy, particularly large and heavy books, in the proper location for copying and yet close enough to the typewriter to make it easy to read copy. The special bars in this room are no more or less successful than most others. While one of these rooms calls for darkness and the other for very good light, the lighting is the same in both rooms—very poor. The ceilings contain down-lights, which seem to be a disease of architects, and the intensity at the typing desks ranges from thirty to forty footcandles of very poor quality light, in this case not due to glare but to lack of diffusion and too few fixtures.[16]

The other three sides of the sculpture court contain two secretarial alcoves, which open directly (without a wall) into the corridor, the curators' offices, and three seminar rooms, one of which is assigned to their Hinman collating machine. All of these rooms are pleasant, handsomely furnished, and poorly lit with down-lights (see p. 68). In two rooms, a column lands in an awkward location, and unfortunately one of these is the office of the librarian. The court, which opens to the sky, is deep enough so that sun is no problem, and the window-walls are equipped with louver-drapes that pivot closed and draw aside when not in use. Anyone who has worked in an office with a window wall knows how very pleasant it feels.

The corridor surrounding the offices is lit with down-lights, which make no particular difference here. They paint the ceiling pleasantly with a row of light circles and give enough illumination for walking. At the extreme east of this floor is a wall 116′ long, covered with glass-enclosed bookshelves which are good looking, very convenient, and extremely useful to the curators.[17]

The Sculpture Court

The court serves as a light well for those working on the library floor (except the processing staff), and contributes to the pleasant feeling of this floor.[18] Isamu Noguchi designed the court, which is paved with white Imperial Danby marble edged with a granite curb. The paving is cut by a pleasant design of arcs and partial circles which radiate from three large, geometrically designed sculptured forms of the same marble—"a 'Sun' symbolizing cosmic energy, a 'Pyramid' symbolizing the geometry of the earth, and a 'Cube' symbolizing chance" (see p. 67).[19] The symbolism is by no means imbedded in these forms, but they nevertheless are pleasantly intellectual, simple, and geometrical, thus harmonizing nicely with the feeling of the cap. The architects said that they avoided landscaping to prevent retention of water that might seep into the stacks directly below the court, but since the ceiling of these stacks had to be penetrated in three places to provide water run-off from the curb drains and a separate column to support the twelve-ton weight of Noguchi's Sun, we wonder if the hazard is not as great.

The Stacks

Viewed from the east in cross-section, this underground building is composed of a south three-floor tier-built stack separated by an internal wall from two floors on the north comprising the library floor and the stack directly below it, which has an 11' ceiling and is separated into three sections by cement brick walls and fireproof doors. This juxtaposition of two and three stories violates the AIA-ALA award committee's remarks about the "pristine simplicity" of this building and makes for awkward movement from the circulation desk to the tier-built stacks. In a rare book library that receives limited use, this is no great drawback.

Burying the stacks simplified most of the problems of protecting the books from hazards. It immediately eliminated danger from hurricanes and lightning, and made the problem of heat and humidity control much easier.[20] In addition, it simplified the construction problem by placing all the book weight on the basement slab, instead of on weight-bearing floors.

The fire-control problem is no easier in this building than in a building above-ground, but it was solved by providing a Cardox system for flooding each of five zones with carbon dioxide on call from sensitive heat and smoke detection units placed throughout the stacks. When the units signal, a bell rings a warning to clear the stacks, and the system then prepares to discharge. When a manual release button is pressed, the zone is flooded with carbon dioxide, heavy enough to prevent combustion, from a great tank in the mechanical area.

The system contains enough carbon dioxide to provide two full charges (presumably they would be in two different zones), and still have enough gas left for a couple of small charges. While the manufacturers designed the system to release the charge automatically two minutes after the bell rings, the Yale authorities bypass the automatic discharge, because they know that people running sometimes trip, and that ice crystals formed in a carbon dioxide discharge would moisten the books when they melt. The system can therefore be discharged only after a human agent has looked to see that the stacks are clear and the fire large enough to require it.[21]

The one hazard increased by placing the stacks underground is the moisture problem, although there is also danger of wall and roof leakage from the plaza and the sculpture court. It is impossible to treat concrete in any way that will make it completely waterproof. The waterproofing depends on covering a layer of concrete with waterproof membranes and pouring a second layer over the membranes. About half of New York City lies under such construction, and a great deal of that half leaks a great deal of the time.

The Beinecke library provided the ideal solution to this problem, by interposing one floor without stacks between the surface through which the water might seep and the stacks. Presumably, it would always be possible to catch the leak before it ran through a second floor. Most of the stacks are protected in this way. But having the solution in hand, the architects rejected it by sinking a sculpture court above the basement stacks, and penetrating the stack ceiling to run drains through it and to support the Noguchi Sun. While the best construction methods for waterproofing have been used, there is some risk involved. There is also risk involved in the fact that the top of the triple-tier stacks is drectly below the plaza paving, which is constantly walked on, a leak-prone condition.[22] Presumably the dials recording changes in humidity would instantly alert servicemen to any serious problem, but they would not record small leaks.

Remington Rand provided the stacks, which are 7'6" high in the tier-built area, and 8'6" high with eight shelves per range in the basement stack area. They are on 4'4" centers, hanging 10" shelves above 24" bases, leaving an aisle of 28", which is adequate. John Ottemiller, whose long experimentation with shelving in the Sterling Memorial Library is responsible for these stack arrangements, had Rem/Rand determine that the same gauge steel used in standard three-foot shelves could be extended to 40" (which he stated is the outer limit) and still hold a shelf full of average-size books without bending. These stacks use 40" shelves.[23] Unfortunately, the bay size of the floor was changed on site, and some 30" shelves and some 28" shelves had to be used to compensate.[24]

Except for the processing room and reading room, the rest of this building is lit by incandescent lights, despite the heavy load they place on air conditioning. In these stacks, which are entered infrequently, and where consequently the air-conditioning load would be comparatively light, the architects have used fluorescent lights. They produce very bad glare, but this is unimportant in a stack area where no browsing will take place. The fluorescent tubes have been fitted with plastic filter shields to minimize the deleterious effects of this light, but to safeguard the rare books completely, incandescent lights should have been used in the stack areas.[25]

Air-Handling

The air-handling system uses a rotating screen prefilter, electrostatic filters and activated charcoal filters (which remove noxious gases) to protect the books from air pollution. Both the air intake and exhaust are screened from view, embedded in the top of the wall south of the library, and the cooling tower for the air-conditioning system is skillfully located on top of the Commons building to the north, high enough to place it completely out of sight.

The ventilation of the cap is unusual. A large volume of air has to be injected to maintain the temperature and humidity in this area, which to accommodate people is kept slightly different from that of the book vaults yet is quite humid. The air descends through four-foot openings in the ceiling, 40' above the mezzanine floor, in great volume. Since it mixes with the room air before it reaches walking level, it must come in at a considerably different temperature than that desired on the mezzanine. Until the very late stages of planning, it was not definite what the facing of the building would be, since the architects were searching for onyx. The mechanical engineers therefore planned the system for the most difficult possible conditions, with the result that the air enters with such velocity that it sucks moisture from the air already in the room. To balance this, they arranged to introduce humidity when needed through peripheral vents on the mezzanine, which were originally designed to blow warm air up along the facings to prevent dripping in the winter. This is not an ideal arrangement for achieving humidity balance. It would not have been designed in this way if an open-ended budget had not allowed the architects to prolong their hunt for suitable onyx. The humidity in this area is kept below 50 per cent in the winter (in contrast to the book storage areas) to avoid dripping, but slight dripping has been observed on the upper facing panels, where it is not dangerous.

Acoustics

In the only area where it matters, the reading room in the library proper, the acoustics are quite good, quiet, without being dead, with a low ventilation sound in the background and no ballast hum. Everything about this room is good. In the cap the architects are reported as having aimed to achieve "stonelike" acoustics, one would surmise to inspire awe, and it is difficult to see how they could have achieved otherwise.[26]

Construction

Although the construction of the stack areas is extremely simple—poured concrete slab and walls, painted, with vinyl flooring—and the construction of the reading floor is conventional, that of the exhibition cap is extremely interesting. Each of its walls, which measure on the longest sides 51' high by 130' long, is a Vierendeel truss, composed of steel crosses welded together into a rigid framework (see p. 69).[27] This frame supports its own weight, the weight of most of the roof, the weight of the 1-1/4"-thick marble facing slabs, and of the granite sheaths which cover the crosses (on the outside with cut granite, and on the inside with precast concrete sheaths into which has been ground the same granite to match color). This is an expensive way to construct a wall, justified only by the amount of free space required inside.

The trusses are supported eight feet above the plaza at all four corners on oilite bronze bearing plates that rest on steel columns embedded in concrete piers that go straight down through the building to bedrock below the foundation. The whole has been described by the architects as a "big box sitting on four points,"[28] the most interesting and elegant box you are likely to see.

The quality of the building's construction, by the George A. Fuller Company of New York, is remarkably high, due partly to the fact that one of the Beinecke brothers was a director of this company. The building has, of course, undergone some mild settling but the construction throughout shows painstaking care that is unusual in this hit-and-run construction period. The stonecutting on the building, by the Concord, New Hampshire plant of the John Swenson Granite Company and the Procter and Rutland, Vermont plants of the Vermont Marble Company, is a joy to behold, on a level of craftmanship that is seldom encountered.

Along the central rib of the granite crosses, where the stone is cut to a sharp edge right down the middle of the arm, it goes true and precise and flawless. Eight feet above the plaza, the underside of the overhang above the glass wall is faced with granite slabs, and the joint between them runs 131' long, as neat and true as if laid out with a transit. The paving slabs in the quadrangle are laid with the fine precision for which New England was once noted. The pointing at the joints of the building is precise and unrippled. The whole building has been done with a pride of workmanship that has nearly gone from the world.

Exhibition Cases

I have deferred discussion of the exhibition cases because although this library has solved more of the problems involved in designing them than any I have seen, there are still more problems to be solved, and cases are extremely important in a rare book library. The ideal exhibition case should keep out all dust, and should therefore be sealed. Yet it must have movement of air within it because stagnant air invites mold. To be dustless, air must be pre-filtered, and forced into the case, preferably through the top to be vented out the sides or bottom. The cases must avoid being heated, but to avoid reflections in the glass facings they should be lit from inside. This means that they must be cooled with great precision, ideally by a separate machine. Since fluorescent lights are much cooler than incandescent, they would seem to be most fit for this lighting, but they produce ultra-violet rays which deteriorate paper and vegetable dyes, and must be properly shielded if used.

The cases must be at the right height for easy viewing, and not so deep that part of the exhibit is too distant from the viewer. They must be easy to load. They must provide a background to contrast with a range of colors and textures. They must be esthetically pleasing in appearance.

It is easy to see how many of these qualifications are violated by the standard flat museum case or its variants, and the common upright exhibition case. To the credit of the architects, they designed all the exhibition cases in the Beinecke library, all of which are esthetically pleasant and, with one exception which is really a bookcase, place the material exhibited in the right position for viewing.

I have already referred to the pleasant feeling produced by the cases at the head of the mezzanine stairs. Though they give the illusion of open bookshelves from the entrance, they are glass-enclosed bronze cases eight feet high, built in the form of two upright flat arcs, which touch where they back into each other. They have curved glass fronts, which slide rather stiffly to open, and are filtered with shelves designed to display the backs of books. They are really enclosed bookcases.

These cases have the worst heat problem, because they are brilliantly lit by round, incandescent lights set in a row in the ceiling of the bookcases just three or four inches from the tops of the highest books. The cases are air conditioned, but the temperature reaches 80° in the top of the cases.

There are two large-headed cases tailored (one a little snugly) to specific books—Yale's magnificent copies of the Gutenberg Bible and the elephant folio Audubon. The Gutenberg case has four glass sides, framed in bronze, that measure 4' by 4', and is set on a single, square pedestal whose diagonal is at right angles to the axis of the case.[29] This case is lit by small, round incandescent lights set in the ceiling of the case whose intensity is controlled by a rheostat. A transformer is built into the case to cut the electric voltage, and its heat, combined with the heat of the lights, raises the temperature to 83° with the lights on full. The temperature is kept to 70° by lowering the lights to a sombre, holy, concealing level of intensity, which partly defeats the purpose of the case. The Audubon case at the other end of the floor has two glass sides that measure 4' by 10', with bronze frames and bronze end panels. It has exactly the same heat difficulty as the Gutenberg case, for exactly the same reasons.[30]

The nine smaller cases on the east and west walls are attractive and well lit. They place materials at the right height for viewing and close enough so that ordinary typing is easily readable on the exhibition labels.[31] They have two glass sides 2' by 4', framed in bronze, and the ends are provided with frosted glass panels against which color slides can be mounted for viewing. These cases are lit by three slimline fluorescent tubes, within the case but above a solid plastic diffuser, below which is a metal louver of half-inch squares. These cases had heat difficulties when they were first used, but this has been completely solved by cutting holes an inch and a half in diameter in the top of the case above the tubes. The holes let in dust, most of which is caught on the diffuser, but allow the temperature to be held to 70°.

The bed of these cases is painted with a textured and toned flat black paint that provides the best background for exhibiting materials that I have ever encountered. Devised by the Yale plant department, it is washable, shows no brush marks, can be applied to metal or wood, and is so inexpensive and simple to apply that they paint them once a year.[32]

The long, flat cases that flank the glass vault on the main floor are totally successful, and this is where material is exhibited to coordinate with undergraduate courses. They measure 4′ by 32′ and are pedestal mounted and air conditioned. These cases completely avoid the usual surface reflections so disturbing in flat cases by lighting their interior with slimline fluorescent tubes mounted out of view in the sides of the cases. Light from the tubes, which are covered with filter shields, is reflected by a curved mirror into the cases through a polarized panel in such a way that the viewer is not aware of the light source. Higher than usual for flat cases, they place the aterial at the right height for easy viewing, and are handsomely well proportioned. Their beds are set on rollers in eight-foot sections that allow them to be pulled out into the open for mounting materials.

Esthetics

As indicated above, the exhibition cap is very impressive, and the reading room floor is on the whole pleasant and appointed in fine taste. But when the ultimate question is posed—is it a beautiful building? the answer is—not quite. Looking at it from across the quadrangle for an hour on a tranquil evening made it clear that in fitting it to the surrounding buildings, the architects had put together forms, in the crosses and the facing panels, that are not completely harmonious with each other. It is an extremely strong building in its impact on the viewer, very interesting, full of character, and highly original, and in a building these are perhaps qualities more to be desired than beauty.

I have tried to make clear that this is, on the whole, an outstanding building, flawed (as are all buildings) at the points indicated, but very good in its most essential elements. It is a building that has pioneered in a number of ways, and one that deserves the AIA-ALA award granted it in 1964. If some of the mistakes made in its begetting are naive at this stage of library building, that is partly because postwar academic library buildings have not been subjected to demanding scrutiny in public statements, and partly because the relationship between architect and librarian has not received sufficient comment to be understood in the library world. Let us hope that both deficiencies in information will be speedily remedied.[33]

Notes

1. This chapter was originally published as an article entitled "The Beinecke Siamese Twins: An Objective Review of Yale's New Rare Book Library Building," in *College and Research Libraries,* May 1965, pp. 199–212. It is reprinted here, with a headnote and some additions and changes in diction, by permission of *College and Research Libraries.*

This review has involved an analysis of the published accounts of the building, prolonged study of floor and furniture layout plans, interviews with Richard Kates of Jaros, Baum and Bolles (the building's mechanical engineers), and Morris Zelkowitz (team captain on this job for Skidmore, Owings and Merrill). In addition I spent two days in New Haven for a careful study of the building's details and extensive conversation with Herman Liebert (librarian of the Beinecke library), John Ottemiller (Yale's associate university librarian), and Kenneth Nesheim (assistant librarian of the Beinecke library). I thank all these men for their patient answers to my probing. They may not be surprised to know that their information did not always jibe, and that I have had to evaluate the evidence available.

2. The Beinecke Rare Book and Manuscript Library was chosen for its inherent significance as a model, and because the writer became conversant with the Skidmore, Owings, and Merrill style while planning the Colorado College library with their Chicago office. The main features of the Colorado College library are clearly related to those of the Beinecke library, although Walter Netsch of the Chicago office stoutly denies it.

3. Since there was feeling among the Yale faculty, as stupid in practical matters as most faculty, that money for constructing the Beinecke should have been diverted to help the central library (never mind that the donors *gave* for a rare book library), no one was willing to state what the cost of that building actually was. When it was announced in articles in the professional magazines, architects estimated that it would cost $8,500,000. In talking to everyone of importance in the university, the architect's office, and the engineers, it was clear that no one had ever suggested at any time that there was any limit on the cost of the building. Indeed, had the architects succeeded in finding onyx slabs instead of marble large enough for the facings, it would have more than doubled the cost of the building.

Anecdote no. 1. In a social gathering Jim Babb, Librarian of Yale University, heard from the elder Beinecke what he thought was an invitation to propose a rare book building. He came home, gathered his best heads together, and a few weeks later went to see Edwin Beinecke with Yale's plan for a two-million dollar building. With enthusiasm Babb described the project and delineated what it would do for the university. Mr. Beinecke heard out the entire project and immediately said "No!" When Babb regrouped his flabbergasted state and said, "Why, Ed, I thought I was following up a line you let out to me two weeks ago," Mr. Beinecke said, "No, you're mistaken. The Beineckes would be interested in nothing except the greatest rare book building in the world."

4. There was a tendency at Yale to think of written programs and library building consultants as inflexible elements that hamper creative architects and produce unsuccessful buildings, rather than indispensible guides through a dark wood. My own experience indicates that library buildings fail most often because architects have a tendency to conceive of (as they talk of) buildings as spatial sculptures rather than spatial functions, and this often leads to building from the outside in, despite pious protestations to the contrary. It's a rare architect who knows how a library works, and the best buildings have resulted from a strong interaction between the special talents of the librarian and the special talents of the architect. On this job the imbalance was much too heavily in favor of SOM.

5. I first encountered this great man in 1938, when I was a pup in the Reference Reading Room of Yale's Sterling Library, then only four years old. McCandless put a light meter directly under a lightwheel containing twenty incandescent lamps hung from the ceiling of that room, and it measured five footcandles! He later worked with us as consultant on the Hofstra University Library, where I learned that in addition to his range of creative contributions to the handling of theatre lighting, he had worked for twenty years as a designer of lighting fixtures for Century Lighting in New York, and had a more sensitive feel for quality in lighting than anyone I've encountered except John Kraehenbuehl.

The stack lighting in the library section of the Yale art school, half a block from McCandless's office, designed by Paul Rudolph, is simply abominable. It is formed of incandescent spotlight bulbs screwed into exposed conduits mounted slightly above head height in the middle of the aisles. The resultant glare is eyeshattering and the heat immediately disturbing even on a cool day. The arrogant disdain of many architects for the basic principles of good lighting would require a four-volume commentary.

6. As initially conceived, the Beinecke Library was to have been faced with thin slabs of onyx which would glow like a lantern when struck by light from within. I saw a model of the building faced in onyx. The slabs required to fill one-quarter of the gigantic granite frames that hold a unit of the library's exterior had to measure, trimmed, about four and a half feet square. Onyx does not exist in nature in slabs this size, as a telephone call uptown to the Columbia University department of geology would have informed the architects. They surveyed the world trying in vain to supply this need.

Turning next to marble for facings, the architects again launched a global search which included a sample from the quarry at Naxos that had supplied the marble for the Parthenon. Finally, they settled on a lovely Yugoslavian marble. Suitable slabs were imported and sent to Vermont, the one state in the union qualified to polish it to nobility.

Anecdote no. 2. When the architects visited the Vermont Marble Company to view the finished Yugoslavian marble, it was polished to high elegance and dramatically lit, in the center of a shed, at the far end of which some other marble slabs half covered with tarpaulin leaned against a wall. The proprietors expressed great admiration of this Yugoslavian marble, which the SOM men also liked. But something about those slabs at the end of the shed caught their eye, and they asked where that marble came from. The proprietors dismissed that marble as some stone cut out of the hills nearby, and went on effusively about the virtues of the Yugoslavian slabs. When the SOM men demanded to see the marble at the end of the shed, reluctantly the proprietors ambled over, removed the tarpaulin, and turned on the spotlight prepared to display in its pristine glory, polished to heartwarming brilliance, the Montclair Danby marble that SOM was intelligent enough to see far exceeded what they had intended to use. New England changes slowly.

7. In a prime example of abstract expressionism in words, which we could do without in architectural criticism, Vincent Scully states, ''All these surrounding buildings are effectively swept out of existence by the Beinecke rare book library . . .,'' *Saturday Review,* May 23, 1964, p. 28. Exactly the opposite is true; the quadrangle now feels close knit.

8. This figure was supplied by Mr. Zelkowitz, but in the Beinecke library most of the computations generally applied to the comparison of buildings have little meaning. Square footage is one of them, because although the square footage of the cap is small, its fifty-foot ceiling makes the corresponding cubic footage enormous.

9. These crosses are derived from those in the screen wall of the Banque Lambert, Brussels, designed by Skidmore, Owings and Merrill in precast concrete.

10. I brought back a flashlight to look at it. This wood is richly magnificent in both grain and color, and it is a pity that the two desks made of it, in other parts of the library where they can be seen, are covered with plate glass to avoid scratches, which effectively destroys their beauty.

11. The rare book gallery discussed in my chapter on the Robarts Library at the University of Toronto is the reverse, probably intended, of the Beinecke exhibition cap. Its books are exhibited on the outer walls, with the center of the area open.

12. A large L-shaped expansion area was built under the quadrangle as a shell large enough to contain triple stack-tiers on the north and west sides of the Beinecke library proper, for the law school library, but its cost was not in the Beinecke budget and its area is not included in these measurements. I should mention that the Beinecke library is also connected to the Sterling Memorial Library by a tunnel.

13. Even in the mechanical room of the Beinecke Rare Book and Manuscript library, the panel board should not spell Gutenberg with two ''t''s, which it does.

14. A study of this building shows the limitations of two materials. Teak is at its best in small pieces. These tables, and the teak desks used in the offices, are quite handsome, but the mass in which it is used in the card catalog room makes it appear a little weak (although that room on the whole is pleasant). On the other hand, polished chrome goes well with such textures as plastic, but is aggressive and hard when used in the frames of the teak desks. None of the commonly used metals—polished chrome, brushed chrome, aluminum, or stainless steel—goes really well with a wide variety of excellent surface textures now available in furnishings, and it is often preferable to use enameled steel in a harmonious color.

15. With the irony that invades human affairs, the students who use this library are so highly motivated that they would wade through seas of blood to reach its treasures, and do not need to be lured in. Given the Yale collections, the occupancy of this room would probably be the same if it were furnished with bales of gunny sacks.

16. Down-lights are round, incandescent lights mounted flush or slightly recessed in the ceiling. They sometimes have a glass lens (these do) and sometimes an ornamental grill. Architects love them, because they think them romantic, like little stars in the sky. To get this effect, they have to be distributed wide apart, and although they are not spotlights, they throw a cone of light that covers no greater an area than a spotlight. To get good coverage in a room, the ceiling must be saturated with them, and even then they do not diffuse light well. When architects are afflicted

with downlightis, which is often, they use them to paint with, not to illuminate, to twinkle or "punch holes through the air," as one put it to me. So we get twinkles and punches, but no good light, and they throw horrible face shadows.

17. The teak shelves in these cases and in the card catalog room are hung on round metal pegs slipped into holes drilled into the siding. This ancient device had been updated in the twentieth century by equipping the peg with screw threads, thereby increasing its efficiency in gouging out the siding. Six months after installation, these pegs when removed droped loose sawdust. After twenty years, especially at heavily loaded shelves, railroad spikes can be slipped into the holes. Since adjustable strip shelf hangers are now available with wooden covers that conceal the metal almost entirely, this is inexcusable.

18. Sterling Memorial Library has two such light wells, one of them around a lovely court, which are probably the ancestors of the sculpture court.

19. *Yale University Library Gazette,* April 1964, p. 129. The old grads in the correspondence columns of the *Yale Alumni Magazine* wielded their heavy-handed irony on the Noguchi sculptures for months.

Anecdote no. 3. As a couple of visitors were looking over the granite railing into the sculpture court, one of them turned to the other and said in an irate voice, "Who's the goddam fool that paid good money for that stupid stuff?" Just at this moment one of the Beinecke staff happened to be passing behind them with Edwin Beinecke, patriarch of the Beinecke donors. Ed walked briskly up to the complainer, clutched and shook his hand, and said, "I'm the goddam fool that paid for that stupid stuff, and I agree with every word you've said."

20. It would have been necessary to provide heavy insulation on the outer walls if they had been above ground to prevent dripping at 50 per cent humidity in New England winters. The stacks, both here and in the glass vault, are kept at a constant 70° temperature and 50 per cent humidity. The mechanical engineers claim they can hold the system to within 2° of this temperature and five per cent of this humidity, but I have long since come to doubt the claims of engineers, because I have never seen any modern building that is uniformly comfortable in warm, cold, and intermediate weather. All areas of the stacks in the Beinecke library, including the glass vault, feel comfortable as you pass through them, and if the engineers can hold to within 8° of the temperature, and 10 per cent of the humidity the books will be more than well preserved. The elaborate dial recordings of conditions in each of the building's zones should make safeguarding the books an easy, if constant, task.

21. In 1977 we would use a Halon discharge system, which is not noxious to humans caught in it for a time.

22. I am informed by architects that it is impossible to build a roof that will not leak sooner or later, even if not subjected to unusual strain.

23. Ottemiller stated that this change saved the University about $85,000 in stack costs (which sounds like a large figure). It is clear that we are now in a position to re-think every dimension of stacks—height, centers (we should really think about aisle width instead, which depends on the width of the bases), length of shelves, and depth of shelves for our libraries. If a library is to shelve three hundred thousand volumes or more, it probably will not increase the unit costs of stacks to depart from standard heights and lengths.

24. This is the most horrendous field change I have ever heard of, the kind of decision that sends librarians up the wall. The original bay size had been planned to accommodate the extra-wide stack sections. There were valid mechanical reasons for changing the bay size, but the change was made on site, without consulting *or informing* the librarians. Who gives a hump about mere stacks in a library? One result is a series of columns in the middle of the outermost aisle, around which the staff have to dodge while paging books.

25. For information on this subject, see note 17, on p. 38.

26. *Progressive Architecture*, December 1961, p. 156. It was surprising to discover in reading through the articles on this library that none of them, even in the most eminent architectural magazines, is completely accurate, and numbers of them are highly inaccurate. It is evident that these magazines push "news" for bulk, just as the daily newspapers do, with no great regard for accuracy. All journalism has now become show-business, and architects cooperate by making dramatic releases for public relations purposes. The result is a large body of literature loaded with undependable facts.

27. Because of the enormous stress on the frame, the crosses were changed in the course of planning from preformed concrete to welded steel, and this building is a great achievement in welding.

28. *Architectural Record*, April 1962, p. 130.

29. The pedestals on all the rest of the cases are of this type, and small enough so they stand recessed below the case and are not very noticeable. They are hollow, and serve as air-conditioning inlet ducts.

30. The most frightening aspects of the strange world of architects to librarians new at library building are its weird imprecision and radical lack of common sense. For instance, having made such a failure in such strategic elements as these cases, the librarian expects a firm with a high reputation to rush in to remedy the situation and wipe the blot from its escutcheon. Not at all! Some six months after the move into the Beinecke library, Skidmore, Owings and Merrill were still blithely ignoring the university's plea to do something about these cases. Since my study of the building, they made an attempt at recovery by increasing the velocity of the air through the cases, when the most obvious solution is to remove the sources of heat from the cases, by placing the transformers remote from them (not easy but possible) and locating the lights outside of the case above a glass diffuser. These special cases were conceived too late in the planning to get a proper duct system. This problem could have been avoided if the building had been programmed to begin with.

31. These cases can be seen in the background of the photograph on p. 66.

32. Yale's formula: one gallon of Devoe's Flat Black oil paint; one pint of Martin Senour Radiant Red oil color pigment. To achieve the same tone and texture, these brands must be used, but your plant department can experiment, too.
By 1977, the painted beds had been covered with a tan-beige velvet cloth to provide a more luxurious foil for the books.

33. By 1977, neither deficiency had been remedied.
Statistics for the Beinecke Library:

> Gross Area—112,000 square feet
> Seating Capacity—36
> Book Capacity—800,000 volumes
> Building Cost and Project Cost are still undisclosed at the request of the Beinecke family.

The following publications on this building are worth reading. Even if the language is not accessible to readers, the photographs and diagrams are instructive:

"Rare Building for Rare Books," *Architectural Forum*, November 1960, pp. 138–141.
"SOM Designs Onyx Shelter for Yale's Rare Books," *Architectural Record*, November 1960, p. 44.
"SOM Joins Notable Architects with Yale Designs," *Progressive Architecture*, November 1960, p. 66.
"Biblioteca per l'Università di Yale," *Domus* [Milan], March 1961, pp. 1–4. [Contains an English summary.]
"Projet de Bibliothèque pour l'Université de Yale," *Architecture d'Aujourd'hui*, June 1961, pp. 98–99.

"Yale's New Vault; Material Structural Analysis for the Beinecke Rare Book and Manuscript Library," *Progressive Architecture,* December 1961, pp. 152–159.

"Rare Book Library at Yale Dedicated," *Architectural Record,* November 1963, pp. 12–14.

D. Ashton, "Sculpture in a Closed Court of the New Beinecke Rare Book Room and Manuscript Library at Yale by I. Noguchi," *Arts and Architecture,* November 1963, p. 6.

"SOM, Rudolph and Johnson at Yale," *Architectural Forum,* November 1963, pp. 30–31.

"Opposites: Expressionism and Formalism at Yale; Rudolph's School and Bunshaft's Library," *Progressive Architecture,* February 1964, pp. 128–133.

"The Beinecke Rare Book and Manuscript Library," *Yale University Library Gazette,* April 1964, pp. 127–130.

"Rare Book Box: SOM's Beinecke Library," *Architectural Review,* June 1964, pp. 391–392.

"Yale University: Bibliothèque des Livres et Manuscrits Rares," *Oeil,* June 1964, pp. 34–37.

"Bibliothèque a l'Université de Yale," *Architecture d'Aujourd'hui,* November 1964, pp. 62–67.

CHAPTER 7

THE ROCKEFELLER LIBRARY
AT BROWN UNIVERSITY

The front entrance of the Rockefeller Library. Note that the peripheral columns come through to the exterior as strong decorative elements.
Photo: Leon Kowal

The main entrance lobby, with the end of the circulation desk at the left and the card catalog beyond the doors at the rear.

The Periodicals Reading Room.

The reference desk and reading room.

The Humanities smoking lounge and reading room.

Peripheral student research carrels.

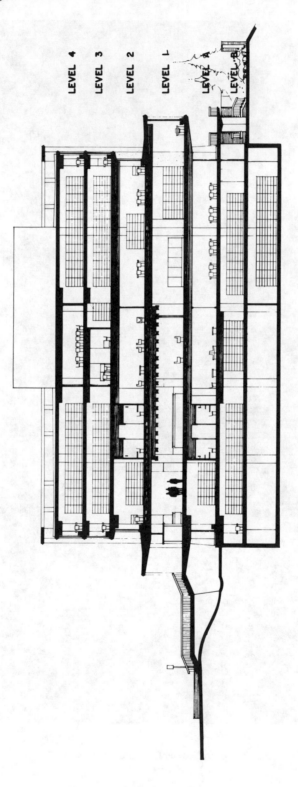

The cross-section of the library, showing the sloping site.

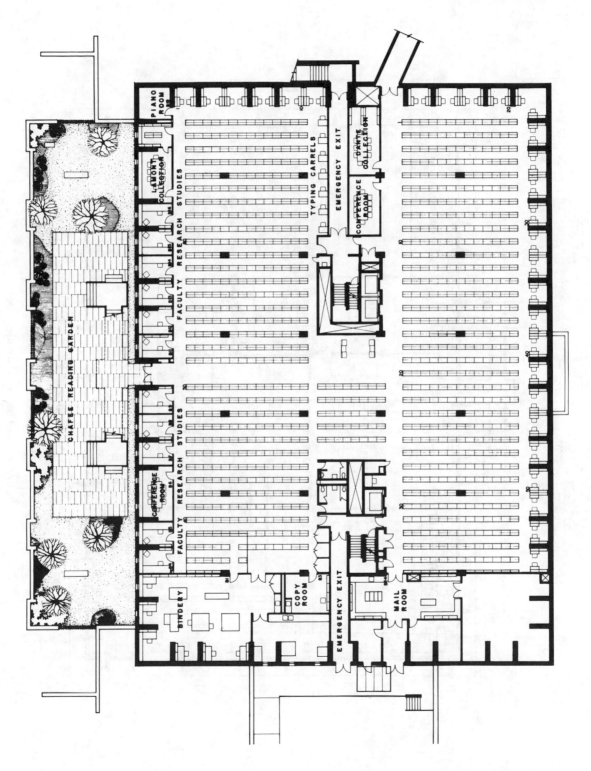

Level B, two floors below the main floor.

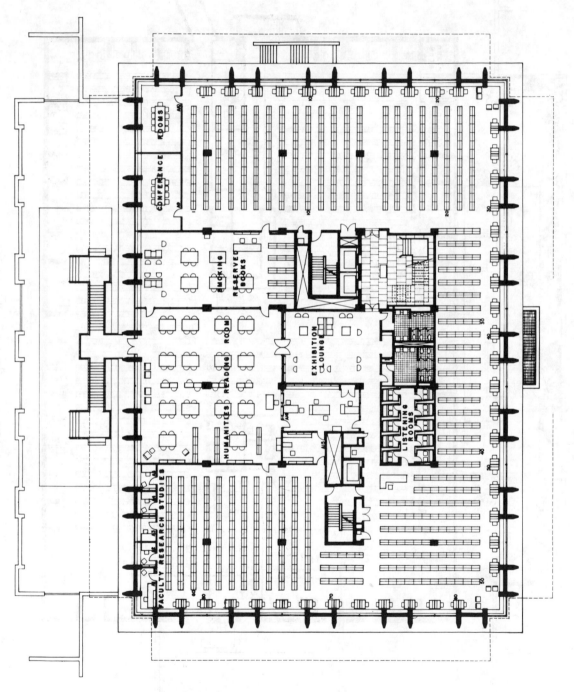

Level A, one floor below the main floor.

The main floor, cantilevered out on all four sides.

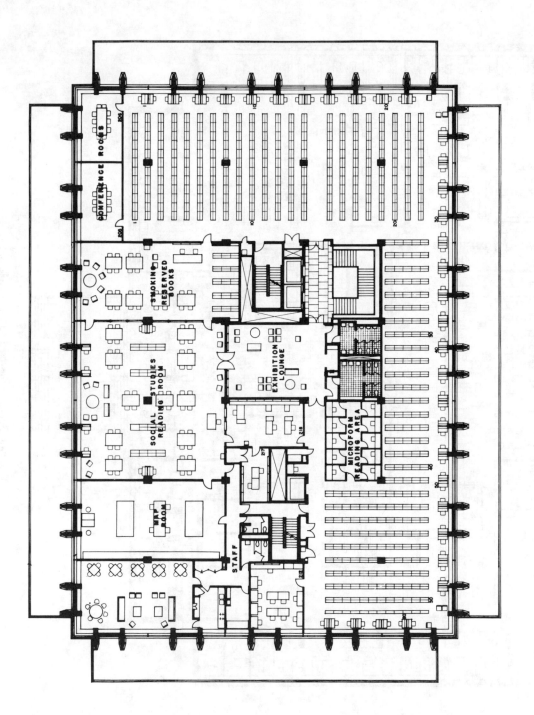

Level 2, one floor above the main floor.

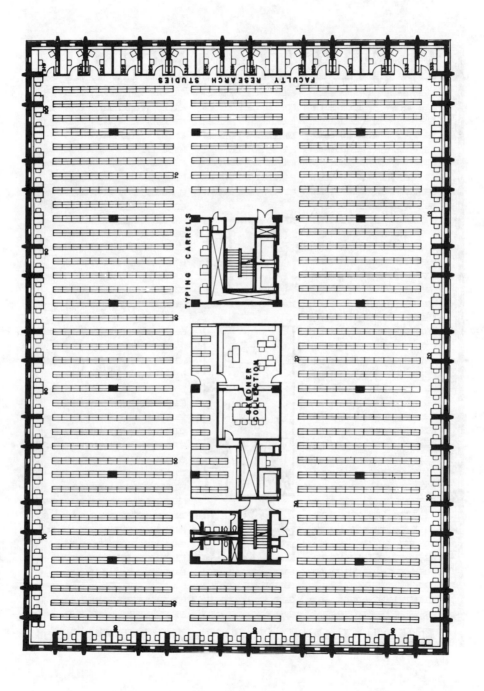

Level 3.

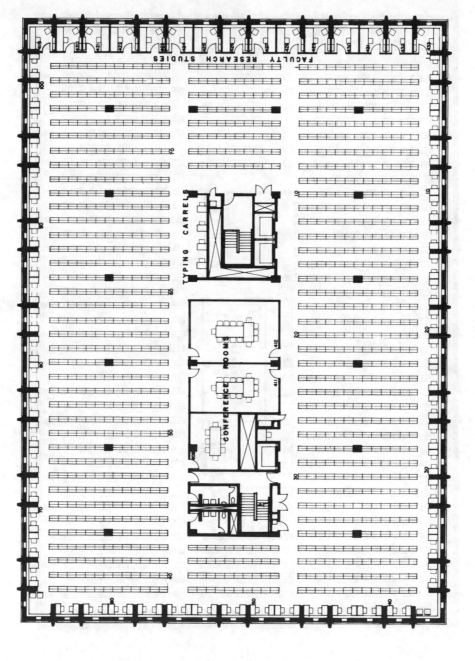

Level 4.

THE ROCKEFELLER LIBRARY AT BROWN UNIVERSITY*

(It often is possible to get some idea of what your new library building would look like by visiting the architect under consideration and viewing the buildings he currently has in the design stage. Architects cannot afford to throw away a concept after using it on one building; they ring variations on it, often very ingenious variations, until they tire of it or they have designed enough of them to call public attention to the similarities. In the case of the Rockefeller library this was not true.

The planning of the Rockefeller library came in the midst of a series of high rise libraries that Warner, Burns, Toan, Lunde had designed for Cornell and were to design for Hofstra University, Brown University (their science library), and Emory University within the span of a few years.[1] All of these buildings contain elements recognizably related to each other. The Rockefeller library has nothing in common with any of them. Its form was produced by the slope and location of the site which posed problems solved brilliantly by the architects. Among the buildings analyzed in this series of reviews, only the Sedgewick Undergraduate Library at the University of British Columbia shows as significant an interaction of the site with the building.[2]

My evaluation of this building in 1967 placed it among the handful at the top of academic libraries. Although a number of new libraries have joined it in that category over the past ten years, the Rockefeller library still stands up very well in comparison with its peers. It is superior to every academic library I know in the way that its entire structural system and floor layout in general reach out to help the users of the library nearly everywhere in the building.)

*   *   *   *

People have great difficulty understanding that flaws in a building have the same significance as flaws in a person.[3] Everyone has lots of them, but you don't just add them up and say, "There; that's the person!" People can emerge above their flaws as distinctive characters of considerable stature. So it is with buildings. It is possible for a building to have a considerable number of faults (most buildings do) and still be a remarkable building. All of my best friends are built like that.

Since this chapter presents reservations about the details of the John D. Rockefeller, Jr. Library, let me make two things clear. First, its architects, Warner, Burns, Toan, Lunde of New York, are remarkably able, reasonable to work with, committed to quality and dogged in pursuing it. Eleanor Larrabee was the associate largely responsible for this building. Second—the Rockefeller is the best library building they have planned to date, out of a series that ranges from reasonably good to extremely good, a series that includes my baby, The Hofstra University Library.

The Brown University library system, compared to the demands on it, is easily one of the finest in the country. Brown was therefore adding to strength when, in the course of considering a second addition to the John Hay Library, the decision was made to build an entirely new library for the Humanities and the Social Sciences directly across the street. Its requirements posed a series of problems.

---

*Footnotes to this chapter begin on p. 112.

First—shelving for 1,250,000 books, and seating for 1000 students could mean a forest of stacks large enough to swallow completely this comparatively small number of seats. Second—room to accommodate the order and catalog departments for the entire university library system, which suggested a preternaturally large main floor area. Third—an exterior that would confront without offense, directly across the campus, a two-century architectural melange that barely avoided eclecticism; an exterior that would also live harmoniously with the John Hay Library across the street, built in an early 20th-century, white marble, monumental style.

All of this leaves out of consideration the undergraduate, who is left out in nearly every library that requires a great mass of stacks to house a research collection. The problem is, as it always has been, how to give young students a feeling that they have a home—to lure them in by appealing to their sybaritic nature, while at the same time so relating their home base to the research collections that they will move on into the stacks, landing eventually at their periphery, in an assigned carrel, not far in feeling from the medieval monk's cell, but higher as a status symbol. The design, and location, and relationship to the stacks of the undergraduate home base have been accomplished remarkably well in the Rockefeller Library, as attested by the fact that the library is called affectionately by the undergraduates "The Rock," or "The John" (depending on whether they view the intellectual world as sterile or fertile, I presume). The road to this accomplishment leads through some very basic elements in the building's structure.

Five structural elements are of critical importance in determining the usefulness of a library building: (1) its shape, that is, the shape of the floor plan of a typical floor on a blueprint—round, square, rectangular, etc.; (2) its massing, that is, the vertical cross sections on the blueprints; (3) the building's system of support columns; (4) the location of the service core elements, especially stairways, elevators, and restrooms; (5) the relationship between spaces assigned to internal rooms and spaces assigned to bookstacks, which determines the flow of bookstacks, a matter of vital importance in a library.

The Shape

The Rockefeller Library is rectangular in shape, with its entrance on the longest side. This is still the most useful shape for a library building, despite the shapes of some recent buildings that would make Mae West look like a rhomboid.[4] All of the "new" shapes are really very old—octagons, used in Navaho hogans and by early New England farmers for barns; circles, probably the most primitive shapes devised; irregular straight lines, used by the Minoans; pyramids, used by the Egyptians and Mayans, and so on. The contemporary frenzy to find a brand new shape for a building is as misguided at this point in history as trying to find a new sexual position. They have all been tried many times before and we keep coming back to one which still seems to do the job best. So it is with buildings. The simple, orderly arrangement of the typical stack floor in the Rockefeller Library (Level 3, p. 103) converts easily to a simple, orderly arrangement, on a floor that has many more complex demands (Level A, p. 100). The rectangular shape makes it easy to convert.

The Massing

If the shape of a building has the greatest effect on its function, its massing has the greatest effect on its exterior esthetics, and the massing of this building, as seen in the cross-section (p. 98), does some very remarkable things. It takes brilliant advantage of the slope on which it is built. An ornamental stairway leads up to the entrance on the main floor of the building, which is cantilevered 11 feet out beyond the peripheral columns on all four sides of the building.[5] This provides a main floor, the most demanding for space of all floors in a library, which is one-third larger than any other floor in the building. The cantilever helps shade the two floors below, and juts out dramatically on the downslope side of the building.

There are three floors above the main floor and three below it. Of the seven stories, five are completely open on all four sides and only the lowest one, which contains mechanical equipment, is completely underground. The floor below the main floor, Level A (p. 100), has large floor-to-ceiling window panels on all four sides, with the dramatic feeling of the cantilever hanging above them visible through the windows. More than half of the wall on this floor is glass, protected by the cantilever from the sun. On the downslope side, the windows look down on the very pleasant reading garden just below it.

The downslope side of Level B (p. 99), is completely open, allowing the use of large slit windows in rooms on that side of the building, and a walkway through the stacks into the reading garden. In short, the building is open on six out of seven floors.

The Column System

This library has two systems of supports, like a well-braced woman—one for the central structure and one for the cantilever. There is a system of great columns around the periphery (Level A, p. 100), that carry the outer wall and the load of the cantilever, and a system of internal columns. The columns on the periphery measure 10″ by 6′ long, and on all open sides of the building they go straight through the outer walls to form a tapered vertical unit on the exterior, one of the very dramatic lines that helps to create the sense of pattern on the building's exterior.

They are laid in pairs on 9′ centers, with 18′ centers between adjacent pairs. This spacing divides the outer wall of the building on all except the main floor into multiples of 9′. That is to say, anywhere that an interior wall must run at right angles to meet the outer wall, this 9′ dimension must be taken into account. The same kind of limitation is imposed in other buildings by window mullions. The dimensions of the unit of space that forms the outer walls, and how it fits library activities, is of greatest importance. Since the 9′ unit divides into two 4-1/2′ units, they fit library purposes exactly.[6]

On Level 3 (p. 103) the wall areas on three sides are used to provide paired carrels on 9′ centers, the peripheral columns serving as baffles for half of the carrels and a facing on which to hang bookshelves above them. The peripheral column system provides, on the fourth side, faculty research studies measuring 9′ × 9′, a generous size. On Level A (p. 100) in addition to a similar arrangement for carrels and research studies, the flexibility of wall lines allowed by the peripheral columns is apparent. The walls terminate either at an intermediate window mullion, or at a column proper, but these walls can be moved to run parallel on any multiple of 9′ on any wall, which makes for a wide range of possible sizes for rooms. On this level, the exterior ends of the peripheral columns are sheathed in precast granite aggregate, making a bold, handsome structural element.

On Level 1 (p. 101), the columns fall internally because of the cantilevered floor. In periodicals, bibliography, and reference, where they fall within stack ranges, they displace exactly two double-face stack ranges, while allowing ranges to stand on 4′6″ centers. In the catalog department, they serve as baffles for catalogers' work stations, helping to achieve some degree of privacy in a heavily populated room. On Level B (p. 99) where the columns fall internally in their full length, they hold a full section of shelving for books alongside of the carrel desk, which is also mounted on the column. On the left side of this floor, the intrusion of the columns makes the use of the wall areas of these rooms much less flexible than they should be. This is the only place in the entire building where the columns do intrude, and in my experience this is a remarkable record.

The system of internal columns is very nearly perfect. Consisting of a series of bays 27' square on centers, with seven bays running north to south and five bays running east to west, it is brilliantly coordinated with the system of peripheral columns. That system is a series of 9' units running along the outer wall. The inner column span is three times 9', with the columns located to fall in line with the center of the 18' outer wall space between the pairs of peripheral columns. This provides twice as much flexibility of choice in placing internal walls as if they were in line with the peripheral columns.

The columns are 24" × 35" in dimension, which is exactly the size to replace one double-face stack section when they fall within stack ranges, with no waste space whatsoever. The 27' dimension accommodates exactly the 4-1/2' multiples of stack range aisles. This is a large, clear span, which allows the accommodation within its pattern of various kinds of library units, with a column falling within a room only rarely, except in the stack areas.

In summary, after studying this lady's props carefully, what they do for her shape, and how they let her work back and forth, we can only gasp with admiration, "What a frame!" It is the best structural system I have seen.

The Service Cores

The service cores at the right contain a mop sink, stairway, public elevators, and a large, L-shaped vertical air duct wrapped around the stairs. The service cores at the left contain the circulation communications system (including a pneumatic blower, an automatic conveyor, and a stack desk), a staff elevator, a large vertical duct, an electrical closet, a small mop sink, a stairway, and two small rest rooms. These elements are repeated on each floor of the building with very little change. The cores are located in the central bays running east and west, with two bays completely free on either side of them, and are only a step removed from the center bays running north and south. They immobilize a very small portion of floor space, and are located in areas that allow maximum freedom of arrangement for the rest of the floor.

This is the most economical core arrangement that I know in a building this large, and its location is crucial. Since we have to walk around the cores, they determine the basic traffic pattern for the floors, and in this building the traffic patterns are ideal. Level 3 (p. 103) has 6' wide aisles the entire length of the floor, and three cross aisles connecting them. Traffic originates at the elevators or the stairs, and moves along the long corridors to the edge of the floor, or through the stacks to the reading areas. This arrangement is flawless, and it is repeated, with very minor alterations, on every floor in the building.

Level B (p. 99) shows how nicely the core locations adjust to a number of requirements. In addition to the usual requirements of the service elements and the traffic patterns, this floor contains the emergency exits required by law at the foot of the two fire stairways. For this reason, the rest rooms on this floor have been separated from the stairway on the left and combined with the duct shaft, to allow access to the emergency exit corridor at the bottom of the stairs. On the right-hand side of the plans, without variation, the emergency exit is head on to the foot of the stairway. In addition, at the ends of the main traffic lane below the core areas are, head on, the mail room and loading dock at one end, and the tunnel to the John Hay Library at the other end. By omitting a single stack range, another wide aisle is developed leading upward in the middle of the building directly to the reading garden. The remarkable achievements of this level demonstrate architectural art of the highest order.

Room/Stack Relationships

The placement of the rooms on a floor determines what spaces are left for the stacks. The shape of these spaces determines whether the call numbers on books can flow in an orderly, logical way so that stack groupings do not suddenly leap, leaving the poor student, like a baffled rat, in a corner wondering where the books go next.

In the Rockefeller Library the relating of rooms to the stack areas is superlatively well done. On Level 3 (p. 103) the total area committed to rooms and service cores (except for faculty studies on the west) is in the center, with stacks flowing around them in a starkly simple, logical way that would have delighted the classical Greeks. They are not quite perfect. The flow at both ends of the long run of ranges breaks, and the student has to hunt to pick up the trail again. However, if the intermediate block of stacks were turned at right angles to its present arrangement, with a loss of only three double-face sections, the flow would turn both corners without a ripple.

On Level A (p. 100) all nine of the internal rooms are grouped with the core areas as one solid block, leaving the stacks to run in a U around them. This time they turn the corner perfectly.

Level B (p. 99) has the unusual requirements of emergency exits running straight out the middle on the ends, a problem difficult to handle. The stacks are laid out in two long equal blocks of ranges, joined by a small block in the middle, again related in a totally logical manner.

Merely to have achieved the logic of the stack flows in this library would have been a great accomplishment by itself, but I have described in addition a shape, and a massing, and a column system, and a service core arrangement all of which are outstanding. A building so excellent in its basic structural elements could not possibly go far wrong. Even if the relationship between its rooms on the floors were all bad, someone could straighten them out easily.

Floor Layouts

I have some reservations about the floor layouts, and we might as well start with the main floor, because it is the most important, and because the architects went to great effort to make it larger than usual by cantilevering it. One of the first things I learned from Ralph Ellsworth, our consultant on the Colorado College Library, is that modular libraries built since World War II show clearly that an entrance placed in the middle of a building handicaps its main floor. The entrance determines the main traffic path that tends to divide the floor in two, and it is impossible to group activities that focus on the card catalog in such a way that they comprise two approximately equal areas.

On this floor, the main traffic pattern runs past the circulation desk, where it forks, to go upstairs or to the card catalog. Space on this floor tends to be tight in technical processes. It is loose in the public catalog area, in the bibliography collection, in the reference room and in periodicals. With the processing load of this library, a primary aim should have been to get all of the space possible for technical processes.

The processing departments would have had more space if they had been placed on the right wall, rather than the left, but ideally, they should occupy the whole north end of this floor, with the card catalog and reference just below them on the right wall, the administrative offices on the left wall and perhaps not so hoggish of space (the administrative area contains more than 2000 square feet), and a smaller periodicals reading room developed on the left side of the lobby.

Without arguing the disposition of space, the present layout has two serious flaws. It should have an entrance door to the periodicals reading room just to the right of the main entrance, rather than forcing the reader around through the magnificent walnut and travertine lobby, past the elaborate chandelier, into a rear entrance. Since there is an inspection point at the main entrance, it was perverse not to provide a more convenient entrance to this room.

In addition, the separation of the reference room from the card catalog by a window wall effectively chops that important function in two. They should be together, and the reference desks should be related much more intimately to the center of the card catalog. And it is a pity that the reference room and the periodicals reading room on this level were not carpeted. The rich carpeting on the floors of the rest of the public areas make their tile floors stand out like stark poverty.

Special Rooms

Level A (p. 100), one floor below the main floor, is home base for the Humanities students. This and its Social Science companion on the floor above the main floor are well designed to provide a feeling of attractive relaxation, with easy access to a core of books in each field, and to such high-use conveniences as the public rest rooms and pay telephones. At the entrance point is an exhibition lounge, through which there is access to the stack facilities or to the reading room. The variety of seating in the reading room is matched by that in the reserve book room to the right. At the right of the reserve room is an access door to the stack facilities. All of this home area is carpeted and richly furnished. Smoking is allowed in the reserve book room. Unfortunately, it is also allowed in the exhibition lounge through which everyone has to walk, and the lingering smell of smoke is offensive to nonsmokers, a growing group in society. The smell indicates that the lounge is not separately exhausted, an important requirement to keep any smoking room in a library fresh.

The listening rooms just outside the lounge are snuggle rooms just large enough for two side by side, designed for listening to stereo recordings with earphones. Really to listen to stereo effectively, speakers must be located in a room at least $10' \times 10'$ placed far enough apart so the sounds mingle before they reach the ear, as they cannot in small booths. Moreover, these booths are not soundproof. They have sand plaster walls and wooden doors with a 4" wide glass panel from floor to ceiling. Sound therefore passes between them.

The conference rooms in the upper corner are the wrong size even for conference. They are used as group study rooms, and if cut in two would provide the proper area for two group studies for six. Their present size does not fit any predictable activity. The same thing is true of the conference rooms on all of the other floors, some of which are used for seminars but are too large even for seminars.

Faculty research studies throughout the library are at least $9' \times 9'$, a generous size, with a built-in desk top dropped at one end to typing level. They have generous bookshelves, and are well lit—overlit, in fact (about 110 footcandles, of which they could easily drop 40). But they are not well ventilated. The periphery of the building is tempered by induction units which introduce fresh air drawn from outside the building in each cycle of the ventilation system through nozzles in such a way that its velocity induces movement of the air in the room into the unit, and up over elements which cool or heat it. These units are the only source of fresh air in the room, and not enough gets into the faculty studies by this system. This is true in summer even in studies that are adequately cooled, which means that the system is not well-designed. The same fact holds true for the conference rooms located at the periphery of the building, where students prop the doors open to alleviate stuffiness. Smoking in the faculty studies, or in the peripheral conference rooms, leaves a smell in the rooms which does not disappear, and makes them unpalatable for nonsmokers. These rooms should be separately exhausted.[7]

Interior Design

This building provides centers of visible pleasure and a touch of luxury in the public areas on the main floor and in the home areas on the floors above and below, where walnut panelling and travertine walls predominate, where the floors are carpeted, and where the most pleasant furniture is located. On the whole the furniture is quite good. Walnut is used throughout, including the top of reading tables and carrels, and while it is handsome to look at and luxurious in a traditional way, one of the things that we know about reading is that presence of a background considerably darker than a book page tends to draw the eye toward the background. To hold the eye on the page strains the eye muscles. Libraries must take this fact into account. In addition, the presence of light reading surfaces in a reading room can double the quality of the lighting in the room through increased interreflection.

The tables are well-designed, combining in different ways wood tops with metal legs. The library uses an interesting flat exhibition case made by Irving & Casson and uses standard stack uprights in lengths that reach from floor to ceiling as decorative strips painted black on the walls of the card catalog room, and of the Humanities and the Social Science lounges. Where utility calls for it, long shelves, or pullout compartments for the CBI, are hung on them, while the total effect of the uprights is still decorative.

Two pieces of furniture in this building I quarrel with. In the main floor reading rooms, the carrel has a short baffle, much too short to baff. This provides a decorative skirt, not a barrier that could be called a baffle, and the carrel has a limited use for reading.[8] A variant of this mini-skirt baffle is used in the stacks for a typing carrel, out in the open along a service core wall. The interior of the short baffle is lined with metal acoustical tile. Every open typing carrel made to date is a complete failure, since none of them encloses the typing noise. This one is even more of a failure since the sound baffles are about half the size of those used in other failures. Since there are no public typing rooms the stack typing carrels are used and their noise bounces loudly into nearby study carrels, resulting in complaints by readers.

In the periodicals reading room and in the stack areas a face-to-face, double carrel is used with a center pedestal. Most center pedestal writing units are unstable, but these are especially unstable, and it must be utter agony for two people to use them at the same time, unless they are playing footsie.[9]

Lighting

The lighting of the building varies in the type of fixtures and the type of diffusers used, and varies greatly in the quality and intensity of the illumination. In the main floor reading rooms the lighting is of reasonably good quality and 60-70 footcandles intensity. The Humanities and Social Science reading areas use $1' \times 4'$ fixtures with prismatic diffusing lenses in 26' troffers on 9' centers. The light is of good quality, and at 45 footcandles provides reasonably good reading light. Moving the troffers closer together, on 6' or 7' centers, would have made very good reading light.

The lighting for the peripheral carrels in the stacks, while of various kinds, is, in general, poor, and this is unfortunate, since a large proportion of the library's seating is in these areas. Sometimes $2' \times 4'$ fixtures are used parallel to the carrels, sometimes $1' \times 4'$ fixtures are used at right angles, sometimes, most horribly, an open bare fluorescent tube is placed at right angles to the carrels, but nowhere in the peripheral carrel areas is the lighting good. On Level A (p. 100), where it drops off to about 25 footcandles of illumination of the worst possible quality, it is atrocious. Under bad lighting conditions, the use of walnut writing surfaces on the carrels and dark walls, especially on Level B where the walls are cement block, conspire to produce the worst possible kind of light conditions.

This is partly due to the practice of keeping lights off in the stacks in research libraries, to save on the air conditioning load and lighting costs. These stacks have time switches for the stack lights. As a result there is infrequently any light drifting out of the stack areas to interreflect with peripheral lights to improve illumination, which to be good quality must be the result of light from many fixtures producing heavy interreflection. Unlighted stacks always cast a dismal aura wherever they are located, and it must be understood that in a research library, to compensate for this condition, special care must be taken and special money spent to assure that the lighting over the peripheral carrels is of good quality and intensity.

The lighting within the stacks is as bad as it has always been in research stacks since the twenties. Illumination is supplied by bare fluorescent bulbs, which provide the most efficient (i.e., least costly) light, but of the poorest possible quality. When, as here, the high, 10-1/2' ceiling provides typically only two 4' tubes for 15' of stacks, the atrocity is compounded. At the bottom shelf, there is a level of five footcandles of the worst possible quality lighting, to compensate for which Brown's processing department would have to affix call numbers in Braille labels.

What to say as envoi? The intellectual demands of planning a building and of appraising building plans are extreme. Once this fact is absorbed, one should not wander around in plans without using consultants, any more than he would enter without a guide into the eastern uplands of Kenya. Dave Jonah's Building Data Sheet lists under consultants "—" (dash, dash). He had none. After helping to plan 120 libraries, had I been planning this one I would have hired three consultants—a library building consultant, other than myself, a lighting consultant to review the lighting layout and fixture schedule, and an air-handling consultant to review the ventilation plans and specifications.

Dave Jonah was lucky in working with Warner, Burns, Toan, Lunde, because they understand well how a library works, but a good library building consultant would probably have produced an improved main floor for the Rockefeller Library. The lighting defects in the building are easily predictable, and a lighting consultant would have picked them up in an eye-blink. The defects of the air-handling system are more subtle but an expert would have picked them up. It is impossible to plan a building thoroughly well, even a building planned under as many advantages as this one had, without a crew of specialists on your side, walking over the documents behind the planners, picking up the broken pieces that have burst open or caved in through the pressures that attend all planning.

This building, like all buildings (which are like people in this respect) has flaws. But it also has virtues which are remarkable, and which greatly outbalance its flaws. Among other things, it has pioneered in providing library facilities for undergraduates within a research-size collection that are human in dimension and warm in feeling. Taken all in all and compared with its peers, this library ranks among the few at the top.[10]

Notes

1. Large variations in building costs in the same area are almost always dictated by the pressures on local contractors to bid low. Contractors have a very large overhead in their highly trained core staff and even more in their equipment. If these are not fully used at the time of bid, they are likely to be satisfied with ten per cent net profit rather than thirty per cent. The two libraries at Brown University were let for bid within a few years of each other. The Rockefeller came in far below its estimated cost. This situation was frustrating for the architects, who had omitted a number of desirable features in the building to come within the budget, then, when the budget could afford them, were unable to add them because of the time it would take to change the designs. Local contractors were running slack on work at the time. However, they were busy when the science library was let, and to get within the estimated budget the building had to be redesigned.

2. I had the great advantage of studying this building in the company of the architects, and of Dr. David A. Jonah, its Librarian (one of the fine unsung library directors of the 1950s and '60s), before I returned for a more thorough study. A year later I was enlightened by the reactions of four South American architects whom I guided through the building while consulting for them on the Universidad del Valle Library in Cali, Colombia.

3. My expenses for a three-day formal study of the Rockefeller library were financed by a research grant from Hofstra University in 1966, for which I am grateful. It was first presented as a paper at the Library Administration Division Buildings Institute pre-conference, San Francisco in June, 1967. It appeared, revised, as the lead article entitled "The Rock: A Critical Analysis of the John D. Rockefeller, Jr. Library at Brown University" in the annual architectural issue of *Library Journal,* 1 December 1968, pp. 4487–4492. It appeared in the form it was given as a paper, a speedy six years after the pre-conference, in the proceedings of that conference, Alphonse E. Trezza, editor, *Library Buildings: Innovation for Changing Needs* (Chicago, American Library Association, 1973), pp. 24–33. It is published here, slightly revised and with headnote and footnotes added, by permission of *Library Journal.*

4. Mae West was a movie actress prominent during the thirties to the fifties, whose dimensions and the way she managed them swept up the sensitive male populace and set obvious standards for the females of that time. This remarkable figure of a woman has just completed at the age of 84 her latest movie, in which she stars as heroine.

5. A cantilever is that portion of a building that juts out beyond the line of its supporting members. At a meeting of building planners held at the Playboy Club in Detroit, it was observed that the bunnies were well cantilevered. The cantilever of the Rockefeller library produces an entirely different but equally notable effect.

6. As discussed elsewhere, four and a half foot centers are not absolutely required for stack centers, but this dimension was normal, with very few deviations, at the time the Rockefeller was built.

7. For the difficulties experienced in completing this air-handling system see note 9, p. 47.

8. To provide the feeling of privacy which students seek when they choose to sit at carrels, baffles must rise at least nineteen inches above the reading surface. If the carrels are arranged on less than five-foot centers or if the population of a university runs heavily to very tall students, the baffles will have to be twenty-one to twenty-three inches above the reading surface. If side baffles are used to separate side-by-side carrels (cowstall arrangement, the most undesirable), they must extend out eight inches past the edge of the carrel.

9. It is possible to provide stability by using a single pedestal with two upright bars (instead of one) bracing the strain between the footing and the under-desk frame of the carrel, but this still leaves the face-to-face position which, despite the baffle, makes users aware of the presence of another person nearby. The elimination of this awareness is what students who prefer carrels desire.

10. Statistics for the Rockefeller Library:

> Gross Area—198,300 square feet.
> Seating capacity—1,048.
> Book capacity—1,250,000 volumes.
> Building cost—$3,546,722 ($17.88 per square foot).
> Project cost—$4,875,000 ($24.58 per square foot).

The following article on this building is worth reading: "The John D. Rockefeller Jr. Library and Science Library at Brown University," *Architectural Record,* September 1966, pp. 204–209.

CHAPTER 8

THE COUNTWAY LIBRARY OF MEDICINE

COUNTWAY LIBRARY OF MEDICINE

SOUTH-WEST

HUGH STUBBIN
A R C H I T E

The architect's elevation of the southwest façade of the Countway Library, showing the distinctive seating bays hung between the paired exterior columns, the entrance bridge (at left), and the sunken plaza in the foreground.

One of four identical façades of the building, whose beauty depends heavily on its exquisite proportions. Photo: Louis Reens

View of the entrance lobby, showing the information desk, the circulation desk, the ornamental staircase and, at its foot, exhibition cases and the periodical index area.

A view of the atrium from Lower I, showing the hanging carrels, the ornamental staircase, and straight ahead the current periodical issues. Photo: Louis Reens

The interior of a hanging carrel. Photo: Louis Reens

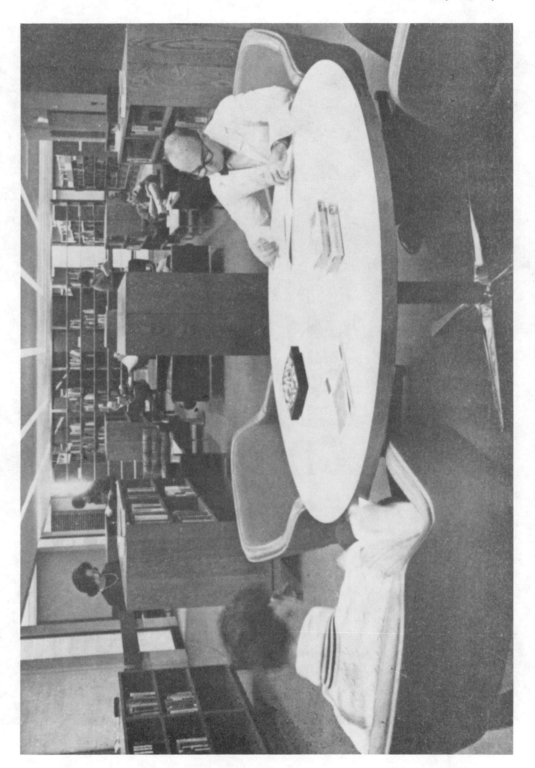

The Aesculapian Room (actually, a reading area) on the Second Floor.

One of the Lelli Ecorchés on the Fifth Floor.

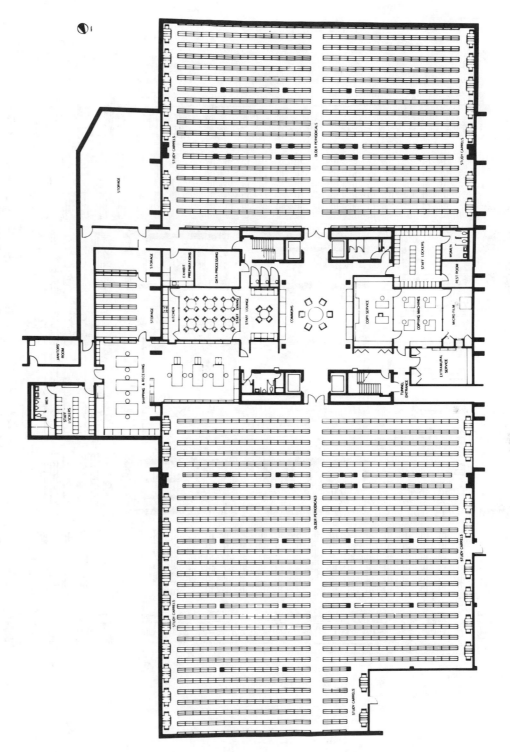

Lower II, two floors below the main floor, completely underground, which contains older periodicals.

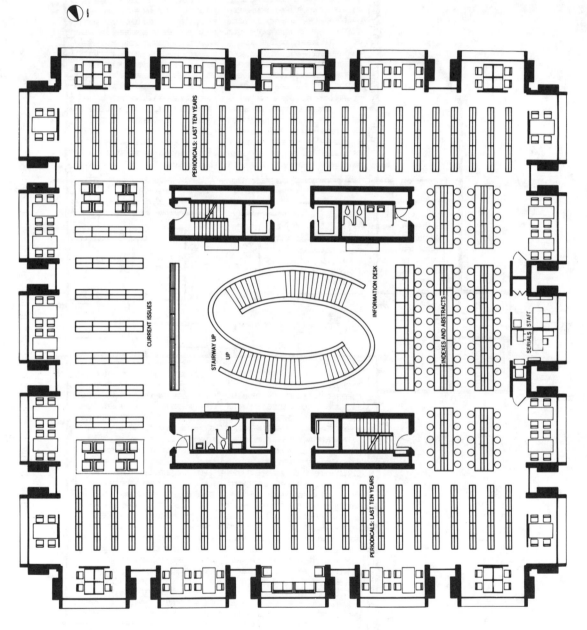

Lower I, one floor below the main floor, which contains the last ten years of periodicals. It is open to the exterior through windows in all the reading bays.

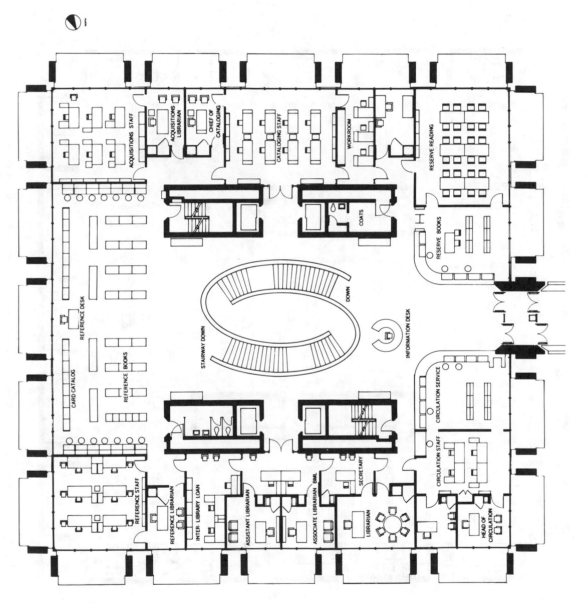

The main floor, completely surrounded by a window wall.

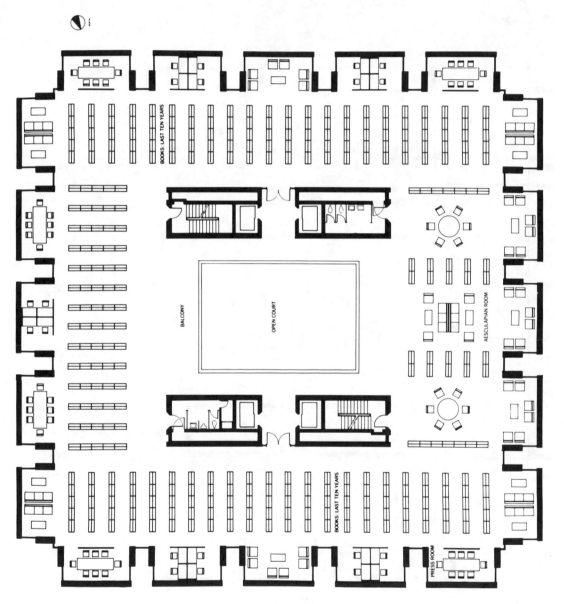

Second Floor, which contains books published within the last ten years.

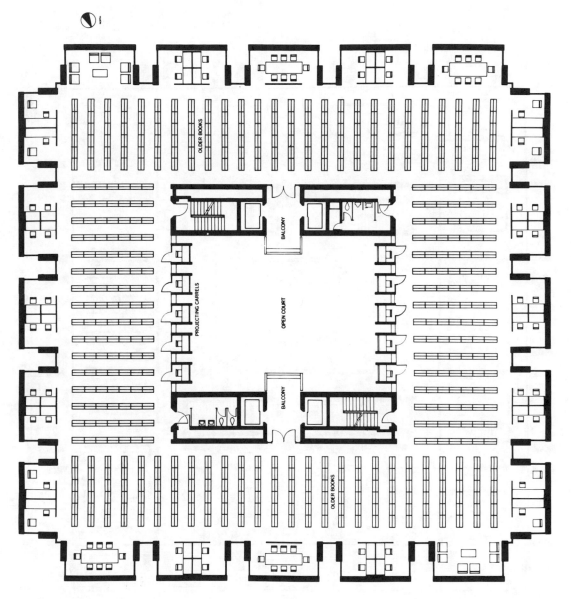

Third and Fourth Floors, which contain older books.

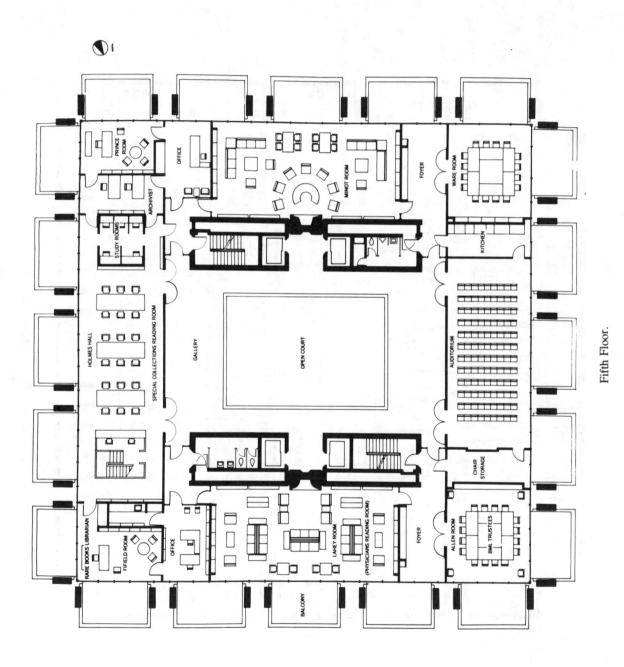

Fifth Floor.

THE COUNTWAY LIBRARY OF MEDICINE*

(In March of 1966, after reading my review article on the Los Gatos High School Library, Ralph Esterquest, Librarian of the Countway Library, wrote to me enclosing a brochure of that building, which had been open less than a year, and suggesting that I write a critical article on it. It had been on my mental list of possibilities after the Rockefeller library review, on which I had already started, but at Hofstra University we were about to move into a new library building and our staff and budget had just been doubled, so the possibility had been forced into the background. I agreed to review his building sometime within the next nine months, if he in return would agree to write a critical review article on an important library building within a year. He accepted this condition.

Late in September, on research funds supplied by Hofstra, I studied the Countway library for two and a half days, and returned with copious notes and a range of printed information about that admirable building. Immediately I was engulfed in the dynamics of my own library, which quadrupled the collection and came current with its cataloging in a period of four years. At the same time we were redesigning its service program to fit a major new library building that doubled use the first year it was open. By the time I was able to come up for air, Ralph Esterquest had died at a very early age, after nearly completing the gathering of information for review of the Tufts University Library, and somehow the project became less important to me.

In the summer of 1976, with the emergence of this book, the Countway at once assumed large dimensions in my mind, and on funds supplied by the Council on Library Resources, I returned to study it for two days nearly ten years after my initial review. This chapter therefore has a unique perspective on its subject from two points in time, and from ten years use of the building itself. It has worn remarkably well.)

*   *   *   *

The Francis A. Countway Library of Medicine could never have been anything other than a monumental building; that it also is highly functional is a tribute to the architect.[1] Largely funded by a gift of his sister Sanda Countway, it was a memorial to the former president of Lever Bros., a man greatly interested in the advancement of science. It was built to house the combination, consummated in 1960, of two of the most extensive libraries of medicine in the world, those of the Harvard Medical Library, established in 1782, and of the Boston Medical Library, founded in 1875 by a group of noted Boston physicians including Oliver Wendell Holmes.[2] When it opened, the Countway collections numbered more than four hundred thousand volumes.

It held nearly all of the great works in the field of medical history from the fifteenth to the nineteenth centuries, including 805 incunabula (the eleventh largest incunabula collection among all libraries in the United States). Its collections are rich in European books from the 16th to the 19th centuries, English books from 1475 to 1700, American books from 1668 to 1820, New England imprints, Bostoniana, medi-

*Footnotes to this article begin on p. 145.

cal Hebraica and Judaica from the 14th to the 19th centuries, and Chinese and Japanese medicine from 1650 to 1850. It has strong collections of medieval and renaissance medical manuscripts and of archives, and important collections of medical medals and portraits.[3]

It was built to serve students, faculty, and research staff of the Harvard Medical School, the School of Public Health and the School of Dental Medicine, the professional staffs of the Harvard Affiliated Teaching Hospitals, as well as members of the Boston Medical Library, which include members of the Massachusetts Medical Society—the human components of one of the world's great centers of medical education and research.

This new building had to be reconciled with five massive, neoclassical marble buildings on the Longwood Quadrangle which have housed the Harvard Medical School since 1906. Unless it was strong enough to confront them as an equal, its impact would be effectively muffled. To all of these demands the Countway measures up in a magnificent way. Worthy of the importance of its contents and the eminence of its clientele, strong enough to command the attention of its elders, it has already influenced the architecture of a new building in the medical complex built since 1965. It is one of the most handsome library buildings in this country, and in my opinion is the only completely successful library building in the entire melange of nearly one hundred libraries in the Harvard library system.

The Site

Siting the Countway posed similar problems to those encountered at the Beinecke library. It had to be a dominant structure in the midst of a group of large and imposing buildings. Though its surrounding architecture was more homogenous than that of the Beinecke, it was planned to contribute to the unity of the Longwood quadrangle. The space available for it was tight in ultimate terms and grindingly tight when it was built. The closest building of the Peter Bent Brigham Hospital complex overlaps the front half of the Countway. Although soon to be razed, it was still standing in the summer of 1976, still overwhelming the feeling of the Countway's entrance ramp and front facade. Its proximity makes it difficult to ignore its presence even in the imagination, which the architects have been able to do.

At the rear of the building Huntington Ave., a main urban trafficway, cuts off the site sharply on a 45° angle, making it impossible to construct a reasonably available loading area on a lower level. Instead, the Countway is served by a walk-in glass-enclosed kiosk about forty feet from the building, with an elevator that descends to a tunnel connecting the kiosk to the library.

The Countway had to be set back on the site far enough to blunt the impact of traffic noise and to allow enough distance for development of space to set off the building. At the same time, in lining it up its east façade had to relate to those of two other buildings in the quadrangle. And it had to leave enough space on Huntington Ave. diagonally northeast of it to accommodate a new School of Public Health building with a footprint almost as large as that of the Countway.

The front entrance to Countway is still constricted by the Peter Bent Brigham Hospital, which is soon to be razed. With its removal, the Countway will address gracefully the long axis of the quadrangle that forms the natural traffic way to its entrance. In every other way when built, this building had solved all the problems of a very difficult and overwhelmingly large-urban site with a high degree of success. By using materials of similar color and texture, by relating the height of the Countway and its facades, and the proportions of solid stone to glass areas, to the older buildings on the quadrangle, the architects have made in the scale and character of this new building a congenial but more elegant addition to the old. At the same time its proportions and shape and the handling of materials on its exterior make it one of the loveliest libraries in existence, a clear declaration of greatness in its design.[4]

The Planning

The planning of the Countway, which extended over a period of six years, involved more extensive intellection than is generally bestowed on buildings and the interaction of unusual talents. Ralph Esterquest was the somewhat scarred veteran of planning the building for the Midwest Inter-Library Center in Chicago, now the Center for Research Libraries, and had learned a good deal about building problems and working with architects at the expense of his hide.[5] The planning of the building, which was largely in his hands, began in 1958, with the first version of the program completed in October 1958 (72 pages). It was widely circulated for criticism among the Harvard medical faculty and the Boston medical community in general. As yet all planning was preliminary. Although Harvard had long felt the need to centralize its scattered medical collections a final decision to build had not yet been made.

In 1959 Miss Countway's gift of $3,500,000 precipitated a commitment to a major new building, and together with their reaction to the preliminary program it brought the Boston Medical Society into the library. For a long time the Boston Medical Library had suffered from ill-housing.[6] For more than a decade the sharply rising expense of maintaining a library had gnawed at the resources of the Society. With the prospect of a major new and well-conceived library, the Society formally contracted with Harvard to participate in a joint library. The program was then radically rewritten to embrace the needs of this new partner and the final version was completed in March 1961 (90 pages).

Parallel to these developments went a prolonged period of gathering information and investigation of library buildings, during which Esterquest visited more than forty buildings, nineteen of them medical libraries (of which very few were good at that time). These visits resulted in serious and prolonged discussions at home and abroad of basic library problems. They included a thorough study of current dynamics and emerging trends in medical education and practice, student-seating ratios, lighting, air-conditioning, after-hour studies, the library habits of medical users, patterns of stack-seating relationships, and such esthetic considerations as the effect of color and art on human behavior. Of these the only problem not solved well in this building is lighting, for reasons made clear in my chapter on lighting.

The selection of the architect was as thorough and unhurried as the conception of the building. Esterquest had a larger voice in the selection of the architects than most librarians ever have. More than twenty prominent firms from all over the country were visited at their home base or called to Harvard for interview, and the final selection of Hugh Stubbins & Associates was based on their proximity in Cambridge as well as their excellence in design as witnessed by their buildings in the Boston area.[7]

During the two-year development of plans for the building, the architects engaged in the most extensive discussions with their clients about major alternatives for choice that have occurred on any project I know. The plans were exposed to criticism at the Library Buildings Institute held at Chicago in July 1963, shortly after they were completed.[8] Two years later the building was opened for occupancy in June 1965. The results of this long consideration and unhurried process, combined with the unusual talents involved in the planning, has produced the handsomest major library in the country, in my opinion, one which is graceful and attractive inside, and extremely easy to use. It well merits its two architectural awards—an AIA/ALA/NBC award for library building architecture, and an American Institute of Architects award for excellence in design among all types of buildings completed in 1965.

The Exterior

The Countway is laid in a square plaza sunken six feet below grade level, which reduces the potential tension between the shape of the library building and that of the site, sliced sharply at an angle. The plaza supplies light to floor Lower I through strip windows set in its upper walls, and provides a surface below which large storage and equipment areas are located. It covers the tunnel to the Harvard Medical School complex, and provides access to an area under which future expansion of the building can be burrowed.

The plaza surface is pitched slightly outward to drains that collect water beyond the furthermost reach of the structure below it, and there have been no leaks into the levels below the plaza. It is paved with light brown brick. Its retaining walls, slanted outward from the building, are paved with the same brick alternated with darker brown vertical strips, which produce a very pleasant effect. The landscaping of the plaza includes large shade trees, including a slip from the Hippocrates tree on the island of Cos, an oriental plane tree which sheltered Hippocrates teaching his students, according to legend. These trees are set on the plaza in large round concrete tubs. Around the edge of the plaza are flowering trees and evergreens.

The Countway is a square building of eight stories, two of which are below grade, but its fine proportions present it as a horizontal building. Its exterior consists of four identical facades of warm-toned Indiana buff limestone (see p. 116). Each facade is divided into fifteen separate facing panels by four couples of paired columns (reminiscent of the Rockefeller library) which support the perimeter of the building, and three vertical sunken relief strips of contrasting limestone which mark the upper floor levels of the building. Each of these panels forms the outer wall of a cantilevered perimeter reading alcove. The sides of each alcove are faced with glass, and glass between the paired columns forms a vertical strip on the facade. All of the glass receives considerable sun relief from the insets.

Above these facing panels stand open balcony alcoves the same size as the reading alcoves, with the window wall of the fifth floor inset behind them. Above the balconies, the facing expands into a splendid series of fifty-seven vertical limestone fins which extend out beyond the building's facade, an impressive contemporary cornice that reflects the classical cornices on the surrounding buildings of the Longwood quadrangle. The windows for the sixth floor between each set of fins receive considerable sun relief from the inset.

Below the fifteen facing panels is the twelve-foot-high window wall of the main floor, and below this a series of five strip windows, inset below limestone canopies, bring light into the floor designated Lower I, which is partly below the plaza level. Not visible from ground level, but a dominant visual feature from surrounding buildings, the four service cores, enclosed within the central structural elements of the building, rise as limestone shafts above roof level. This is a rare building in its treatment of the roof area as an esthetic factor in relation to surrounding buildings. All of its machinery is concealed in the shafts above the roof, and a court sunken in the center of the roof to the level of the sixth floor conceals the large skylight lighting fixture containers above the building's central atrium.

Variations of the exterior emerge rather directly from interior needs. The main floor, with offices flanking main traffic lanes and views out across the plaza, has rather solid interior walls and a window wall exterior. The fifth and sixth floors, with views out over tree- and rooftops, are largely window-walled. The reading floors between, which do not have particularly engaging exterior views, open directly to the central atrium and are predominantly solid on their outer walls.

The exterior columns and inset strips of smooth limestone frame the facing panels made of random-width strips of rough, shot-sawn limestone.[9] The combination produces a strong texture that carries a considerable distance from the building. It has improved with ten years' weathering, the Boston pollution having emphasized the variations in the surface levels of the panels.

The total effect of all these elements is a stately, ordered building, warm in its appeal, varied in its conception and imagination, and in the fittingness of its proportions (wherein dwells most of the secret of beauty), in the balance of its colors and textures, in the interplay between its solids and glass it is a building of commanding beauty.[10]

The Entrance

We enter the Countway across the sunken plaza by a limestone bridge that leads to a windbreak vestibule. Just inside the vestibule, the Main Floor lifts suddenly to a 12'-high ceiling that extends in front of us for thirty feet. The eye is immediately drawn to a very handsome wood-railed elliptical double-stairway sweeping down to Lower I before us, with a wide vertical rack for latest periodical issues, shining stark white below 100 footcandles of illumination, directly athwart the view beyond the bottom of the stairs. The white intensity and apparent closeness of materials excite our library bones.

As we move toward the stairhead our vision, at first gradually and then abruptly, is drawn radically upward as the bold and dramatic forms of the atrium burst suddenly into view straight ahead of us. The atrium opens to a skylight 65' above floor level, and from the third and fourth floors of its far wall are cantilevered ten handsome carrels, five from each floor. Light from the skylights dramatizes the warm tones and fine texture and distinctive forms in limestone that border the atrium. As our vision recovers from the sudden delight of this initial impact we note balconies cantilevered laterally out on both sides of the third and fourth floors (see p. 119).

On all floors the atrium is contained by four vertical core towers, 14' × 24', faced with smooth limestone to match the exterior. These serve as visual boundaries for the atrium and baffles for the floor areas beyond them. A solid railing faced in limestone encloses walkways on all sides of the atrium above the Main Floor, with openings above them to the ceiling marking the height of the floors. In a single bound the atrium invites us further into the library and draws our inquiry up or down to those floors in view, a vivid example of the "active educational instrument" that the building committee called for in their library.

Straight ahead on the Main Floor beyond the stairwell the card catalog and catalog reference desk are in full view. As we move toward them we pass eight-foot wide lateral aisles between the cores and are at once aware that they contain elevators on both sides of the lobby. The one beckoning finger lacking on this floor is that of the stairway to ascend. There are two of them, enclosed behind doors in the northwest and southeast cores, but one must learn their location from experience. Consequently, most travel to the Second Floor is by elevator.

The Atrium

Ever since the Countway opened, the atrium has been a subject of consistently ignorant controversy. Before I saw it, I was warned that the Countway was an extravagantly expensive building. It is not, although it is rich in a dignified, practical way. In 1973 when the contract was let, $30.92 per square foot for a building faced with good building stone, and constructed in a major metropolitan area, was a reasonable price. Considering the quality of the materials used in the building and the high quality of workmanship evident throughout, Harvard got very good value for its money.

There have been cries about the enormous "waste" space in the atrium and how much this costs. At the Library Buildings Institute in 1963 Alderson Fry decried that the "hole" cost "$410,000." The cost of opening up a building in this way is the cost of the square footage of the floor and of the roof. These are the only additional areas added when a building is opened up. The idea that the square footage of the atrium could be recaptured for usable space on each floor at no extra cost is mad. Each square foot built would cost the building's basic unit price. Since the atrium space measures 30' × 42', or 1,260 square feet, the total space added to the Countway by the atrium is 2 × 1,260 square feet or 2,520 square feet in all. Assuming that the roof costs as much as the floor (and it really costs less), at $30.92 the cost of this additional square footage would be less than $78,000. Add $12,000 for the railings on the four open floors above the main floor, and the total cost of the atrium was about $90,000. If there were no offsetting savings to balance against this, it still would be a very modest sum to pay for the magnificent impact the atrium has on the feeling of a six million dollar library. This is especially true in view of the basic requirement in the program that the building should provide an experience of esthetic renewal for medical staff who dwell in clinical environments when not coping with human offal.

However, there are very large offsetting savings in this building. Totally aside from the visual delight provided by the atrium, and ignoring the fact that if the building were squished together to fill in the atrium as its opponents desire it would completely destroy the fine proportions of the exterior, we still have the fact that the atrium is the air-return duct for the entire air-handling system. The floor plan for the Main Floor (p. 125) indicates how little duct space is required for a building this size: the four elongated spaces on the extreme left and the extreme right of the cores.

Three different systems of arranging the core elements were proposed to the library staff, and after prolonged discussion it became clear that the alternatives to this split core arrangement with atrium air-return would occupy nearly as much space as the arrangement chosen, without adding anything visually distinctive to the building, because of very large additional space requirements for air-return ducts. The atrium, therefore, has added very little to the square foot requirements of the building, and in addition to its function as an air-return, the atrium serves wonderfully as an acoustic blotter, absorbing in its cubic volume the noise of entrance traffic along the Main Floor, and traffic from Main to Lower I, the three heaviest noise generators in the building.

Architectural Strategy

The three most important qualities called for in this building by the program were simplicity, ease of use, and attractiveness of feeling. Ease of use was especially important, because medical staff and practitioners, by virtue of their high location on the hog, are more demanding than most library clientele, and very often in a hurry to gather information. There can be few more demanding positions than that of a librarian responding to medics. The building's simplicity begins with that view described above from near the entrance, down to the periodicals and up to the library floors. It continues in the highly visible cores containing the elevators, which can be approached at four locations on each floor. When the elevator stops each floor is very simple to use because of the building's structural system.

As can be seen in the floor plans, except for Lower II, and only at the point where that floor spreads out beyond the perimeter of all of the floors above it, there are no columns in the entire building. For a library of 153,000 square feet, with a floor load throughout of 150 pounds per square foot live load to accommodate book stacks anywhere, this is a prodigious accomplishment. The poured concrete floors span the distance everywhere between the exterior columns and the center cores. As a result the layout of the floors proceeds in an entirely unencumbered, completely simple, startlingly logical manner.

Each floor that contains materials (except Lower II) comprises a series of concentric squares, seen in their purest form on the plans of the Third and Fourth Floors (p. 127). In the middle is the square formed by the core areas surrounding the atrium. This is surrounded by a square band of traffic aisle on the inner side of the stacks. This is surrounded by a broader square band of stacks. This is surrounded by a square band of traffic aisle at the outer side of the stacks. Beyond this aisle are all the reader spaces, located at the perimeter of the building in cantilevered alcoves. Nowhere in the building, except in older periodicals of low use on Lower II, is a seat more than 23' from the shelf where a book is found, a remarkable accomplishment in any library. This arrangement provides an impeccable traffic flow up through the cores, along the inside aisle, through the stacks to seating. The broad band of stacks provides excellent protection for the readers against the noise and distracting movement of the traffic. This arrangement could not be better or simpler.

Seating

Another aim of the program, similar to the problem solved in the Rockefeller library, was to provide convenient and attractive reading areas in contact with a mass of stacks in a research library. The perimeter alcoves on the materials floors provides a large variety of seating choices:

    two enclosed individual studies with sliding doors;
    four individual carrels with center and side baffles, and a partial wall on the traffic aisle;
    six lounge seats, around a coffee table or back-to-back;
    one table for eight;
    one table for four, with a partial wall on the traffic aisle;
    two tables for four;
    two locked studies, with custom desks and a side chair, assigned for research projects;
    group conference room, for typing, dictation, or conversation.

The variety is enhanced by the fact that most alcoves have lateral windows that afford pleasant and unusual views of the exterior, especially at the corners of the building. These windows have sun protection from the insets, but in addition each is equipped with full-height sliding oak louvers to shed what sun does come in. The alcoves are carpeted, very attractively furnished, and their ceiling has acoustical treatment.

Organization of Materials

This library is lent a further dimension of simplicity by the nature of medical literature and typical uses of it. The rule of thumb is simple—if you want periodicals, go down, if you want books, go up. The library usage is more than 60% in periodicals. Upon entering, the first thing that seizes the eye is the white rack holding current periodicals on Lower I. Also on Lower I are periodical indexes and periodical volumes for the last ten years. Below it on Lower II are periodical volumes more than ten years old. Up one floor from the Main Floor are all books of the last ten years, above it on the Third and Fourth Floors are all books more than ten years old. On the Fifth Floor are Special Collections and Archives. The organization could not be simpler. In the Countway, although there is an active service program, there is no excuse for not finding the floor on which your materials are located, even if you are a doctor or a professor.[11]

The Main Floor

On the Main Floor, the entrance is flanked on the left by the Circulation Desk and offices, on the right by the Reserve Desk and Reading Room. Shortly ahead, at the edge of the atrium, is a circular Information Desk. On the left oblique, running in a band between the window wall and the north cores, are offices for the Financial officer, Librarian, Associate Librarian, Assistant Librarian, Computer Consoles, and Reference department. On the right oblique, in a band between the window wall and the south cores, are offices for the Circulation head, Cataloging department, and Acquisitions department.[12] At the far end of this floor, between reference and technical processes, are the reference desk and collection and the card catalogs. This is a floor to use for business purposes, or to check the location of materials.

All offices on this floor have a twelve-foot ceiling, a height that generally makes for awkward proportions. The problem was solved here by solid walls seven feet high, extended five feet to the ceiling by quarter-inch glass. The glass provides good sound protection, occluding even typing noise, and makes the offices feel quite pleasant. The window wall with a view down to the plaza provides an especially nice touch to each office. All window walls are protected by lightly-woven pull draperies.

The Information Desk serves for interception and registration of all except authorized users of the Countway library. It also serves as a book inspection point for people leaving the building.

The circulation and reserve desks are handsome, matching, and custom designed. They curve gracefully at right angles away from the traffic lane, and both are recessed to hold a number of slipping stations for charge cards. These slipping stations, designed by the architects, the most attractive that I have seen, are no longer used at either desk, time having passed them by.

A booklift connects the circulation desk with the photocopy room on Lower II. Controls for the lighting on this floor, for the public address system (used to announce the closing of the building, the only effective device for this purpose in my opinion), and for the radio-alert system for physicians are all at the circulation desk. This system allows a doctor to pick up a beep device bearing a number for which he signs his name when he enters. If a telephone call comes for him, pressing a button for his number alerts him anywhere in the building to come to a red telephone to receive the call. There are two phones on each floor mounted on prominently visible and attractive oak and limestone panels located near the elevators. These telephones also are used to phone inquiries from the stacks to service desks about the location of books.

The selective lighting switches used in the Countway should never be used in any building. They consist of a dial marked with numbers 1 to 12. Twisting the dial to the proper number and pushing it in activates or extinguishes the lights controlled by that number. No one remembers what number controls which lights, and exactly the same results are obtainable far cheaper and more simply by flip switches, which are much easier to use (and to correct, if you flip the wrong one).[13]

Passage in and out of the Reserve area is through turnstiles. By locking them and unlocking the outside door to the Reading Room, a closed reserve condition is established. Locking the outside door to the Reading Room and unlocking the turnstiles establishes a closed reserve condition. As indicated in note 12, the use of this entire area has changed.

At the far end of this floor is a reference complex consisting of a service desk, the reference collection, the national bibliographies, the card catalog and consultation tables, and six atlas cases. The reference shelves of custom-built oak are arranged in double-face cases 4' high with three wide shelves mounted on limestone pedestals. They provide shelving for about three thousand volumes, and are attractive units. The oak card catalogs against the east wall of this floor are in 50-drawer units separated by a relief strip. The catalog is in two sections of eight units each, separated by a space designed for the service desk between them. Someone was intelligent enough to realize that walking from one side of the catalog to the other, around in front of the desk, tripping over the reference librarian along the way, was a sub-maximal arrangement, and the desk has been moved forward to a more appropriate location. The catalog is still separated into two halves.

Consultation tables are located opposite the catalogs. High swivel stools on fixed pedestals with a circular footrest accompany them. The skirt of the consultation table is too low for users sitting at the stools, who touch the skirt. These tables and the consultation shelf below the high bookcases that hold the national bibliographies against the north and south walls are covered with white satin formica, a smooth finish that reflects glare and should never be used on work surfaces or in large quantities anywhere in a library. As discussed in my chapter on interior design, matte-finished plastic must be used. This mistake is made wherever plastic surfaces are used in the Countway, which fortunately is not in many places.

The layout of this entire area could be greatly improved by giving a little on the precise symmetry of it all, and with little loss in appearance. The service desk should intercept users at the outer edge of the area. Card catalog cases arranged in short, double-face ranges should open at right angles to the lobby, with consultation tables between them and the reference collection beyond them. The national bibliography bookcases should remain on the walls as they now are. This arrangement would present the user the facilities he needs in their most logically used arrangement, would speed use of the catalog, and make the service desk more invitingly available.

Access to the administrative offices is through the alley between the northwest and northeast cores, off the north side of the lobby, which leads through double doors directly into the reception area for the offices. Behind the receptionist's desk, an inset alcove accommodates black, four-drawer filing cases within an oak liner, and shelves for ready-use books. It forms a distinctive and pleasant functional wall. The offices are well-appointed, though neither too large nor opulent. The Librarian's office opens off his secretary's office, and also has a French exit that leads directly out to the central area of the Main Floor. The administrator's offices, as well as offices of department heads, all have a wardrobe closet.

The department rooms, furnished with oak desks and attractive chairs, are all pleasant if a little snug in 1976. Lateral filing cases are used where needed, and the desks tend to have two-shelf bookcases beside them, rather than booktrucks, for work in progress. The card catalog and the Library of Congress catalogs are located near Acquisitions and Cataloging in the reference area, off which they open.

The center lobby of this floor, around the railing of the double-stairway and directly below the atrium skylight, is impressively clad in smooth limestone panels which face the core tower walls to a height of twelve feet. One wall bears a large portrait and inscription to the honor of Dean George Packard Berry of the Harvard Medical School. Attractive leather-covered benches are against each wall. This entire floor is carpeted in a lightly-ribbed tobacco colored carpeting, a very good-looking floor covering which in this large unbroken area shows ripples in the traffic lanes. Carpeting laid over an underpad, rather than fastened to the floor, tends to ripple wherever it is not held in place by many pieces of furniture, which means on all walkways of any extent. It can be pulled taut and refitted at the edges (as Countway's was) once, but further tautening is prevented by protrusions through the carpet, such as lighting fixtures, openings for stairwells, and other fixed elements on the floor. It should never be used in libraries unless fastened to the floor. The limestone panels, which come down to floor level, have been soiled by cleaning equipment along the bottom edge on this level.

The effect of this area has been diminished since 1966 by the energy shortage. Because the tops of the skylights are sunken one floor below the roof line, sun hits them only at certain times of the day. To accommodate this fact, the mercury vapor lights in the skylight coves were turned on, some of them during the day, all of them at night, to enhance the richness of materials in the atrium. These lights are now kept off except for very special occasions. At times, the center court of the library gets dull through dimness.

Lower I

Only the lobby of this floor is covered with the tobacco colored carpeting used above. The rest of the flooring is an antique white vinyl. Two pieces of furniture in the lobby catch the eye. An oak desk for reference use (lightly staffed these poor days) is accompanied by a striking, handsomely designed swivel arm chair upholstered in orange and black nylon tweed. On the other side of the lobby is a free-standing bulletin board six feet high, formed of three concave arc surfaces fastened together into an upright triangle. Lights for this bulletin board are fed from a floor plug.

At the east edge of the lobby, head on from the stairs that lead down from the entrance, are the Weekly Arrival Display racks, so vividly noticed from the entrance way. This unit, 36' wide, is formed of vertical slots of white enamelled metal, terraced to provide multiple display of single periodical issues, above a consultation shelf at stand-up height covered with white satin formica. This area is violently lit to 100 footcandles by downlights directly above. Both the high glare and heat load assure brief consultation only. Nearby are two inviting lounge islands, each with six black leather armchairs on red oriental rugs, separated by a travertine coffee table, inviting the reader to linger.

At the opposite edge of the lobby, head on from the stairs that lead down from the reference area, is a row of five exhibition cases. These cases, in oak, are 6' long and 26" deep, with a facing of glass set in metal frames 3' wide and hinged to lift upward. The cases are 36" high, too low by six inches for easy viewing, and are set on limestone pedestals. The bed of the cases is covered in light beige cloth. They are lit by a 60"-long slimline Verd-a-Ray fluorescent tube concealed below an overhang inside the rear of the case. An air fan cools the cases but the glass surface still is slightly warm to the touch. There is too much heat in the cases to accommodate really valuable books.

Beyond the Weekly Arrival Display racks, at the east end of the floor are seven ranges of custom-made current periodical cases that hold about half of Harvard's current subscriptions to four thousand periodicals. These cases are not totally successful. They are placed in double-face ranges four cases long. Each case is 5'7" high and 4' wide, with eight terraced mounting slots for display issues set above twelve flat storage shelves 15" deep. These shelves, which astonishingly enough are not adjustable, provide only 3" clear distance between shelves. This is enough to hold only three issues of the *Physical Review*, which is a bi-weekly publication.

Beyond the exhibition cases at the west end of this floor, a battery of periodical index tables supplies nearly 600 linear feet of shelving for indexes and abstracts. These tables have double-face shelves made of oak two shelves high, with provision for adding a third shelf on top if needed. In front of the shelves is a 17"-deep reading surface, of white satin formica with an oak edge. These heavy oak tables are set on limestone center pedestals, with steel support beams running their entire length.

These tables are flanked by rows of swivel stools with a low 9"-high back set on fixed pedestals. Fixed stools at consultation tables (which are used upstairs at the card catalog consultation tables, and in the Northwestern University Library and elsewhere) are attractive to architects because they assure continual visual symmetry; they never move. They are anathema to people, who come in different sizes and shapes and want to locate stools the proper distance from the table to suit their needs. Along the north and south ends of this floor, flanking the current periodicals, the center cores and the periodical indexes, are the stacks that house bound volumes of the last ten years of periodicals.

Twenty reading alcoves set in window bays formed by the exterior columns have a very pleasant feeling on this floor, although we are partly below plaza level. Each bay has a strip of windows a foot and a half high at the top of the wall, which look out on the overhung limestone canopies that frame the window strips and partially protect them from the sun. In these 8' × 18' alcoves seating is provided for 124 readers in the variety that is characteristic of this library.

For ease on this floor, we go to alcoves that contain two love seats and two lounge chairs, with small travertine coffee tables separating them in the corners. For privacy we choose individual carrels in groups of four, with an oak writing surface 26" × 38", 25" high center and side baffles, and a partial wall on the traffic aisle. The carrels are hung from the walls by brass straps. For company, we sit at 3' × 6' tables for four, custom designed by the architects in dark oak, with specially finished writing surfaces for ease of writing and maintenance. Seating is in armchairs with black oxhide seats set in sculptured oak frames that match the tables.

At these areas the feeling is very pleasant, slightly on the dark side, with good-grained wood, but the writing surfaces in this medical library defy our basic medical knowledge of what happens to readers at dark surfaces. Library writing surfaces must be light toned, for reasons discussed in my chapter on lighting.

Lower II

The ceiling of this level, two floors below the Main Floor, is 4-1/2' below the plaza level, and the spaces are entirely interior, totally unrelieved by windows. In addition, this is the largest floor in the building by far, reaching out considerably below the exterior columns that support the rest of the building. Here are shelved periodical volumes more than ten years old. This floor observes the principle of simplicity that governs the rest of the building, but in a different manner. The entire east-west axis to the outer edge of the core towers is occupied by service facilities, with the entire north and south areas occupied by stacks.

The center is largely occupied by a large photocopy service area, that was forced to cut back from its ambitious intent to provide free photocopies to all authorized users, and by a staff lounge connected to a lunchroom and kitchen. This totally interior staff area is pleasantly furnished and brightly lit. In the northwest corner of the center service area a shipping room provides enough space for a small brigade with forklifts. When I visited it, the man in charge was running it all from one single table in the corner of the room. Adjacent are large open storage areas and stack storage. The shipping room connects by tunnel to the delivery kiosk up at ground level. Also in this area are the men's and women's staff locker rooms and toilets. The tunnel to the Harvard Medical School complex begins on this level.

Between these service areas and the tower cores is the commonly used entrance to this floor, to which most users travel by elevator. In the middle is an area designated, New England-like, a Commons, paved in dull mottled-brown brick (the rest of this floor is vinyl). In the center is a five-foot-diameter coffee table and in a nearby alcove coffee and snack dispensing machines. The coffee table is ringed by five swivel lounge chairs upholstered in black naugahyde. Both sides of this area contain four wall-mounted exhibition cases 3' high by 4-1/2' wide and 2' deep. They are not successful. They are lighted by the general overhead light, which in this area is only 22 footcandles, largely swallowed up by the highly porous wall surfaces. The cases use one glass shelf, and the visibility of books exhibited on the top shelf is poor, and that of books on the lower shelf which are shaded by those above is atrocious.[14]

Opening through double doors on the north and south edge of the Commons are large areas with unbroken stacks in long ranges on 4' centers.[15] Seating is provided along the walls in double-carrels, different from the carrels on other levels of the library. They have a 2' × 3' writing surface, a 25" high center baffle and 17'' wide side baffles, all in dark oak. The carrels are provided with a bookshelf 10'' deep, with a canopy above at the top of the baffle, which makes the carrels feel unnecessarily dark and enclosed. The side baffle is composed of a panel that extends to the floor as a support, and the carrel is fastened to the wall and to this side panel in a way that provides extreme solidity to these face-to-face carrels.[16]

When I visited the Countway in 1966, the south stack room was closed and entirely unused. By 1977, it was completely activated, with a sizeable collection and carrels along the walls. By that time, the southwest corner of the north stack room had been converted to house a tenant, the New England Regional Medical Library Service staff and collection. The area had converted nicely to this new use.

Second Floor

One floor above the Main Floor are the most used books. Typically, there is a floor plan guide on the wall of the elevator niches, but at 6″ by 6″ it is too small for easy comprehension.[17] All ceilings on the stack floors are dropped around the core area. On this floor we notice a refinement carried up through the Third and Fourth Floors as well. The limestone walls around the core towers are variegated on the side facing the stacks by a series of vertical raised relief strips in limestone, with eight strips measuring ½″ × ½″ and six measuring 1″ × 1″ producing a pleasant change in texture on the inside walls.

From the atrium to the alcoves on the west side of this floor is the Aesculapian "Room." Though not enclosed, this area is defined by the atrium railing and by two long standard stack ranges at right angles to the general bookstacks. Here are kept humanistic books for high-level recreational reading and a change of pace from medical literature, as abominably written as all technical literature. The area is dominated by a relaxed, loungy feeling.

At the west end are three alcoves of lounge chairs accompanied by standing floor lamps. Toward the atrium are three reading bays separated by two rows of 47″-high wooden bookcases. The two outermost bays are furnished with a 5′-diameter round coffee table, topped with white formica with an oak trim, surrounded by five swivel armchairs upholstered in tobacco colored fabric. The center bay contains two sofas back-to-back and four lounge chairs, all in pleated black leather, separated by low travertine-top tables. There is a separate card catalog here for this collection, and the two custom-designed magazine-holding racks in this area are handsome and very functional. This area is carpeted.

In the northwest corner of this floor is an alcove Press Room for science journalists working in the library. In addition to a large table and chairs there is a small reference collection, a selection of periodicals, and a typewriter. The remainder of the alcoves on the perimeter seat 116 at the usual variety of user accommodations, including on this floor conference rooms, separated by a wall on the traffic lane with sliding doors. They contain 3′ × 9-½′ tables for eight, and grey chalkboards. All the alcoves are carpeted.

The other three sides of this floor contain the bookstacks, on 5′2″ centers here, all with oak end panels. They hang 9″ nominal shelves above 18-½″ bases. The flow of call numbers is totally logical and extremely easy to follow. Seating is always very nearby.

Third & Fourth Floors

These floors are identical, and in general differ from the Second Floor in few ways except that the side of the building used for the Aesculapian Room below is filled with stacks on these floors, where they flow in an unbroken band around all four sides. Books more than ten years old are shelved here, and as a consequence only two of the alcoves (which seat 114 on each floor) contain lounge chairs. The four corner alcoves each contain two locked studies of seventy-five square feet, reserved for long-term research writing projects. The outer walls in these studies are covered with an off-white vinyl. Each contains a 2′ × 8′ oak desk top the width of the study, with a bookshelf above, hung from the walls by brass straps, two handsome side chairs, a lounge chair and a standing lamp containing two 75 watt bulbs. All the alcoves are carpeted.

Two distinctive architectural elements appear on these floors only, jutting out into the atrium space in a very dramatic way. On the north and south edge, the walkway cantilevers out 6′ in a balcony ten feet wide. On the east and west edges five hanging carrels are cantilevered completely out into the atrium space (see p. 127).

Their brilliantly balanced proportions, and the simple device of insetting their face about five inches under a three-sided overhang, make these carrels strikingly handsome. The separation between them is faced with fire-resistant glass that makes them seem to float independently in the air.[18] The hanging carrels are made of precast poured concrete sandblasted to give them a texture that harmonizes with the limestone. They are entered from the stack floor traffic lane through an oak door flanked by a vertical glass relief strip. They are carpeted. The front end of the carrel is solid to a height of three feet, then glassed to a height of 8'6", giving the occupant an exhilarating view down into the atrium space. Each carrel contains a 22" × 50" dark oak writing surface, hung from the walls and slightly turned up on the sides, and a black leather side chair. These carrels, twenty in all, provide highly unusual and extremely pleasant spaces for study, and they are in high demand by users.

The stacks on these floors are on 4'4" centers, with 9" nominal shelves, and contain two distinctive stack units. The end ranges near seating supply a number of coathanging units mounted on stack uprights, with a hat shelf, a rod for coathangers, and a drip pan below for umbrellas. In part of the stacks, freestanding locker units of 8 lockers, each 12" wide by 17" high, replace a stack section. These floors are pleasant in feeling and easy to use, although they shelve more than 150,000 volumes each.

Fifth Floor

This History of Science Floor is addressed to an unusual component of the library's clientele, consisting of donors and the most broad-gauged intellects of the Harvard medical faculty and the Boston medical profession. As a consequence it is opulent and its facilities are extremely popular and highly used. The floor is covered with rich, bright red carpeting that comes as a stimulating contrast to the tobacco carpeting of the reading areas below. The lobby around the atrium is faced with limestone on the north and south, which contrasts nicely with dark oak panelled walls of a bold wood grain on the east and west. The large ancestral portraits of hallowed medical saviors of the area's past include one painted by Gilbert Stuart. Around the limestone railing enclosure are custom-designed exhibition cases in dark oak, related to the nature of this floor and the presence of the rare book room. In 1976 they were engulfed in dismal light (partly through bad initial light design, partly by more recent economy moves) that fairly well defeated their purpose.

Set in limestone niches specially built for them on the walls between the elevator cores are the two Lelli "Ecorchés," as they are known locally, and these are kept lighted by a single incandescent downlight (see p. 122). "Ecorché" literally means "de-barked," and these 18" by 72" rather magnificent and extremely rare engravings, which depict a human figure stripped of its skin down to the musculature, are graphic representations done in the 1780s of two figures carved in wood for the anatomical theatre in Bologna by Ercole Lelli.[19]

This floor in many ways reflects the pattern of the Main Floor, to which it is related in function. It is the only other floor completely carpeted. Its entire perimeter is shielded by draperies exactly like those on the Main Floor. The exterior walls of the floor are, again, window walls inset below the overhang of the cornice above. Sliding panels in the window walls open out to balconies formed by the uppermost reaches of the reading alcoves set between the exterior columns below.

Similar to the Main Floor, the space between the center core and the outer walls is occupied by enclosed rooms, and the simplicity of design that governs the building continues to operate here. Broadside to the court, two large lounge rooms occupy the north and south sides of this floor; on the east side is the special collections reading room, on the west side an auditorium for 120. The corners are for smaller occupancy rooms—offices connected with the rare book room on the east, and on the west a trustees room for the Boston Medical Society and a seminar room.

The Lahey Room on the north is a reading room exclusively for the Fellows of the Boston Medical Library and members of the Massachusetts Medical Society. Books and periodicals of dismal literacy (why is Economics the only dismal science?) are on wooden shelving on the end walls, and the rest of the room is occupied by two writing tables and black leather lounge furniture. A large open fireplace on the south wall of this room incorporates the handsome ornately-carved wood panelling and the iron liner formerly in the main reading room fireplace of the Boston Medical Library.[20]

The Minot Room on the south side of this floor, reserved for groups interested in the history of medicine, is used for small lectures and discussions. Like the Lahey Room, it has an open fireplace, but in a modern style, confronted by an arc-shaped coffee table which is related to the information desk on the Main Floor. Swivel arm chairs around this coffee table, groups of lounge chairs in pleated black leather set beside glass-topped coffee tables, and two writing tables of dark oak complete the furniture of this room.

The planning of the Special Collections areas lacked the guidance of any totally competent special collections librarian (the present incumbent not yet on the spot). As a consequence some of its features are badly designed and its stack capacity was grievously underplanned. It is only fair to say that the additions to Harvard's special collections from the Boston Medical Library greatly exceeded expectations, but we still shudder to recall that less than a year after opening (when I first visited this library) half its collection had been forced down into grilled areas of the Fourth Floor which were never intended for them. By 1976 more than a third of that floor was occupied by special collection materials.

Although the staff has improvised around these difficulties, there was no room provided for the card catalogs, and no workroom. Specially designed booktrucks were noisy and unsatisfactory. Virtually all of the collection is one floor from the reading room (above, on the Sixth Floor, as planned for a rare book stack, and below on the Fourth, not as planned), and retrieval of material is not easy.

The reading room, named after Dr. Oliver Wendell Holmes, is more than adequate, with three very large tables, 5′ × 12′ for six readers, to allow ample space for handling large and valuable materials. The dark oak tables are attended by Knoll chairs in black leather. At one end of the room is the librarian's desk, raised on a dais for better supervision of users, and behind this the stairs to the stacks above. At the other end, behind eight-foot-high partial partitions, are five typing rooms with desk tops hung from the wall and oak side chairs. The offices of the Rare Books Librarian and the Archivist, both handsomely appointed, open off this reading room. Wooden bookshelves fill the west wall of this room with reference books. The feeling of the room is pleasant, and dignified enough to engender respect for use of these books in the reader.

The special collection areas are air conditioned by a separate system (that also feeds the entire Sixth Floor) which is kept operating around the clock even when the tempering capacity of the rest of the building is lowered during times when it is not occupied. A special humidity control system is provided for these stacks. Lighting in the stacks is incandescent, but by downlights, which are ineffective in distributing the light and hot enough to feel when you stand below them. The reading room is lit by fluorescent fixtures set in the transverse coffered beams of the ceiling. These were not provided with ultra-violet shielding.

Sixth Floor

The sensible future of this library would call for converting the entire Sixth Floor to stacks for special collections. At present, as tenants since 1966, the editorial offices of two major journals, *The New England Journal of Medicine* and *The Journal of Bone and Joint Surgery,* occupy the three sides of this floor not occupied by the special collection stacks. Offices are separated on both sides of a central corridor on each side. The roof of the library is at the floor level of this floor above the atrium, providing a window wall on the interior for offices that face inward. Exterior offices have windows between the fins of the building's cornice.

Air-Handling

The Countway uses a double-duct system that distributes air at high velocity through vertical ducts in the core towers to horizontal zones on each floor. The large areas on Lower II are broken into several zones, each controlled by its own thermostat. On other floors, the stack zones are fed through a vent-spline system in the ceiling, and the reading alcoves are provided with individual thermostats that control air fed from above the lighting louvers. This system is excellent, and the temperature and humidity are comfortable throughout the building with a few exceptions.

On the Main Floor the rooms that contain long window walls on the south side complain about extremes of temperature in summer and winter. Rooms on the north side, which have less exposure per room, complain about some discomfort in summer. The southeast corner room, with window walls on two sides, complains about excessive cold in the summer, a condition we encountered in a similar room at the Colorado College Library. We must conclude that the air-handling system provides inadequate tempering along these window walls, which are 12 feet high.

This system allows for smoking anywhere in the library. Smoking is permitted everywhere except in the stacks, in the Special Collections areas, and in areas set aside for non-smokers, now a large portion of the seating areas.

Lighting

The only totally good quality lighting in the entire building is in the Hanging Carrels, which use a $1' \times 4'$ fluorescent fixture that indeed has open eggcrate louvers, but is so located in relationship to the desk surface that it produces 40 footcandles with no reflected glare, and the rooms are small enough to produce good interreflection from this single fixture.

In general the lighting throughout the building uses eggcrate louver fixtures. These control direct glare completely, but do nothing to control reflected glare. Given the Countway's unique conditions—with reading in alcoves no longer than $18'$, a distance that minimizes direct glare, and with half of its collection in periodicals printed on coated paper, which registers reflected glare most intensely, we would have chosen the exact opposite if necessary, the control of reflected glare at the expense of ignoring direct glare.

The quality of the lighting is no better than adequate in any reading area in the building. On floors Two to Four each reading alcove has a ceiling formed entirely of bare tubes hung above eggcrate louvers with a half-inch grid. This provides about 100 footcandles of partially diffused light that is reasonably bright in most alcoves but has high reflected glare directly below the tubes. On Lower I the alcoves use strips of $1' \times 4'$ two-tube fixtures with eggcrate louvers on $4'6''$ centers, which produces light that varies considerably with the furniture in the alcoves. Those with four individual carrels with baffles have 45 footcandles of poorly diffused, heavily shadowed, poor quality light. Lounge alcoves, where the carpeting and furniture absorb what interreflection there is, have 50 footcandles of cheerless light. In alcoves with open tables for four, there is 50 footcandles of brighter light, but the glare is perceptible. The definitive commentary on the quality of lighting in the reading areas is the fact that occupants of seven of the eight locked studies on the Fourth Floor use a standing incandescent lamp and a desk lamp in preference to the overhead lighting (which is controlled by switches in each alcove).

The stack lighting on Lower I is contained in units 4' × 20' hung in the coffers of transverse beams, which use three tubes above eggcrate louvers. At the index tables there are 70 footcandles of reasonably bright light with high reflected glare. In the stacks, where lighting runs parallel to the stacks, there are 20 footcandles to 50 footcandles (depending on whether the stack falls under or to the side of the fixture). Here reflected glare is of no importance.

The stack lighting in the bulk of the stacks, on the Second to Fourth Floors, uses a Columbia fixture that was specifically designed for stack lighting. Its reflection has been increased by enamelling the two-way baffles white. However, this fixture must be used on stack aisle centers, as discussed on p. 33, to be effective. One of the basic requirements of this library, with different stack centers on different floors, was that stack centers could be changed without remodeling the lighting. This requires lighting strips at right angles to stack ranges. As a consequence, to get the lighting level desired in the stacks, these lighting strips run on 4' centers.

These are expensive fixtures. Four-foot centers use 50 per cent more fixtures than would be expected from stack lighting at right angles, which can easily be run on 6' centers. The result is an installation that cost about 75 per cent more than it should have to achieve the conditions produced in the stacks, which read 30 footcandles about 30" above the floor. Reflected glare is of no importance in these areas, but it would be impossible to convert these stack areas to reading areas without changing fixtures.

Interior Design

The interior design of the entire library is in good taste. Units custom designed by the architects are good, and there is sufficient variety of color and texture to provide change without scattering the feeling of the building. The quality of the furniture is good throughout. The color coordination is done with a fine eye. All is nicely related to the structure of the building, which participates heavily in the interior design in the limestone that it brings inside, in the four walls of the four core towers and the inside of the exterior columns.

While I do not quarrel with the harmony of the effect of the interior I do question the conception of the gentlemanly convention of dignity that restricted the imagination of the designer. There are enough black chairs here to tickle the innards of any Wall Street lawyer. Dark oak dominates the view from almost any angle of the library. The carpet used predominately is a medium toned tobacco color. The only relief to these tones is the antique white vinyl in the stack areas, which is so overwhelmed by the oak end panels that it scarcely impinges on the general feeling of the library (except on Lower II, where it indeed picks up the feeling of that floor, which is completely below grade). A few surfaces of white formica and travertine interrupt the darker tones. On the Fifth Floor, the bright red carpeting picks up the feeling of its rooms. But on the whole, the feeling of the interior design is subdued. Not enough to be sombre or a depressant (an effect we shall see in another library), but far more than is required by either human need or the status of Harvard University or the dignity of Boston medical men.

The same tinge of tepidity is apparent in the imagination that chose the shapes of the furniture selected for the building. All of it is just barely distinguished; nothing rises to the level of true distinction. It is possible to create a dignified and conservative feeling in a brighter palette of colors and shapes than was used in this building, and by so doing to improve the feeling of the library and make it a place that more people would feel happier to be in. It is just barely possible that a reaction to the subdued quality of the Countway led to the insane wildness of colors in the Harvard Education Library discussed in my chapter on interior design.[21]

Summation

The architectural properties of the Countway achieve rare qualities of feeling and function not completely matched by the lighting and interior design of the building. With all its flaws properly adjusted for their various degrees of importance, it remains after twelve years one of the most successful library buildings in the country, and in my opinion it still is the handsomest and most impressive of them all.[22]

Notes

1. Although I grew up in it in the thirties, when endowments stretched splendiferously far, the lavish scale of living in the upper Ivy League still is surprising when one returns to it these meager days. Last summer, at a time when academic construction everywhere was in the doldrums, there were six or seven large construction projects in process at Harvard. The visible portions of the Pusey Library addition to Widener are opulent, and around its light court adjacent to the stacks are the most elegant faculty studies imaginable.

   The funding of the Countway, as related to me by Ralph Esterquest, reflects this happy condition of affluence. The very first meeting with the architect, Hugh A. Stubbins of Cambridge, attended by Esterquest, the Dean of the Harvard Medical School, and the fiscal vice-president of the university, was opened with the remark by the money-manager that the first order of business was to establish a budget for the building. In reply, the Dean said, in effect, "I don't like that kind of talk. Mr. Stubbins is an artist, and we don't want to inhibit his creative approach to our building design by practical matters." Since the Deans at Harvard are responsible for raising funds for their buildings, the vice-president was reduced to a gulp. After some conversation, all four men agreed that they all were highly disciplined and responsible people, and that they would be wary of extravagance, but that a budget for the building would not be set until after its design had proceeded considerably. As events turned out, the Dean of the Harvard Medical School retired before he had raised the entire cost of the Library. On the other hand, it is not an extravagant building.

2. This joint venture fused the collections and staff of the two libraries while providing a very badly needed new building for the Boston Medical Library. The Countway opened with an Associate Librarian for Boston Medical Library Services, a Joint Committee of the Library representing both groups, and a room for the Boston Medical Library Trustees on the fifth floor of Countway.

   In the flush of generous feeling toward the Boston/Cambridge medical community that ensued, the Countway library offered free Xerox copying to all legitimate users, backed up by twelve Xerox machines, when it opened. Within a year they had begun to charge for copies, and had cut to three machines.

3. In 1978, the Countway held 474,000 volumes.

4. This building's success is attributable to a large degree to Peter Woytuk, Collaborator in Design for the firm of Hugh A. Stubbins & Associates and one of the finest architectural designers of recent times. Since there are only a few major talents in this field at any time, it is sad to record his death in his early forties a few years ago. He was representing Stubbins as associate architect on the Ohio State University addition. I was working with him in that capacity at the time of his death, and can testify to his stature as a person as well as a talent. The Countway library may well be his most significant building.

5. When I first met Esterquest in 1953 he expounded to my ignorant ears the discoordination of architectural planning in the Midwest InterLibrary Center. In one room, the door was prevented from swinging fully open by two ceiling light fixtures. There ensued a negotiation on the "re-shaping" as the architects called it, or "mis-shaping" as Esterquest called it, of the reflecting shield on the fixtures to accommodate the door swing. Neither seemed to realize, nor did I of course in 1953, that this very bad light fixture was being further warped into uselessness by this change.

   Ralph Esterquest had a freer hand in the development of this library than most librarians have ever had. The only parallel I know is my experience with the new Hofstra University Library. Although the architects had been hired before I joined that staff, the planning and working with the architects was totally in my hands, without even a committee of any kind to muck-up affairs.

6. For example, when Lee Ash was brought in to sort out the usable material from the uncataloged miscellany in the Boston Medical Library, he discovered a huge basement nearly solidly full to the ceiling with a cubic mass of heterogenous materials, which ranged from single-sheet brochures through books and periodical issues. The books included, hidden in the mass, twelve incunabula!

7. Proximity is frequently a deciding factor in selecting an architect. While it is convenient to work with a nearby architect, the demonstrated talent of the firm for building library buildings should be the decisive factor, no matter how far away he is located. In planning buildings I have often worked, as consultant and as librarian-planner, with firms more than a thousand miles away, and I find the distance no drawback.

Telephone conversation, which settles most detailed problems in the course of a building's planning, ignores distance. Major decisions always require large group meetings, which are easy to arrange disregarding distance. Proximity of the architect is a positive factor only if the local planning officers are weak or non-existent, or if a Clerk-of-the-Works is not to be hired to supervise construction closely. But, as I have already pointed out, not to hire a very good man for this critical function is to invite destruction.

8. A highly uninformed critique of the plans was given by Alderson Fry, then Medical Librarian of West Virginia University at Morgantown. His misguided rant against the Countway's atrium, which is discussed at length in this review, might have been more credible if he had not demonstrated a weak ability to understand the floor plans, and included the statement that the library "has a transformer room to hold the fluorescent light transformers which have a bad habit of degrading to an anoying hum," a fiction that trips on the fact that fluorescent fixtures do not have transformers. Ballasts, which he has in mind, are not transformers, and although they can be located remote from the fixtures, rather than in the fixtures, to locate them in a single room in an eight-story building of 150,000 square feet, wired back individually to each fixture and identified to indicate which fixture they control, would have cost about a quarter of a million dollars in 1963 money. The architects wisely did not provide such an arrangement.

Fluorescent lighting ballasts are not much of a problem if they are replaced as soon as they begin to hum. Unfortunately, most buildings of any size do not have anyone assigned to monitor their physical properties on a daily basis, so prolonged hums may occur.

These proceedings will be found on pp. 16–27 of William A. Katz and Roderick G. Swartz, editors, *Problems in Planning Library Facilities* (Proceedings of the Library Buildings Institute conducted at Chicago, July 12–13, 1963). Chicago, American Library Association, 1964.

9. The new Kresge School of Public Health building, whose northeast corner is about twenty-five feet from the southwest corner of the Countway, rang a later variation on the Countway's exterior. It uses solid vertical limestone panels separated by raised limestone relief strips to counterpoint the Countway's random-strip horizontal panels and inset relief strips.

10. I will send at cost a copy of a good color slide of the Countway taken by my librarian wife, a good amateur photographer whom I drafted into architectural photography, to anyone seriously interested in this building.

11. My apologies to that five per cent of teachers and professionals who can use a library, but my constant observation over forty years of librarianship indicates that higher intellectual skills equate with lower library skills. New instructors fresh out of graduate school and on the make tend to be splendid bibliographers and library users, since they have spent four years sharpening their skills. By the time these same instructors have made tenure they tend to be sloppy and library-vague. Eminent research professors can be inexcusable.

I think that the worst example of a library user in my experience was Bernhard Knollenberg, Librarian of Yale University from 1938 to 1942. Knollenberg was a remarkably admirable man, highly intelligent and informed, had been a very successful lawyer, and was one of the country's leading authorities on George Washington. His hand-scrawled citations to books, that he handed over to the reference department when I was at the bottom of their totem pole, invariably took a skilled reference librarian two weeks to equate with any known book.

Mr. Knollenberg, who succeeded Andrew Keogh, a fine librarian, was intelligent enough to realize after a few years that he had about as much skill in running a library as we had in running a law office, and resigned under no pressure at all. Indeed, the Trustees, including Wilmarth Lewis, thought he was doing fine!

12. The following changes in function occurred during the ten years between my study visits to this library. The bookkeeping function was moved out of Acquisitions to the northwest office that had been used by the Circulation head. This allowed the move to Acquisitions of the serials-checking Kardex, which was working ad-hoc and unhappily out of an alcove on Lower I, which had not converted well to this change, in 1966. The Circulation head moved to an office on the south wall that was unassigned in 1966. The Interlibrary Loan office had given way to a Computer Console room by 1976, and had been absorbed into the Reference office.

Although the Reserve area had been planned to convert easily from open to closed reserve, by 1977 the desk area was being used for Computer Assisted Instruction fed by a computer in the Massachusetts General Hospital, and audio and visual equipment filled the Reserve Reading Room (the materials were issued at the Circulation Desk). The reserve books have been moved behind the Circulation desk, where they should have been planned for this kind of a library from the beginning. There are enough electric outlets in the former Reading Room to accommodate these machines, but they are not conveniently located for this multiple demand and electric cords trail in a disorderly fashion around the room.

13. The fascination of architects with complicated technical devices is a constant factor. So many times I have heard the statement, ''We can give you that in a far more sophisticated system.''! Exactly at that point, the client should put his foot down hard. The rule of thumb in planning buildings should be—indeed, do what you need to have done, but do it in the simplest way possible.

Elevators, for instance, are frequently overprogrammed. The two worst instances of oversophisticated devices I know are the flushing of the urinals at Northwestern University Library and the stack entrance control at Emory University Library. Northwestern was sold a system that we vetoed when the same architect proposed it at Colorado College. When the john door is opened, it activates a device that flushes all the urinals automatically three minutes later, thus saving the enormous manpower required to pull a simple flush lever.

At Emory, the entrance gate to the closed stacks (which resembles subway control gates in New York) is activated by plastic cards issued to authorized users. Each card has a separate number, and it is possible to prevent that card from opening the gate, if it is lost or the holder proves to be a low character, by inserting push pins in a master control panel designed specifically for this purpose. Of course the system worked highly erratically, and consequently is no longer used at all.

14. By 1976 these cases hung empty, looking defeated by staff costs and their own ineptitude.

15. The year 1965 was very early in the move to cut back to narrower than 4-½' stack centers. These hang 9" nominal shelves above 18-½" bases, leaving 29-½" wide aisles (which we should worry about, instead of range centers). They are adequate, especially for a low use area. Through most of the rest of this library the stack centers vary.

16. My opposition to the face-to-face carrels in general, and those in the Rockefeller library in particular, remains unchanged by the fact that these carrels, with great stability in their mounting and a very high baffle, are acceptable in a low use area.

17. This is quite in contrast to floor plan guides on the Rockefeller library stack floors, which are about 24" by 30" (as they should be), with sheets easily changeable by slipping them behind glass enclosures.

18. This German-made glass has a very delicate reinforcing wire running in a vertical direction only, in contrast to the heavy two-way wire reinforcement in most fire-resistant glass. As a result, the wire is nearly invisible only a short distance away. A great relief from the very obtrusive counterpart used in most buildings, it was approved by the Boston fire authorities. I have never seen its equal anywhere.

19. The two engravings cost $5,000, and Ralph Esterquest's adamant refusal to buy them at this price was softened, as he told me, when the bookseller convinced him that he was viewing the price in the wrong manner, as simple engravings, whereas he could consider an entirely different dimension of price if he viewed them as a major element in the interior design of the building. See how the devil woos with a soft tongue! Even in Boston.

20. The Boston Medical Library is heavily involved in the Countway library. The Associate Director specifically represents it, the Joint Committee of the Library contains three representatives each from Harvard and the Boston Medical Library, the Lahey Room is nearly its exclusive preserve, and a handsome room is set aside for its Trustees. Nevertheless, they feel that they have been swallowed up and become owned by Harvard in this joint venture. This feeling is reflected in a decrease in the number of their Fellows since the merger in 1960. Recently a fund drive for the refurbishing of the Countway has been initiated by the Boston Medical Library to repair broken furniture, provide a fund for internal changes in the building and furnishings, etc. Another room on the Fifth Floor, originally intended for the Harvard Professor of the History of Medicine, has been turned over to their fund-raising staff, and their morale is said to have improved.

21. Statistics for the Countway Library:

> Gross Area—153,600 square feet.
> Seating capacity—720.
> Book capacity—750,000 volumes.
> Building cost—$4,750,000 ($30.92 per square foot).
> Project cost—$5,310,000 ($34.57 per square foot).

22. The following are worth reading about the Countway:

A Descriptive Handbook; The Francis A. Countway Library of Medicine. N.p., n.d.
This handbook, to which this chapter is considerably indebted, is superlative, by far the best of its kind that I
　　have ever seen.
"The Countway Library of Medicine of the Harvard Medical School and the Boston Medical Library," *Architectural Record,* March 1963, pp. 133–136.
"The Countway Library at Harvard," *Progressive Architecture,* November 1965, pp. 166–177.
"The Francis A. Countway Library of Medicine," *Arts and Architecture,* April 1966, pp. 20–23.
"1966 AIA Honor Awards: Countway Library of Medicine, Harvard Medical School," American Institute of Architects, *AIA Journal,* July 1966, pp. 48–49.
"Francis A. Countway Library of Medicine della Scuola Medica di Harvard," *Architettura,* September 1966, pp. 326–327.

CHAPTER 9

THE DALHOUSIE UNIVERSITY LIBRARY

Photograph of a model of the building, showing the raised plazas to the west and southwest, and the inner court that penetrates the entire library.

View of the front façade, with the entrance to the inner courtyard just left of the window wall to the left of the tree.

View of the Main Floor access shaft, looking toward the Directory and the window wall entrance to the Information desks. The Main Entrance is lcoated out of sight to the left of the elevators near the Directory.

The Information desks, with the main card catalog directly behind. Note the glass clerestory collar around the upper rim of this room.

The Reference Reading Room, showing the clerestory collar around the upper rim of this area.

The ornamental main stairway to the Second Floor.

The Special Services room, Second Floor.

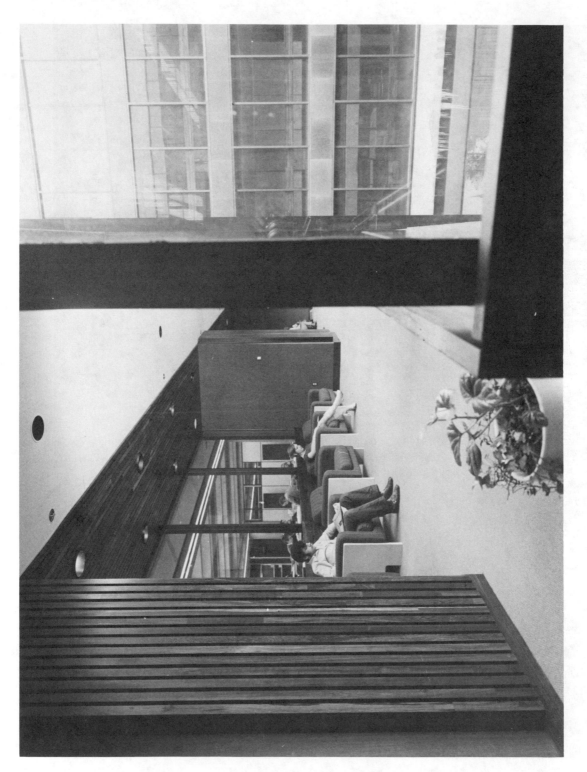

A typical section of the perimeter lounges on the three upper floors, with the stack reading area behind the glass at left and the inner court to the right.

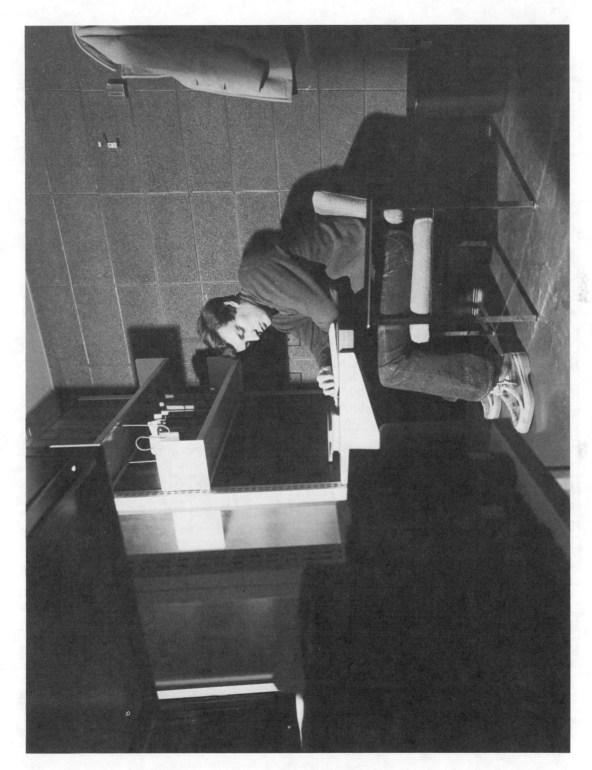

A typical carrel on the outer walls of the three upper stack floors.
The two wall plates to the left of the student's shoulder contain wiring for audio-video-computer access.

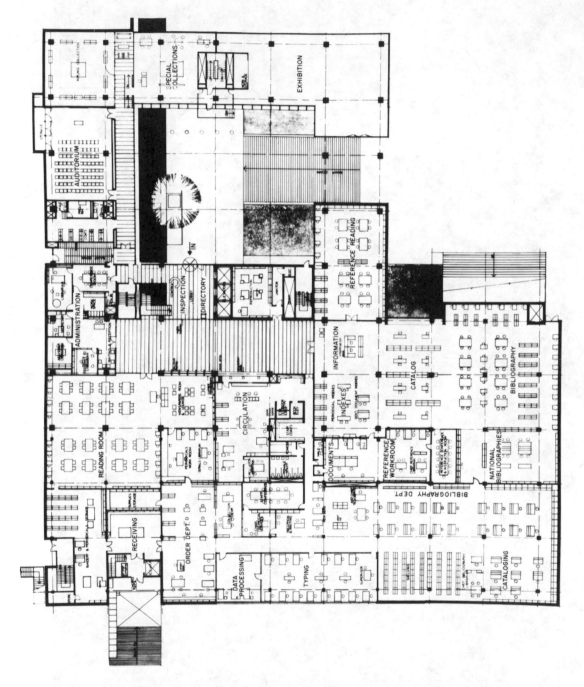

Main Floor Plan.

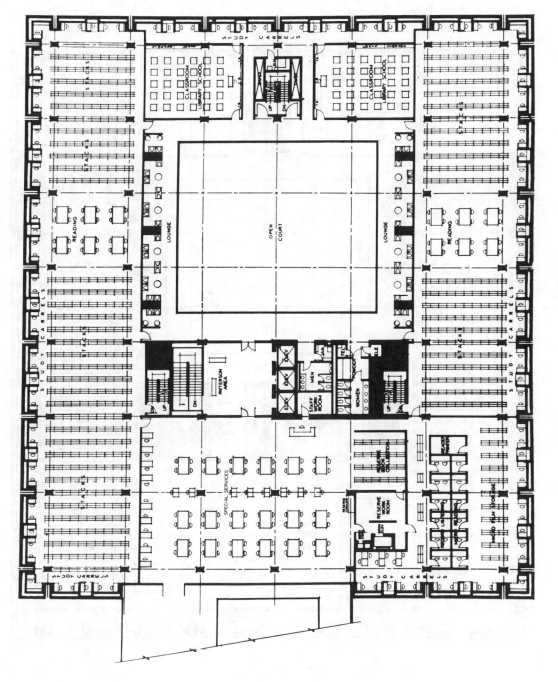

A modified stack floor plan (Second Floor).

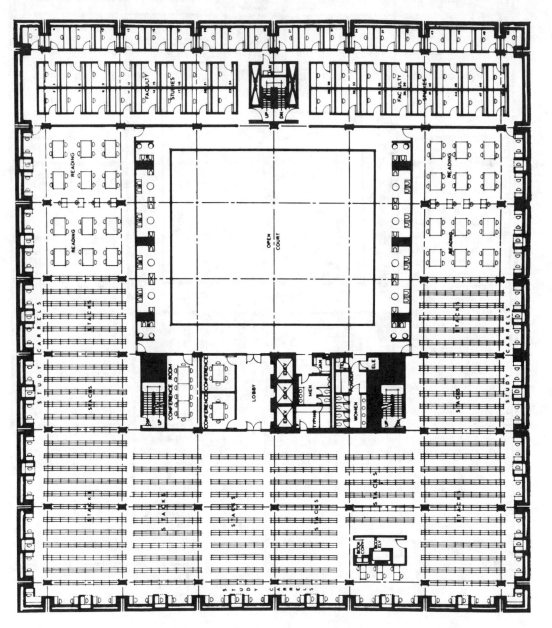

A typical stack floor plan (Third and Fourth Floors).

THE DALHOUSIE UNIVERSITY LIBRARY*

The Killam Library at Dalhousie University in Halifax, Nova Scotia, has been highly regarded in Canada since its completion in 1969, but until the summer of 1976 I had been unable to see it. Halifax is not a stop-over on any beaten path, a fact that accounts for a good deal of its charm. It can be reached by air about 450 miles northeast from Boston. The last 135 miles of the flight over territory of the province span wooded areas so dense they seem impenetrable, with only a few clearings hacked out of the woods, until the air strip northeast of the city comes into view.

Though its population is but 125,000, Halifax is the most important educational center of all the Atlantic provinces. Of the eleven colleges and universities in the city Dalhousie University is the largest, with 8,500 students in 1976. It has major commitments to professional programs, with 400 students in law, 400 in medicine, 100 in dentistry, and large commitments to collateral health service disciplines. The building of a new central library to replace severely inadequate quarters was a major event in the history of this university, which had expanded radically, like all Canadian universities, since 1959. Its concept, the selection of its site, and the development of the layout and massing of the building emerged from prolonged and careful planning. They were translated by a receptive local architect, Leslie R. Fairn & Associates, into a good library building that contains a number of unusual elements of flexibility.[1]

The Exterior

A nearly ideal location was available for this library on a site 275′ × 375′ which was central to the master plan of the campus development, easily accessible to the arts and science departments and to the professional schools, and had very few buildings to contend with nearby. The one limitation on shaping the library was the requirement to relate it to one adjacent building, whose height limited the new building to 70 feet.

On this plot of ground was built a library whose impressive exterior is shown on pages 151 and 152. It stands beyond a large entrance patio paved with sandblasted rough aggregate concrete slabs 3½′ × 5′ each. To the left of the patio is a 24′-wide monumental stairway that leads up two sets of risers separated by an 8′-wide landing to a patio that flanks the southwest and west sides of the building. Directly in front of the entrance to the building (an opening which passes under the second floor), the name of the library, mounted in large letters on a large concrete slab 8′ × 12′, is visible from a considerable distance.

The walls of the main floor are of large black and brown field stones set in light grey mortar. Inset directly above these walls is a 3′-high clerestory collar that runs in a strip around four sides of the building to form the upper part of the interior walls of most rooms on the main floor. The façade above, which contains floors two to four, presents a massive, nearly solid wall cantilevered out 11′ on all sides of the building. The floor of this mass is marked by a foot-wide strip of light concrete that reads through to the exterior as a decorative band on four sides. Above it loom enormous sandblasted aggregate concrete panels

---

*Footnotes to this article begin on page 173.

that produce a rough brown texture as the dominant feeling of the building's facade. These panels are 27' × 35', separated by foot-wide full-height strip windows, at the bottom of which vertical concrete bars 3'-high jut out a foot from the building's face. Seven of these panels form the north and south walls and six the east and west walls, joined by 11' panels set at right angles to form the corners.

Above the facing panels, the inset strip window of the Fifth Floor is capped by impressive poured-in-place fascias, in a lighter tone of concrete, that taper from top to bottom in a decorative manner.[2] The whole effect is one of very pleasant rough stonework highly appropriate in appearance to the north country and highly effective in conserving energy.

The Plazas

The stairway to the left of the entrance patio leads up to the southwest and west plazas laid on the level of the clerestory collar. These plazas are paved with rough aggregate concrete slabs. Around the edges pre-formed concrete units support lighting fixtures and form benches for seating, although the tranquillity of the western patio is disturbed by the constant roar from the air outlets of the ventilation system. At the south edge of the plaza are angular concrete units with slit windows that provide light-relief for the stack areas below. At each end of the west plaza twenty great round concrete drums, 12' in diameter, contain small trees, which were still struggling for survival when I was there in 1976.

The Structure

The module of the building is a bay 27' by 27', with seven bays running from west to east and six bays running from north to south (as seen in the floor plans, pages 161–162) with a cantilever of 11' on all sides of the building above the Main Floor. The upper floors are about 38,900 square feet. The Basement Floor is built out underground two additional bays to the west of the main structure. (The underground area on the plans is marked by columns smaller than the basic columns.) The Main Floor, on which so many library functions must be located to be efficiently related to the card catalog, the most demanding floor for space, is extended out under the raised plazas three bays to the west and three bays to the southwest (marked by columns smaller than the basic columns), for a total of 50,000 square feet on this floor.[3]

The Basement Floor contains totally interior space. The Main Floor has sizeable window walls on its north, east and west sides, located to relieve interior working and reading areas. In addition, the clerestory collar that forms the top of the interior walls of the Main Floor brings a good deal of exterior feeling inside. The Second Floor has a sizeable window wall not needed by the room it is in, and facing, perversely, west. The rest of the building is relieved by vertical slit windows on the exterior of the building (Floors 2 to 4) or strip windows (on 5).

All floors of the building except the basement are built around a 90'-square central open court, entirely enclosed in glass, which provides a major feeling of light to the entire building.[4] No area on floors above ground is very far from exterior glass. This court is offset to the right in the floor layout, making the north, south and east sides of the building a bay and a half wide and the west side three and a half bays wide. On all four sides of the open court wide corridors form the major walkways of the building (see page 161).[5]

Flanking the west corridor on each floor a major central core area contains three elevators and a lobby that opens to the east and west, two stairways, a typing room, a telephone booth, restrooms, two group studies and a conference room.[6] The doors to the stairways are quite unobtrusive and as a consequence are not much used, forcing more traffic to use the elevators than is necessary. These doors should be painted a flaming pattern, because most passage from floor to floor should take place by the stairs.

As the Modified Floor Plan shows (page 161), it is extremely easy to close off any of the sides of the building, but difficulties in finding books arise when the enclosed sides leave two stacks separated from each other, as occurs on the Second Floor of this Library where both the east and west sides are used for purposes other than shelving (page 161).

The Entrance

Immediately behind the upright slab on the entrance patio, the main walkway into the building beckons, leading to the inner courtyard. As we pass below the underside of the Second Floor, a distance of forty feet, we see the poured-in-place truss and beam structure that forms the exposed ceilings of the entire building. Their 18"-deep coffers contain at this point one-foot-square fluorescent lighting fixtures. The walkway slants gently down to a slate-paved patio, and we are suddenly aware of the three facing sides of the open court, the movement along the walkways just beyond their glass walls, and the cantilever of the upper floors above the patio level. A roar of air from the ventilation system discharges low on the east side of the patio and disrupts its quiet.

Tri-level concrete seating areas on the west side of the patio invite students to congregate in the open, in weather that in Halifax is usually moderate throughout the year. At the far end of the patio flows a pool of running water which originates just inside the entrance as a small spray-fountain with a retainer pool directly behind the Inspection Desk. The pool turns users at right angles to the traffic lane, through the main entrance.

Main Floor Layout

Immediately inside the main entrance the user is struck with full force by the strong visual quality of the building. The mass of concrete in the walls of the lobby that rise 20' to exposed ceiling waffles continues beyond the lobby in the waffle ceiling of the Reading Room directly ahead, which extends for another 60' clearly visible through the glass wall of that room. This massiveness is emphasized by a 30"-square horizontal beam that rims the lobby at a height of 15', below the 3' clerestory collar, and by the 32"-square columns used on this floor (their size varies slightly around the building), and by the huge expanse of black slate floor. The impression is a combination of a feeling of great volume, which is pleasant, and a feeling of unrelieved grey and black, which is powerful but not enlivening.

The feeling of cheerful attractiveness which should greet the user of every library at the entrance is lacking here. I have already complained about the overdark interior of the Countway Library in Boston, and will register a similar complaint against the University of Toronto Library. This is a kind of northeastern tradition which still persists, born of the need for enclosing buildings against the weather, which excluded light during all seasons, and colored darkly the feeling of the entire interior. Growing up in this tradition in the early years of my life, I came to believe that it was the offspring, in a way, of the stern and rockbound coasts and the stern and rockbound religion, with its emphasis on denial, which dominated this region's early history.

On the left side of the lobby are three elevators, separated by a wall of dark-brown rosewood panelled with battens from floor to ceiling.[7] At the right is the Inspection Desk, and beyond that a monumental cantilevered staircase of concrete with dark slate risers and 18″-wide, laminated dark rosewood railings leading to the Second Floor (see page 156).

Straight ahead from the entrance is a five-sided interior-illuminated Directory stand, complete with floor layouts of all five floors of the building and a cross section of its elevation. The top of the stand (mounted on a concrete pedestal) is formed of 28″-square lighted panels which illuminate color-coded layouts of each floor, with space below for directory information (see page 153). One such panel is used on each floor of the building directly opposite the elevator to orient the users to its layout, and it is extremely effective.

Beyond the Directory and the lobby, the main access shaft to rooms on this floor crosses as a "T", some 30′ wide, running north and south (see page 153). On the west side of this shaft are the Reading Room and the Circulation Desk and workroom, on the east side is a room containing coin-operated photocopiers (centralized here, there are none elsewhere in the building), at the south end of the shaft is a glass wall beyond which is the reference area, labeled "Information," and at the north end is the Administration complex.

Reading Room

The Reading Room directly opposite the Entrance functions as a newspaper reading room, a general reading area, and a reserve book room, serviced from stacks adjacent to the circulation work room through a window in the south wall of the Reading Room. The newspaper alcove off the main reading area contains ingeniously designed special units hung on standard stack uprights, to hold newspapers. One upright section contains a single newspaper title on shelves 17½″ wide, on 2″ vertical centers, numbered 1 to 31 from top to bottom. Each shelf holds a single issue of the newspaper for the date of the month that correlates with the shelf number. Earlier issues of select titles are located nearby on wall-hung 10″-deep shelves.

The reading area varies in feeling with the ceiling height and the lighting intensity. The outer half of the room has a 20′-high exposed waffle ceiling, with the clerestory on all four sides. Lighting in this area is of very good quality but only 22 footcandles intensity. The inner half of the room, with a dropped ceiling 9½′ high, provides 75 footcandles of good quality lighting. This area was greatly favored by readers during my three-day visitation.

This room is furnished with 2′ × 4′ tables for four readers, with dark wood tops, a black metal skirt, and chrome legs (typical of the reading tables throughout the building). They are accompanied by a version of the Breuer skid chair, slightly wider than usual, with arms (shown on page 154). Though any variation in the proportions of that original Breuer chair reduce its magnificence, these are reasonably attractive, upholstered in blue. All of the chairs have arms, and since they were not coordinated with the table clearance they bang into its skirts, which have been marred. All chairs with arms must be tested with the tables they intend to fit before purchasing them to make sure the arms slide freely under the table edge.

The south end of the Reading Room outer glass wall, which separates it visually from the Circulation Desk, contains a series of six exhibition cases 4′ wide by 4′ high by 2′ deep. Each is lit by two fluorescent tubes above white, ¾″-square eggcrate diffusers, which provide very good light but create a serious ultra-violet light damage problem and cause heat rise in the cases. The glass shelves in the case are adjustable, and the cases are attractive and so placed that they attract attention by their brightness when users enter the building.

Circulation Desk

South of the exhibition cases is a handsome Circulation Desk 30′ long with a black slate front topped by a dark wood butcher block counter, with a dark panelled wood wall beyond it. The desk area is shallow, 10′ from desk edge to wall, similar to that of the Brown University Library, and it also uses the book return device of that library, an opening in the desk wall that transports books back into the circulation workroom by an industrial roller strip.[8] Opposite the Circulation Desk a series of dark wood benches, mounted on concrete slabs at right angles to the axis of the shaft, are located beside dark wood bookcases containing the latest book acquisitions of the library (see photograph on page 153).

The Detached-L

On this floor, intended largely for public uses, are rooms that form an L around the north and east sides of the entrance courtyard (see page 160). The access to these rooms is outside the Inspection Desk, by a corridor immediately to the right inside the library entrance, by a separate entrance just west of the Auditorium area, and through the south end of the Exhibition area. Since there is no access to the rest of the library from these areas there is no security problem and no harrying of the public through inspection.

The Auditorium, connected to a projection room, seats 100. Beside it is a large coathanging area and two rest rooms. The room in the corner of the building is equipped with special exhibition cases to hold general exhibitions. They are poorly designed for such use, and have very bad lighting.

The Special Collections area, up eight steps from the corridor, is a combination Music Resources Center and Audio-Visual Services. Between columns in the north-south axis of this room are 20′-high exposed waffle ceilings, with the 18″-square lighting fixture typically used in waffles in the building. They provide 40 footcandles of good quality lighting. Along the sides dropped ceilings contain downlights (similar to the lighting arrangement in the reference reading room shown on page 155), which supply extremely bad lighting. Small rooms built on the west wall of this area for the use of practice pianos with muffled sound are "lit" (actually darkened) by such downlights. Standard stack uprights in the room accommodate stack-hung phono-disc holding tubs, and carrel desks to hold record players. The room contains a few carrels with tape decks similar to those used in the language laboratory in the basement of the library.

This area is lightly screened from the Exhibition area by panel walls 48″ wide × 92″ high, held upright by two force screws in their top (like floor to ceiling light poles). Easily set up, totally movable, they are useful for compartmentalization and for art exhibition panels. A snap-in lighting rail, the length of both sides of this room, brings electricity from the rails down through stack uprights to the carrel desks. In addition, of course, they provide an infinite variety of possibilities for exhibition lighting. There is also an art-hanging rail below the clerestory collar in the center of this room. To add to the uses of the room, a battery of 18″-square upholstered foam cushions serve students for concert seating, and at the north end of the wall a glass door set on a roller that runs on a curved steel track in the floor opens to a width of six feet to accommodate movement of pianos into the room. A pleasant orange carpeting is used throughout this area.

Information

The reference elements of the library are centralized in a large area at the south end of the Main Floor, available through swinging glass doors in a glass wall at the south end of the main access shaft. The entire area has pleasant orange carpeting. Head on from the entrance are two standard Steelcase desks (which are used throughout the building), butted together to form a single unit, with a typing-L on each end. Behind them are low bookcases with ready reference books (see page 154).

Behind the reference desks are the card catalog cases, formed of standard 60-drawer card units slipped into double-face customized covers, four double-face units long, mounted on foot-high support stands, faced by carpeting, which form a raceway for future computer lines. The catalogs were made by Art Laboratory Furniture Ltd., of Quebec. The catalog ranges are on 14' centers. Between them are custom made consultation tables, 42" high, 2' × 6', with white formica tops and compartments on each side to hold P-slips and books. The split catalog division is indicated by orange and green labels. Lighting in the catalog area is 60 footcandles of good quality at consultation tables and 30 footcandles at the drawer faces 30" high.

West of the reference desks a series of low bookcases and standard bookstacks hold periodical abstracts and indexes, with consultation on tables nearby. These stacks have dark wood end panels. East of the reference desks, through a glass wall, is the reference collection (too far from the reference desks and ill laid-out for quick access) in the reference reading room, furnished with dark wood tables and the variation of the Breuer skid chair upholstered in blue (see page 155). The stacks are off-white, as are all steel stacks in the Information area, and hold 3,500 volumes, mostly on wall hung stacks at the periphery of the room, causing a long walk along walls to reach a book.

Two of the walls in this room are covered with blue vinyl. Between columns, the center of the room has a 20'-high waffle ceiling, with an 18"-square fixture in each, surrounded by a clerestory on all four sides. This area has very good quality lighting, but only 22 footcandles intensity. The round downlights in the 9½' dropped ceiling at the perimeter of the room supply about 30 footcandles of extremely uneven and very bad quality light.

South of the card catalog are ranges of current periodical stacks composed of six slant-faces shelves per section. The top and bottom shelves are fixed; the others flip up for storage behind the display shelf. The lower lip of the top shelf is 6' 6" above the floor, and too high for me to reach (they are built for the likes of Keyes Metcalf). These stacks have dark wood end panels.

Through the wall south of the current periodicals (not shown on the floor plan), up six steps, and accessible by truck only by a sharp pitched ramp, is a stark area called the "Documents tunnel," about 12' wide by 120' long. Lit by bare fluorescent tubes, it has harsh glare, relieved only by light from a number of slit windows and by light drifting down from the concrete shafts in the seating units on the west Plaza, above. This room is used to store little-used documents.

In the southwest corner of the Information room the foreign national bibliographies are shelved along the wall, leading naturally (if you know their location) through a door to the English-language bibliographies immediately inside at the south end of Technical Services.

Technical Services

These services are contained in one great unbroken area 40' wide by 200' long, running west of the Information, Circulation, and Reading Room areas. The long outer wall is broken by a window wall that relieves the central third of the area, but most of the technical services are in essentially interior space.[9] This area has a 9½' ceiling which provides 80 footcandles of good quality lighting throughout.

Immediately inside the door to the Information area the English-language national bibliographies and the shelflist are available to the public during the work day. North of Bibliography (moving against the normal flow of materials) is the cataloging area, composed of 30 cataloging stations. Each station is supplied with a Steelcase modular unit, which can be assembled in a variety of ways, that includes a desk with a drawer pedestal, an 18″ × 30″ L-extension, and baffles 5′ high at the rear of the desk and the side of the extension. Nearby are personal lockers, 24″ × 51″, combined with a 3′-wide adjustable shelf unit to hold materials in process. These stations are used singly or paired side-by-side. Their disadvantage is that any typing must be done on movable typing stands. Only three typewriters were in the vicinity of these stations when I was there.

Opposite the Cataloging area are desks for the Bibliographers. North of this area are ranges of holding stacks on the east, opposite long rooms that hold the Typing operation, a graphics department that serves the entire university, and a Data Processing Room, with half-window walls on the interior to help bring the light in through the exterior window wall.

North of these areas are the Order Department, and the Receiving and Bindery areas, with two large conference rooms on the east wall. This entire area contains 4″-wide walker ducts in the floor as conduits on 12′ centers, and they had already been used to relocate electrical outlets many times when I studied the building. The work areas of Technical processes, with the exception of the Typing and Data Processing areas, leave much to be desired in terms of esthetics, but they are reasonably comfortable to work in, unusually well lit, and arranged for efficient work flow.

Basement

This building has a large basement which contains mostly non-library functions—the computer center, the printing center, language laboratory. It also houses the Government Documents collection and services. Access to this area is by an elevator near the Circulation area on the Main Floor. The reading room, totally internal, is well lit, and the Government Documents stacks open directly off of it, running the entire width of the basement from East to West, an area of 35′ × 280′ containing stacks to shelve the volume equivalent of 120,000 books.

Second Floor

This floor is the Modified Stack Floor shown on page 161, the last floor in the building that provides any specialized facilities for users. The entire west side of the floor is occupied by Special Services, most of the east side is occupied by two classrooms of the Library school, housed mostly on the floor above, and the remaining space north and south of the court is dedicated to general stack shelving, reading areas, and study carrels. The difficulties presented by stacks split on two sides of the building when they are not connected along a third side are clear from the plan. The user in one stack has to guess what call numbers are in the opposite stack. However, the ease of converting the library's stack space into special facilities is just as clear.

Special Services

Special Services, located at the head of the monumental staircase that leads up from behind the Inspection Desk on the Main Floor (see page 157), is an unusual melange of material forms that require special attention in their use and special preservation in their care. Here are microforms, videotapes, spoken records, computational machines, and rare books. Twenty-six enclosed viewing carrels, all equipped with dimmer switches, are located in the south section of the room. They double for computation and record listening. Videotape players are mounted in a number of enclosed carrels. This entire area, which includes shelving for the special materials, is separated from the central reading area and is less brightly lit.

The central reading area is furnished with 4' × 6' tables accompanied by secretarial chairs. A number of tables are used for microform readers. The entire area is carpeted in orange, as in the other carpeted areas of the library. The west wall of this reading area is completely glass, a perverse violation of common sense. It is provided with a coarse-woven string net drape, which does little to keep the sun out of this area, where invaluable materials are used and exhibited, such as the Sir Francis Bacon materials on display when I was there.

Lighting in this area varies radically. Where fixtures with a diffusing lens are used, they provide 150 footcandles, far more than needed but of good quality. Part of the ceiling is supplied with exposed fluorescent tubes, which provide 150 footcandles of hideous glare, both direct and reflected.

The exhibition cases specially designed for this library are as perversely difficult to use as only highly ingenious furniture designers can make them. The low cases are side-loading, with wooden drawers on slides, usually very easy cases to load. But these have split-beds covered by a single loose piece of facric, and sliding them back simultaneously after loading without dislocating the arrangement of materials is impossible. The upright cases are rear-loading, extremely difficult to move out from the walls, and the difficulty of moving them back dislocates materials set up on their shelves. Neither case has anything special in esthetics or function to compensate for these burdens, and it would be fascinating to know what torments Dante would provide for their designers in his Inferno.

This area has incorporated a portion of what were formerly the general stacks for shelving rare books. In doing so, it absorbed three slit windows on the north end of the stacks, and one slit window plus about 5' of window wall on the west side of the stacks, which provide an extremely great sun problem for the preservation of books in these stacks. No special atmosphere control or fire protection is provided, and on the whole these stacks are ideally bad for the housing of rare material.

The Inner Court

From the central walkways and lounges on this floor, the full expanse of the inner court is visible, down to the entrance courtyard and up to the roof. The top and bottom are marked by poured concrete bands about two feet wide at the level of the Main Floor ceiling and the roofline. Between these are four floors of glass wall that form the outer facing of the lounges and walkways, varied only by thin vertical window mullions and wide metal bands at each interim floor level painted a flat grey-black. The general feeling is somewhat industrial and not very exciting, only slightly relieved by a foot-wide window-rail of rosewood on each floor and the orange carpeting of the walkways, which can be seen from the third to fifth floors. These window walls are unshaded and the rosewood of the window-rails on the south, east and west, which had been stained dark brown, has bleached to a less opaque tone which makes them far more interesting than the darker wood in most of the building.

Third Floor

The layout of the Typical Stack Floor plan (page 162) serves for both the Third and Fourth Floors. On the Third Floor, the entire east side of the building is occupied by the Library School classrooms and offices.

The rest of the floor is exactly like the plan, which shows clearly the basic functional elements on stack-and-reader floors.

In the southwest corner is the book conveyor and stack elevator core; two bays to the east is the users' service core, directly connected to the elevator lobby. The walkways in the center of the floor are 12' wide, with window walls on both the court and the stack sides. All other elements of the floor open off these walkways on all four sides of the building. On the north and south sides, they become smoking lounges, located directly outside the reading areas at each end of the stack flow (see page 158). They are furnished with overstuffed chairs, with ash urns beside them. The lighting provided in the walkways are round downlights, which I have already roundly cursed, and although quite adequate for traffic purposes, they provide extremely bad light for reading in the lounges, which are prime reading areas. At each corner of the walkways are located attractive cylindrical planters, but the plants provided are too small to make much impact on such large areas.

Stack Areas

The stack areas are stark and pragmatic and economical, with concrete ceilings, cement block walls, and vinyl floors. Their poured concrete ceilings are specially designed to fit the requirements of the stacks. Ceiling coffers are, with some variations in length, 24' long, and on 4½' centers. The stack uprights are fixed, 10' high (similar to those at Brown), and nailed to the structural underbeam of the ceiling coffers, providing vertical space for nine or ten shelves per section at ultimate capacity.

There is a price paid for this convenience and economy. All stacks must run north and south, since the east-west span of the 4½' coffers will not accommodate 3'-wide stack sections. This prevents the stacks on the west side of the building from being oriented east and west, so that stacks can turn the corner nicely, and the user can continue to follow range labels in a continuous flow in his search for call numbers, as is possible in the Rockefeller Library stacks.

These stacks, by Steel Equipment Company of Ontario, are provided with one pullout shelf per range face, painted orange to attract attention among the beige shelves. The stacks are lit by troffers of bare fluorescent tubes mounted in the ceiling coffers on stack centers. Their glare is no great drawback in stack lights that are only intermittently turned on, and they provide sufficient light to read labels on the lowest shelves. One pushbutton light switch is provided on every other stack range to turn on the fixtures on both sides of the stack. They are timed to turn off in twenty minutes. These stacks are saved from the gloom that plagues the peripheral carrels in the Rockefeller Library by two single-tube lighting troffers equipped with diffusing lenses that are mounted on the slotted air diffusers that run at right angles to the stacks at their periphery.

The stack ranges are equipped with end panels everywhere except on the outside ends of the extreme north and south ranges, where they are omitted to keep the open carrels on the building walls from feeling enclosed. Since label holders are mounted on the stack endpanels, there were none on the unpaneled stack ends when I was at Dalhousie.

Research Carrels

The peripheral carrels are typical of those used throughout the library, which will ultimately provide 400 open carrels and 100 closed carrels in stack areas (see page 159). The interior wall is divided into niches on 27' centers, formed by slit windows inset between support piers of the building, as shown on the floor plan. Each bay contains five carrels, with a closed carrel in the center separating two open carrels on each side of it. Throughout the building there are never more than two open carrels in a row.

The carrel desks, 23″ × 34″, are hung by cantilevered brackets on standard stack uprights fastened to floors and ceilings or to the face of the piers.[10] Their dark wood desk tops are as bad a writing surface (as previously discussed) as all the other dark wood writing surfaces in this library, with two bookshelves hung above them. A troffer of 1′ × 4′ lighting fixtures with a good diffusing lens runs at right angles directly above the center of the carrel desks, providing 50 to 60 footcandles of good quality lighting, controlled by a light switch at each end of the niche. The closed carrels are 3′ × 5′, with a 36″ desk top and bookshelves above, all hung on stack uprights. They have open-slotted lockable doors of dark wood. There are seven modules of five carrels each on the north and south walls and six on the west wall. All of the carrels, all perimeters and conference rooms, and the main card catalog are fully wired for audio and closed circuit television reception from central production, and for computer terminals and telephones, with outlet boxes beside each carrel desk. None of these had been activated when I visited Dalhousie.

A considerable amount of pigeon debris is heaped at the bottom of the inset window, about at waist height, consisting of abandoned nesting, live pigeons, and guano, which only a steeplejack could remove.

The remaining seating in these stacks is provided in reading areas at the two ends of the stack flow, located to take advantage of the window wall on the inside of the lounge areas. They do get some of the feeling of the exterior from the inner court, but in other respects they are highly undesirable seating areas. Each is equipped with 12 tables for four and three tables for one, all with matte finish white formica tops and orange upholstered chairs. The flanking wall is panelled with white formica, the floor is of dark grey-brown vinyl tile, and the ceiling is exposed concrete. The combination is sterile and forbidding. The walls, the floor and the ceiling are acoustically very bad, and the lighting, from ceiling troffers of double, exposed fluorescent tubes, which provides 110 footcandles of horrendous direct and reflected glare, eliminates any hope of making these reading areas acceptable.

Fourth and Fifth Floors

The Fourth Floor is identical to the Third Floor, except that it provides enclosed faculty studies on the east side of the building. Twenty of them are on the perimeter and 32 are totally interior in double-face rows. These carrels, measuring from 6′ × 9′ to 8′ × 8′, contain a desk top, a filing case, 12 bookshelves, and an inset on the desk top for a typewriter or microfilm reader. They are assigned for one semester.

The Fifth Floor was designed to work as a separate part of the building. For a long time it will be occupied by Faculty department offices, although at present the library is using part of it for a very embryonic Archives and for the staff lounge, pleasantly located at a corner overlooking the campus. The present vertical division of the library floors is: First and Second Floors—library users, Third and Fourth Floors—research, Fifth Floor—separate.[11]

Summation

This library has a handsome and impressive exterior which is enhanced by elements of surprise and discovery, at the entrance patio in the facade of the inner court and the pool, at the building entrance in the powerful feeling of space, and throughout the Main Floor in the effect of the clerestory collar. Its layout is extremely good, making it simple to understand and easy to use. It has excellent convertibility, more than half the Main Floor having been converted to alternative uses, with unusual ease. Despite some failures, the quality of its lighting is mostly good (which can be said of very few libraries). Its stacks are economical, with a large number of research carrels for a building this size. Its range of unusual furniture and equipment—the directories, newspaper holders, music room panels, piano-access door, card catalogs, catalogers' stations—lend it a freshness that makes it continually interesting. Finally, one notices the considerable influence of the Rockefeller Library on the Dalhousie University Library, translated to Canada by Louis Vagianos. It is a worthy offspring of a noble ancestor. The building was awarded the Nova Scotia Association of Architects Design Award for 1971.[12]

Notes

1. Planning of this building was slowed down for a year through lack of a library director. Louis Vagianos, who filled that position, was selected partly because as a junior administrator in the Brown University Library he had very good experience in librarianship working with David Jonah, Director of that library, and had participated in the planning of the Rockefeller Library building. Vagianos was centrally in charge of planning this building, and with one exception, recorded below, was able to get everything into it that he wanted.

2. By now the reader should be aware that a basic pattern of solutions to interior and exterior library design can be seen in large or small fragments in many library buildings. This does not mean that the repetitions produce the same results in different libraries. Although this building has different proportions and produces a strikingly different visual effect, a careful comparison of this facade with that of the Countway Library shows close similarities that become all the more convincing when we learn that the interior of the building is constructed around an open court.

The similarity would be even greater except for one major miscarriage in the planning of the building. It was designed to be faced in rust-tone Indiana limestone panels, but at one point when Vagianos was out of town for a few days, the Board of Trustees voted to face it with aggregate panels to give local companies some business. Vagianos was not told of this decision, and discovered it far too late to reverse it. Fortunately, he had strong enough character to resist cutting his own or someone else's throat.

3. Compare the enlargement of the main floor of the Rockefeller Library at Brown, the extension of the lower levels of the Countway Library out under its sunken plaza, and the placement of most of the Beinecke Library's stacks under its plaza.

4. Compare the internal central court in the Countway Library, and the internal central glass-faced stack in the Beinecke.

5. Compare the central walkways in the Countway.

6. Compare the core areas of the Rockefeller library, and the movement of stacks around them, although Dalhousie has a unified core rather than a split core.

7. The wood used throughout this building is rosewood, whose essential quality has been destroyed by staining it dark brown, which obliterates its distinctive texture. Much the same kind of expensive idiocy occurs in the staining of mahogany in the University of Toronto library, as we shall see.

8. I believe that the Brown University Rockefeller Library was the first to use these simple rollers for book returns. Their success lies in testing the pitch of the roller unit by placing materials to roll on it before it is fastened down. Those at Brown would roll small pamphlets in a Gaylord into the circulation work area. The same device is used at the Circulation desk in the new addition to the University of Colorado Library at Boulder.

9. The grim irony is that this exterior window wall, whose feeling is brought deep inside by half-window interior room walls, serves to relieve—you guessed it, the holding stacks directly opposite the rooms on the west wall of technical services.

10. These carrels are quite similar to those at the periphery of the Rockefeller Library.

11. Statistics for the Dalhousie University Library:

> Gross area—230,000 square feet.
> Seating capacity (library area)—1,269.
> Book capacity (ultimate library area)—1,250,000 volumes.
> Project cost—$6,880,000 ($29.91 per square foot) in Canadian dollars.

12. The following article about this Library is worth reading: A. H. MacDonald, "Planning for the Second Century," *APLA Bulletin,* March 1968, pp. 7–20.

CHAPTER 10

THE ROBARTS LIBRARY

AT THE UNIVERSITY OF TORONTO

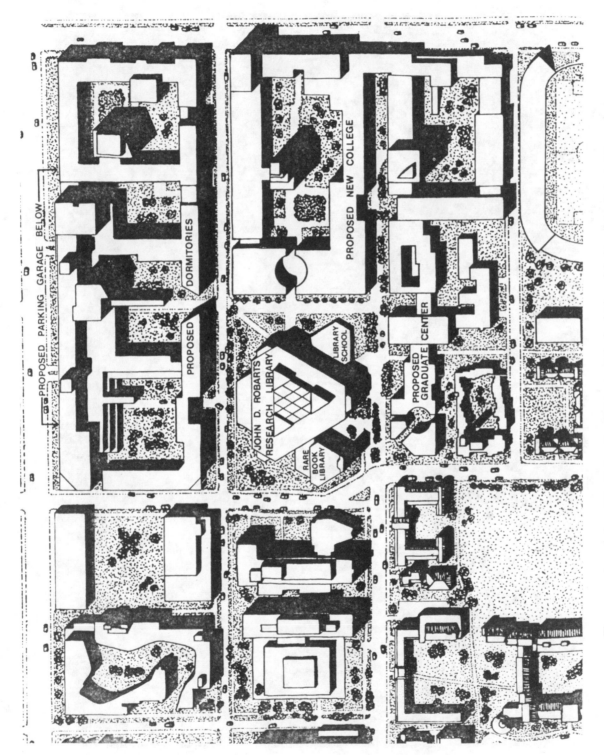

The proposed expansion of the University of Toronto at the beginning of design of the Robarts Library.

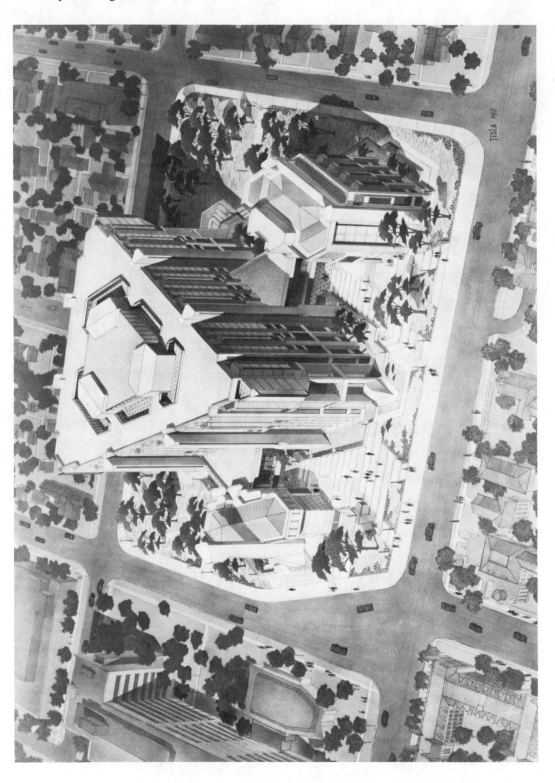

Photograph of a basic model of the building.

The south façade of the Robarts Library, with the Fisher Rare Book Library and tower in the foreground.

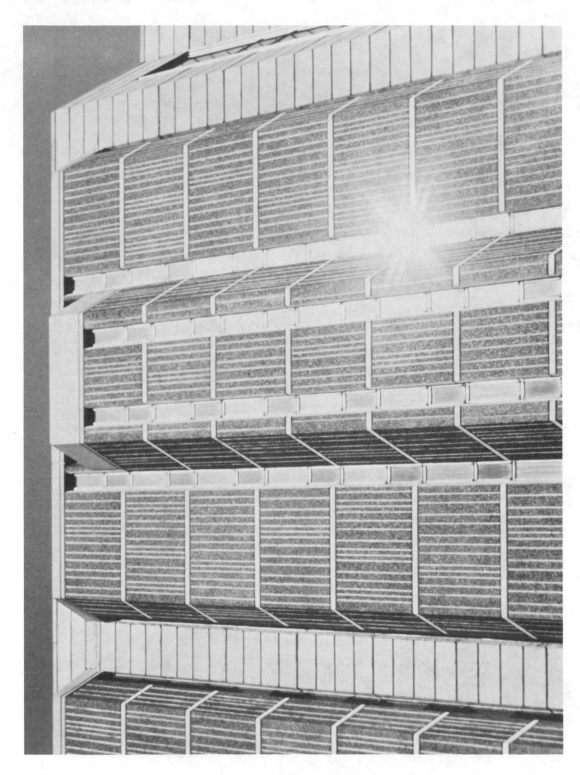

Photograph of the projecting bays on the upper floors of the library, showing the facing panels, the carrel window strips, and the light colored exterior faces of the large and small cup columns.

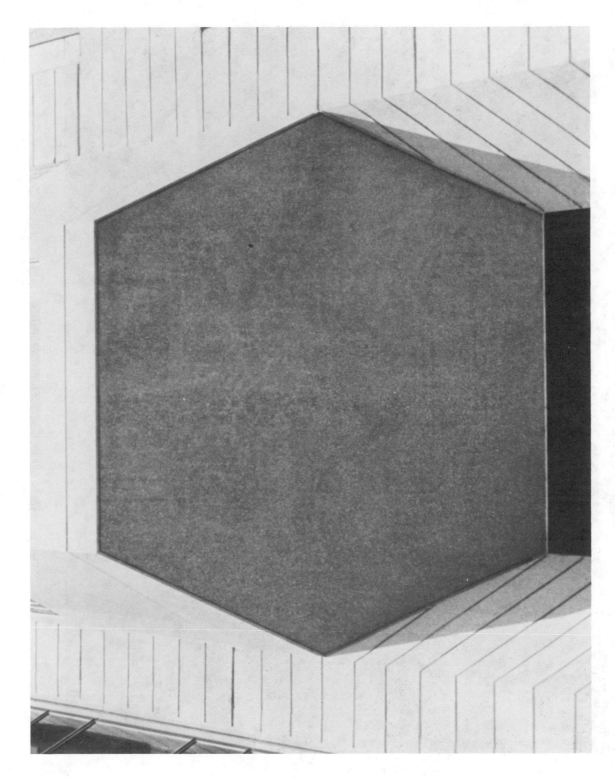

The dramatic geometry of the underside of a projecting bay.

View of a typical column head and pattern of triangular ceiling coffers.

The massive detail of an open stairway in the current periodicals area.

The south entrance lobby, Second Floor, looking into the traffic core toward the escalators to the right of the column.

A corner of the General Reading Room, Second Floor, showing the two-story height and the overhanging balcony looking toward one of the cup columns beyond the window wall. The free standing panels, lounge chairs, reader tables, and side chairs are typical of the furniture.

Lateral view of the Reference area, Fourth Floor, showing periodical index tables (foreground), the main card catalog and reference tables (rear), the stairway to the Government Documents floor, and open carrels overhanging the reference area.

The Circulation delivery desk, Fourth Floor.

A manual hoist for lifting book tubs into the book conveyor system on the stack floors.

The observation floor, exhibition areas, and wall bookshelves of the Fisher Rare Book Library book gallery room, one of the great architectural spaces on this continent.

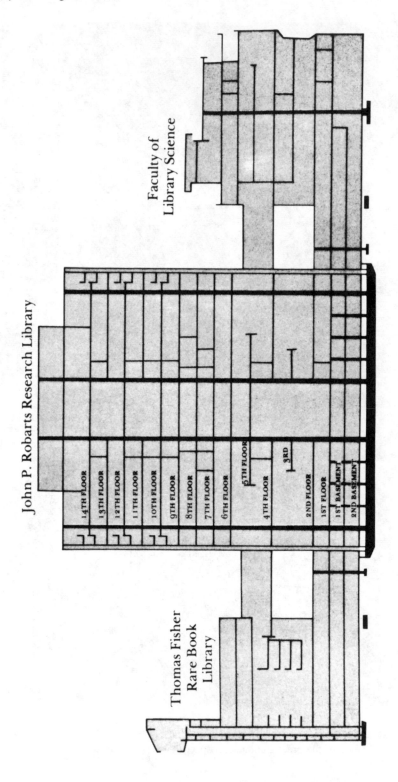

Faculty of
Library Science

John P. Robarts Research Library

Thomas Fisher
Rare Book
Library

14TH FLOOR
13TH FLOOR
12TH FLOOR
11TH FLOOR
10TH FLOOR
9TH FLOOR
8TH FLOOR
7TH FLOOR
6TH FLOOR
5TH FLOOR
4TH FLOOR
3RD
2ND FLOOR
1ST FLOOR
1ST BASEMENT
2ND BASEMENT

The cross section of the building.
Note the mezzanine levels at the periphery of the upper floors of the Robarts Library.

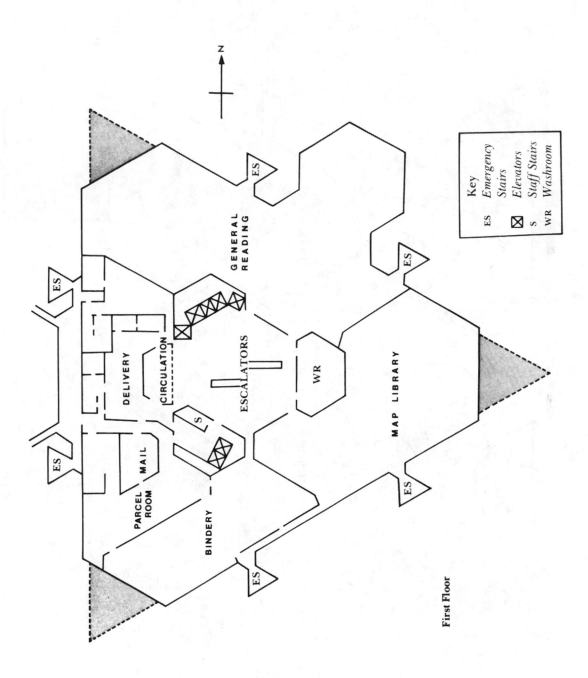

First Floor

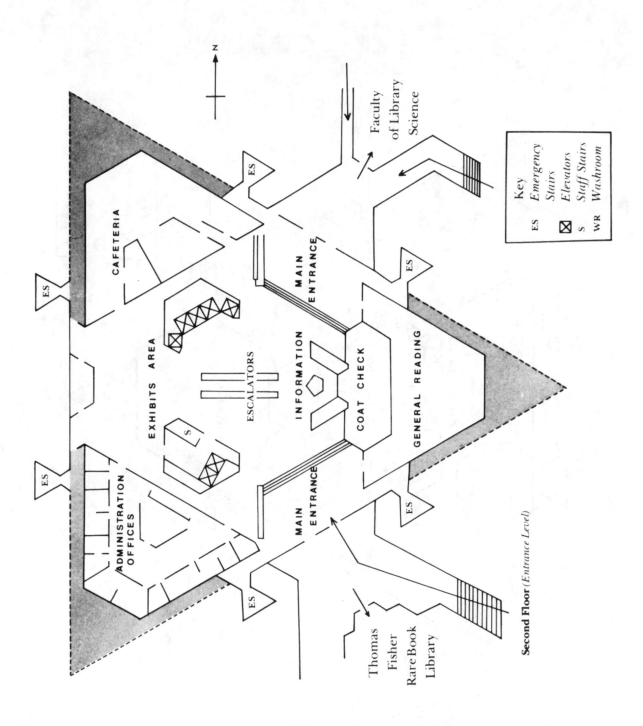

Second Floor (Entrance Level)

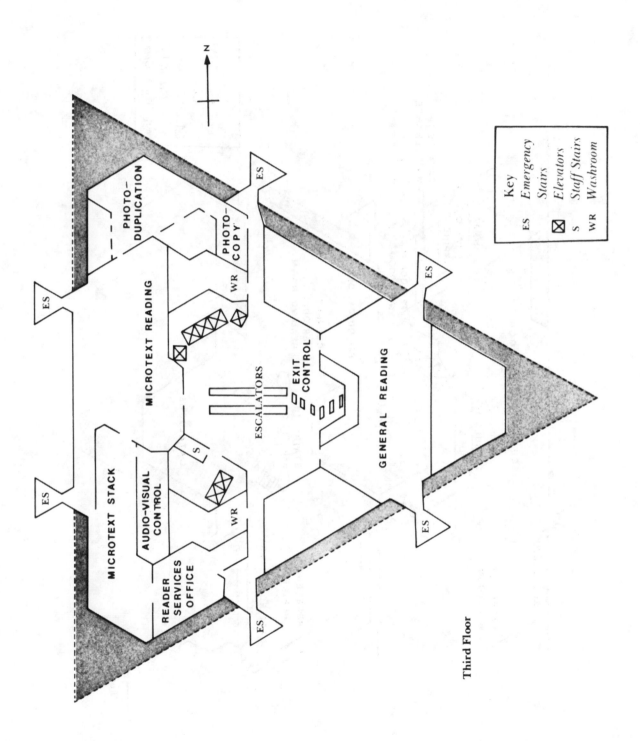

Third Floor

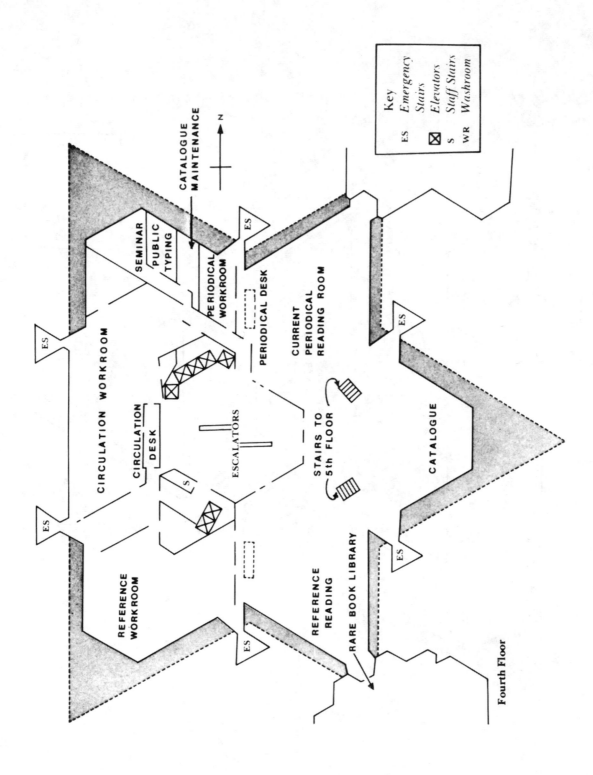

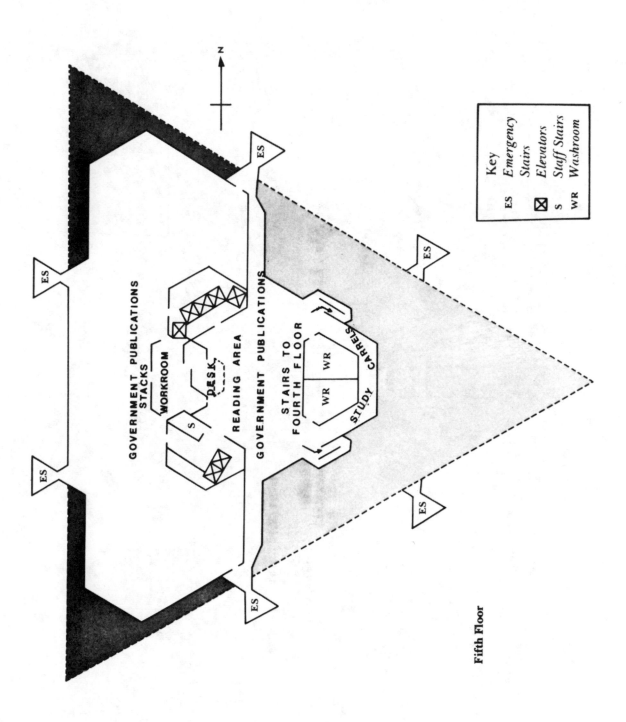

Key
Emergency Stairs
ES

Elevators
⊠

Staff Stairs
S

Washroom
WR

GOVERNMENT PUBLICATIONS STACKS

WORKROOM

DESK

READING AREA

GOVERNMENT PUBLICATIONS

STAIRS TO FOURTH FLOOR

STUDY CARRELS

WR

WR

Fifth Floor

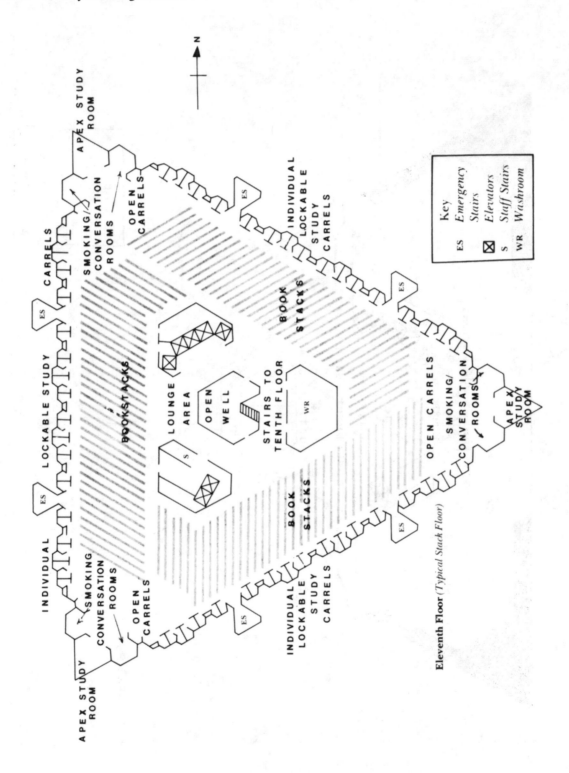

Eleventh Floor (*Typical Stack Floor*)

Key
ES Emergency Stairs
⊠ Elevators
S Staff Stairs
WR Washroom

THE ROBARTS LIBRARY AT THE UNIVERSITY OF TORONTO*

(Soft music from the Italian bands marching below on Fifth Avenue floated up to the 8th floor offices of Warner, Burns, Toan, Lunde on Columbus Day in 1966.[1] We had just finished discussing the interior design of the Hofstra University Library, when Dan Toan asked with some excitement if I'd like to see the models of the three alternative concepts they were to present to the University of Toronto Library in a few days. Natch! With some scurrying three small wooden models were assembled for view, while I was filled in rapidly on the unbelievable statistics connected with it (which changed somewhat as plans developed)—a million square feet/thousand faculty carrels/four million books/five thousand readers/a trintegrated building for library, rare books, library school.

The architects' solution to the handling of these enormous spaces was in all three proposals the building as a city. The least integrated model separated vertical units considerably, another model presented a single building with large straight-sided vertical blocks balanced against each other in various ways, but the most integrated version, one close to the present shape of the Robarts Library, was a triangular building with two connected satellites for rare books and the library school. It was the most attractive of the solutions, and the one I preferred, although I cautioned against the waste space unavoidable when a library shape departs from rectangular or square forms.

Over the ensuing year I had occasion to see the development of design plans for this building in that office.[2] As planning at Toronto proceeded, after we had settled into the Hofstra University Library, groups of Toronto librarians and architects involved in specialized aspects of the building visited us to see what Warner, Burns, Toan, Lunde had produced in our library, which had won four architectural awards.[3] When bids were called on the Robarts Library they were seven million dollars over budget, and again I was involved in discussions of what they were planning to do. The building was under construction over an entire city block when I visited the University of Toronto on a Council on Library Resources Fellowship in 1970 to study how they were solving problems we were into at Hofstra, and I was able to review completed floor plans with the Chief Librarian's assistant, who was working nearly full time as building coordinator.[4]

These personal experiences in watching it develop and the fact that the Robarts is the largest academic library building in the world *by fifty per cent,* made me eager to see it. The opportunity occurred shortly after it opened when the Association of Research Libraries met in Toronto in the Spring of 1974 specifically to provide an opportunity to view the building. The significance of its size became apparent during a three hour tour of the building, which is so massive that I was unable to orient myself in the building, to have a sense of where I was in it, even after fifteen years experience in library planning and visitation to more than four hundred libraries.

In June of 1976 the Council on Library Resources financed my study of the Robarts Library, specifically for this book, that absorbed eight ten-hour days. After assimilating to some degree the information gathered, I was in Toronto for a rare book conference a year later, and was able to check my impressions, answer outstanding questions, and review carefully the library floor devoted to computer operations. Even

---

*Footnotes to this chapter begin on page 222.

after such long and variegated contact with the building, there is still much to be learned, and the reader should profit from the following account of the building, then go visit it personally.)

* * * *

On the lawn south of the Robarts Library is a small, late twentieth century shrine. Four slender columns twelve feet high support gracefully a hexagonal canopy of six triangular ceiling coffers. On a low wall between two columns a bronze plaque dated October 14, 1970 reads:

> IN THE HOPE THAT THIS TIME CAPSULE WILL BE FOUND BY
> A CIVILIZATION WISER THAN OURS, WE HAVE BURIED HERE
> A RECORD OF MAN'S FOLLY ON THE PLANET HE'S OUT-
> GROWN.

Here in the Robarts Library can be read some of that wisdom and folly writ in poured concrete.

Fraser Poole posed the central question about the library the minute we began to discuss it: "Why?" It sits near the northwest corner of a large campus, a massive fourteen story building surrounded mostly by two-story residential houses. It occupies an entire block and students have to walk around it to reach other buildings. It is triangular in shape in defiance of bad experience with this shape in library buildings.[5] It is essentially a closed stack. It is largely a solid-face building in a city whose nearby downtown areas are replete with glass-screen, thin wall office buildings.[6] How did this building come to be?

The Mass

The Robarts Library is a monument to a peculiar stage in North American mentality, which believed for a time that higher education was the answer to all things, the bridge to heaven, and that it would continue to expand indefinitely. That time coincided with an extremely ambitious president of the University of Toronto who determined that Canada would have one supremely great research university, that it would be the University of Toronto, and that it would have a supremely great research library. How earnest he was is marked by the fact that for two years or more annual acquisitions at the University of Toronto surpassed that of Harvard.

When the Canadian universities began to stir significantly in 1959, Toronto was a university on the model of Oxford, with ten loosely connected colleges.[7] This scattering made development of a strong graduate program extremely difficult, and good students were being lost to the United States. Moreover, the university felt itself in the shadow of McGill University. It needed major new research facilities, practically, to expand its graduate programs, and symbolically, out of pride and to declare and solidify its aspirations.[8] The jewel in the crown was to be a research library for the Humanities and Social Sciences.

Accordingly, a planning committee programmed in the early 1960s a major library to provide 4,000,000 volumes, 950 locked carrels for research scholars and faculty, and total seating for 4,500. This library would contain technical service space for a massive acquisitions program, projected at 150,000 volumes per year but actually reaching more than 250,000 before the new building opened. It would provide study facilities and scholarly carrels for all fourteen of the provincial academic libraries, and all serious students in Ontario would come to the university library to use its great collection.

To accommodate space for such an enterprise, an entire block in the northwest corner of the campus was made available. With the planned growth of enrollment to 70,000 students and movement of the campus north and west this site would soon become more nearly central. The master plan for growth of the university, prepared by the architect John Andrews, called for extensive building of dormitories, colleges and other academic buildings in the five blocks immediately surrounding the new library, with a large graduate center directly across the street (see page 177). These buildings would surmount underground parking, where students would arrive, with five- and six-story structures of large occupancy. The scale and mass of these new buildings would balance nicely a very large central structure, the Robarts Library. The buildings around Robarts would be to a considerable extent open on the first floor level, allowing students to walk through to the Library easily from all sides. Robarts itself would have access to its entrance level by extremely broad stairways from the east, the north and northwest, and from the south and southwest.[9] Acquisition of the urban property required was assured, since the university had the power of eminent domain, (the Canadian term is "expropriation rights"). It therefore was not difficult to justify the planning of a new building of a million square feet thirteen stories high (ultimately to be fourteen stories).

In the ten years between the conception of this library and its completion in 1973 nearly every premise on which it was based disappeared. The envisioned increase in enrollment did not materialize; therefore the campus has not spread significantly, and the library is in a peripheral location. Surrounding buildings were not built to the scale of the Robarts Library, and it looms as a super-giant among pygmies. All the other provincial libraries were calling for great libraries on their own campuses instead of storming the collections at Robarts; therefore the generous accommodations provided in the building for outside students and scholars are lightly used. Had these changes not occurred, the university would have had great difficulty in buying surrounding city blocks, since in the interval the ability to exercise eminent domain was greatly weakened by law.

The Triangle

The requirement to provide 950 locked carrels in the building was triply compounded in difficulty by the university's decision that all of them should have an outside window. The architects were, moreover, encouraged to develop areas contiguous to the stacks that would provide identification for the academic subject departments in the university. These requirements generated the triangle, the geometrical form that provides the greatest perimeter area for any given square footage. Even with this advantage, the architects had to stretch into split-level carrel pods on the exterior walls, as we shall see, in order to get in enough carrels.

The points of the triangle invited use as home base for the academic subject departments, and in a collection this size, they could be related to bookstacks that contained books in their field. The triangular library also gave the rare books library and the library school buildings prominence and identification of their own, instead of being submerged in the massing of a more conventional form. The triangular form was carried inside into the building's bay system in order to provide stack ranges that are longer in angle stacks than in rectangular stacks, and to establish a stack arrangement on the extremely large upper floors with different colored stacks on each of the three sides of the building, to provide users a way of orienting themselves on the floors.

Obstacles

Three other givens had to be accommodated in the layout. Documents had to be in contact with both the Reference Department and with the current periodical reading room. The Reference Department had to tie in with the rare books library. The current periodical stacks make contact with the library school building.

The university's intention to build storage stacks for lesser used books at a later time was accelerated to build them into Robarts on two enormous levels below the lowest library user level. This made necessary special provisions to keep those lower two levels dry on a site with a twenty-foot water table. A huge mat of concrete seven feet thick had to be designed to be poured in this watery subsurface to hold up the enormous weight of the building.

Late in the design development, the Ontario government proposed to enlarge the building specifically to serve other provincial library needs. These were to include expansion of the research collection (with an initial fund of $10,000,000 specifically for acquisitions for provincial needs), a large number of reader seats where provincial users would have priority, and a provincial bibliographical center with its own computer operation. This proposal led to the addition of two entire floors to the building, one effect of which was to raise its entrance level a full story above grade.

The original design of the building was severely hampered by the bid overrun of $7,000,000, and the most serious losses occurred in the building's interior, where qualities of building materials had to be cut, where once budgeted sculptural and textural art works (for which this building cries out) were eliminated, and where control of the interior design of the building became dispersed. Warner, Burns, Toan, Lunde had already established the interior design of elements that were integral parts of the building—wooden walls, some carpet colors, the main card catalog cases, and the three bookstack colors, but when their proposal for an interior design was turned down (for reasons described by a staff member as "Presbyterian thrift"), the design of the furniture and equipment was turned over to the design department of the University, and the Canadian architects Mathers and Haldenby sometimes had to make decisions on colors and textures, presumably in consultation with the American architects. The result was a hybrid situation, lacking one authoritative control, with superlatively sensitive taste, to make the decisions on shapes, colors, and textures chosen to interact to produce the best feeling of the interior of the library's spaces. As a consequence, as we shall see, the building's interior design often acts to depress its feeling.[10]

The Scale

The size of the building is hard to believe until you actually see it, and, as I indicated above, it is impossible to comprehend it in a quick view. A few statistics will indicate its magnitude:

Site—3 acres.
Building gross area—23.8 acres.
Linear shelving capacity—110 miles.

Exterior building face—330' long.
Floor to floor height—14'.
Bay spans—36'.
Bay area—650 square feet.

Escalator well (floors 1-4)—1,500 square feet each floor.
Single floor area (library proper)—45,000 square feet

Catalog Department area—35,000 square feet (NOT including related areas of conference rooms (3), rest rooms (2), staff lounges (2), union catalog room.)

As a yardstick, compare the Yale University Library's 668,000 square feet housed in 34 buildings, with this building of 1,036,000 square feet, 934,000 square feet for the library areas alone.

Structural System

The structural bays of the library are formed of equilateral triangles measuring 36' on a side, supported by three great poured concrete hexagonal columns that measure 4' through the column and 5' from point to point of the hexagon. They are faced with sandblasted concrete panels 28" wide. forty of these columns hold up the building, with collateral central support from a triangular center core, and exterior support from two large triangular emergency stair towers and seven cup-columns that run the height of the building on each side (see page 179).

The cup-columns are ingeniously designed vertical shafts combining load bearing columns with ducts for the transmission of tempered air, water and electricity. Their cross section is a hexagon sliced in half: (see page 180) of which the outer three sides are thickened and reinforced to bear loads, with the inner part of the column forming an insulated hollow that carries smaller pipes and ducts for vertical distribution of utilities. The inner face of these columns are painted metal panels when they form part of the interior. From the Second to the Sixth floors, where they form part of the colonnade around the exterior of all three sides of the building, they are faced by precast concrete lids. These cup-columns widen the interior spans within the floors by removing vertical ducts to the periphery, and serve the economic and esthetic function of allowing exposure of a great deal of the structural ceiling which otherwise would require dropped ceilings.

The structural ceiling is an exposed concrete grid of triangles 62" on a side, which form a beam where their bases come together (see page 182). These beams are parallel to the outer walls of the building, so that, with the exception of the extreme corners of the floor they can accomodate parallel walls of various lengths. To use them for end walls for rooms, however, they would have to enclose space in the form of a hexagon or a parallelogram or a full or truncated triangle. The tendency in forming rooms in the building is to make them rectilinear by dropping ceilings 27 inches below the structural ceiling.

The First and Second Basement Floors, constructed for compact storage, hold 300 pounds per square foot live load (the rest of the building holds 150 pounds per square foot). On these floors, the great hexagonal columns are supplemented by a grid of 18" square columns on 16' centers. These have 14' clear space between columns, or 12½' clear space when they pair with the great columns. Neither dimension coordinates with standard stack sizes so equipment for this area would have to be manufactured to fit.

The center core of the building from floors one to four is an open shaft that contains escalators. Floors ten to eleven and floors twelve to thirteen have a two story central atrium, with stairs that connect the floors, to lighten the feeling of the enormous unrelieved area of the stack and research floors.

The Exterior

The top of Robarts Library can be seen four blocks away above the thick foliage of Queen's Park near the center of the University of Toronto's spread of buildings. Three blocks away, its mass looms large across the playing fields near Hart House and Soldier's Tower. As you approach, the building becomes larger and more detailed until a maximum view is reached about a block away from it. The views from much closer are partial, falling short of viewing the entire fourteen stories of the building without a contorted effort to look up, which distorts perspective on it.

Its massiveness is impressive, and the complexity of its great variety is apparent at once (see page 179). The architects have ingeniously lightened the feeling of this mass in a number of ways. The central library structure is played against the two lower satellite buildings, which rise to the 6th or 7th story of the main building. They are laid out on axes that exactly bisect the library's triangle.[11] The large façades of the building are broken into three equal units by two large emergency stair towers that rise fourteen stories from ground level. The five lower floors, devoted to library user facilities, are kept relatively open by the use of sizeable glass areas inset below balconies. The three floors above, which contain technical processes, are more enclosed, and the stack floors above these are relieved only by vertical strip windows that run the entire height of those floors. The upper floors are cantilevered out over the lower floors at the three corners of the triangle beginning at the Eighth floor level. They are separated from them by the use of darker precast rough concrete facing panels (see page 180). These are marked by a horizontal stripe of light concrete at each floor level, which is carefully related to inset stripes on the face of the emergency stair towers and the poured concrete supports of the building. There are four inset stripes for every vertical floor stripe on the facade.

These devices, in addition to the ingenious use of variety in the window enclosures and the geometrical forms of exterior components (see page 181), break up the enormous square footage of this facade into a myriad of visual components that greatly reduce the feeling of heaviness inherent in its size. The use of outset and inset areas on the periphery of the stack floors (see page 196) is designed to provide the extremely large number of windows required for the locked carrels in the building. The most remarkable achievement of the exterior is its total avoidance of any appearance of triangularity. The outer walls are varied everywhere, both horizontally and vertically, to escape the stark and oversimple appearance inherent in any triangle. From most angles it gives the impression of being rectilinear. The functionality within of these seemingly decorative elements on the outside will be seen as we examine the interior.

Vertical Arrangement

The floors of the building are arranged vertically into four distinct functional groups:

Floors 1–5   User facilities.
Floors 6–8   Technical services.
Floors 9–13 Stacks and research facilities.
Floor 14   Faculty departments and offices.

More specifically, the functions on each floor are:

I.   User Facilities

First Floor
1.   Provincial reader facilities, including:
       Circulation delivery desk.
       Reading room with assignable carrels.
2.   Map library.
3.   Bindery.

4. Mail/shipping room, including Fumigator.
5. Storage, refrigeration, and preparation area for Cafeteria above.
6. Loading dock.
7. Supplies storage.
8. Caretaker's office.

Second Floor (Main entrance floor)
1. Covered walkways to:
    Library School building.
    Fisher Rare Book Library.
2. Coat checkroom.
3. Information desk.
4. Administration suite.
5. General reading room.
6. Cafeteria.
7. Exhibition area.

Third Floor
1. Readers Services offices.
2. Microform reading and stacks.
3. Photocopy area.
4. Photoduplication.
5. Photography studio and dark rooms.
6. Workroom for sign preparation, servicing of A-V equipment.
7. General reading room.
8. Exit control.

Fourth Floor
1. Circulation delivery desk and workroom.
2. Main card catalog and Catalog maintenance office.
3. Reference area and workroom.
4. Current periodicals and workroom.
5. Public typing room.
6. Seminar room.
7. Entrance to bookstacks (elevator).
8. Interior entrance to Fisher Rare Book Library.
9. Stairs up to Government publications.

Fifth Floor
1. Government Publications reading, workroom, and stacks.
2. Study carrels.

II. Technical Services

Sixth Floor
1. Order department.
2. Serials department.

    3.   Book selection department.

    4.   Joint Technical Services for Scarborough and Erindale Colleges.

Seventh Floor
1. Catalog department.
2. Searching department.
3. Union catalog.
4. Technical Processing department.

Eighth Floor
1. East Asian library.
2. Centre of Criminology and its Library.
3. Council of Ontario Universities.
4. Library automation systems (UTLAS).

III.   Stacks and Research Facilities

Ninth Floor
1. Bookstacks.
2. Book lockers.
3. Reading areas.
4. Locked peripheral carrels.
5. Stack delivery workroom.
6. Subject reading area for Philosophy/Psychology.
7. Two seminar rooms.

Tenth Floor
1. Same basic areas, plus:
2. Center atrium with stairway to 11th floor.
3. Subject reading areas for:
    History.
    Medieval studies.
    Sociology/Social work.

Eleventh Floor
1. Same basic areas, plus:
2. Subject reading areas for:
Political Science.
Slavic/Russian.
East European.

Twelfth Floor
1. Same basic areas, plus:
2. Center atrium with stairs to 13th floor.
3. Subject reading areas for:
    Classics/Fine Arts.

Islamic/Near Eastern.
Linguistics/German.

Thirteenth Floor
1. Same basic areas, plus:
2. Subject reading areas for:
English literature.
Drama.
Romance literature.

IV. Faculty Departments and Offices and cafeteria—Fourteenth Floor.

The Library Floors

Although set below street level, the earth has been scooped out on three sides of the First Floor to place it completely above ground, allowing the building to provide full-height window walls in most of the areas. Two basement floors below this level are provided for compact storage equipment, some of which has been installed already to house rare books, connected to the Fisher Rare Book Library through a common wall. The First Floor contains a large hexagonal projection on the north face of the building, which makes it the largest floor above ground in the building (see page 191).

The core area at the foot of the escalator that leads down from the main entrance floor, above, contains free standing exhibition cases and wall exhibition cases, a few lounge chairs in a pleasant beige upholstery, and a number of side chairs in a good tone of orange. On the west side of the core, head on to the escalators, is a large circulation desk with light indicators for fifty numbers above it, intended for paged closed stack book delivery. The use of the reader facilities on this floor intended mainly for provincial students has been far short of anticipation and this delivery desk has never been activated. It presently is closed off by locked accordian panels that mock the large APPLY FOR BOOKS HERE sign to the right of it. The book return drop to the left of the desk is heavily used.

First Floor—Provincial Reading Room

Off the north side of the core opens a very large reading room, about 16,000 square feet, for non-University of Toronto readers. This has been very lightly used to date, mostly by students from York University ten miles away. The architectural design of this area is very good. Except where they lift around the perimeter for exterior views, the ceilings are of dropped acoustical tile 8½' high, fitted with 1' × 4' lighting fixtures with a diffusing lens that provide 50 footcandles of reasonably good quality lighting. Most of the perimeter contains 10' high floor to ceiling window walls looking out to upward sloping greensward, and laterally to the many interesting aspects of the exterior of the library that are visible through the perimeter glass walls, whose angles form varied alcoves pleasant in shape on the interior. The large square footage of the room is broken visually by the cup-columns of the building, some of which come down on this level as piers thirteen feet wide. This room provides a great variety of feeling in its spaces.

Unfortunately, the basic elements of what could be a brilliantly successful reading room, are undermined by the details of the interior design. This begins what persists throughout most of this library as a conflict between the building and its interior, in which the struggle goes sometimes to the building, sometimes to the interior, the total effect of which is far short of what this building should have achieved in the feeling of its interior spaces.

The interior is not entirely bad, it is mixed. The building contains many areas that require brightening, the more so when they are removed from exterior windows. The most damaging aspect of the interior design is its overwhelming and consistent darkness of tone, in the wood, in the furniture, and in the upholstery for the most part. In mass, this combination works as an active spirit-depressant. The wood is mahogany, but stained dark brown or dark red, too dark in both colors to enhance the grain of the wood, which is deprived of a feeling of richness. The frames and divider panels of carrels and reading tables are dark brown mahogany, with a dark greenish-brown formica writing surface, which helps depress the feeling of reading areas and violates good vision practice for reading.

The shapes of the furniture while not ugly are completely undistinguished in their proportions (although they do provide larger than usual reading surfaces for students). Fabrics used on chairs tend to be dark in tone and dull in color, although the orange upholstery is good. The carpeting used in variations throughout the user areas, with the exception of the cores, provides a reasonably good green, and a good orange color, but the tone of the red carpeting used is distinctly unpleasant, and when these three colors are juxtaposed on the same floor the effect ranges from bad to horrible, not as bad as the color combinations in the Harvard Education Library but surely second worst in my experience.

This provincial reading area uses the green carpeting, but also uses large areas of the unpleasant red carpeting, at one point bordered by a 32 inch strip of green for a long distance. The color conflict is horrible to contemplate. Two large end walls covered in reddish orange vinyl, the orange fabric used on some of the side chairs, and the pleasant beige in the lounge chairs (used mostly on the periphery) help to brighten the feeling of the room. But these elements are overborne by the wood in the dark, undistinguished 4' × 8' tables for four, the 2' × 3' tables for one, and the carrels, by large areas furnished with chairs with dark brown fabric, and most of all by the dark red mahogany of the locked assignable carrels that help compartmentalize the room and act as a highly visible element in it.

Seventy-nine of these carrels are arranged in three double face rows of carrels separated by two aisles containing reading tables. They are 4' × 6' each, with a door 6' high containing an inspection panel. Each contains an attractive swivel arm chair (one of the few distinctly attractive pieces of furniture in the building), and two book shelves above a wall-hung desk. The dark red mahogany is especially depressing in the interior of these carrels, where the small space cries out for color relief. This problem is intensified by the fact that the carrel walls are too high to allow the overhead lighting fixtures, which are not correlated with the carrel rows, to provide good lighting for enclosed carrels of this size. The lighting in the carrels varies from inadequate to poor, and although the desks are provided with local lighting underneath the lowest bookshelf, as is usual with such an arrangement, it lights only the rear of the reading surface and not the outer edge where reading takes place. The impact of the carrels and the other wood furniture on this room as a whole is sombre and not very appealing.

First Floor—Map Library

This very large area of about 10,000 square feet is a completely open space nearly rectilinear in feeling. It has two long tack-panel walls at the entrance, well used for map display, and a small office and workroom on the north side of the room. Bookstacks for atlases and reference books and nine tables for four are located at the west end of the room, the rest of which is occupied by 110 standard blueprint cases, to hold sheet maps, arranged in double-face sections on 11' centers.

The area is provided with the green carpeting, which with orange fabric chairs and beige blueprint cabinets and the black bookstacks once made a reasonable interior design. But with the wantonness that attends human affairs, and seems to work more virulently in library interiors, a large mass of additional blueprint cases and a number of additional chairs have been added to the original quantities, all of them *plum purple,* a color that nearly makes the green carpeting retch. Despite this atrocity, the high 10½′ ceilings of exposed triangular coffers, which provide 50 to 65 footcandles of reasonably good quality light, and two long sides of the room composed of window walls make this area reasonably pleasant to be in.

The attendant in this room on the Sunday I visited it, a student at Victoria College (Toronto has nine small college libraries more or less self-sufficient except for research purposes) was free in her complaints about the Robarts Library, which she asserted she did not use because it intimidated her. She found the mass of concrete in the building cold, and the interior design depressing.

First Floor—Bindery

A staff of fifteen in this room handles binding preparation of the material that goes to outside binding (95 per cent), minor mending, pamphlet binding, portfolios and recasing. This is one large open room with work stations arranged for the logical progression of its tasks. A glass enclosed office serves for the unit head, and a fifty-foot long window wall at one end of the room makes the room pleasant. Stem-hung troffers of 1′ × 4′ fixtures with a diffusing lens provide 60 footcandles of lighting of better quality than is usual in this building, for the visually demanding tasks of this staff.

Going Up?

The core centers of floors 1–4 are occupied by up and down escalators that cross each other in the middle of a large hexagonal space surrounded by poured concrete retaining railings at each landing. These in turn are surrounded by a terrazzo-paved hexagonal traffic dispersal area, off which open all the rooms on each floor. A metal slat ceiling with fluorescent tubes above it provides lighting for the traffic area and sometimes, as on the Fourth Floor, extends into reading areas. The escalators are lit by an ornamental metal slat ceiling, dropped above the escalators parallel to the pitch of their rise.

The feeling of the cores tends to be cold, with surfaces of concrete and terrazzo, of brown painted metal and stainless steel (on the escalators), only slightly relieved by the dark metal slats above. From the Second to the Fourth Floors there is little in the traffic areas to halt one; everything seems to signal: Move on! Nothing beckons to stay. I repeatedly arrived at the wrong end of the escalators, through lack of prominently visible "Up" and "Down" signs on the floors.

Second Floor—Main Entrance
The Approach to the Library

As we approach one of the two main entrances, at midpoint on the north and south sides of the building, we are immediately aware of the size of it, 206′ high, and of the angularity of its details. Stairways lead up past the Fisher Rare Book Library or the Library School to an open covered plaza between the buildings. (A wheelchair ramp is on the north side, west of the Library School.) Twelve steps lead up to an intermediate landing; sixteen more lead up to the plaza. The steps are 20′ wide and divided into up and down lanes by a railing in the middle. Careful observation reveals that these risers, of precast brown pebble aggregate, are very slightly beveled from both the top and bottom to meet at a slight angle on the nose of the riser, beginning the feeling of angularity in the building's decorative details. This feeling is expanded as the steps flare outward, on an angle at the sides, from the landing to the plaza level. The faces of the satellite buildings, both elongated hexagons, are set fifty feet across from the entrances to Robarts that protrude from the outer wall of the Library. The plaza areas reach back around the entrances to the buildings to measure 100' over all.

The plaza ceiling is part of the Fourth Floor, whose exposed concrete underside displays in a decorative manner a great truss and beam triangular ceiling containing the smaller triangular ceiling coffers lighted by triangular fixtures that is distinctive of so much of this building. This plaza ceiling is thirty feet high!

The Entrance

We enter the building through two revolving doors in a hexagonal unit set in glass panels 10' wide by 30' high. The cylinder of the doors, of magnificent polished granite, contrasts in form and feeling with the hexagon that contains it.[12] Immediately inside the lobby, we are aware of the ceiling supported by three great hexagonal columns, typical of those used throughout the building, which measure 4' through from face to face, and 5' from point to point (the width of your office desk). Thirty feet in height, they are greatly impressive, the closest one only three paces away.

Directly ahead, the area faces an open mezzanine, marked by the concave hexagonal face of a poured concrete railing (see page 184). This is flanked on both sides by huge areas of dark mahogany wall that drop to the level of the Second Floor ceiling, defining the height of the floor above. Over this area the triangular ceiling coffers contain in a pattern triangular lighting fixtures that drop 6" below the bottom of the coffer. Below the mahogany, the concrete facing of the lobby is decorated by 2"-wide inset Palladian stripes, similar to those on the building's exterior, on 2' vertical centers.

From the entrance point the ceiling of the first floor traffic dispersal area can be seen 14' above the entrance level, made of 1" slats of dark brown metal set on edge into the ceiling on 6" centers. The ceiling is lit by 1' × 4' lighting fixtures, partially inset into the ceiling in a pattern on 5' centers laterally and 6' centers longitudinally. The fixtures are offset in rows so that every other row is in line with the open spaces of facing rows.[13]

The entire experience of approaching the building from a distance, the effect of its variety of facings in form and color tone, the reduction of the building to eye level as we get near it, the upward gaze which accompanies the ascent of the staircase, the enormous height and size of the covered plaza, the movement into Robarts through the confined and lowered space of the revolving door, and the emergence into a space with a monumentally lifted ceiling above a lobby filled with architectural elements of an impressive and varied nature is a process through spectacular architectural spaces that are unusual in any building and rarely achieved in libraries. If for no other reason, the Robarts Library would be an outstanding building for its approach.

Second Floor—Lobby

The Second Floor opens up directly in front and at the sides of the lobby. Nearby, to the left oblique, a concrete wall 5' high conceals a wheelchair ramp that connects the two levels of the entrance floor. Two Book Return slots appear in the lobby walls ahead, and clearly visible, for the benefit of visiting firemen, is a large Fire Annunciator Panel in each lobby, with 130 active stations identified, and blank panels for 50 more as needed. On each side of this lobby is a 4′ × 6′ table with chairs, for student activity use, or for readers.

Straight ahead and up four steps 45′ wide that rise to the general level of this floor, a large service desk for the collection of coats, which must be left at this level in the coatroom, is clearly visible.[14] In the center of the core can be seen the St. Andrew's cross of ascending and descending escalators. Opposite the ascending escalator is an Information Desk faced with precast terrazzo panels that match the poured-in-place terrazzo on the floor, separated into slabs by brass division strips.[15]

At the main level of this floor the corners of the triangle are occupied by the Administration suite on the south, and the Cafeteria on the north, with an Exhibition area between them on the west wall. The east corner of the triangle contains a General Reading area on the entrance lobby level.

Second Floor—General Reading Room

Semi-hexagonal in shape, this room winds around the wall of the Coat Checkroom. In all its architectural details it has the potential of being a great room. The inner twenty feet of ceiling drops to a height of 14′, beyond which the room lifts grandly two stories high to a 30′ ceiling, with the triangulated ceiling and the triangular lighting fixtures appearing remarkably decorative at this distance. The Third Floor Reading Room above looks down from a balcony over the outer half of the room, at the far end of which window walls look out to a 30′ high gallery 10′ wide formed by great columns that support the 11′ overhang of the Fourth Floor. Through the side window walls appear fine views of details of the Library School and of the Fisher Rare Book Library (see page 185).

Yet, though it cannot completely suppress the grandness of this space, the interior design works hard to depress it, in its overdark wood panelling on the inner walls, in the dark wood of the tables and carrels with their dark greenish brown writing surfaces, in the dark wood panels that separate reading areas, and in the dark greenish brown fabric on the side chairs. Though not of the same darkness of tone, the unpleasant red of the carpeting does nothing to enhance the feeling of this room.

There are reader seats for about a hundred, with room to accommodate sixty more easily. The lounge chairs are comfortable, and the reading space is generously large on all the furniture—2′ × 3′4″ single tables, 4′ × 8′ tables for four, 25″ × 44″ carrels with baffles.

Second Floor—Administration Suite

This area occupies eight complete bays, about 6,500 square feet, in the south corner of the floor, with ceilings that drop to 9½′. The rooms are lit by 1′ × 4′ fixtures with a diffusing lens that give 70 footcandles of reasonably good light. They also contain the air returns. The area is an elongated semi-hexagon (see page 192), with a service core on the inner wall, surrounded by a corridor, with administrative offices on the outer walls.

The service core contains two rest rooms, a mail/duplicating room, a coffee room, supply room, and a conference room (a totally interior room with only down lights that supply abominable illumination). The corridor contains dark red mahogany reception desks, black filing cases, and black floor tile with a dark brown drift through it, continuing the darkness without lightness that mars this building. The reception desk has a signal station for short voice messages to key members of the public service staff. On the outer window walls overlooked by the 30′-high gallery are 12 offices of 150 square feet and two offices of 300 square feet. The Chief Librarian's office has a private rest room and a separate door to an exterior balcony.

These administrative offices are more successful in feeling than any rooms we have considered in the library to this point, since they are balanced by lighter tones and colors. Most of them are nearly rectilinear in feeling; their angularity where it occurs is not intrusive. They have 70 footcandles of good quality lighting. The usual dark mahogany desk with a dark brown formica surface is balanced by an attractive Steelcase swivel armchair upholstered in light brown nylon fabric. The outer walls of sandblasted aggregate panels are broken by floor to ceiling window walls, supplied with beige louver-drapes that swivel and pull open. The other three walls of the office have a clerestory window above off-white walls.

The walls separating adjacent offices, identical on each side, are decorative and functional, composed of a wardrobe beside two lateral filing drawers, in matte black, below six bookshelves of dark brown mahogany.

The door to the gallery from the Chief Librarian's office leads to a balcony large enough to hold thirty people. The top of this balcony, of poured concrete, meets the top of a decorative architectural form on the building, which, at the three points of the triangle (of which this is one) serve also as a gently sloping escape ramp that drops to within three feet of the ground.

Second Floor—Cafeteria

The Cafeteria which occupies the north point of the triangular floor is more pleasant in feeling than the Reading Room. It has dark terrazzo floors, similar to those in the core, and dark red mahogany interior walls, but these are lightened by the expansive exterior window walls. The 3′ × 3′ tables have the same dark mahogany frame, but their off-white formica tops (which ironically are far better reading surfaces than the dark formica used in this library) brighten them up. They are accompanied by chairs in a very pleasant plum purple fabric. The cafeteria provides human service for hot and cold meals during normal hours, and coin-operated service at other times. It is open during all the hours the library is open.

It should be mentioned that the room signs on this floor, as is true throughout the building, are exceptionally good and easy to read—a simple, pleasant LETRASET system with letters 3½″ high and numbers on all doors 3″ high.

Third Floor—Core Area

This is the first floor that contains a complex of services in the building, and it is immediately apparent at the head of the ascending escalator that the directional signs are inadequate here and at every other core area in the library. Most of the areas on this floor are not visible from the landing point, and some are around behind two or three sharp angles. Nothing short of an elaborate system of directional signs, repeated until the room is in view, could keep the user from confused wandering.

Third Floor—Reader Services Office

One floor below the main reader services departments are the offices for that division, including a service desk for reader services registration (where I was duly issued a pass to use the library and stacks), a workroom, and the division head's office. This area connects through a door to internal photocopy facilities located beyond the microtext stacks. The staff of six that occupies this space has offices on the exterior wall that vary from large to commodious (for the division head), and are quite pleasant in feeling and well lit. An interior office for the assistant head is very pleasant, with beige vinyl walls, white tile floor, burnt orange lateral files, and very good lighting.

Third Floor—Microtext Area

The very large reading room for this area has two windows at the far north end, but for the most part it is internal space, supplied with readers on open tables, 2′ × 4′, with a fixed center panel and two sliding panels on either side. It has the same unpleasant red tone carpeting and dark wood-and-formica furniture whose poor feeling is somewhat lessened by the dim overhead lights, kept at 45 footcandles intensity by rheostat control.

A control desk at the south end of this room services microtexts from a closed stack behind it. There is also an audio-visual control room, equipped with a raised floor, for sending programs to fixed locations in the room, now in use for internal photocopy facilities. On the west wall of the reading room are 13 enclosed rooms, 5½′ × 8½′ with a 2′-wide bar built in on the long side for audio and video use. The walls are light, to supply a screen for projection. Each room has its own air supply and individually controlled rheostat lighting. Each has a slit window in its door, 6″ × 36″, which makes it impossible to darken the room as much as one would like to for visual projection.

In the north point of the triangle on this floor are the photocopy facilities, serviced at a handsome cast terrazzo desk set in a mahogany wall at the entrance to the area. Beyond it is a complex of a microfilming room, a film processing room, a negative room, and a finishing room, all with enough room for elaborate equipment, adjacent to an open workroom, staff lounge and three enclosed offices.

Third Floor—Reading Room

The east point of this floor contains a Reading Room, similar to the one below on the Second Floor, but about half its size. It has a pleasant view straight ahead to the upper part of the 30′ window walls, and down over the balcony to the room below, but it is weighted down by the same unsuccessful decor as used below, now aided by a ceiling dropped to 8½′ high. This floor, which is the lowest floor containing any library materials, has an Exit Control through which users must pass to reach the down escalators. A human inspection system was in use when I was there.

Fourth Floor—Reference Area

This floor is a phenomenon, since not until he is three floors above street level and two floors above the entrance floor does the library user have access to circulation services, reference services, the card catalog, and the entrance to the stacks. The core area is flanked by numbers of mahogany benches and large ash urns, smoking still being a universal habit in Canada and very noticeable to anyone accustomed to our recent reformed practice.

The east side of the core area where one comes off the escalator opens through large doors into a huge unbroken tri-point room, formed by bridging the sides of this point of the floor into the Fisher Rare

Book Library and the Library School. Straight ahead is the card catalog, to the left is the Current Periodicals Area and to the right the Reference Area.

Straight ahead from the entrance doors a large hexagonal, quite accessible mahogany Catalog Information desk greets the user, who must walk around it to reach the catalog beyond. Consultation tables 20" × 60" × 42" high hold microfilm reading machines that contain the current Computer Output Microform catalog in film reels. This catalog is in brief information by author, title and subject, form, while to the right in the Reference Area are machines with the same catalog in full LC form. Beyond these tables ranges of custom designed catalog cases contain cards for retrospective holdings. These cases, 5' high, are double-faced cases 12 drawers high by 40 drawers long, arranged in ranges on 15' centers, with consultation tables between them.

As we move toward the catalog, twenty feet beyond the door the dropped ceiling raises dramatically to an exposed decorative ceiling 30' high, with most of the periphery within view composed of enormous window walls (see page 186). This is exactly the condition of the Second Floor Reading room, discussed above, the correlate area to this one. However, this area and its flanking areas for Reference and Periodicals have a very good feeling despite the unpleasant red tone carpeting (except at the edges, where it collides violently with a 10'-wide green border), and the use of the same dark red mahogany in catalog cases, office walls, stack end panels, and in the frames of all the library furniture in this room. The mass of the card catalogs blankets the carpet area and the stacks with their contents brighten the darkness that weighs down the feeling of other areas in the library.

The Reference Area proper, south of the Catalog Information desk, has its own set of entrance doors opening off the core at an angle. Directly inside is a large reference desk 30" wide × 42" high × 21' long, made of cast terrazzo panels with a matte black formica writing surface. Behind this desk is a large Interlibrary Loan book return box with a lock and a door that opens into the Interlibrary office, part of a large reference office-workroom area directly behind the desk.

The rest of the Reference Area is filled with periodical index tables, atlas cases, stacks for 30,000 reference books, and concealed behind a very large column, a Diebold Power File 9' wide by 9' high by 4' deep that contains telephone directories, biographical clippings, and short bibliographies on standard subjects of inquiry. This file makes a noticeable noise when it rotates. At the far end of this room a door opens to a lobby with views through glass of the Fisher Rare Book Library and an elevator down to that library.

The reference office-workroom is a completely open area with three private offices. The interlibrary loan librarian's desk is immediately inside the door behind the Reference Desk. The outer fifteen feet of this room are partitioned off by freestanding panels to form a very attractive staff room on a window wall, with colorful furnishings behind the panel.

The Current Periodicals Area, to the north of the Catalog Information Desk, is supplied with a duplicate of the Reference Desk, but it is not manned. The rest of this room is filled with book stacks with ten flat cantilevered shelves per section with two dividers per shelf. There are clusters of lounge chairs adjacent to the stacks, and in the northeast hexagon of the room, upholstered in a reasonably good grey fabric and extremely comfortable. Along the window wall, inviting leather-slung lounge chairs are arranged beside low 2' × 2' tables. Some newspapers are out on hanging stacks, but most of them are kept behind the desk in a small periodicals workroom adjacent to this area. West of the periodicals workroom, opening off a corridor, are a small office for Catalog Maintenance (whose department is two floors above), a public typing room with 12 custom built typing stands, and a seminar room with good quality lighting in the northwest point of the triangle. Two ornamental staircases that flank at a distance the Catalog Information Desk lead up from the Current Periodicals Area and the Reference Area to the Government Documents reading room on the mezzanine above.

Fourth Floor—Circulation Area

On the west side of the core area is the Circulation Desk, made of cast terrazzo panels, 20' long × 32" wide × 42" high. The desk height drops to 32" on the inside edge. Above the desk are light panels numbered from 1 to 50 for paged books (see page 187). The book conveyor system, which we will encounter again in the book stacks, terminates at one end of the desk. At the opposite end is a large sorting area. The wall behind the desk is of dark red mahogany panelling.

Behind this wall is a very large unbroken area for the circulation workroom, staff desks and department head office. It is a very pleasant area, light and open, with acoustical tile ceilings 8½' high containing 1' × 4' lighting fixtures with a diffusing lens that give very good quality light of 65 footcandles intensity. The far wall of the room is a window wall. The department head was in a pleasant office with white vinyl walls below clerestory partitions. Her two reservations about the area were the inability to see the Circulation Desk, in order to give supplementary help when it is rushed, and the loss of a staff elevator planned to go directly from this room to the stacks which was eliminated in the cost overrun. A staff lounge for this department set off by floor to ceiling panels provides a very pleasant area for thirty, playing beige and brown fabrics in the seating against white floor tiles and off-white and orange walls in the panels. This lounge is one of the most pleasant areas in the library.

The department head reported that most of their book returns come through the book return drop on the First Floor, which they have to empty every hour.

Near the Circulation Desk a turnstile-controlled area allows authorized users, mostly research students and faculty who must show a card, access to the elevators that go directly from this floor to the Fifth, and Ninth to Thirteenth Floors which contain the government documents and the book stacks.

Fifth Floor—Government Documents Department

This floor of the Library is unsuccessful in almost all of its parts. To reach it, you must come up to the Fourth Floor and either walk through Reference and up the stairs (if not stack authorized), or go through the turnstile to the stack elevators and up one floor (if you have a stack permit). If you have a stack permit, you can exit through a turnstile in a glass wall to the elevators on this floor only when the Service Desk is manned. At other hours, the staircase down to the Reference Area is the only exit for everyone.

When you reach this department it is on the smallest floor in the Library, little more than half the square footage of most other floors (see page 195). Its small reading room has a limited capacity for reference aids on periodical index tables and in ten stack sections. Below 8½' metal-slat ceilings, which give 60 footcandles of reasonably good light, its plum purple upholstery (good in itself) shrieks at the green carpeting, as it does in the Map Library on the First Floor.

All is dark here. Dark red mahogany furniture, dark red mahogany stack end panels, dark red mahogany service desk with a black matte formica writing surface, and the rear wall of the workroom behind the desk, visible through glass walls is painted dark brown, although the small area of that room calls for relief. Despite its good illumination at 70 footcandles the staff does not like it. The entire documents collection, which is restricted, is shelved in stacks behind the workroom, which places the nearest stack 25' from the Service Desk, far too distant for effective service.

The lateral aisles above the Reference and Current Periodicals Areas are equipped with twelve assignable carrels, 5' × 6' with a 25" deep desk top built in, that are open on top and overlook the areas below. This excellent concept is totally destroyed by the interiors. These lateral aisles are the most shatteringly depressing areas in the Library, with the unpleasant red carpeting on the floor, one dark-red mahogany wall 14' high by 30' long, and the study carrels covered with dark-red mahogany vinyl on the other.

The interior of the carrels is dark-red mahogany vinyl, with dark-brown mahogany dividers. The desk tops are black formica with dark-brown mahogany frames. So much darkness in such a tiny area is devastating, and these carrels fail much in the same way as the carrels in the Provincial Reading Room on the First Floor. Eighteen additional carrels on the perimeter of the mezzanine, although they share the same gloomy interiors, are relieved by the sandblasted concrete walls with horizontal inset stripes that form the corridor walls behind them (see page 186.)

Sixth Floor—Technical Services

Floors 6–8 are occupied by technical service departments, with a few exceptions as noted. No public elevators have access to floors 6 and 7, which are serviced instead by two staff elevators. The center core of each floor, which is occupied by escalators and traffic dispersal areas on floors 1–4, are occupied here by conference rooms, staff lounges, and staff rest rooms, within a single hexagonal outer wall. This center core is surrounded by departments that are enormous areas, separated from each other by lateral walls, which span the floor from center core to exterior wall.

On the Sixth Floor the walls of the core, painted dark blue, are surrounded by a brown-drift black tile walkway. The conference rooms, one for 25 and one for 50, have off-white tile flooring, off-white vinyl walls, one equipped with a long chalkboard, and reasonably bright illumination of good quality. Completely light in contrast to the darkness below, they nevertheless feel sterile. Instead of ascending to heaven, we have reached at this height a kind of clinical Purgatory.

The staff lounge is furnished with comfortable lounge chairs upholstered in three tones of brown stripes which are not great but are acceptable. A spider-pedestal chair in beige, white tables, and white General Fireproofing chairs complete the decor, which is clearly not distinguished. A service hexagon is located at one side of the area, which has seating for 30.

All of the peripheral areas have off-white tile floors with light brown speckles and off-white vinyl walls when they are not concrete panels or window walls on the exterior. This floor contains the Order Department, Book Selection Department, Catalog Maintenance, Serials Department and the Joint Technical Services of Scarborough and Erindale College Libraries, each of which covers an enormous area. There are sixteen single offices built of demountable partitions on the peripheral north and south walls, and three pairs of administrators' offices with solid walls, one in each of the apexes of the triangle.

Seventh Floor—Technical Services

The Seventh Floor has the same core arrangement with much the same feeling as that of the Sixth Floor, with the exception of the core walls, which are painted orange. It has the same kind of enormous peripheral departments with the same light floors and walls. On this floor, the areas are much more heavily occupied, and some freestanding panels are used for separation of areas. These 6'-high panels are designed in poor proportions and covered with an unappealing brown fabric. The insensitivity to colors and textures in the interior design of this building is remarkably consistent. Two thirds of this floor is engulfed by the two Catalog Departments in a great unbroken area that winds around the center core. The other third is occupied by the Searching Department, a Coding room, two small Audio rooms, a Union Catalog Room, three department head offices, and the division head's office.

Eighth Floor

This floor was originally intended for the special processing of a single $10,000,000 purchase of books for the provincial libraries, a project that developed during the planning of the building and required insertion of one additional floor. The money was never appropriated and that additional floor is now pretty much surplus space for the program of this Library. It is occupied by one technical process—Library Automation Systems (UTLAS) and two library branches, the East Asian Library, the Center for Criminology and its Library, and one rental facility, the Council of Ontario Universities. A public elevator is programmed to stop at floors 2, 8, and 14 only.

Eighth Floor—Library Automation Systems (UTLAS)

This department of the Library, which has a long history of erratic performance, has recently begun to deliver solid products, and in the past three years has launched a kind of Canadian equivalent of OCLC, charged with becoming self-sustaining or terminating. These changes, and those that lie ahead, require radical changes of space in those areas of this floor which they occupy. The spaces do not readily adapt to multiple small offices for computer specialists. Privacy is impossible to achieve without interfering noticeably with the balance of air distribution of the floor.

Eighth Floor—East Asian Library

This Library uses the unpleasant red carpeting at its entrance and in the center reading area, but the rest of the floor is a pleasant light beige tile. The dark red mahogany card catalog cases, service desk, and reading tables are relieved by wooden end panels on the stack ranges which are stained plum purple and chinese red, both of which are attractive in this setting. The beige lounge chairs in the center reading area, and a chinese red fabric used on some of the side chairs are pleasant. Two walls just to the right of the entrance have attractive exhibition cases with black metal frames and sliding glass doors that exhibit rare Chinese material, among which are the oldest books owned by this Library. The area is small enough to be easy to use, and on the whole it achieves a much better feeling than most rooms in the Library.

Eighth Floor—Center of Criminology Library

This small library, adjacent to the Center itself, uses the same dark red mahogany table with greenish brown tops, but the rest of the interior of this room is attractive. It has a saffron carpet, an orange formica service desk with a medium brown top, and orange fabric upholstered side chairs. An alcove is furnished with red leather slung lounge chairs against red and orange striped drapes. One end wall holds yellowish brown slant-face periodical display stacks, and the wood panels on the stack ranges are stained a medium tone of walnut. The room has an 8½′ ceiling, containing 1′ × 4′ fixtures which supply good quality lighting which enhances the good taste in the colors of the library. Though it lacks the architectural qualities we have seen in some of the library spaces below, it is the best feeling room reviewed so far.

Eighth Floor—Council of Ontario Universities

This area, rented to an organization not part of the University, is a painful reminder of how unsuccessful the library interior design is on the whole. It was designed by a local business interiors firm, and although it is not great interior design it is distinctly good interior design in all of its elements and is especially good in its color combinations. Good taste may have nearly fled from the world, but when it is encountered, like everything of high quality these days, it looms like Mont Saint Michel.

This room has a tan tweed carpeting, and attractive beige vinyl interior walls. It uses office landscaping panels of good proportions covered with extremely attractive fabrics of royal blue and burnt orange and a light wood edging, which brighten areas of the floor remote from exterior walls as nothing in any of the Library areas does. The use of low dividers combined with landscaping panels defines small areas for single desks and larger areas for multiple desks. A totally interior workroom for Xerox copying, mailing and sorting is made very attractive by the use of a light beige fabric on the walls. This area rises in the quality of its feeling far above the rest of the Library.

Floors Nine through Thirteen

These stack floors are quite simple and almost identical in their floor layout (see page 196). In the center of the floor is an open area between three cores at its points, which contain, in one core, the rest rooms, in another, the staff workroom, two staff elevators and two vertical conveyers, and in the third the public elevators. Beyond a walkway outside the bookstacks are the locked carrels on the peripheral walls. Since carrels occupy the entire perimeter, the stack floors are entirely internal spaces except for the points of the triangle, which contain the reading areas for the subject departments, terminating in window walls. General seating is in the center of the floor, at its three points, and in reading areas that occupy two open bays at each of the three corners of the bookstacks. Each floor can house 500,000 volumes, with shelves two-thirds full, and seat 430 students. The center of the 9th floor contains two seminar rooms designed to accommodate 30 to 40 students each. On the 10th and 12th floors, the center core area is opened up by an atrium that accommodates an ornamental stairway connecting the 10th and 11th and the 12th and 13th floors. Otherwise, passage from one stack floor to another is by the six fire towers on the periphery of the building, by internal stairs adjacent to the staff elevators, or by public elevators in the core.

The Bookstacks

Three enormous banks of bookstack ranges, one on each side of the building, occupy the outer edge of free floor space on each floor. They are formed of ranges of free-standing cantilevered stacks 15 sections long, run at 60° angles to the outer wall. The stacks in each row are brightly and distinctively colored. The same color is used on the same side of the triangle on each floor: bright blue, bright yellow, and chinese red. On the wall opposite each stack row, a 3½′ dropped ceiling fascia above the locked carrels, the carrel doors, and the walls and equipment of the reading rooms in each point is of the same color as its corresponding row of bookstacks. These colors are extremely helpful in orienting the user to where he is located in these huge, totally internal spaces. At each public elevator landing, a large floor plan $3\frac{1}{2}' \times 4'$ displays the call number layout of the floor, and on the concrete slabs between elevators a detailed guide to all call numbers in the library gives the location of books by floor, range number and color of the section it is in.

The stacks are lit by stem-hung troffers of $1' \times 4'$ single-tube fixtures with a prismatic diffusing lens on the aisle centers, which give 25 footcandles of good quality illumination on the lowest shelf.[16] The stack areas and walkways are floored with light beige tile, which increases the illumination in these huge areas.

Stack Reading Areas

A mixture of freestanding carrels and reader tables occupies the reading areas on each floor, with a number of lounge chairs in the center core reading area. The feeling of these floors is heavily dominated by the colors of the stacks, and the high $12\frac{1}{2}'$ coffered ceilings exposed above most of the floor. Reading areas are lit by $1' \times 4'$ fixtures with a diffusing lens set in an offset grid similar to that of the main area on the Second Floor. Lighting is 65 footcandles of good quality lighting.

The three subject-oriented reading areas at the apexes of the triangle on each floor are semi-enclosed by bookstack panels at their entrance. The outer side is composed of book lockers. On the opposite side are bookshelves, which contain reference books in some of the subject areas. The area includes two smoking/conversation rooms, which are enclosed, four tables for four, and six lounge seats in the point formed by the joining of two outer walls of the triangle. These walls terminate in two glass window panels $8\frac{1}{2}'$ high by $6\frac{1}{2}'$ wide that meet at a 60° angle, providing fine views out over the city at all points of the building. These subject-oriented reading areas and the reading areas between them and the bookstacks are floored in the black tile with a dark brown drift used elsewhere in the building.

Locked Carrels

The very large number of locked carrels required in the building led to a simple but brilliant architectural solution to this problem, which defeated all other architects who were considered for this building. On floors 9, 11 and 13 the carrels are at the periphery on the level of the floor, but on floors 10, 12, and 14, they open off of corridors carried by balconies located at half-levels up and down from the library floor level (see page 190). This ingenious solution provides nine levels of locked carrels that open off six library floors. Access to the balconies is at two points on each side of the building directly opposite the entrance to the fire tower stairs.

Each carrel is $6\frac{1}{2}'$ deep by $4'$ wide, with a built-in desk top $2'$ wide, set at an angle to the exterior wall, covered with the same greenish-brown formica used on reading surfaces throughout the building. Each includes an attractive Knoll arm chair upholstered in dark blue fabric. The black-tile floors of the outer walkways of each of these stack floors is brought into the carrels, even when they open off of the balconies, and although they are lightened by off-white walls and by a $1' \times 4'$ two-tube fixture with a good prismatic diffusing lens above the desk, which provides good illumination, the persistent use of dark colors in small areas that cry out for lightening invades these research carrels. Each carrel has a 10″ wide slit window 53″ high in its exterior wall (protected by a louver-drape), with a somewhat smaller window in the door. Each carrel is equipped with a bookcase $2'$ wide, containing four shelves and two lateral filing-case drawers.

The Paging/Delivery System

Call slips are sent to stack floors by pneumatic tubes, of which only one of three is presently in use. When a slip is sent up the stack attendants get a beep signal on a radio receiver in their pocket, but they say they can hear the tube land from most parts of the floor. A horizontal book conveyor operates on all the stack floors. It is hung from the ceiling to run above the second stack section out from the center core on all three sides of the floor (see page 188). Trays from the horizontal system are automatically picked up by the vertical book conveyor in the staff work area on each floor and delivered to the system terminal at the Circulation Desk on the Fourth Floor.[17] The conveyor trays hold books up to 10″ × 15″ in size; larger books must be taken to the Circulation Desk by hand.

Since the horizontal conveyor is rather slow, and there is occasionally trouble with trays getting hung up at the angles in the horizontal system, pages take books directly to the vertical conveyor in the staff workroom when they have time to do so. The stack attendants complained about the noise that occurs when book trays are inserted into the horizontal system, but I heard no such complaint from any of the users I consulted, and there is no discernible noise in the overhead movement of the conveyor.

Fourteenth Floor

The Fourteenth Floor is completely occupied by faculty department offices and a cafeteria to serve them, in the center of the floor, with locked carrels at the periphery. This floor is reached by express elevator from the Second Floor that stops only at the Eighth Floor on the way up, to service the public areas there.

The Thomas Fisher Rare Book Library

This building is in the foreground of the photograph of the library façade on page 179. It contains the rare books library on six floors (plus two underground floors) below the cantilevered overhang, and the archives in the two stories mounted above the rare books library. The pylon on the street side of the building was originally planned to contain a carillon, then was cut back to contain a clock, but in the final budgetary squeeze it was stripped of anything functional and remains as a decorative element.

Entrance to this building is from the Second Floor plaza, through its main entrance opposite the Robarts Library's southeast entrance, or through a lobby off the southeast angle of the Fourth Floor Reference Room connected by elevator to the lobby of the Fisher Library.

This library consists mainly of a great, lofty rare book gallery that competes with the grandeur and responds to some of the qualities of the central glass rare book vault in the Beinecke Library at Yale (see page 189). It is conceived, somewhat more conventionally than the Beinecke's display piece, as the architects' reflection of the English feeling of the city of Toronto and its life style. Whereas the Beinecke vault is viewed across open space as books enclosed behind glass, the Fisher book gallery is the reverse, with visitors looking across space through a central glass enclosure to book-lined walls. The scholar seems to be reading in a grand version of the Bodleian book-lined scholarly study. The vast loft space provided by this concept allowed the architects to place columns inside of the space without diminishing its feeling, so the two floors of the Archives are mounted on top of this building.

Just inside the main entrance, an elegant name plaque appears at the right, carved into black slate in Eric Gill letters. Immediately ahead is a receptionist at a desk in cast terrazzo who controls access to the building through a turnstile. Just outside the turnstile a coatroom opens off of the entrance area. An elevator opens off one side of the foyer beyond the control point. Straight ahead visitors enter the observation island, a glass-enclosed hexagon 35' wide that spans the center of the building from gallery to gallery. From here the view drops 14' to the reading rooms below on either side, with scholars' desks and exhibition cases partly visible on the floor below.

Upward the view reveals one of the great architectural spaces on this continent, one that presents almost unbroken the immense volume of this building (see page 189). The gallery book room is an elongated hexagon 45' wide by 120' long (try pacing that out), with a 60' high ornamental ceiling. Book shelves line all sides of the room within 5' wide galleries that run entirely around the room at five levels.[18] They are lit by incandescent lights, shielded from the visitor, that hang from the edge of the gallery above. The galleries are edged by railings, from which hang grey-tinted glass protective panels held in place by simple ornamental frames which leave the view of the book-lined walls almost completely unobstructed.

The galleries are supported on their outer edge by fourteen enormous hexagonal columns, 2' through from tip to base, that extend unbroken from the reading floors below to the ornamental ceiling 50' above the observation point. Each column is brilliantly lit by two enormous 3' high downlights (light-washing up and down) mounted on its two inward faces at a height of 12' above the observation island. In the center of each great open space on either side of the observation island a monumental lighting fixture drops 20' from the ceiling. These hexagonal fixtures, 20' from top to bottom and 3' from point to point, each hold 72 clear glass incandescent globes 5" in diameter, behind ornamental glass facings composed of grey-tinted glass, banded by six clear glass horizontal stripes. These highly ornamental and strikingly handsome fixtures supply precisely the right feeling in the right form to balance in the open spaces the impression of the book-lined walls of this great room.

After recovering from the grandeur of the gallery room, which immediately commands attention, we are aware of the exhibition areas that flank the observation island on four of its glass walls. These are formed of shelves 3' deep by 12' long cantilevered upward from the mullions of the glass enclosure at a height of 32" from the floor. The shelves, covered with black velvet, are loaded from the gallery walkway on the staff side of the glass, and are well lit by adjustable incandescent spotlights hung on a trellis 7½' high at the top of the mullion frames. They are easy to load, easy to view, but in all, they supply too little exhibition area for a rare books library of this size and importance. A major exhibition cannot be mounted in this building.

One floor below the entrance is the Reference Lobby, a hexagonal room which contains service desks for reference and paging and the card catalog. Off this room, doors at either side lead into the two reading rooms. These contain large 4' × 5' desks, some with slanting tops to hold large books and maps. There are two built-in exhibition cases in corners, which are very little used. Each reading room has seats for 25 users, and is pleasantly commodious in its space, in addition to the feeling of awareness of the great loft space of the book galleries above. The rare book areas are carpeted throughout with pleasant orange and burgundy carpeting.

From this central room there is access to a microfilm storage and reading room, a map storage and reading room, and six enclosed studies for long-term scholars using materials in this library. From this room, materials are paged from the gallery floors, reached by elevator, and the distance of retrieval for most of the items is very great, one of the costs of creating the great gallery space.

This room also has access to the library work areas, which are scattered in odd angles of the building as it is developed at the lowest level above ground. With a staff of 24, this makes for separation of functions, and inefficient groupings of staff and movement between them. The functions include a rare book bindery, headed by a fine binder, which contains a remarkable collection of 18th- and 19th-century gold stamping tools, put to practical use daily in the binder's work. Most of the work areas have pleasant window views to the outside.

The book stacks are in space below entirely within the perimeter of this building and that portion of the Robarts Library connected to it. With 7½' stacks with canopies, 9½' ceilings, fluorescent lights covered by ultra-violet shields, these are stark, pragmatic economical spaces.

Most of the building is protected for security by an ultra-sonic system wired directly to the university security office. There is no special fire protection except in the areas below ground, where local fire regulations required a sprinkler system.[19] The entire building has its own separate air-conditioning with a refined dust filtration system. However, the books stored on the sub-levels of the Robarts Library, which had already begun to be used for rare books in 1976, participate in the general air conditioning system of the Robarts Library, which is not refined in any way.

Archives

The top two floors of the Fisher Rare Book Library are occupied by the Archives Department. These floors are cantilevered 6' beyond the walls of the rare book areas below. The uppermost floor, dedicated mostly to workrooms, offices, and reading rooms, is opened by floor to ceiling slit windows 10" wide. The floor below, that contains the archive stacks and map room, has only two windows.

The elevator deposits users at the top floor, which contains a reception lobby, an archives reading room, a microform reading room, the Archivist's office, two seminar rooms, a staff lounge, and two stack rooms. They are the least satisfactory areas in the entire library. The Archivist's office is the only office in the Library completely hexagonal in shape, and the waste space in it is perceptible. Of the two seminar rooms, designed for eighteen students each, one is trapezoidal and one a truncated triangle. The shape of both hampers their full use of the space they contain for seminars and they are cramped. One seminar is totally interior, the other relieved by three slit windows. Both are lit by downlights, and the lighting glares with intensity.[20]

The reading room is marked by the same dark feeling of decor as most of the rest of the library. It contains ten 3' × 7' tables, for large boxes and spread space. The stacks were not specifically designed to hold archival loads; they lack web stiffeners and tilt under the load of boxes full of papers. As originally installed, the wall-hung shelving pulled off the wall when it was loaded. These stacks have 10"-wide shelves, which is inadequate for archival boxes. The aisles between stacks are not wide enough for easy passage of trucks loaded with materials wider than usual, which comprise a great part of archival storage.

This area lacks any enclosures for student typing, which must be done out in the open reading room. It lacks a proper receiving room, with room for sorting, and it is dependent on the elevators which service the entire building (for both rare book and archival uses) to transport materials from the floor below the top floor, where the bulk of materials is stored, to the reading room above. The archivist registered the eternal complaint of his trade that there was not enough unbroken space with facilities for massive sorting.

Summary of the Library Complex

Any attempt at a general summary of a building this large must oversimplify; yet specific things can be said about a range of the building's properties that will lead to some general conclusions. Speaking exclusively in terms of the functional and esthetic qualities of the spaces, as a working library the Robarts Library and its satellites have three very good *Service Areas,* and they are in the right place—on the entrance floor:

Information Desk
Coat Checkroom
Cafeteria

Of the *Work Areas,* three are clearly unsuccessful:

Government Documents
Library Automation
Archives

However, there are a number of good ones. Working our way upstairs:

Bindery
Administration Offices
Reader Services Offices
The entire Circulation area (an extraordinarily rare accomplishment)
Reference Lounge

The Technical Service areas are huge and unbroken and provided with extensive window areas on their periphery. Yet they are largely untested, since their occupancy is still too light to require many partitions. They are easily convertible, but it is already clear, in the Library Automation area, that any partitions used will have to remain open at the top to avoid blocking the ventilation flow.

Of the *Reader Areas,* the good ones are:

Map Library
Microform Area
Reference/Current Periodicals Area
East Asian Library
Center for Criminology Library

Many of the reader areas are depressed by the feeling of the interior design, which often blankets or obliterates the excellence of the architectural spaces. The glorious exception to this condition is the gallery book room in the Fisher Rare Book Library.

The *Stack Floors,* although much plainer in appearance than the rest of the reader areas, are highly successful and quite economical. In a research library these are critically important spaces. Their layout is simple and repeated from floor to floor, their reader areas are all good, their lighting is reasonably good, and the architects' highly imaginative solution to the demand for a huge number of locked carrels is turned to decorative effect on the façade.

The *Mechanical Systems* include a lighting system of reasonably good quality at 55 to 60 footcandles (which is economical) everywhere except in the few areas equipped with downlights. The ventilation system is adequate; there were a few complaints of stuffiness and unevenness in temperature in certain areas. Vertical traffic movement is good throughout the building. The book delivery system and circulation communication system are good.

The *Architectural Spaces* that have achieved great success esthetically are all monumental:

The Façade
The Approach to the Entrances

Lobby

N. Reading Rooms spanning Floors 2–4 (though these are marred by the interior design)

The Fisher Rare Book Library Gallery Book Room

The size and complexity of this library emerged directly from the program to which this building had to respond. There are at present some reactions against this monumentality, yet they are of our time and probably will be short-lived.

Architecture is already moving into more ornamental and monumental styles in reaction to the starkness of the international style, which has long ago gone sterile. As constricting economies lead us to build on a smaller scale and skimpier, the Robarts Library will loom as an outstanding example of a high style we have lost. Taken all in all it is a good library building. If its present interior design could be scoured and re-designed on a highly successful level, it would be an excellent library building.[21]

Notes

1. That was on October 12th, kiddies, as it always was before we sold our heritage for a mess of three-day vacations, poor exchange for a nation that needs a great deal more heritage and much less vacation.

2. The designation of Warner, Burns, Toan, Lunde as "Design Consultants" in the documents is very misleading. They were *the* architects for the building during the entire design phase, through very complete design development drawings almost to the stage of pre-working drawings. After this time the working drawings and final bid documents were developed by the good Toronto architects Mathers and Haldenby. WBTL recalls that the Toronto architects were very careful to preserve the original design of the building, and that, indeed, the importance of design in Toronto (as seen in a series of fine buildings, including the city hall, the art museum and the public library) reflected a higher design level in Canada than in the United States. Even more to be wondered at, the workers on the building and suppliers of castings had greater respect for design, and the acceptance of the importance of design by the university administration was unusually high.

3. This is probably the most honored library building in the country. WBTL learned a number of things in its design that were carried over to the Robarts Library:
—Divider walls in the Administration area that incorporate bookshelves above a recessed telephone shelf above filing drawers.
—A sunken moat that allows all rooms on the lowest reader-use floor to have floor to ceiling windows.
—Walk-in exhibition cases on the Second Floor, whose counterpart is in the Hofstra rare books room.
—Microform reading tables, fathered by John MacDonald at Washington University, St. Louis, and translated via Hofstra, that measure 2′ × 4′, with a fixed center panel and two pull-out side panels for note taking.
—Rheostatically adjustable fluorescent lighting in the microform reading room.
—Decorative cobblestones *set in mortar* around the wheelchair ramp north of the Building. At Hofstra they were filled in loosely around the lower level window walls, providing urchins with convenient missiles to hurl through the windows. We had to cement them down.

4. This obviously necessary step was inadequate. No one on the University of Toronto Library staff had adequate knowledge of library building planning, and in a building like this one which was remarkably ambitious, pioneering in the range of functions it proposed to integrate, and on a scale of size never before attempted in an academic library, the refusal to hire a corps of highly experienced library building consultants was nothing short of ostentatious folly. Many of its flaws could have been removed at first reading.

5. The triangle was a common cliche which did very poorly for school libraries in the 1960s. The worst triangular library I have seen is at the former Pennsylvania Military Academy, presently Widener College, in Chester, Pennsylvania.

6. The Robarts Library is one of the few energy-conserving recent buildings in this city on Lake Ontario, which has very rigorous winters, like its neighbor, Buffalo, N.Y. Toronto rivals our own Chicago in pretending that glass-wall buildings are appropriate for such a climate. In addition to its prudent use of glass the Robarts Library has double exterior walls connected by a thermal break, an arrangement that prevents outside temperatures from penetrating directly except through insulators. In a building that began construction in 1968, this was extremely farsighted.

7. Most of the information immediately following came from a luncheon query of Danforth Toan, architect extraordinary, in 1977. Toan is a remarkably articulate man with a clarity of mind that communicates immediately to an academician. As I listened to him talk effortlessly and with total clarity about the bases of planning of this library, which he had completed ten years previously, I recognized in his deep understanding of what the Robarts Library was trying to accomplish a basic reason why his firm is one of only three that I trust without reservation to design library buildings (subject to informed review, of course, which any architect thrives on). It was no fault of the architect that the basic premises on which the Robarts Library was launched were changed before it completed construction.

8. How badly they needed a new library is well known to anyone who was in the old building. Robert Blackburn, its Chief Librarian, told me in 1970 that at one time, while the building was torn up for alterations to make it a little more liveable, there were seats for only eight students in the entire library.

9. When bids for construction came in over budget, the Canadian architects had perforce to eliminate two of the stairways and drastically cut the size of the others, making the building far less approachable.

10. This interior, through lack of central control by someone with superlative taste and knowledge of a wide range of alternatives, demonstrates better than any building I know what a fine interior designer actually does, in relating all of the visual aspects of the interior, to achieve excellence. This design often falls between two or three stools, which is regrettable because Warner, Burns, Toan, Lunde had a very fine interior design department which I worked with on the Hofstra Library interiors.

Although the decision not to use them for interior design was primarily an economic decision, this firm felt increasingly, toward the end of their work with the University, the rise in Canadian nationalism that turned against British and American participation in their educational build-up that began in 1959. In 1968, while conducting a workshop on consulting for the Canadian Association of College and University Libraries at Jasper, I pointed out to the Canadian librarians that although they were not yet as confused as we were, I thought that they had enough talent and resources to become so. By now they have joined the club in earnest, as witness the recent solicitation for head librarian of a university in Alberta, restricted by their regulations to Canadian citizens and "landed immigrants."

11. A large auditorium, designed to open off of the second level in the same way on the third side of the triangle, to make all three sides of the building symmetrical, had to be eliminated when bids came in drastically over budget.

12. As originally bid, the entire flooring on this level and the facings on all of the service desks were of polished granite. The cost overrun on the bids cut this material back to terrazzo.

13. As is true of many buildings these days, numbers of the lighting fixtures in the Robarts Library have been disconnected to save energy. This fact was aggravated by the change in the color of tubes in many lighting fixtures from warm white fluorescent (yellow tone) to cool white (blue tone). Both changes greatly impaired in this building, as in many others, the esthetics of the pattern originally planned in the lighting layout.

14. The Coatroom holds 3,360 coats on oval, mechanized hanger tracks, similar to those in large dry-cleaning shops, 424 hats on racks, and storage racks for luggage. In the winter both sides of the coatroom are staffed.

15. The Information Desk is the nerve center for a range of important activities in the library. It is the telephone answering service for outside information calls, the only library telephone number listed in the Toronto directory. It contains a two-way elevator emergency intercom system, the emergency power control to bring elevators down to the main (Second) floor in case of power failure, and the control panels for snow melting units on the outside patios, stairs, and ramps.

The staff member on duty at this desk felt that this main floor was cold and lacked color, that it should develop a lounge area, using colored fabrics, at the west end of the floor. She added that many people, including professors, say that the library is "scary."

16. I repeat my assertion, see page 37, that lighting fixtures hung above the aisle between stack ranges are far more efficient than those hung at right angles, although they do not allow the same flexibility in adjusting range centers. These stacks are on 4½' centers, and if they were to be moved to 4' centers, which is happening many places these days, the overhead fixtures would all have to be relocated.

17. The conveyor system can also deliver books to the conveyor terminal at the circulation desk on the First Floor, but that part of the system is very lightly used.

18. Access to the books in the galleries, is, of course, restricted to staff. They are reached by an elevator which can be brought to the gallery levels only by special keys. The elevator has public access to the paging room below and the archives above the control lobby.

19. This worst of all possible conditions under the law should be avoided at any cost whenever it is possible to do so. Given a water pipe, sooner or later it will burst, although it cannot be predicted when it will burst. In a building as huge and complex as the Robarts Library and its satellites, there are endless possibilities for vandalism, as was seen in this very library during a strike of the staff union two years ago. If forced to use sprinklers, a drypipe system should be used (as is done in the Fisher Library) that does not have water fed under pressure to the sprinkler heads until it is called for by one of the heads.

20. The worst headache I ever had was caused by downlights in just this size meeting room, where the table placed me at such an angle to the downlights that the glare was driven straight through my brain.

21. Statistics for the Robarts Library:

> Gross area—1,036,000 square feet.
> Seating capacity (library areas)—3,700.
> Book capacity (ultimate)—5,235,700 volumes.
> Building cost—$34,500,000 ($33.30 per square foot in Canadian dollars).
> Project cost—$41,700,000 ($40.25 per square foot in Canadian dollars).

The following publications on this building are worth reading:

University of Toronto, *John P. Robarts Research Library.* Toronto, U. of Toronto Press, 1974. (A 16-page detailed and illustrated handbook.)

"New Humanities Library for the University of Toronto," *Architectural Record,* June 1975, pp. 92–95.

I have made no attempt to evaluate the 102,000 square feet of this building dedicated to the Library School (an integral part of this building and the first to be completed) because I am not competent to do so.

CHAPTER 11

THE SEDGEWICK UNDERGRADUATE LIBRARY AT THE
UNIVERSITY OF BRITISH COLUMBIA

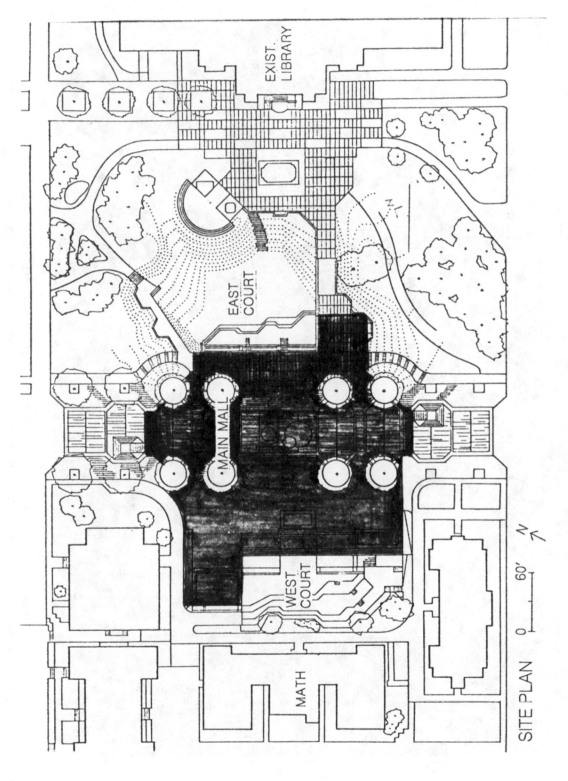

SITE PLAN 0 60'

The extent of the underground floor areas of the Sedgewick Library.
Note the traffic shaft of the Mall and the eight round drums, each containing an oak tree, that penetrate the building.

The main entrance façade of the building showing the Upper Floor (one level below the Mall),
the Lower Floor, the oak trees in the drums, the truncated skylight cone penetrating to the Upper Floor, and the East court.

A view of the library from the main entrance level. Note the planters on the building's overhang.

A view of the truncated skylight cones from the Mall.

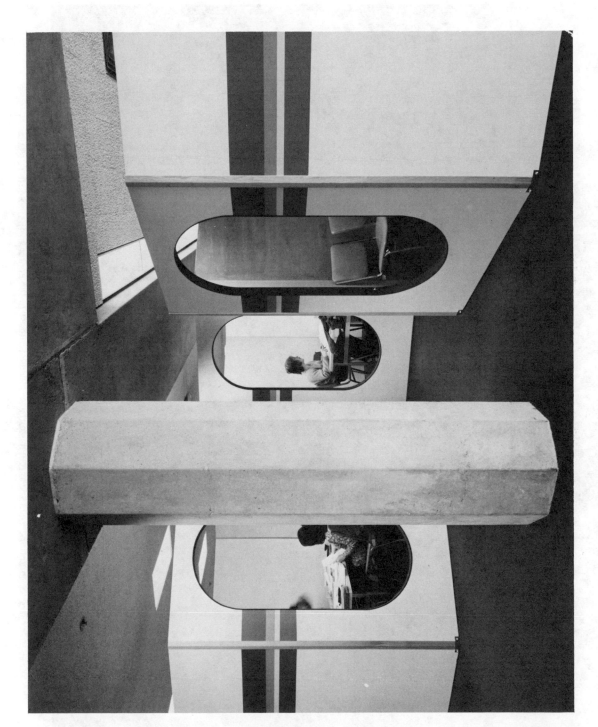

Demountable octagonal group studies. Note the open doors and tops.

The open and the enclosed circular staircases, located almost in the center of the bookstack ranges.

A portion of the supergraphic on the Lower Floor.

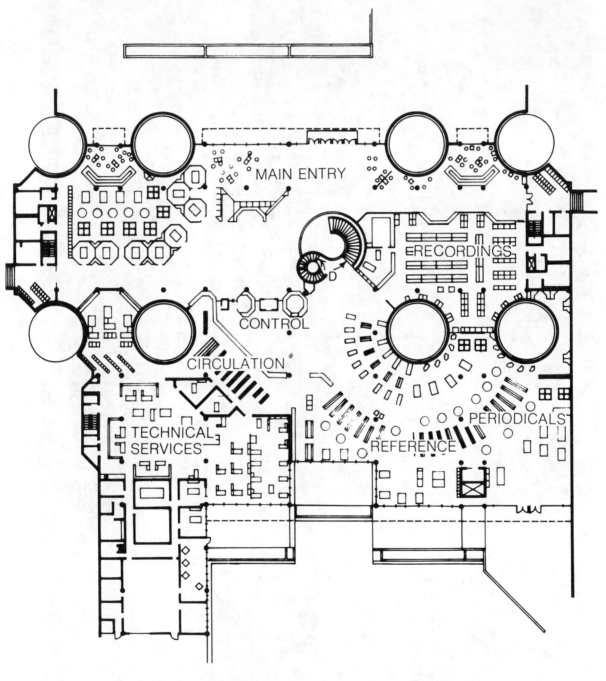

UPPER FLOOR PLAN

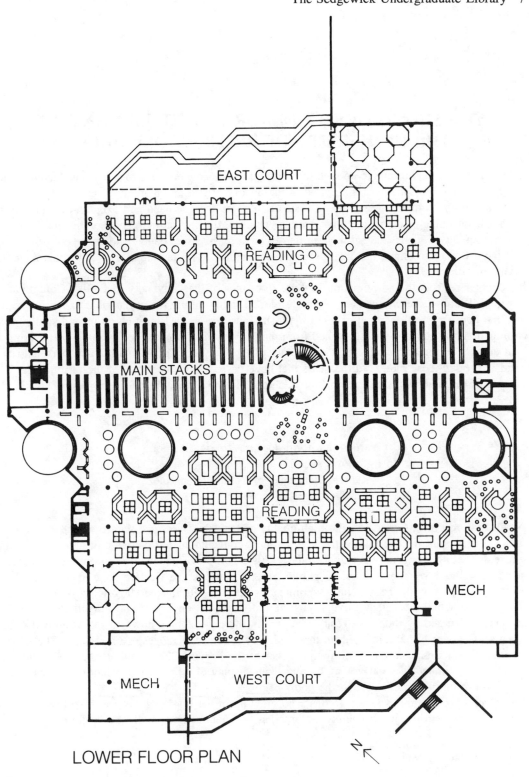

EAST COURT

READING

MAIN STACKS

READING

MECH

MECH

WEST COURT

LOWER FLOOR PLAN

THE SEDGEWICK UNDERGRADUATE LIBRARY AT
THE UNIVERSITY OF BRITISH COLUMBIA*

(From 1967 to 1973 I was fortunate enough to be called to Vancouver four times to visit, lecture, study library processes, and consult, during a period in the history of that city marked by prosperity and growth. I was much taken by its international flavor, Asia-oriented on the one hand and London-oriented on the other, with a wide range of compact ethnic groups visible in the city on the streets and in its shops and restaurants.[1] Vancouver's physical setting can hardly be surpassed for beauty, and its urban growth, as is true of all large Canadian cities, has incorporated architectural styles far superior to those that have marked most American cities.

This chapter reflects the participation in these dynamics of the University of British Columbia, the crown on the hill above the city center, which developed richly during the remarkable expansion of higher education that occurred in Canada after 1959. I finished the writing in Birmingham in mid-summer 1973 on a scrounged typewriter and time snatched from tending our five-year old son who was recovering from open-heart surgery at the remarkable Medical Center of the University of Alabama. This personal trauma I believe did not touch these pages. In the years that have passed, my conviction of the rarity of the achievements of the Sedgewick Library has not changed. In many ways it still is the best of its kind.)

*   *   *   *

"I learned that form does not follow function;
form follows site."
—Richard Henriquez of Todd & Henriquez,
Urban Designers, Vancouver.

You can tell that you're in Canada by the high quality of taxicab drivers and waitresses; that you are in Vancouver, at this point in time one of the world's most congenial and attractive cities, makes the change all the more appealing.[2] Legend has it that in the 1920s a group of students walked out from their cramped urban site and staked a squatter's claim on public land to a knoll at the western edge of the city which was subsequently validated by the Provincial government as the new site for the University of British Columbia. Whatever the actual facts, that university is presently laid out on a thousand magnificent acres of "endowment land," fringed by the finest residential area in the city, sloping down to the Strait of Georgia on the west, with the near horizon marked on three sides by spectacular ranges of mountains. The view across the bay to the mountains from the balcony at the rear of the Faculty Club is one of the most remarkable views imaginable, enhanced in early May by a brilliant display of tulips in the balcony planters, and the meticulous grooming of gardens around the pools below.[3]

The university is impressive even to one who grew up in the Ivy League when it still was solid ivy, and as we walk eastward from the Faculty Club across the main campus mall, the visual quality continues

---

*Footnotes to this chapter begin on p. 244.

in the landscaping and plantings, in the arrangement and architecture of the buildings (most of them recent), and in the attractiveness and intelligence of the directional signs, which are unusually good on this campus.

The Introduction

Straight ahead beneath a mall seventy-feet wide and flanked by huge oak trees, lies Sedgewick Library, marked only by two truncated cones that rise from the mall to a height of about ten feet. The truncated slices form skylights that provide views into the library. Before reaching the cones, a stairway at either end invites you down to a commodious main entry area of the building. Outside of the library control point, running from south to north there is an informal seating area, a snack area with lounge seating, and open formal seating at small tables and carrels surrounded by the attractive octagonal group studies designed by the architects that form a distinctive feature of the furniture of this library.[4]

One level below the mall, the main entrance to Sedgewick (four double doors set in a long glass wall which faces the Main Library) provides a fine view over the terraced open-court garden between the two buildings. Early in the exploration of Sedgewick a pleasant feeling is aroused by the substitute for the chair-rail or visual-graphic barrier generally used to prevent people from walking through glass walls. Here and throughout the building we have instead a continuous line of quotations from Shakespeare, all of which contain allusions to glass or the word "glass" in handsome black lower-case letters two inches high, which reinforce intellectually the visual impression of the octagonal group studies. Here is a building, they seem to say at the very entrance, created by thought and taste to expand the capacities of the young.

The Site

An unusual combination of sensitivity and intelligence marked all aspects of the planning of Sedgewick Library, which posed from the beginning a seemingly insoluble site problem—the addition of a large undergraduate library building in a very limited area just west of the existing Main Library, where studies indicated the center of student travel was located. Almost certainly it would crowd the existing buildings around it and probably would have to encroach on the Main Mall of the campus, a wide walkway flanked by forty-year-old northern red oaks which frame a vista that traverses the entire campus. Rhone & Iredale, the Vancouver architects assigned the task of designing a two-story building without destroying the traditional feeling of the Mall and surrounding areas, detected in the course of their studies what escaped easy notice through distance—that the elevation of the Mall was twelve feet higher than the entrance to the Main Library.

They concluded that excavating additional depth lower than the Main Library would allow them to build directly below the Mall an underground structure not unduly submerged. By exposing both the east and west sides of the library, the only underground library to date that has done so, they changed the entire range of considerations that governed the building and allowed themselves a great deal more freedom in shaping it than would have been possible in a building above ground, where exterior esthetics would have limited the form (see p. 227).[5] It gave them the freedom of shaping it into irregular nooks and compartments for varied study areas, and of providing angles on the lower floor from which the building looks back on itself (a very pleasant feeling). It emphasized the importance of views looking out from the building, which is completely surrounded by sunken courts on its open sides, and invited glass walls that enjoy unusual freedom from sun because of the excavation. The north and south ends, of poured concrete entirely below grade, became logical places for the core units—peripheral stairs, rest rooms, utility closets, elevators, mechanical areas—and for noise producers such as typing rooms, completely removing them from intrusion on the rest of the building.

There remained the considerable problem of the trees, which were finally encased in brickwork that penetrates both floors of the library as a strong design element interrupting in most pleasing fashion the very large areas, more than 50,000 square feet, on each floor. One wonders how these spaces could have been divided without some such monumental interior design feature, here given to hand by the solution of the site problem. The simplicity and ingenuity of the architects' use of the underground concept is remarkable, as the floor layouts show (see pp. 234–235).

The remaining problem of the esthetics of the exterior sides that faced the courts, a problem inherent in the use of glass walls (which, on balance, the next century will probably consider the Curse of Mies), was solved by using overhangs containing planters that produce varied and interesting facades very much in keeping with the landscaped gardening of the terraced courts and the well-groomed feeling of the UBC campus, as the photograph shows, p. 229.

Traffic Flow

Within, the traffic flow and functional layout of the library match the general concept of the building in their high degree of success, as is seen in the main floor plans (see p. 234). Head on from the main entrance the tapering walls of the large truncated skylight cone come down through the ceiling. They are covered with the green carpeting used on floors throughout the building. Slotted windows in their sides afford a view of the lower level from the main floor. To the left is the building directory. To the right a wide natural walkway into the building leads, on the oblique, past a sixteen-foot-long communication wall made of handsomely textured, vari-brown-colored resawn cedar which is used throughout the building for interior separation panels. It contains a suggestion box, a wide shelf for writing, and above the shelf on P-slips clipped to the wall typed responses to each question, over a hundred of which were posted when I was there. They make instructive reading about the building and how it works, and about the preferences of undergraduates in library facilities. Nearby is a blackboard for students to use for messages, and briefcase storage units.

This communication wall points the student toward another wall, along the entrance allée from the northwest mall stairway, that contains book return drops, right beside six turnstile entrance and inspection points, which define the working areas of the library. Rolling grills are lowered from overhead to close off each exit and entrance for flexibility of control.[6] When all are lowered the library is closed to access; the elements in the main entry area then serve as an after-hours study area complete with snacks, smoking areas, rest rooms, coathanging units, study units and book return slots, with three different outside entrances. That the area outside the working library has been arranged without clutter, and that the main entrance also provides a pleasant, visually interesting, and clear avenue leading into the library demonstrate a high degree of architectural skill.

Inside the turnstiles we encounter the oblique angle of the circulation desk, which points us to the Reference Desk, directly in front of the small reference collection, and opposite the card catalog. Having located our call number, the next logical movement is through six doors at the end of the catalog, to the staircase, and down to the numbered books. If our need is for periodicals, they are just beside the reference collection. Sound recordings are located together with machines in the Recordings Collection that opens off the main floor beside the doors into the stairwell. From the entrance to the library, we are led past a series of specialized library facilities and directly along a traffic artery that is clearly marked, indeed, almost dictated, by the arrangement of partitions and furniture. Few library layouts are so self-explanatory.[7]

Adjacent to the Recordings Collection a lightwell, extending from skylight to lower floor, draws us down to the lower level by a large open spiral staircase or a smaller spiral staircase enclosed in a concrete turret.[8] A slot in the wall of the turret conceals slide and film projectors which occasionally project images high enough on the upper wall of the lightwell to be visible from outside the building. These projectors provide a prime facility to project images that produce a quick, pleasant feeling about the building on the way down to the working floor; but, to date, they seem to have been used for delivery of information that really requires seating and concentration to absorb.

Compartmentalization

The foot of the stairs lies between the avenue of bookstacks that runs between the great circular tree drums.[9] Head on, the center aisle that penetrates the north stacks leads users through stacks to seating. Beyond the stacks to the east and west extend seating areas, which provide a very successful solution to the problem of compartmentalizing large quantities of seating into humanly congenial areas, as is seen in the lower level floor plan (see p. 235). No seating group contains more than forty seats in one visual expanse. To the east and west of the stairs seating areas on platforms raised 15″ and surrounded by 6′-high resawn cedar panels provide bench seating on their inside and outside faces. These panels are penetrated on all four sides to provide easy access. Similar but lower bench panels are used throughout the floor to interrupt and define this very large area of more than 50,000 square feet.

In the north and south corners of this level, raised floors are carved into circles, banks and steps covered with carpeting for sprawl seating. These interesting islands, together with the three-foot-square hassock used throughout the building, provide materials for students to build the ingeniously tortured positions favored as comfortable by many contemporary students.[10] In the east and west corners of this floor, the octagonal study is used in clusters of six within enclosed or semi-enclosed rooms, one of which doubles as a library orientation room. Everywhere, an intelligent mixture of single or cluster carrels and tables provides a variety of writing spaces and good esthetic balance, completely avoiding the institutional feeling generally produced by heavily furnished libraries.

Visual Activity

While the feeling of the upper floor is light and airy, dominated by open traffic areas, with window walls inviting views down to the garden courts, this larger, heavily furnished floor finds its greatest interest in a range of visual activity. Beginning with the spiral staircase in the center, our first impression is dominated by the stacks, whose yellow endpanels play against the bone white tone of the shelving, the green carpeting, and white painted coffers overhead. One orange book-return shelf in the outer section of each stack range forms a pleasant pattern as the eye flows down the aisle between ranges.

At the perimeter, the glass walls look out to the east and west garden courts. Seen from this level, the west court, with its five terraced levels of retaining wall built of rough cedar, becomes five sharply stepped levels of flower and shrub planters above a court planted with moss. The east court slopes more gently in a garden-punctuated lawn flowing up to brilliant plantings and to a clock tower at the entrance level to the Main Library.

The other walls on this level, far more extensive than on the main floor, are painted white and enlivened by the purple-orange-yellow-green band of the supergraphic used on all solid walls in the library. It occasionally explodes into a fine burst of romanticism for emphasis, as shown in the photograph on page 233.[11]

The Tree Drums

The thirty-two-foot diameter tree drums make their most striking contribution on this level, covered with a light-brown brick with a slightly red tint and a beige pepper texture. The meticulous mortar work between the bricks formalizes the drums into curving walls, as seen from any one spot. The design of spaces related to the drums, and the irregularities of the east and west window walls, with the main floor planters jutting out overhead, are used to full advantage by the architects to create effective, irregular spaces for relaxed and secluded reading, and to produce vistas of great interest from within the library back through the library. This building contains a dozen different kinds of atmospheres distinctly different from each other and varying from the most casual and informed to aloof, quiet and protected reading areas.

Furniture and Carpeting

The heights of chairs in Sedgewick Library follow the recommendations of the Arkansas Agricultural Experiment Station (with adjustment for their local students), in favor of a lower chair than is usually found at writing surfaces.[12] Since this is the only side chair used in public areas, the tables and carrel tops in this library are twenty-seven inches high instead of the conventional twenty-nine or thirty inches.

The library uses $4' \times 6'$ tables for four, $4' \times 9'$ tables for six, and a $5'$-diameter round table with a five-footed center pedestal (which is unusually stable), but their carrel, with rear and side baffles is undersized—$23\text{-}\frac{3}{4}'' \times 31\text{-}\frac{1}{2}''$ on its writing surface, due to budgetary pressures. Since it also lacks a bookshelf, the floor around it must be littered with books and personal belongings at high use periods.[13] All writing surfaces are matte white plastic. Unusual furniture includes an $18'' \times 72''$ table $40''$ high, placed at the outside ends of bookstacks for consultation of books before proceeding to a seat. This excellent idea has not yet received response at Sedgewick where the table is not much used, perhaps because the loosely-packed shelves provide book-browsing niches in the stacks.

The Reference area contains a good double-faced triple-shelf index table, made in units $4\text{-}\frac{1}{2}'$ long and $5'$ wide, that provide $14''$ clearance for index volumes. The special microfilm tables, with two pull-out writing shelves and a reader mounted on a slide, are a failure, in my opinion.[14] A totally good microfilm reading table has yet to be designed.

The carpeting is made of polypropylene, with an anti-static wire woven in, completely without padding of any kind, cemented to the concrete floor. The lack of cushioning should have made the carpet wear out much faster, but the cost was about seven dollars per square yard, and after three years of very heavy use it has proved to be easy to maintain (it has not required cleaning yet), and except at extremely vulnerable points (at turnstiles and stairs) it has shown no signs of wear.

Interior Design

The feeling of the lower level is not dominated by the forms of furniture and equipment but rather by colors and textures—the stern grain of concrete overhead relieved by white painted coffers, the red-tinted brown of the tree drums, the green carpeting matched by the vinyl covering of the hassocks, the orange vinyl covering of bench seats, and looming everywhere the variegated brown tones and rough texture of the resawn cedar panels.

The overall effect of the interior design, which emerges most strongly on the lower level, is not completely successful. The tones of colors fall short of blending sensitively and enhancing each other. The weakest item visually is the carrel. With its baffles of an undistinguished tone of pale green and disappointing proportions it falls pathetically short of meeting the demands made by the other forms, colors and textures. In addition, the use of resawn cedar in such numerous and prominent masses, often rising 6' high, overwhelms and submerges to a considerable extent other elements of the interior design. Its overabundance should have been relieved by varying its surface or color in ways that could have been managed simply.

As great as were Rhone and Iredale's contributions to this building, their interior design, planned by an architect, falls short of maximum performance. In my experience, architects have never demonstrated the refinement of taste and synthesizing esthetic skills necessary to create a totally successful integration of forms, colors, and textures into an outstanding interior design. Architects, as they must, think and feel differently from interior designers, and why they generally refuse the interior designers with whom they collaborate (even those in their own firm) enough freedom of sway to take full advantage of the distinctive sensibilities of these specialists, I am unable to say.[15]

Lighting

The fluorescent lighting, with three different light sources, is of better than reasonably good quality and intensity in most locations throughout the building. The best quality lighting is in the bookstacks, where open tubes are mounted on top of the canopies to provide indirect lighting of superb quality that provides 40 footcandles at the lowest shelves. Troffers of 16″ × 48″ fixtures, hung from the ceiling nearly to the edge of the beams, are contained within coffers formed by the T-beams. The ceilings dropped around the tree drums contain 1′ × 4′ flush-mounted fixtures. Both of these fixtures use a plastic prismatic lens with a good degree of diffusion but both lenses have overbright tube show-through, a source of reflected glare, due to the shallow (3-½″) depth of the containers.[16]

Where the building's huge 2′ × 4′ support beams cross at right angles to the T-beams that hold the light troffers, a six- or seven-foot stretch of ceiling has no lighting fixtures, and the intensity at reading surfaces below drops to 40 footcandles. Everywhere else, the library has intensities of 50 to 75 footcandles, even within the confines of the baffles of the small carrels. In general, the light distribution throughout the building is good and even.

All the fixtures in T-beam coffers have a sheet of colored plastic that comprises the top of the container. Light passing through these sheets reflects the color off the white-painted coffers down to the areas below, in the first substantial use of color in library lighting in my experience. Five different colors are used, alternated in areas of three strips each—yellow, orange, red, green and blue. The sheets can be easily interchanged at will. Although this venture into overhead color was launched by the architects on very simple conceptual grounds, it is a matter of infinite complexity, requiring an outstanding degree of skill in handling colors in a total interior environment. As indicated above, no one involved in this planning had such skill.

The architects first proposed the use of color in lighting to code the areas of the library by their use—reading, book storage, service—or to code sections of the stacks by content. Since this turned out to be far too complex a problem, they settled on a theory that warm colors would invite readers who preferred "active"-feeling areas for study while cool colors would invite those who preferred "quiet"-feeling areas. Unfortunately, they planned the color areas too small to keep them from scattering.

Sitting at a table in a corner of the lower level, within my sight line three shafts of blue merged uneasily into three shafts of yellow which merged into three shafts of green. On my left flank, and feeling brighter because of the angle and the color, were three shafts of yellow, and through the slits above the support beams ahead appeared two shafts of green and some reds. None of the colors blended especially well with the tables, resawn cedar, or concrete textures within sight. The result is scattered and unharmonious.

On the other hand, the area in which I sat was well defined as a visual unit by the support beams, tree drums and wall, and the use of a single lighting color, not juxtaposed with any other, could have lent this area a special feeling for those who prefer a change from the usual feeling produced by fluorescent lighting. Providing a few areas using no more than two different colors could add to the variety of choice already available to readers in Sedgewick. The problem would require the total elimination of contact with other lighting colors, which would make these areas emerge as color islands in the white lighting. This is a simple problem of coordinating the lighting layout with the furniture layout.

The far more complex problem, requiring the highest levels of sensitivity and taste, involves the selection of every color, texture and form in the area below this lighting to be enhanced by the overhead color while still remaining harmonious with each other as they appear under the color tint. This early pioneering effort at UBC suffers from multiplicity of colors and from a nearly total lack of consideration of what the lighting colors would do to the furniture and equipment below. The effect sometimes impairs the achievement of the interior design which, as indicated, rises only to the middle level of success. The use of colored lighting in Sedgewick should be studied to achieve in other libraries higher degrees of success.

Construction

The very simple construction of the building resulted in a cost of $25.41 per square foot, excluding site work, landscaping and fees, in a city where costs are roughly equivalent to those in the suburban areas of New York. The lower floor slab and the end walls are cast in place concrete. The rest of the building is constructed of 2′ precast octagonal concrete columns, which support 2′6″ × 4′ precast concrete beams, which in turn support precast double T-beam floor panels 7′4″ wide. The space between the downstrokes of the Ts, about 4′ wide, provides white-painted coffers about 2′ deep and 40′ long, with 3′ to 3-½′ clear space between Ts. The top of each coffer is lined with white acoustical tile, which, together with the carpeting and the cedar panels, provides extremely good acoustics in the library.

The coffers hold the lighting troffers and the white ducts and diffusers of the air-handling systems. At one large air-return grille on the lower level enough sound is generated to disturb a small seating area. Otherwise, the system is admirably quiet. The plumbing pipes, painted white, are also run in the coffers. No attempt is made to conceal these mechanical elements and their appearance in no way detracts from the feeling of the building. The ceilings measure 10′ to the underbeam of the Ts and 12′ to the coffer, except for around the tree drums and along the end walls, where acoustical tile ceilings drop to about eight and one-half feet high.

This structural system allowed the development of very large clear spans, which use a basic module of 22′ × 44′. Between the tree drums on both floors, where the direction of the spans is at a right angle to the spans elsewhere, the module is 22′ × 52′. The bay containing the central stairwell is 44′ × 52′. The spans allow total flexibility of layout for the bookstacks which at present are on 4′4″ centers. The use of precast floor panels to achieve longer spans and minimize the restrictions of columns is bound to increase in library construction. This library was required by the local fire marshal to use sprinklers throughout.

Achievements

A balanced evaluation of this multi-faceted library would sum up its achievements as follows:

Site—a brilliant solution that turned difficulties completely to the advantage of the building.

Traffic layout—outstanding; surpassed by no other building in my experience.

Compartmentalization—the best in any large-seating library in my experience.

Visual interest—very high.

Architectural elements (stairwell, tree drums, window-walls, garden courts)—extremely good.

Interior design—in the medium range of success.

Lighting—better than reasonably good.

Construction—simple, functional and inexpensive.

To be able to say this much about a single library is a rare opportunity; but in addition, Sedgewick Library is probably the most venturesome library built since World War II, incorporating these unusual elements, some of which are pioneering:

1. Its placement beneath an existing main pedestrian mall, without disrupting the character of the area.
2. The opening up of both sides of an underground library.
3. The enclosure of existing trees in the interior of the library.
4. The variety of library elements located outside of the control point.
5. The communication wall.
6. Unusually wide stacks.
7. Unusually long spans between columns.
8. The heights of furniture.
9. The size of carrels.
10. The stripped, backless carpeting.
11. The four-color supergraphic wall stripe.
12. The Shakespearean line window wall barrier.
13. The use of color in the lighting.

Not everything ventured has achieved maximal success, but most of the results are admirable, and everything will serve as an example to test the potential of what was attempted. If you're short of money, see how stripped carpeting and a small carrel have worked at UBC.

Those of us who have watched the amazingly high professional achievements of Canadian librarians since 1959 have urged them to step forth and teach us what they have learned by thinking originally under very different circumstances. They still defer to the long-held leadership of librarianship in the United States, although I note with interest significant articles by Canadians beginning to emerge in recent years.

It is time to recognize that during the 1960s, while the seemingly endless cornucopia of this country was blowing our brains into fatuousness and hanging Hero Medals on all the hollow men (the most disruptive period in librarianship in my lifetime, despite its material cumulations), the librarians of Canada and Great Britain were quietly laying sound, comprehensive, and long-range bases that have radically increased the potential of their libraries in a short time. The supremacy of U.S. librarianship has staggered, and we now have a great deal to learn from abroad.

Sedgewick Library will remain a supreme exemplar. It has already won the 1970 Award of the Canadian Architecture Yearbook, and the 1973 First Award of the Royal Architectural Institute of Canada, the highest architectural award in Canada in a competition including all kinds of buildings. Additional recognition will swiftly come from abroad, and Sedgewick will be a seminal influence in the design of new library buildings during the coming years.[17]

Notes

1. Among other benefits derived from Vancouver is a set of direct reading scaled rulers that I use with library plans scaled from $1/16'' = 1'$ to $1/2'' = 1'$, manufactured in Australia, which have no counterpart that I have seen elsewhere and are now indispensable to me. Practical artifacts made in the Pacific are difficult to get in this country.

2. This chapter was published as an article entitled "Underneath the Oak Trees; the Sedgewick Undergraduate Library at U.B.C.," in *Journal of Academic Librarianship* for January 1977, pp. 286–292. It is published here slightly revised by permission of that Journal.

This chapter departs from a policy of silence about library buildings with which I have been connected (I refused to evaluate good library buildings at Colorado College and Hofstra University for which I was librarian-planner). Although I was consultant on this building for two days, my contribution was largely advice on the planning process, and very little of the detail can be attributed to me. I therefore feel capable of evaluating it objectively. The distinctly good features of the building are the result of the superlative information bases for planning generated by the UBC librarians, and the talent of the architects.

My travel to Vancouver for a formal study of the Sedgewick Library was supported by Dr. Harold Gores, President of Educational Facilities Laboratories, whose small but extremely stimulating staff has had a larger impact on educational buildings and equipment than any comparable group in the country.

3. One has to visit UBC to realize how low on the hog American academicians really live. Though I frequented the luxurious Williams College Faculty Club from 1948 to '50, the UBC Faculty Club, a private gift to the university, must be the finest in existence in its architecture, size, range of services and especially of its decor. It is appointed in unusually good taste in every aspect of the building.

4. This octagonal study is esthetically the most successful component of the many imaginative devices created by the architects to compartmentalize by office landscaping methods the large number of seats (1,650) used in comparison to the small number of bookstacks (for 193,000 volumes). Its eight sides are connected by bolted braces, and it is movable. One entire room filled with these cubicles on the lower floor is cleared at the proper season to provide open space for orientation. About ten feet separates opposing interior walls, and an oval, open, step-in doorway (similar to a ship's door-hatch) provides entry. One inside wall is a chalk board, and another a tackboard.

These studies are furnished with a $3' \times 6'$ table, which should be able to seat six (one at each end and two at each side), but support stretchers at each end of this table prevent it from being used by more than four, even when such groupings are desired by students (which, in my experience, is often). From the outside, the shape of the oval doorway in the seven-foot-high white-painted walls, striped with the four-color (purple-orange-yellow-green) super-graphic strip used throughout the building, makes them visually striking and pleasant furniture elements (see p. 231).

Their open top, thin walls and open doorway, however, make it impossible for them to contain sound, and they cannot be used for group conversations. The single most important flaw in this building is the total lack of conversationable group study rooms, where intellectual ferment can pour forth without disturbing nearby readers.

5. The University of Illinois Undergraduate Library opened the center of its underground building to bring the feeling of outdoor light into the library, which it does well. Harvard is also using this solution. The effect of opening both sides of this underground library is far superior.

6. Due to a lapse in communications during the planning of the building, these grills, intended to be stored behind an overhead beam, had to be stored at the bottom of the beam. As a result, the grill in storage position allows only 6'6" above the turnstiles, which makes for a close feeling as you pass under it.

7. This is overwhelmingly a public-use building, but it should be said that all its work areas for librarians are conveniently and efficiently arranged, and sized for future expansion. The staff lounge opens onto a very pleasant cedar plank deck overlooking the west garden court.

8. Circular or spiral staircases should be avoided in libraries except where there are clearly overriding reasons for having them, because the width of treads, which vary according to the point on the tread on which you walk, is almost never a dimension that accommodates a normal stairstride. The widths of the treads in these two spirals vary from 11" on the side to 19" on the outside of the tread of the large staircase and 11" to 21" on the small staircase. Eleven inches is just a little too wide for a normal stride and nineteen or twenty-one inches splits the mind between taking giant strides, one per tread, or mincing steps two per tread. This schizophrenic choice varies slightly at other points on the tread. Consequently the use of spiral stairs inflicts a constant, if slight, discomfort on users. In addition, they take up considerably more space on each floor than comparable square or rectangular stairs.

Balanced against these factors is the consideration that, in the hands of a good designer, these staircases can be highly ornamental. This fact alone cannot justify their use. However, in Sedgewick Library, coupled with the smaller enclosed spiral, and surrounded by a circular lightwell that extends up into the truncated cone skylight, the whole reflecting in an open form the great circular tree drums that penetrate the building, the staircases justify their existence (see p. 232).

The provision of a second staircase as an alternative means of reaching the lower level, instead of a larger single staircase, resulted from questions posed by the Environmental Psychologist on the faculty of the UBC School of Architecture, about the desirability of allowing students an alternative. Since the vast majority of books and seats are on the lower level, and the student must go down to use them, and since he is totally committed to do so by the time he reaches the stairhead, providing twinned alternative routes down reflects a conception of people as incredibly delicate creatures, rather than the sturdy fellows we are, to survive all that the psychologists try to do to us.

9. Two items of the stacks are of considerable interest. I don't know what made me measure them, because three-foot-wide stacks are even more maternal than motherhood, but these stacks, manufactured by Johl, are exactly thirty-six and three-sixteenths inches wide. If this is standard with Johl, Canadian and other librarians considering these stacks must be sure to correlate their bay systems to accommodate this dimension.

The shelves use the best end bracket I have seen, a triangle 9" high by 2-½" at the base, fastened to the shelves in an easily removable manner. Custom made, they cost $1.68 each. When the brackets have to be removed because of crowded shelves, there no longer is any fear of books toppling over.

10. What they do to the circulatory and reproductive systems I leave to cardiologists, gynecologists and human engineers.

11. This extremely pleasant graphic was designed by Virginia Chapman and Terry Harrison of Penthouse Studios Ltd., a Vancouver firm. The handling of graphics of all kinds in this library is admirable, but the supergraphic is the most impressive.

12. Clara A. Ridder, *Basic Design Measurements for Sitting,* Fayetteville, Arkansas, 1959 (University of Arkansas Agricultural Experiment Station Bulletin 616). These measurements resulted from the actual choice of dimensions in an experimental adjustable chair by subjects seated in it as positions of total comfort for a chair at a writing surface. The exact complex of dimensions of the seat is given on pages 38–42 of the Bulletin. UBC had its chair made to order to its own measurements based on the Arkansas design by Flexsteel, a Canadian company, at $24 each. Its appearance is reasonably good, but not striking, as one would wish in the only side chair used, but budgetary pressures at the end of the construction also caused the development of a carrel smaller than normal.

13. Observations of study habits at carrels with baffles and a generous bookshelf in the College Library section of Norlin Library, University of Colorado, indicate that more often than not, students forego the bookshelf in favor of laying their materials on the floor. We should systematically study such behavior to see if carrel bookshelves are really needed.

14. The reader is mounted on rollers that move on fixed tracks parallel to the width of the table. It is difficult to push it left and right, and it allows no adjustment from front to back, making it impossible to position the reader at just the right spot in relation to the note-taking shelf.

15. The one basic lack on the otherwise outstanding planning team at UBC was a person with sure and sensitive esthetic judgment.

16. The tubes should be at least four and a half inches clear of the surface of the lens to obtain totally good diffusion and low showthrough in fluorescent fixtures even if they have totally good diffusing lenses.

17. Statistics for Sedgewick Library:

> Gross area—113,349 square feet.
> Seating capacity—1,646 seats.
> Book capacity—192,625 volumes.
> Building cost—$2,880,270 ($25.41 per square foot construction cost).
> Project cost—$3,894,808 ($35.15 per square foot project cost).

The following article on this building is worth reading: "Understatement," *Progressive Architecture,* March 1973, pp. 86–91.

APPENDIX I

One Hundred Five Buildings Evaluated

The following is a list of buildings within my span of knowledge from which something either positive or negative can be learned about planning a contemporary library. The evaluations of their parts are my opinions after looking at them carefully. The few that I have not seen or seen only partly completed are so designated. The others are evaluated as of the time that I visited them, and they may have changed since that time. Verification of their present condition should be obtained before visiting them.

The designations Excellent, Good, Fair, Poor and Abominable can be thought of in terms of academic grades of A, B, C, D, and F. Abominable *really* means that it shouldn't happen to an outhouse.

Adelphi University Library, Garden City, New York
  Size—Minuscule
  Layout—Good
  Lighting—Fair
  Esthetics, interior—Excellent
         exterior—Good

Amherst College, Amherst, Massachusetts
  Layout—Fair
  Lighting—Fair
  Esthetics, interior—Good
         exterior—Fair

Arizona State University, Tempe, Arizona
  Layout—Poor
  Lighting—Poor
  Monumental stairs—Poor
  Moveable partitions—Cost of moving prohibitive
  Esthetics, interior—Poor
         exterior—Fair
  Feeling of the building is depressed (in Arizona's shining clear light)

Atlantic Union College, South Lancaster, Massachusetts
  Layout—Good
  Not seen completed

Auraria Library/Learning Resource Center, Denver, Colorado
  Lighting—Poor
  Glass—Abominable (reached 138° on main floor first summer)

Two Atrium Courts—Poor
Air ducts—Poor
Orientation—Poor
Esthetics, interior—Poor
        exterior—Poor

Ball State University, Main Library, Muncie, Indiana
Size—Enormous
Layout—Good
Lighting—Good
Esthetics, interior—Good
        exterior—Good

Bismarck Junior College, Bismarck, North Dakota
Layout—Good
Lighting—Excellent
Esthetics, interior—Fair
        exterior—Fair

Bowdoin College, Brunswick, Maine
Layout—Good
Lighting—Good (except for periphery)
Glass—Considerable sun glare
Fireplace—Abominable, except to devoted arsonists
Esthetics, interior—Good
        exterior—Good

Bowling Green State University, Bowling Green, Ohio
(A tower building on a 2-story platform)
Layout—Fair
Glass—Good
Esthetics, interior—Fair
        exterior—Fair

Bryn Mawr College, Bryn Mawr, Pennsylvania
(A faculty committee library)
Layout—Fair
Lighting—Fair
Esthetics, interior—Fair
        exterior—Fair

Butler University, Indianapolis, Indiana
Layout—Poor
Not seen completed

Cabrillo College, Aptos, California
Layout—Abominable
Lighting—Good
Esthetics, interior—Poor
        exterior—Fair

California State College, Los Angeles, California
  Layout—Poor
  Lighting—Poor
  Articulation of the Addition—Poor
  Esthetics, interior—Fair
          exterior—Fair

Cazenovia College, Cazenovia, New York
  Layout, main floor—Good
        upper floor—Poor
  Esthetics, interior—Good
          exterior—Fair

Center College, Danville, Kentucky
  Library floors flanked by classrooms convertible to reading rooms
  Not seen

Chabot College, Hayward, California
  Layout—Poor
  Shape (round)—Abominable
  Lighting—Poor
  Esthetics, interior—Poor
          exterior—Fair

Clark Art Institute Library, Williamstown, Massachusetts
  Layout—Fair
  Lighting—Poor
  Esthetics, interior—Fair
          exterior—Good

Clark University, Worcester, Massachusetts
  (John Johansen's Folly—a fixed function library)
  Layout—Poor
  Lighting—Poor
  Sound transmission—Poor
  Flexibility—Abominable
  Esthetics, interior—Fair
          exterior—Garbled

Colgate University, Hamilton, New York
  Layout—Fair
  Lighting—Poor
  Esthetics, interior—Fair
          exterior—Fair

Colorado College, Colorado Springs, Colorado
  (This is my product and I am prejudiced)
  Layout—Excellent
  Upper Atrium—Good
  Central roof skylight—Fair

Lighting—Excellent
Glass—Good
Esthetics, interior—Good
       exterior—Fair

Colorado State University, Fort Collins, Colorado
  (An L-shaped library)
  Layout—Fair
  Central grand stairway—Abominable
  Esthetics, interior—Good
       exterior—Good

Cornell University, Research Library, Ithaca, New York
  Layout—Good
  Lighting—Fair
  Esthetics, interior—Fair
       exterior—Good

Dickinson State College, Dickinson, North Dakota
  Layout—Good
  Lighting—Fair
  Esthetics, interior—Good
       exterior—Fair

Douglass College, New Brunswick, New Jersey
  Layout—Fair
  Lighting—Poor
  Open eggcrate pseudo-"luminous" ceilings—Poor
  Floor air tempering ducts—Good
  Esthetics, interior—Fair
       exterior—Good

Earlham College, Richmond, Indiana
  (An L-shaped library)
  Layout—Good
  Lighting—Fair
  Esthetics, interior—Fair
       exterior—Fair

Elmira College, Elmira, New York
  Layout—Fair
  Audio visual elements—Excellent
  Not seen completed

Emory University, Atlanta, Georgia
  (A tower building on a two-story platform)
  Layout—Fair
  Lighting—Fair
  Center Staircase—Poor
  Rare Books Floor—Good

Entrance Floor, only half used—Poor
Esthetics, interior—Good
   exterior—Good

Fieldstone School, Riverdale, New York
Layout—Excellent
Lighting—Fair
Esthetics, interior—Good
   exterior—Good
Relation to site—Excellent

Foothill College, Los Altos Hills, California
Layout—Poor
Lighting—Good
Esthetics, interior—Fair
   exterior—Good

George Washington University, Washington, D.C.
Layout—Good
Lighting—Fair
Esthetics, interior—Fair
   exterior—Fair

Georgetown University, Washington, D.C.
Layout—Good
Lighting—Poor
Esthetics, interior—Fair
   exterior—Good

Grinnell College, Grinnell, Iowa
(A faculty committee library)
Layout—Poor
Lighting—Poor to Abominable
Glass—Poor
Extremely small (13') bay system
Esthetics, interior—Good
   exterior—Fair

Groton School, Groton, Massachusetts
Layout—Good
Lighting—Excellent
Esthetics, interior—Fair
   exterior—Fair

Guelph University, Guelph, Ontario, Canada
Layout—Fair
Lighting—Poor
Esthetics, interior—Fair
   exterior—Good

Harvard University, Pusey Library, Cambridge, Massachusetts
  (An underground library)
  Layout—Good
  Lighting—Fair
  Esthetics, interior—Good
         exterior—Good

Haverford College, Haverford, Pennsylvania
  (The original library has had four additions)
  Layout—Good
  Lighting—Fair
  Esthetics, interior—Excellent
         exterior—Fair

Hofstra University, Hempstead, New York
  (This is my product and I am prejudiced. A detached Reserve Book wing, tower building)
  Layout—Excellent
  Lighting—Excellent
  Esthetics, interior—Good
         exterior—Fair

Indiana University, Bloomington, Indiana
  Layout—Good
  Lighting—Fair
  Esthetics, interior—Fair
         exterior—Good

Jamestown College, Jamestown, North Dakota
  Layout—Poor
  Lighting—Fair
  Esthetics, interior—Fair
         exterior—Good

John Crerar Library, Chicago, Illinois
  Layout—Fair
  Glass—Abominable, especially in Chicago's weather
  Floor air tempering ducts—Good
  All offices interior—Poor
  Esthetics, interior—Good
         exterior—Good

Lakehead University, Thunder Bay, Canada
  Layout—Poor
  Lighting—Fair
  Esthetics, interior—Fair
         exterior—Fair

Loretto Heights College, Denver, Colorado
  Layout—Fair
  Lighting—Fair

Esthetics, interior—Fair
          exterior—Fair

Lincoln University, Oxford, Pennsylvania
(An L-shaped library)
Layout—Excellent
Lighting—Good
Esthetics, interior—Fair
          exterior—Good

Long Island University, C.W. Post College, Brookville, New York
Layout—Abominable
Lighting—Poor
Esthetics, interior—Fair
          exterior—Poor

Loomis School, Windsor, Connecticut
Layout—Good
Lighting—Poor
Esthetics, interior—Good
          exterior—Fair

Los Gatos High School, Los Gatos, California
Layout—Excellent
Lighting—Fair
Esthetics, interior—Good
          exterior—Good

Miami-Dade Junior College, North Campus, Miami, Florida
Layout—Good
Lighting—Excellent
Esthetics, interior—Fair
          exterior—Fair
Connected to an expansive Audio-Visual Department
Uses multi-layer polarized lighting

Montana State University, Bozeman, Montana
Layout—Fair
Lighting—Poor
Center atrium—Poor
Interior fountain on main floor—Abominable
Esthetics, interior—Fair
          exterior—Fair

New York University, New York City, N.Y.
Layout—Fair
Lighting—Poor
Center atrium—Abominable
Esthetics, interior—Fair
          exterior—Fair

New York Public Library, Lincoln Center, New York City, N.Y.
  (A combination museum/library)
  Layout—Good
  Lighting—Poor to Good
  Esthetics, interior—Good
        exterior—Good
  The carpeting was destroyed by constant voluminous street dirt

North Dakota State University, Fargo, North Dakota
  Layout—Good
  Lighting—Fair
  Esthetics, interior—Good
        exterior—Fair

Northwestern University, Evanston, Illinois
  Layout—Poor
  Lighting—Poor
  Traffic patterns—Abominable
  Triple-tower stacks—Abominable
  Security layout—Abominable
  Esthetics, interior—Fair
        exterior—Fair
  Uses a 3-story escalator

Oberlin College, Oberlin, Ohio
  Layout—Fair
  Not seen completed

Ohio State University, Addition and Renovation, Columbus, Ohio
  Layout—Good
  Not seen completed

Pembroke-Country Day School, Kansas City, Missouri
  Layout—Good
  Lighting—Fair
  Esthetics, interior—Good
        exterior—Fair

Radcliffe College, Cambridge, Massachusetts
  Layout—Poor
  Lighting—Poor
  Esthetics, interior—Fair
        exterior—Fair

Ridgewood High School, Norridge, Illinois
  Layout—Poor
  Lighting—Fair
  Ceiling height—Poor
  Compartmentalization—Poor

Esthetics, interior—Poor
    exterior—Fair

St. Andrews Presbyterian College, Laurinburg, North Carolina
Layout—Poor
Lighting—Fair
Esthetics, interior—Fair
    exterior—Fair

St. John Fisher College, Rochester, New York
Layout—Poor
Not seen completed

Sarah Lawrence College, Bronxville, New York
Layout—Good
Lighting—Good
Esthetics, interior—Good
    exterior—Good

Scarborough College, West Hill, Canada
(Part of a megastructure)
Layout—Poor
Lighting—Fair
Esthetics, interior—Fair
    exterior—Fair

Simmons College, Boston, Massachusetts
Layout—Poor
Lighting—Fair
Esthetics, interior—Fair
    exterior—Fair

Simon Fraser University, Burnaby, Canada
Layout—Poor
Lighting—Poor
Elongated shape—Abominable
Esthetics, interior—Poor
    exterior—Poor

Southern Illinois University, Carbondale, Illinois
Layout—Good
Lighting—Fair
Esthetics, interior—Fair
    exterior—Good

Stanford University, Undergraduate Library, Stanford, California
Layout—Poor
Lighting—Good
Center atrium—Poor
Esthetics, interior—Fair
    exterior—Good
Uses multi-layer polarized lighting

SUNY at Albany, Albany, New York
   Layout—Poor
   Lighting—Poor
   Ceiling height—Poor
   Esthetics, interior—Fair
           exterior—Fair

SUNY at Stony Brook, Stony Brook, New York
   Original building—Unspeakable
     (no academician was involved in its planning)
   Wrap-around addition—Multiply by two

Swarthmore College, Swarthmore, Pennsylvania
   Layout—Abominable
   Lighting—Poor
   Interior fieldstone walls and monolithic fieldstone piers—Abominable
   Sunken main floor lounge—Abominable
   Esthetics, interior—Fair
           exterior—Fair

Syracuse University, Bird Library, Syracuse, New York
   Layout—Fair
   Esthetics, exterior—Good
   Not seen completed

Taft School, Watertown, Connecticut
   Layout—Good
   Lighting—Fair
   Esthetics, interior—Good
           exterior—Good

Temple University, Philadelphia, Pennsylvania
   Layout—Poor
   Lighting—Fair
   Esthetics, interior—Fair
           exterior—Fair

Texas A & M University, Addition and Remodelling, College Station, Texas
   Layout—Good
   Not seen completed

Towson State College, Baltimore, Maryland
   Layout—Poor
   Lighting—Fair
   Heating system—Poor
   Esthetics, interior—Fair
           exterior—Fair

Tulane University, New Orleans, Louisiana
    Layout—Fair
    Lighting—Fair
    Esthetics, interior—Fair
                exterior—Good

U.S. Air Force Academy, Air Force Academy, Colorado
    Layout—Fair
    Lighting—Poor
    Glass—Abominable
    Circular grand staircase—Poor (but grand)
    Esthetics, interior—Fair
                exterior—Poor

University of Alberta, Main Library, Edmonton, Canada
    Wrap-around addition
    Not seen

University of Arizona, Main Library, Tucson, Arizona
    Layout—Good
    Lighting—Good
    Stack levels not connected directly to each other—Poor
    Esthetics, exterior—Good
                interior — Architecturally good
                            Not seen furnished

University of Calgary, Calgary, Canada
    (A tower library)
    Layout—Poor
    Lighting—Fair
    Articulation of Addition—Fair
    Esthetics, interior—Fair
                exterior—Fair

University of California, Berkeley, Undergraduate Library, Berkeley, Calif.
    Layout—Good
    Lighting—Fair
    Not seen completed

University of California, Los Angeles, Research Library
    Layout—Good
    Lighting—Poor
    Esthetics, interior—Fair
                exterior—Fair
    Uses 125 pound per square foot live load floor

University of California, San Diego
    Layout—Good
    Lighting—Fair
    Glass—Abominable

Vertical movement—Poor
Esthetics, interior—Fair
        exterior—HOLLYWOOD SUPER-SPECTACULAR!!!!!

University of California, Santa Barbara
  Layout—Poor
  Lighting—Fair
  Articulation of Addition—Poor
  Esthetics, interior—Poor
        exterior—Poor

University of Chicago, Chicago, Illinois
  (A split stack/seating floor building)
  Layout—Good
  Lighting—Poor
  Faculty study wing—Excellent
  Esthetics, interior—Good
        exterior—Good

University of Colorado, Addition and Remodelling, Boulder, Colorado
  (This is my product and I am prejudiced)
  Layout—Good
  Lighting—Good
  Articulation of Addition—Excellent
  Esthetics, interior—Good
        exterior—Fair
  Integrates huge bay window wall into the library

University of Colorado, Colorado Springs, Colorado
  Layout—Good
  Lighting—Fair
  Esthetics, interior—Fair
        exterior—Fair
  Air tempering controlled by a remote computer in Denver

University of Denver, Denver, Colorado
  Layout—Good
  Lighting—Poor
  Glass (Reflective)—Abominable
  Esthetics, interior—Excellent
        exterior—Poor

University of Georgia, Addition and Remodelling, Athens, Georgia
  Layout—Poor (except for Tech Services)
  Lighting—Good
  Articulation of Addition—Abominable
  Esthetics, interior—Poor
        exterior—Fair

University of Illinois, Undergraduate Library, Urbana, Illinois
  (An underground library)

Layout—Crowded
Central light court—Excellent
High ceilings—Excellent
Esthetics, interior—Good
        exterior—Fair

University of Illinois, Chicago Circle Campus, Chicago, Illinois
Layout—Poor
Lighting—Fair
Glass—Abominable, especially in Chicago's weather
Esthetics, interior—Fair
        exterior—Fair
Fin-tube peripheral heating—Poor

University of Lethbridge, Lethbridge, Canada
(Part of a megastructure)
Layout—Abominable
Lighting—Poor
Shape—Poor
Esthetics, interior—Fair
        exterior—Good

University of Massachusetts, Amherst, Massachusetts
(A 28-story tower above a 2-story platform)
Stack and study floors alternate
Not seen completed

University of Miami, Miami, Florida
Layout—Fair
Lighting—Fair
3-Story central grand staircase—Poor
Esthetics, interior—Fair
        exterior—Good
Uses a 3-story escalator

University of Michigan, Undergraduate Library, Ann Arbor, Michigan
Layout—Good
Lighting—Fair
Esthetics, interior—Poor
        exterior—Fair

University of Minnesota, West Bank Library, Minneapolis, Minnesota
Layout—Good
Lighting—Fair
Esthetics, interior—Fair
        exterior—Good
Uses a 2-story escalator

University of North Dakota, Grand Forks, North Dakota
Layout—Poor
Lighting—Poor

Esthetics, interior—Fair
            exterior—Poor

University of Pennsylvania, Philadelphia, Pennsylvania
  Layout—Fair
  Lighting—Fair
  Esthetics, interior—Poor
            exterior—Fair

University of Pittsburgh, Pittsburgh, Pennsylvania
  Layout—Fair
  Lighting—Fair
  Esthetics, interior—Good
            exterior—Fair

University of Washington, Addition and Remodelling, Seattle, Washington
  Layout—Fair
  Lighting—Fair
  Articulation of Addition—Good
  Esthetics, interior—Fair
            exterior—Good (for the Addition)

Washburn University, Topeka, Kansas
  Layout—Good
  Not seen completed

Washington University, St. Louis, Missouri
  Layout—Excellent
  Lighting—Fair
  Thin slab floor—Excellent
  Entrance stair tower—Good
  Adaptation to site—Excellent
  Esthetics, interior—Fair
            exterior—Excellent

Weston High School, Weston, Massachusetts
  Layout—Good
  Lighting—Fair
  Esthetics, interior—Fair
            exterior—Good

Wichita State University, Wichita, Kansas
  Layout—Poor
  Lighting—Poor
  Esthetics, interior—Poor
            exterior—Fair

Widener College, Chester, Pennsylvania
  (A triangular library with an open atrium center)
  Layout—Abominable

Lighting—Poor
Shape—Abominable
Esthetics, interior—Fair
       exterior—Fair

Williams College, Main Library, Williamstown, Massachusetts
Layout—Abominable
Lighting—Poor
Entrance—Abominable
Articulation—Abominable
Esthetics, interior—Fair
       exterior—Poor

Yeshiva University, Main Library, Bronx, New York
Layout—Abominable
Lighting—Poor
Tri-level main floor—Abominable
Sunken main floor court—Abominable
Split stack/seating level—Abominable
Esthetics, interior—Fair
       exterior—Good

APPENDIX II

A Demonstration Model Program for a New Library

This model omits the section on the nature of the university and its library, which can easily be written by any informed librarian. It concentrates rather on the practical and technical details that must be developed into an ordered and related statement for the architect. It projects a library larger than many will build, a size that requires all of the basic elements that go into a library. In practice, of course, the shelving and seating capacity will emerge from the demands of the institution. The stack space requirements assume 4½' centers, although considerable variation from this standard is now being used in libraries.

The library elements included are not intended as recommendations, nor do we recommend against any omitted. They rather demonstrate kinds of facilities useful for a library of this size, what furniture and equipment might go into them, and how much space they would require. They demonstrate the kinds of details that must be thought through carefully as they emerge from the dynamics of any specific library, imaginatively projected for the life of the building, in order to write specifications for the program areas.

CONTENTS

	Page No	Public Seating	Public Shelving (volumes)	Area Required (square feet)
V. *Administrative Offices*				
25. Director	305	—	—	250
26. Associate/Asst Directors	305	—	—	730
27. Administrative Assistants	306	—	—	345
28. Secretaries	306	—	—	675
29. Machine/Supply Room	306	—	—	80
30. Conference Room	307	—	—	200
VI. *Technical Processes*				
31. Acquisitions Department	307	—	—	6,500
32. Catalog Department	311	—	—	4,290
33. Processing Department	313	—	—	7,300
34. Serials Department	315	—	—	3,850
35. Receiving & Shipping Dept.	317	—	—	3,330
VII. *Miscellaneous*				
36. Staff Lounge	319	—	—	1,600
37. Staff Toilets	320	—	—	400
38. Public Toilets	320	—	—	1,200
39. Custodial Rooms	321	—	—	600
40. Public Elevators	321	—	—	(in gross area)
41. Staff Elevators	321	—	—	(in gross area)
42. Exhibition Walls	321	—	—	—
43. Bookdrops	321	—	—	—
4. Photocopy Machines	321	—	—	—

Index (omitted here, but
    extremely important
    in a library building
    program)

TOTALS	1,500 seats	1,000,000 vols.	144,110 Net s.f.
		Add 40% to convert to gross	57,644
		Total Gross Area Required	201,754 s.f.

PREFATORY—SPECIFIC CONCERNS

Special attention is called now, so they will not be forgotten, to the need for providing the following elements in the building:

Ash trays and urns, in all smoking areas.
Book return shelves, specially painted and sized, along stack walkways.
Bookdrops, Outdoor, near the main entrance.
Change machines, near all coin-operated machines.
Clocks, simple, plug-in electric clocks, so time can be told everywhere in the building.
Coat Hanging units, in stack sections.
Door handles, that cannot be unscrewed by students.
Drinking fountains, enough, on main walkways, throughout.
Hours Sign, near the main entrance.
Mail chute, through all floors.
Message board, inside, near main entrance.
Mirrors, wherever useful.
Pencil sharpeners, near drinking fountains, obvious.
Photocopy machines, coin-op, in all active-use areas.
Suggestion Box, Reply wall, in an obvious place.
Telephones, coin and house, near main entrance.
Time clock, in a central work area, to serve entire students and staff.
Vending Machines, for pens, etc., in obvious places.

STANDARDS FOR THE HANDICAPPED WILL BE FOLLOWED THROUGHOUT THE BUILDING.

PREFATORY—SCHEDULES

Separate schedules of numbers, kinds and locations will be agreed upon for the following items when floor layouts are completed:

1. Bulletin Boards.
2. Computer conduits.
3. Keys.
4. Electrical outlets.
5. Electrical switches.
6. Fire extinguishers.
7. Intercom systems.
8. Public Address system.
9. Telephone outlets.
10. Separate exhausts for smoking, etc.
11. Clocks.
12. Exit door alarms.
13. Under floor electrical ducts.

VITAL ELEMENTS OF SPECIAL CONCERN

1. Lighting.

The effect of lighting on the use of libraries is considerably greater than generally realized because it works in subtle ways. Unless the intensity is quite low, the reader is not aware that the lighting is poor, yet poor lighting will make him feel generally uncomfortable at his reading and will color his reaction to the library. Moreover, because it completely permeates the building, lighting is as important as the decor in producing the atmosphere that transmits a feeling of pleasantness in the building. When lighting is ideal, the reader is totally unconscious of its presence as light, but perceives it as a feeling. But despite its great importance, there are few well-lit libraries in the United States. We therefore invite the architects' careful attention to this problem.

In this library, we want troffered, fluorescent fixtures recessed flush with the ceiling throughout the building, unless there are cogent reasons in particular areas for departing from this norm. We do not want open-bottom louvres, which are less efficient and considerably poorer in quality of light than a covering lens. At no place should the bulb be exposed to the work task below it to produce reflected glare. If financial reasons make it necessary to compromise on the lighting, it is preferable to reduce the intensity of the lighting rather than to use fixtures that produce glare.

We should avoid depending on window areas for illumination, because the intensity drops off precipitously as you move away from the sill.

We should cut ballast hum to a minimum by specifying selected ballasts, since a loud hum is disturbing in a library.

In the stack areas, wherever possible, light fixtures should run at right angles to the stacks.

We want to achieve the following illumination intensities in the areas designated:

55 footcandles, maintained, measured 30″ above the floor, throughout the library, except in the following areas:

Circulation Desk.	70 f.c.
Card Catalog.	70 f.c.
All staff workrooms.	70 f.c.
Faculty Studies.	70 f.c.
Typing Rooms.	70 f.c.
Toilets.	40 f.c.

All lights in the building should be controlled by as few switches as possible located at the circulation desk, except the night lighting, which will be on at all times.

It will be necessary to provide emergency lighting, that is activated to evacuate the building in case of a power failure.

In open areas of the building that are logical candidates for enclosure into rooms in the future, provision should be made now so that access to wiring for future switches to control overhead lighting will be possible without major expense.

2. Heating and Air Conditioning.

A good ventilation system is as important as a good lighting system in affecting the reader's reaction to a library, and as in the case of lighting, good quality in the air distribution is more important than the temperature settings. We would therefore like the architects to give special attention to the following aspects of the ventilation system.

We want the system to provide a comfortably low level of background noise throughout the building, to play against the lighting system hum and casual noises of movement and talking and make them less noticeable. On the other hand, we must avoid a noise level that is distracting. The air masses must be moved slowly enough and the ducts must be padded or insulated enough to avoid noises in ducts or air diffusers.

The location of diffusers is extremely important, since 72° air is much colder than that when blown from a short distance on a reader's shoulders. Ceiling diffusers should be located at a height and in a position to prohibit direct drafts on readers. We should, if at all possible, avoid having *cold air* blown from floor or low-level ducts.

It is extremely important to have good air filtration to avoid dust, which is destructive to books. We would therefore like to consider a system which combines a high level of filtration with low cost of maintenance. The Rare Book Stacks will be controlled by a small machine separate from the main system, and in addition to filtration similar to the above, it must have an activated carbon filter to remove noxious gases from the air, and humidity removal capacity to insure constant humidity.

Engineers complain that architects take little pains in designing mixing chambers adequate to homogenize the variant temperatures of outside and inside air before it hits the heating or cooling coils. We assume that our architects will do so.

We would like this building to be slightly pressurized to inhibit the entrance of dust through tiny crevices. We would like to maintain a temperature of 70° in winter and 76° in summer and humidity of 40%–50%. In the Rare Book Stacks, we would like to maintain 70° temperature and 50% humidity at all times.

3. Electrical Outlets.

We want outlets to accommodate three-prong grounded plugs, to be distributed in sufficient numbers so that custodial and maintenance workers will have them convenient to their tasks throughout the building. This requires careful thinking; most buildings have either too few or too many.

4. Windows.

We want to minimize the use of windows to conserve energy while at the same time maximizing their effect. We therefore want the architects to provide window areas throughout the building of reasonable size, strategically located with regard to the human activities in the building and the vistas available outside, and shielded from the sun. We should avoid having glass on both sides of corner walls, which has caused difficulties in some libraries. That glass can be used successfully, in moderation, shielded, and arranged in an irregular pattern to fit the functions of the building, is demonstrated by the top floor of the Washington University Library in St. Louis.

5. Walls.

All walls built in this library now should be easily and cheaply removable without much damage to walls and floors, unless they separate noise from non-noise areas, in which case special precautions must be taken to make the walls sound barriers. The walls for enclosed rooms that must provide privacy should go completely to the structural ceiling to prevent voice transmittal through dropped ceilings.

The walls of the Rare Book stacks must be 1½ hour fire-preventive walls.

6. Floors and Floor Covering.

Every attempt should be made to keep the floor slab as thin as possible, consonant with the load it must carry. At least one large library has been built with a 9″ floor slab.

We should avoid using cork on the floors, which pock marks easily, and terrazzo, which is noisy and terribly hard on the feet. In a building this size, the librarians will walk seven miles on some days. Carpeting should be used in all public areas, and vinyl tile in work areas.

7. Acoustics.

Special provision should be made for the control of sound transmission in this library. We would like to achieve a condition of quiet, with a low background noise from the ventilation system, but we do not want a condition that is acoustically dead. People should be free to talk in a reasonable tone of voice without fear of disturbing others, but we do not want all sound to be absorbed in an inhuman gulp of acoustical materials.

8. Traffic Patterns.

It is important to plan stairs and walkways so that well-used paths do not cross. It is especially important for the reference librarians to have access to the card catalog and the indexes without crossing walk-ways. In stack areas, it is important to plan so that readers go through the stacks to reading areas, rather than through reading areas to stacks.

9. Energy Conservation Measures.

A major contribution of the architects will be information about improved technological and physical means of reducing energy consumption in this building while still supplying it with comfortable, high quality facilities. Careful thought about glass exposure, insulation, the number of thermostat controls (to reduce tempering of some areas when the library is closed), and the cubic capacity of areas is extremely important.

10. Economy Measures.

Throughout the planning and construction of this library, every reasonable measure to reduce its costs must be taken while at the same time providing comfortable and high quality facilities. Among other things, the architects should consider the comparative costs of a dispersed air-tempering system, and automatic controls for reducing the tempering of areas of the library, and at times of the entire library, during hours when it is closed.

SPECIFICATIONS OF THE LIBRARY AREAS

I. INTRODUCTION TO THE LIBRARY

The facilities described in this section all must be near the main entrance to the library. Their relationship to each other and to the main entrance are critical in establishing the user's reaction to the feeling of the library and its ease of use. Its planning by the architects is therefore of the first order of importance in the success of the building as a whole.

1. VESTIBULE

Primary Function—This unfurnished area will serve as a weather-lock to protect the facilities inside from extreme of heat or cold outside.

Relationship to Other Facilities—Must be immediately inside the main entrance.

Special Requirements
    Special lighting outside, to call attention to the main entrance.
    A recessed mat to remove water and dirt from shoes.
    Sufficient doors to permit easy access to users who will number——per day.
    Separation of the entrance space from the exit space to provide security of the collection.

Net Area Required—240 sq. ft.

2. TRAFFIC DISPERSAL AREA

Primary Function—This open area will allow users to identify the main facilities to which they will move from the entrance—Reference Desks, Card Catalog, Circulation Desk, Stairways and Elevators to other floors—and allow them to move to these different facilities without the main traffic patterns crossing.

Relationship to Other Facilities
    1. Immediately inside the main entrance.
    2. Leads directly to the facilities listed above.

Special Requirements
    Bright lighting.
    Heating/Ventilation/Air conditioning.
    Carpet tile, or other flooring to suppress noise, yet be easily replaceable in a heavy wear area.

Other Design Considerations—The feeling of the building immediately inside the vestibule sets the tone of the users' reaction to the feeling of the building. Therefore, special attention must be paid to esthetics.

Net Area Required—1,000 sq. ft.

3. EXIT CONTROL AND SECURITY GUARD STATIONS

Primary Function—To inspect books passing out, to make sure they are properly charged.

Secondary Function—To serve as the center for a Security system that patrols the library.

Relationship to Other Facilities—Immediately before the exit point, yet not inhibiting traffic dispersal near the entrance point. Near the Circulation Desk, to which it reports.

Special Requirements—Conduits for Tattle-Tape Security system.

Other Design Considerations—Must be as unobtrusive and as esthetically acceptable as possible, yet it is probably necessary to use lockable turnstiles to provide security. The location, and the esthetics are the most difficult problems to solve.

Built-in Furniture and Equipment—The entire area is built-in.

Movable Furniture and Equipment
1. 2 entrance, and 3 exit turnstiles
2. 1 lockable bar or panel wide enough to let wheelchairs in or out
3. 2 seats for inspectors, each at a small flat area for placing books, briefcases, etc. for inspection, about 1' × 6', in an L, for each station.

One exit control station, which we will designate as the one always manned, will have space for the door security alarm panel, and the fire alarm panel, drawer space, and shelf space.

Net Area Required—200 sq. ft.

4. CIRCULATION DEPARTMENT

This Department comprises the following areas, all near the main entrance:
1. Central Circulation Desk
2. Central Desk Office
3. Circulation Workroom
4. Department Head's Office
5. Assistant's Office

Primary Function—To charge out and discharge library materials, keep control records, reshelve books and maintain central bookstacks.

Secondary Function—The Central Circulation Desk and the Exit Control are often the only points manned in the building, during low use periods.

Relationship to Other Facilities—Must be close to the main entrance, public elevators, and main stairwells, but must not lie athwart entrance traffic as a barrier.

Special Requirements

Fluorescent lighting
Heating/Ventilation/Air conditioning
Acoustics—specially suppressed
Floors—carpeting
Shelving uprights on most walls

Ceiling—Acoustic tile
Utility services—Dedicated electric lines
Communication Systems Telephones
Computer
Intercom System

Built-in Furniture and Equipment—Central Circulation Desk, book return track, as specified.

Movable Furniture and Equipment

Central Circulation Desk
1. 1 - custom build desk 2' wide, 35' long, 40" high, on which will be mounted 4 computer data collection terminals. Special wiring and conduiting. Roll-down ornamental screens to lock it. To be detailed as building plans progress.
2. 4 - swivel chairs with backs, counter height.
3. 3 - microfilm readers, mounted on the desk.

Net Area Required—280 sq. ft.

Central Desk Office (to supervise Central Circulation Desk)
1. 2 - 30″ × 60″ desk, with typing L.
2. 2 - secretarial chairs.
3. 1 - side chair, for item 1.
4. 1 - vertical file.
5. 1 - section of wall-hung shelving.
6. 1 - bulletin board.

Net Area Required—200 sq. ft.

Keypunch Area (easily accessible from Special Service Station at Circulation Desk)
1. 1 - keypunch machine, 3′ × 5′.
2. 1 - secretarial chair.
3. 1 - 2′ × 4′ table, with drawers.
4. 1 - vertical file.
5. 1 - section of wall-hung shelving, 12″ nominal shelves.

Net Area Required—165 sq. ft.

Holding Shelves (easily accessible to Circulation Desk)
1. 6 - sections of wall-hung shelving.

Net Area Required—54 sq. ft.

Behind these areas, separated by a wall, which will require sound control for a noise generating area, with doors to the Central Circulation Desk will be a large unbroken area including the following interrelated functions. There is heavy movement between the Circulation Desk and the functions just behind the wall, which are:

Circulation Processing Area
1. 6 - 30′ × 60″ desks, with typing L.
2. 6 - secretarial chairs.
3. 3 - 3′ × 8′ tables.
4. 15 - secretarial chairs.
5. 1 - computer terminal on 2′ × 4′ table, with grounding pad.
6. 2 - microfilm readers.
7. 1 - microfilm reader-printer.
8. 7 - tab card open file bins, 3′ × 4′.
9. 1 - vertical file.
10. 10 - sections of shelving (1=12″ shelves, 9=8″ shelves).
11. Bulletin Board.
12. 10 - book trucks.

Net Area Required—1,352 sq. ft.

Discharge Area
1. 1 - book return track, rollers pitched for a gentle roll of books from a book return slot, prominent at the Circulation Desk, to this area. It should run along an end wall.
2. 1 - Computer terminal, on 2′ × 4′ table.
3. 1 - secretarial chair.

4. 1 - open tab card file for 2′ of cards, 3′ × 4′.
5. 2 - sections of wall-hung shelving, 12″ shelves.
6. 6 - rolling depressible book bins.

Net Area Required—570 sq. ft.

Sorting and Shelving Area (not far from service elevator)
1. 80 - sections of shelving on 6′ centers.
2. 20 - book trucks.

Net area required—800 sq. ft.

Shelving Office (enclosed room, to supervise sorting and shelving)
1. 2 - 30″ × 60″ desks with typing L.
2. 3 - secretarial chairs.
3. 1 - side chair, for item 1.
4. 1 - 2′ × 4′ table.
5. 1 - vertical file.
6. 1 - section of wall-hung shelving.
7. Dispatch Board/Bulletin Board.

Net Area Required—300 sq. ft.

General Work Area (near the center of Workroom)
1. 1 - 30″ × 60″ desk with typing L.
2. 1 - secretarial chair.
3. 4 - 3′ × 8′ tables.
4. 4 - secretarial chairs.
5. 1 - tab card open file bin, 3′ × 4′.
6. 1 - electric paper cutter, 3′ × 6′.
7. 1 - sink, with cupboard below and mirror above.
8. Bulletin Board on wall.

Net Area Required—700 sq. ft.

Closing Utility Controls
1. General light control panel, for the entire building.
2. Public address system, to be used only for closing, and emergency announcements, in a lockable cover to prevent horseplay.

Both on a wall easily accessible to the Central Circulation Desk.

Net Area Required—None.

Supply Room
1. 1 - 2′ × 4′ table.
2. 1 - side chair.
3. 8 - sections of wall-hung shelving, 16″ cantilevered shelves.
4. 25 - stacking chairs on dolly.

Net Area Required—220 sq. ft.

Machine Room (needs special acoustical treatment)
1. Various computer units, which will change.
2. 1 - 3′ × 8′ table.
3. 1 - tab card sorter, 2′ × 5′.
4. 3 - secretarial chairs.
5. 1 - tape storage cabinet, 2′ × 3′.
6. 1 - vertical file.
7. 1 - supply cabinet.
8. 2 - sections wall-hung shelving, 16″ cantilevered shelves.

Net Area Required—400 sq. ft.

Department Head's Office
1. 1 - 30″ × 60″ desk, with typing L.
2. 1 - secretarial chair.
3. 1 - 3′ × 6′ table.
4. 4 - side chairs.
5. 1 - vertical file.
6. 2 - sections of wall-hung shelving, 12″ shelves.
7. Planning Boards/Bulletin Board.

Net Area Required—250 sq. ft.

Department Secretary (in an open alcove looking out into Workroom)
1. 1 - 30″ × 60″ desk with typing L.
2. 1 - secretarial chair, for item 1.
3. 1 - movable typing stand.
4. 1 - secretarial chair for item 3.
5. 1 - 3′ × 8′ table.
6. 2 - side chairs for item 5.
7. 3 - vertical files.
8. 2 - sections of wall-hung shelving, 12″ shelves.
9. 1 - coat rack for 25.
10. 24 - garment lockers.
11. Planning/Bulletin Boards.
12. 1 - heavy steel safe.

Net Area Required—350 sq. ft.

Total Net Area Required for Circulation Department—5,650 sq. ft.

5. INTERLIBRARY LOAN DEPARTMENT

Primary Function—To be easily available for faculty and students to request loans from other libraries.

Secondary Function—To receive requests from other libraries to lend our books, to perform work tasks connected with these functions, to contribute to inter-campus movement of books from one branch to another.

Relationships to Other Facilities—Must be close to Reference Stacks, which are used heavily, and not far from Circulation Desk. It must be in an easily located location to encourage use.

Special Requirements

Outside windows	Ceiling—Acoustic tile
Fluorescent lighting	Utility services—Dedicated
Heating/Ventilation/Air	electric lines
conditioning	Communication Systems Telephones
Acoustics—Specially suppressed	Computer
Floors—carpeting	TWX

Other Design Considerations—None

Built-in Furniture and Equipment—None

Movable Furniture and Equipment

Department Head's Office
1. 1 - 30″ × 60″ desk with typing L.
2. 1 - swivel chair without arms
3. 2 - side chairs
4. 1 - vertical file
5. 1 - section of wall-hung shelving
6. 1 - 2′ × 3′ table.

Net Area Required—160 sq. ft.

Interlibrary Loan Office
1. 5 - 30″ × 60″ desks with typing L
2. 5 - secretarial chairs
3. 2 - side chairs for Item 1
4. 1 - 3′ × 6′ work table
5. 4 - side chairs for Item 4
6. 1 - 3′ × 6′ writing table
7. 4 - side chairs for Item 6
8. 5 - vertical files
9. 1 - supply cabinet
10. 8 - sections of wall-hung shelving, with 16″ cantilevered shelves
11. 1 - TWX

Net Area Required—800 sq. ft.

Total Net Area Required for Interlibrary Loan—960 sq. ft.

6. REFERENCE DEPARTMENT

Areas of Responsibility—The Reference Department is responsible for the following areas:
1. Information Desk
2. Public Reference Desk Area

3. General Reference Office
4. Consultation Offices
5. Department Head's Office
6. Reference Stacks and Reading Area
7. General Microforms
8. Computer Terminal Room

It would be highly desirable to have this entire complex so arranged that there is a minimum of exits, preferably one, preferably past a point generally staffed by librarians, to keep materials from wandering throughout the building.

Information Desk

Primary Function—To be the obvious place, shortly inside the main entrance, where students can ask questions about directions or about their library needs. These are brief questions, quickly answered, and from here the student goes to another point in the building, often to the Public Reference Desks or the Card Catalog.

Relationship to Other Facilities—This must be easily seen from the main entrance, be physically the obvious place to ask such questions, and must be at least within easy eyesight of the Reference Desks.

Special Requirements
Fluorescent lighting
Heating/Ventilation/Air conditioning
Acoustics—Normal
Floors—carpeting

Ceiling—Acoustic tile
Communication Systems—Telephones

Other Design Considerations—Must wave itself as the obvious Information Point; must call attention to itself. Gimmicks, if in good taste, would be appropriate here.

Built-in Furniture and Equipment—The Information Desk itself, with room behind the desk for shelves to store materials, and for two people to sit at one time. Should be 40" high.

Movable Furniture and Equipment
1. 2 - chairs, of the appropriate height to sit comfortably at the desk.

Net Area Required—100 sq. ft.

Public Reference Desk Area

Primary Function—To locate professional reference librarians at a point where they are obviously at hand to help students with their bibliographical problems, and where they can identify by sight students who are having difficulty finding the information they are looking for. To this end, they should be located in a line, at right angles to the axis of the Card Catalog, which should have aisles wide enough so that students fumbling in their efforts to use the Catalog can be easily seen.

Secondary Functions—To instruct students in the value and use of the General Microforms, and the Human Relations Area Files; to give mass group instruction on how to use the library.

Relationship to Other Facilities—Must be immediately adjacent to:
Card Catalog.
Periodical Indexes.
Reference Stacks.
Reference Information Office, and must be nearby:
General Microforms.
Human Relations Area Files.

The use of these facilities, in the order of importance will be (1) Card Catalog, (2) Periodical Indexes, (3) Reference Information Office, (4) Reference Stacks, (5) General Microforms. The librarians will move directly to each of these points as needed, but should be able to move from the Reference Desks to the Reference Stacks with students, and when materials are found they should be able to move through the Reference Stacks to the reading area beyond the stacks.

Special Requirements

Fluorescent lighting
Heating/Ventilation/Air conditioning
Acoustics—Normal
Floors—carpeting

Ceiling—Acoustic tile
Utility services—Dedicated electric lines
Communication Systems Telephones
Computer

Other Design Considerations—Blatant sign, in good taste, indicating that this is an important information center.

Built-in Furniture and Equipment—None.

Movable Furniture and Equipment
1. 4 - 30″ × 60″ desks with typing L.
2. 4 - swivel chairs without arms.
3. 4 - side chairs.

Net Area Required—360 sq. ft.

The following equipment should be near the Public Reference Desks, but in no way inhibiting movement of librarians and students to the other main use points in the Reference Department:
1. 4 - sections counter-height shelving, with sliding, lockable, glass doors, for Ready Reference.
2. 3 - 40″ high tables, 30″ × 60″ for large dictionaries, guides, eventual computer, visual consoles.
3. 4 - wall-hung sections of standard shelving with one wide sloping shelf each section, for CBI, Union Lists, and other large and heavy bibliographical tools.
4. 2 - 3′ × 6′ tables, for using bibliographical tools.
5. 8 - side chairs for item 4.
6. 8 - 4′ × 9′ periodical index tables, with double-face, 2-tiered shelves, 12″ clearance for the lower shelf.
7. 48 - wooden stools for item 6.
8. 1 - 60 drawer card catalog for the Reference Collection.
9. 12 - vertical files.
10. 2 - sections of standard, slant-face display shelving.

11. 1 - photocopy machine.
12. 1 - bulletin board.

Public seating required—56.

Public shelving required—1,440 vol.

Net Area Required—1,600 sq. ft.

Total Net Area Required for Public Reference Desk Area—1,960 sq. ft.

General Reference Office

This office will house most of the reference staff of Library Faculty, Support Staff and Student Assistants. It should be one large office with a common wall dividing it into two offices. Each should have its own outside entrance, as well as a door in the common wall for passage from one to another.

Primary Function—To provide work areas for reference, research, and book selection activities connected with this department, and serve as a home base for the Reference Librarians when they are not working at the Public Reference Desks. Consultations with the Faculty will take place here, and projects in progress will be stored here.

Relationship to Other Facilities—Near the Reference Stacks and the Card Catalog.

Special Requirements
    Outside windows   Ceiling—Acoustic tile
    Fluorescent lighting   Communication Systems Telephones
    Heating/Ventilation/Air   Computer
    conditioning
    Acoustics—Normal
    Floors—carpeting, walls

Other Design Requirements—Compartmentalization of desks without using walls.

Built-in Furniture and Equipment—One 3′ deep supply cabinet, detailed as item 8 of Support Staff Office below.

Movable Furniture and Equipment

    Faculty Office
    1. 10 - 30″ × 60″ desks with typing L.
    2. 10 - secretarial chairs.
    3. 10 - side chairs.
    4. 10 - vertical files.
    5. 10 - sections of standard wall-hung shelving.
    6. 1 - supply cabinet.
    7. 10 - coat-length lockers for garments.

Net Area Required—1,200 sq. ft.

Support Staff Office
1. 4 - 30″ × 60″ desks with typing L.
2. 4 - secretarial chairs.
3. 1 - 3′ × 8′ table.
4. 4 - side chairs to go with item 3.
5. 2 - typing stands.
6. 10 - coat-length lockers for garments.
7. 1 - vertical file.
8. 1 - supply cabinet 3′ deep built along one entire end wall, for exhibitions supplies.
9. 1 - 3′ × 8′ table to go with item 8.
10. 2 - side chairs to go with item 9.

Net Area Required—800 sq. ft.

Total Net Area Required for General Reference Office—2,000 sq. ft.

Consultation Offices (2 are required)

Small offices adjacent to the General Reference Office for private conversations.
1. 1 - swivel chair.
2. 1 - 2′ × 3′ table.
3. 2 - side chairs.

Net Area Required—180 sq. ft.

Department Head's Office (must have window)

This must be a separate office, enclosed for privacy in delicate conversations, and large enough to hold small meetings here, near the General Reference Office.

It can be located variously, but should not be very far from the General Reference Office. It should not, however, open into that office.

Movable Furniture and Equipment
1. 1 - 30″ × 60″ desk with typing L.
2. 1 - executive chair.
3. 3 - standard sections of wall-hung shelving.
4. 1 - vertical file.
5. 4 - side chairs.

Net Area Required—200 sq. ft.

Reference Stacks and Reading Area.

These stacks will be used constantly by the Public Reference Desks, and frequently by the Reference Information Office and the General Reference Office. However, they should be as close as can be arranged to the Interlibrary Loan Department, which uses the reference collection heavily.

The stacks should be in ranges, which will be used to screen the reading area from movement and noise produced in other parts of the Reference Department. They must also be used to compartmentalize seating in the Reading Area, and must, in their total arrangement, be visually pleasant. At the same time, they must be continuous, to facilitate students finding call numbers they are looking for.

Relationship to Other Facilities—Near Reference Desks and Office.

Special Requirements
Fluorescent lighting
Heating/Ventilation/Air
conditioning
Acoustics—Normal
Floors—carpeting

Ceiling—Acoustic tile

Other Design Considerations—Stack end panels in this area, to make it feel pleasant.

Built-in Furniture and Equipment—None.

Movable Furniture and Equipment
1. 260 - standard, 6-shelf sections of 10″ normal depth shelving, on 5′ centers, to house the following:

    3,672 vol. National Bibliographies (34 sections @ 108 v./section)
      650 vol. Telephone Directories (6 sections @ 108 v./section)
    22,000 vol. Reference Books (220 sections @ 100 v./section)

2. 10 - 2′ × 3′ carrels, with baffle.
3. 13 - 2′ × 3′ tables for 1.
4. 10 - 3′ × 6′ tables for 4.
5. 2 - 3′ × 8′ tables for 6.
6. 75 - side chairs for the above.

Public seating required—75

Public shelving required—26,322 vol.

Net Area Required—4,130 sq. ft.

General Microforms

Primary Function—This area will house and service all of the microforms, in any form, for the entire collection.

Secondary Function—To provide security for the microforms.

Relationship to Other Facilities—While ultimately the desk in this area, through pressure of use, will be separately staffed to service General Microforms, for some time they will be serviced from the Public Reference Desk, so this area should be reasonably close to those desks.

Special Requirements
Suppressed lighting
Heating/Ventilation/Air
conditioning
Acoustics—Normal
Floors—carpeting

Ceiling—Acoustic tile
Utility services—Other—Separate outlet for each reader table.

Other Design Considerations—Ornamental grill (available from stack manufacturers) to enclose microforms shelved here.

The microform readers must be in a light-controlled area. Some libraries use rheostat controls, but they are not very satisfactory; others use overhead lights that are kept switched off. We invite the architects to solve this problem imaginatively, in a way that will provide a solution in esthetic terms that is much better than darkened ceilings, such as a rod-dropped ceiling under the standard lit ceiling, to keep light from coming through to the reading machines. Wide open to suggestions.

Built-in Furniture and Equipment—None.

Movable Furniture and Equipment

1. 1 - 30″ × 60″ des, with typing L.
2. 1 - secretarial chair.
3. 1 - side chair.
4. 1 - 60-drawer card catalog.
5. 1 - section of standard double-face shelving, or the equivalent, to shelve Indexes to the microform collections.
6. 1 - 4′ × 4′ table for 2, for item 5.
7. 2 - side chairs for item 6.
8. 20 - 2′ × 4′ special microform reading tables, connected in a double-face range of 10, with a baffle separating the two ranges of tables, and an electrical outlet at each table.
9. 20 - side chairs.

A grilled section will enclose the following:

10. 60 - sections of standard shelving, with 9″ nominal shelves to shelve:
     33,000 reels of film @ 864/9-shelf section.
     2,000 European microfiche boxes @ 432/8-shelf section.
     630 boxes of microprint @ 70/7-shelf section.
     1,135 boxes of IDC fiche @ 189/7-shelf section.
11. 4 - 8-drawer microfiche cabinets to house 40,000 sheets of microcards and microfiche.

Public shelving—7,500 vol.

Public seating required—22

Net Area Required—1,325 sq. ft.

Computer Terminal Room.

Primary Function—To provide facilities for bibliographical retrieval from remote computer databases, often with the user present to assist in the procedure.

Relationship to Other Facilities—Should be easy to indicate its location from the Public Reference Desks.

Special Requirements
Heating/Ventilation/Air conditioning
Acoustics—Normal
Floors—Wire wove carpeting, grounded for static electricity

Ceiling—Acoustic tile
Utility services—Hollow duct around the entire baseboard.

Built-in Furniture and Equipment - None.

Movable Furniture and Equipment:

1. 2 - terminal tables 2' × 5', with grounding mats.
2. 2 - secretarial chairs.
3. 6 - low stools to go with 1 and 2.
4. 1 - 30" × 60" desk, with typing L.
5. 1 - secretarial chair to go with 4.
6. 1 - vertical file.
7. 1 - 2' × 3' table.
8. 2 - sections of standard wall-hung shelving.

Net area required - 380 sq.ft.

Total Public Seating Required - 153.

Total Public Shelving Required - 35,262 vols.

Total Net Area Required for Reference Dept. - 10,275 sq. ft.

7. *CARD CATALOG*

Primary Function—To serve as a finding list for the entire campus collection of materials.

Relationship to Other Facilities—Ideally, this catalog should be within view of the user when he comes in the main entrance. It must be adjacent to the Reference Department, and immediately flanked by the Public Reference Desks.

The Catalog is also used intensively, by Interlibrary Loan Department, Circulation Department, Acquisitions Department, Catalog Department.

Special Requirements
     Fluorescent Lighting—70 f.c., maintained
     Heating/Ventilation/Air Conditioning
     Acoustics—Normal
     Floors—carpeting

     Ceiling—Acoustic tile
     Communication Systems Telephone jacks
                                        in catalog cases
                            Computer

Other Design Requirements—The catalogs should be arranged in long double-face ranges (we suggest 22 cases per range) on 18' centers, with one pass-through aisle through them, and with stand-up consultation tables at the end and between ranges.

At the end of each range will be a special table to hold the LC Subject Headings book.

Parallel to the ranges will be four small sit-down tables, for those requiring lengthy consultation of catalog drawers.

Large signs to designate the two kinds of catalogs.

Built-in Furniture and Equipment—None.

Movable Furniture and Equipment

1. 66 - 60-drawer card catalog cases, divided into 44 for the Author-Title Catalog, 22 for the Subject Catalog, to hold 4 million cards.
2. 20 - 30″ × 60″ tables, 40″ high, with shelves below, compartmentalized to hold P-slips.
3. 4 - high stools for item 2.
4. 3 - 2′ × 3′ tables, 40″ high, to hold LC Subject Catalogs.
5. 4 - 2′ × 4′ tables, parallel to card catalogs, but separated by an aisle from them.
6. 4 - side chairs for item 5.

Net Area Required - 3,450 sq. ft.

II. SPECIAL SERVICE AREAS

8. RESERVE DEPARTMENT

Primary Function—To house and service books and other materials for short-term reading by many students, mostly in the library.

Secondary Function—To serve as a convenience point to circulate other materials that are restricted.

Relationship to Other Facilities—This area must be easily found by students from the main entrance. It must be adjacent to reading areas of considerable size. It should be near the Circulation Department, which controls it.

Special Requirements

Outside windows (for enclosed rooms)	Ceiling—Acoustic tile
Fluorescent lighting	Utility services—Dedicated electric lines
Heating/Ventilation/Air conditioning	Communication Systems Telephones
Acoustics—Normal	Computer
Floors—carpeting	Intercom

Other Design Considerations—The Reserve stacks should lie at right angles between the Reserve Desk and the Workroom, so that the books can be reached easily from either point.

The restricted reading area can be developed by office landscaping, so long as its exit is past the Reserve Desk to provide control.

Built-in Furniture and Equipment—Reserve Desk, as specified.

Movable Furniture and Equipment

Reserve Desk
1. 1 - custom built desk, 2' wide, 20' long, 40'' high, with 2 computer terminals, book return slot, drawers and shelves, to be detailed as plans progress.
2. 3 - swivel chairs with backs, counter height.
3. 1 - depressible book truck, under desk.
4. 2 - microfilm readers, on counter.

Net Area Required—190 sq. ft.

Reserve Stacks
1. 100 - sections of standard shelving on 5' centers in ranges set at right angles to the Reserve Desk, with 10" nominal shelves, beginning no more than 6' behind the Desk.
2. 5 - vertical files, to hold pamphlets and reprints.

Net Area Required—960 sq. ft.

Reserve Workroom
1. 3 - 30" × 60" desks with typing L.
2. 5 - secretarial chairs.
3. 2 - 3' × 8' table.
4. 2 - side chairs for item 3.
5. 2 - vertical files.
6. 6 - sections of wall-hung shelving.
7. 4 - booktrucks.
8. Coat rack for 8.
9. 8 - lockers.

Net Area Required—600 sq. ft.

Department Head's Office (needs glass panel in door to supervise Reserve Desk).
1. 1 - 30" × 60" desk with typing L.
2. 1 - secretarial chair.
3. 1 - side chair.
4. 1 - 2' × 4' table.
5. 1 - vertical file.
6. 1 - section of wall-hung shelving.

Net Area Required—200 sq. ft.

Restricted Reading Area (suggest office landscaping).
1. 3 - 2' × 3' tables.
2. 3 - lounge chairs.
3. 6 - side chairs.

Public seating required—6

Net Area Required—150 sq. ft.

Public seating required—6

Net Area Required—2,100 sq. ft.

9. PERIODICALS AREA

Primary Function—To bring together all the bound Periodicals in the collection, beside display of all current periodicals in the collection, to make them more easily available for use.

Secondary Function—To provide service for bound and unbound periodicals, and to provide security for the collection at an exit control from this area.

Relationship to Other Facilities—Close to the Photocopy Room, a great deal of whose volume comes from copying periodicals.

As close to the Serials Department as is possible, given the above constriction. As close to the Reference Department as possible, given the above constrictions.

Special Requirements
Outside windows
Fluorescent lighting
Heating/Ventilation/Air
conditioning
Acoustics—Normal
Floors—carpeting

Ceiling—Acoustic tile
Utility services—Dedicated
electric lines
Communication Systems Telephones
Computer

Other Design Considerations—Should be all on one floor, not more than one floor from the main floor.

The far end of this enclosed area (the end furthest away from the entrance-exit control) should be an ornamental grill, separating the bound periodical stacks from adjacent stacks which are part of the General Bookstacks, to provide expansion in the event that our estimate of capacity is in error.

Built-in Furniture and Equipment—None

Movable Furniture and Equipment

Current Periodicals Area.
1. 134 - sections of standard shelving, to hold current periodicals.
2. 8 - 2′ × 3′ tables for 1.
3. 3 - 3′ × 6′ tables for 4.
4. 20 - side chairs for items 2 and 3.
5. 30 - lounge chairs.
6. 1 - coin-operated photocopy machine.

Public seating required—50

Public shelving required—16,750 vol.

Net Area Required—1,825 sq. ft.

Current Newspaper Area.
1. 12 - sections of standard shelving to hold 120 stacks of newspapers @ 10/5-shelf section of 12″ cantilevered shelves, set on 13″ vertical centers.

2. 2 - special newspaper reading tables, 5′ × 18′, with slanting shelves, double-face.
3. 20 - side chairs for item 2.

Public seating required—20

Public shelving required—120 vol.

Net Area Required—600 sq. ft.

Workroom (adjacent to Current Periodicals and the Exit Control).
1. 2 - 30″× 60″ desks with typing L.
2. 1 - typing stand.
3. 3 - secretarial chairs.
4. 4 - side chairs.
5. 1 - 2′ × 4′ table.
6. 2 - vertical files.
7. 1 - supply cabinet, 2′ × 3′.
8. 3 - book trucks.
9. 10 - sections of standard shelving, 16″ shelves.
10. 2 - lockers.

Net Area Required—455 sq. ft.

Bound Periodical Stacks (should be an extension of newspaper stacks and current periodicals stacks).
1. 934 - sections of standard shelving to hold 112,080 volumes of bound periodicals @ 120/section.

Public shelving required—112,080 vol.

Net Area Required—8,130 sq. ft.

Periodicals Reading Areas (distributed through the stack areas specially compartmentalized if necessary).
1. 45 - 2′ × 3′ tables for 1.
2. 45 - 2′ × 3′ carrels with baffle and bookshelf.
3. 12 - 3′ × 6′ tables for 4.
4.   7 - 3′ × 8′ tables for 6.

Public seating required—180

Net Area Required—4,090 sq. ft.

Exit Control (at a narrowed entrance-exit point).
1. 1 - 30″ × 45″ desk.
2. 1 - secretarial chair.

Net Area Required—150 sq. ft.

Total Public Seating Required—250

Total Public Shelving Required—128,950 vol.

Total Net Area Required—15,250 sq. ft.

10. CURRICULUM MATERIALS CENTER

Primary Function—To shelve, service, and provide for reading at tables curriculum sheets, school textbooks, Realia, audio and video cassettes used in classroom teaching below the college level.

Relationship to Other Facilities—Must be on the same floor and adjacent to the Education books.

Special Requirements
Outside windows
Fluorescent lighting
Heating/Ventilation/
Air conditioning
Acoustics—Normal
Floors—carpeting

Ceiling—Acoustic tile
Communications Telephones
                    Computer

Other Design Considerations—Students will be allowed browsing access to this material. Since it is arranged in a special order and small enough to be easily stolen, it must be carefully controlled by the staff on duty both in going out and returning to the shelving area. A work bar should be arranged so that students leaving these stacks must pass it on exiting.

A special display wall should be designed to exhibit advertising brochures, pamphlets, small instructional devices, etc. In an attractive way. This requires a system of interchangeable panels and small shelves that can be rearranged for different needs.

Built-in Furniture and Equipment—A work-bar 26″ wide by 108″ long by 42″ high.

Movable Furniture and Equipment
1. 3 - 30″ × 60″ desks, with typing L.
2. 3 - secretarial chairs.
3. 3 - side chairs for item 1.
4. 2 - 3′ × 8′ tables.
5. 2 - side chairs to go with item 4.
6. 10 - legal size vertical files.
7. 48 - sections of standard shelving to hold a book equivalent of 6,000 volumes.
8. 3 - 3′ × 8′ tables.
9. 4 - 3′ × 6′ tables.
10. 48 - side chairs for items 9 and 10.

Public Seating Required—48

Public Shelving Required—6,000 vols.

Net Area Required—1,785 sq. ft.

11. GOVERNMENT DOCUMENTS/TECHNICAL REPORTS LIBRARY

This Library includes the following areas:

1. Reference Area.
2. Reference Office.

    3. Shelf List.
    4. Microform Area.
    5. Closed Shelving.
    6. Open Shelving.
    7. Reading Area.
    8. Workroom.
    9. Department Head Office.
  10. Instructional Room.

Primary Function—To collect, process and service government documents and research reports.

Secondary Function—To instruct in their use.

Relationship to Other Facilities—No specific relationship, but MUST be in an obvious place in the library, since documents are not widely known to users, and contain a treasure-hoard of materials pertinent to most subjects.

Special Requirements

Outside windows	Ceiling—Acoustic tile
Fluorescent lighting	Utility services—plumbing
Heating/Ventilation/Air	Communication Systems Telephones
conditioning	Computer
Acoustics—Normal	
Floors—carpeting	

Other Design Considerations—None

Built-in Furniture and Equipment—None

Movable Furniture and Equipment

Reference Desks (at entrance, offering a welcome).
1. 2 - 30″ × 60″ desks with typing L.
2. 2 - swivel chairs without arms.
3. 2 - 4′ × 9′ periodical index tables, double-sided and double-headed.
4. 8 - stools for item 3.
5. 1 - 2′ × 3′ table for microfilm reader.
6. 1 - wall exhibition case.
7. 50 - sections of standard shelving.

Public seating required—8

Public shelving required—6,250 vol.

Net Area Required—845 sq. ft.

Reference Office (near Reference Desks).
1. 4 - 30″ × 60″ desks with typing L.
2. 4 - secretarial chairs.
3. 2 - side chairs for item 1.

4. 4 - vertical files.
5. 2 - sections of wall-hung shelving.
   and, just inside the door,
6. 5 - 60-drawer card catalogs, with pull-out shelves.
7. 2 - high stools.

Net Area Required—525 sq. ft.

Microform Reading Area (noisy area; must have dimmed lighting).
1. 10 - 2′ × 4′ special microform tables, in a range of five double-face sections, with baffle between.
2. 10 - side chairs for item 1.

Public seating required—10

Net Area Required—250 sq. ft.

Closed Shelving (near Reference Desks and Workroom).
1. 72 - microfiche cabinets, 24″ × 28″.
2. 15 - vertical files.
3. 180 - sections of standard shelving.

Public Shelving—22,500 vol.

Net Area Required—2,750 sq. ft.

Open Shelving
1. 1,281 sections of standard shelving to supply 19,214 lineal feet of shelving by 1980.

Public shelving required—166,125 vol.

Net Area Required—11,144 sq. ft.

Reading Area
1. 4 - 4′ × 6′ tables for 4.
2. 8 - 2′ × 4′ tables for 1.
3. 24 - side chairs.
4. 3 - sections of wall-hung slant-face shelving.
5. 18 - sections of standard shelving.
6. 1 - dictionary stand.

Public seating required—24

Public shelving required—2,250 vol.

Net Area Required—1,125 sq. ft.

Workroom
1. 3 - 30″ × 60″ desks with typing L.
2. 3 - secretarial chairs.

3. 1 - 2′ × 4′ marking table.
4. 1 - side chair for item 3.
5. 1 - Se-lin Labeler on typing stand.
6. 1 - secretarial chair for item 5.
7. 1 - 3′ × 12′ table for sorting.
8. 1 - supply cabinet.
9. 10 - sections of wall-hung shelving.
10. 4 - book trucks.
11. 1 - coat rack for 8.
12. 1 - sink, with cupboard below and mirror above.

Net Area Required—690 sq. ft.

Department Head's Office
1. 1 - 30″ × 60″ desk with typing L.
2. 1 - swivel chair without arms.
3. 2 - side chairs.
4. 1 - 3′ × 6′ table.
5. 2 - vertical files.
6. 2 - sections of wall-hung shelving.

Net Area Required—250 sq. ft.

Instructional Room
1. 1 - 3′ × 10′ table.
2. 10 - side chairs.
3. 1 - section of wall-hung shelving.
4. Blackboard/ceiling-mounted screen.

Public seating required—10

Net Area Required—160 sq. ft.

Total Public Seating for Government Documents—52.

Total Public Shelving for Government Documents—188,625 vol.

Total Net Area for Government Documents—17,750 sq. ft.

12. AUDIO-VISUAL LIBRARY

This Department consists of the following areas:
1. Reference/Circulation Area.
2. Workroom.
3. Listening Area.
4. Viewing Rooms.
5. Department Head's Office.

Primary Function—To collect and service non-book instructional materials of any kind, to provide for their use and to service them. Much of the function is advisory.

Secondary Function—To duplicate materials, and produce a limited range of materials for library use.

Relationship to Other Facilities—This library should be in an obvious place near walkways, so that it will become known by being seen by students.

Special Requirements

Outside windows (except viewing rooms)	Ceiling—Acoustic tile
Fluorescent lighting	Utility services—special wiring
Heating/Ventilation/Air conditioning (special heat loads)	Communication Systems Telephones
	TV
Acoustics—specially suppressed	Wireless listening system, to be detailed
Floors—carpeting	

Other Design Considerations—None

Built-in Furniture and Equipment—Circulation desk, storage-bin wall as specified.

Movable Furniture and Equipment

Reference/Circulation Area (at the entrance)—
1. 1 - circulation desk 9' long, 2' wide, 40" high, to be detailed.
2. 2 - swivel chairs with backs, counter height.
3. 12 - sections of standard shelving.
4. 2 - microfiche cases, 24" × 28".
5. 3 - record cabinets 24" × 28".
6. 1 - slide storage cabinet, for 30,000, 3' × 5'.
7. 1 - filmstrip cabinet, for 1200, 28" × 40".
8. 2 - supply cabinets, 2' × 3'.
9. 1 - pegboard wall.
10. 2 - 60-drawer card catalogs, near, but outside, the Circulation Desk.
11. 3 - sections of record shelving, 3' wide.
12. 5 - sections of standard shelving.

Net Area Required—500 sq. ft.

Workroom (near the Reference/Circulation Area)—
1. 5 - 30" × 60" desks with typing L.
2. 5 - secretarial chairs.
3. 4 - side chairs.
4. 4 - sections of wall-hung shelving.
5. 2 - 3' × 8' tables.
6. 4 - side chairs for item 5.
7. 1 - entire wall of custom storage bins, with compartments 2½' square and 2' deep.
8. 1 - copy stand/dry mount press, 3' × 8'.
9. 1 - audio duplicator, 3' × 3'.
10. 2 - equipment carts.
11. 1 - pegboard wall.

Net Area Required—1,000 sq. ft.

Listening Area (Plan the esthetics of this arrangement, it generally looks bad)—
1. 60 - wired carrels, 2′ × 4′ and tables 2′ × 4′ for 1.
2. 120 - side chairs (2 per carrel).
3. 30 - lounge seats.
4.   1 - TV receiver.

Public seating required—150.

Net Area Required—3,225 sq. ft.

Viewing Rooms (must be soundproof and windowless).

Previewing rooms, for each:
1. 4 - chairs, with flip-out writing boards.
2. 1 - wall-mounted screen.
3. 1 - equipment cart.
4. 1 - TV receiver.

Net Area Required—80 sq. ft.

Identical units required—6

Total Public Seating required—24

Total Net Area Required—480 sq. ft.

Viewing Rooms, for each:
1. 15 - chairs with flip-out writing boards.
2. 1 - equipment cart.
3. 1 - wall mounted screen.

Net Area Required—300 sq. ft.

Identical units required—2

Total Public Seating Required—30

Total Net Area Required—600 sq. ft.

Department Head's Office—
1. 1 - 30″ × 60″ desk with typing L.
2. 1 - swivel chair without arms.
3. 3 - side chairs.
4. 2 - sections of wall-hung shelving.
5. 1 - vertical file.

Net Area Required—175 sq. ft.

Total Public Seating—204.

Total Net Area Required for Audio-Visual Library—6,000 sq. ft.

13. MAP LIBRARY

Primary Function—To collect and service a large collection of sheet maps and atlases in all disciplines.

Secondary Function—To provide special equipment for users to work on maps.

Relationship to Other Facilities—Should be in an obvious place, where students will know it exists because they pass it; however, its unusual floor load dictates a lower floor.

Special Requirements
Outside windows
Fluorescent lighting
Heating/Ventilation/Air conditioning
Acoustics—Normal
Floors—carpeting
Ceiling—Acoustic tile
Communication Systems Telephones
Computer

Other Design Considerations—Ultimate capacity will make the 3'6" × 4'6" cases weigh 3,600 pounds, or 225 pounds per square foot Dead Load, considerably more Live Load. When stacked in double-face ranges, the floor load increases even more. Ideally, this room should be on a slab; if not, then on a lower floor with floor bracing from the floor below. We invite the architects' attention to the solution of this problem.

Built-in Furniture and Equipment—None

Movable Furniture and Equipment

Map Room
1. 1 - 30' × 60" desk with typing L.
2. 1 - secretarial chair.
3. 1 - 60-drawer card catalog.
4. 1 - vertical file with item 1.
5. 1 - mobile step ladder.
6. 1 - display panel, cork, 8' × 15'.
7. 4 - double-face ranges 7 cases long, total 56 stacked cases, 3½' × 4½'.
8. 24 - 5-drawer vertical files.
9. 1 - cabinet for plastic relief maps, 28" × 40".
10. 4 - atlas cases.
11. 4 - sections of wall-hung shelving.
12. 2 - 3' × 8' tables.
13. 4 - side chairs for item 12.
14. 1 - light table, 3' × 5'.
15. 1 - secretarial chair for item 14.
16. 1 - drafting table, 3' × 6'.
17. 1 - drafting chair.

Net Area Required—2,685 sq. ft.

Map Librarian's Office
1. 1 - 30″ × 60″ desk with typing L.
2. 1 - swivel chair without arms.
3. 2 - side chairs.
4. 1 - 3′ × 8′ table.
5. 1 - map truck, 3′ × 5′.
6. 1 - supply cabinet.
7. 2 - vertical files.
8. 2 - sections of wall-hung shelving.
9. 1 - coat rack.

Net Area Required—400 sq. ft.

Total Seating Required—6

Total Net Area Required for Map Library—3,100 sq. ft.

14. SPECIAL COLLECTIONS DEPARTMENT

Primary Function—To make available rare books and special collections of materials for use under surveillance and to preserve these materials for eternity (give or take a few weeks).

Relationship to Other Facilities—No special relationships, but it should be located where it is easy to find in the library.

This department includes a Reading Room and a Department Head Office, which have one set of special design requirements, and a stack/workroom area that has radically different special design requirements.

Reading Room.

Special Requirements
Outside windows, but minimized, on a North wall.
Fluorescent lighting, with UF-II Plexiglas sleeves, and fused ballasts.
Heating/Ventilation/Air conditioning.
Acoustics—Normal.
Floors—carpeting.

Ceiling—Acoustic tile.
Communications—Telephones.
Security provisions Unusually tamper-proof locks.
Motion detection burglar alarm system.

Other Design Considerations—This room must be unusually attractive, suggesting luxury as inexpensively as possible, to inspire respectful care of the books used here, and to attract potential donors. Fine paintings, attractive woods, special upholstery, etc. are ways of achieving the desired feeling.

Built-in Furniture and Equipment—wooden wall-hung bookshelves for reference books, and wall-hung air conditioned exhibition cases, lighted from outside the case.

Movable Furniture and Equipment.
1. 2 - 3′ × 10′ tables for 6.
2. 3 - 4′ × 6′ tables for 2.
3. 6 - 3′ × 4′ tables for 1.
4. 24 - side chairs for items 1 to 3.
5. 4 - flat exhibition cases, 4′ × 6′.
6. 2 - 30″ × 60″ wood desks, with typing L.
7. 2 - secretarial chairs.
8. 2 - side chairs, for item 6.
9. 1 - antique-styled round table, 4′ diameter.
10. 4 - side chairs for item 9.
11. 1 - antique-styled upholstered divan, for 2.
12. 2 - low ornamental side tables.

Public Seating Required—30

Net Area Required—1,800 sq. ft.

Department Head Office.
1. 1 - 30″ × 60″ des, with typing L.
2. 1 - executive swivel chair.
3. 3 - side chairs.
4. 1 - wooden table, 3′ diameter.
5. 1 - wood bookcase, 6′ long.
6. 1 - vertical file.

Net Area Required—250 sq. ft.

Special Collections Stacks/Workroom.

Primary Function—to preserve against destruction and deterioration the rare materials and special collections, housed on standard stack ranges and in vertical files.

Secondary Function—to serve as a workroom for processing new collections, annointing books, etc.

Special Requirements
No Windows.
Incandescent lighting.

Heating/Ventilation/Air conditioning—the most important physical facility in this entire area. Air tempering systems connected with the general library system are highly unsatisfactory. Once the desired temperature and humidity are attained in rare book stacks it is critically important that they be held within narrow limits of variation, to preserve books.
We recommend the use of a separate air conditioning unit located within the stacks, with all its ducts in the stacks, for recirculation, refiltering and retempering the air in the stacks. It should be sized to control with extreme sensitivity the temperature and humidity for the cubic capacity of the stacks alone. Ideally, there should be two such units connected to the ducts, each capable of tempering the entire stack area to provide a back up system when one machine is down for repair or maintenance.
This unit should be designed for extremely heavy duty service. Such machines are manufac-

tured for use in computer rooms, where sensitive atmospheric control is necessary to keep from distorting electronic data. Many of them have a high incidence of breakdown, and a machine must be chosen with a proven record of low maintenance requirements in actual use. The machine must run quietly.

Each cycle of air turnover should pass through filters that remove any noxious gas that it contains and 95% of the dust in the air.

Fireproofing—All walls, ceilings, floors and doors must be 1½ hours fireproof. Every effort should be made not to penetrate the walls and floors with duct openings. If any are used, they must contain fire-drop dampers.

Acoustics—No requirements.

Floors—Vinyl.

Alarm systems—Unusually sensitive ion detection fire detectors must be used. They should be wired to shut off the air-conditioner if a fire starts, and should be wired to ring a loud fire bell locally, and to ring a signal in the campus Security Office. Unusually valuable collections should be further protected by having the alarm system wired to ring in the nearest municipal fire station.

—A high humidity detector, wired to ring a loud fire bell locally, and to ring a signal in the campus Security Office.

Security Systems —Unusually tamper-proof locks.
      — Motion detection burglar alarm system.

Extinguishing System—A Halon system that discharges automatically on signal from fire detectors, and that retains a second charge for additional protection, should be used. These systems have been known to blow shelves full of rare books out of their stacks at a distance from their discharge ducts, which should be designed to prevent this serious problem.

Other Design Considerations

Location—This area should be on a North or interior wall, to minimize the impact of the outside temperature on the inside, and should be heavily insulated.

It should not be adjacent to any structural element that could transmit fire from floor to floor, such as large vertical air ducts, elevator shafts, and the like.

Waterproofing—This entire Special Collections area should NOT be on the top floor of the building if protected only by the roof. It should be underneath a structural floor, which should contain over the entire area a waterproof membrane constructed for extreme conditions, to protect against water seepage from above.

Ceilings & Walls—These should be free of any water pipes and any electrical conduits except the minimum necessary to supply the needs of this stack area.

Built-in Furniture and Equipment—None.

Movable Furniture and Equipment—
1. 800 - sections of standard shelving, to hold 100,000 volumes.
2. 24 - legal size vertical files.
3.   3 - 3' × 12' work tables.
4.   1 - 4' × 8' table.
5.   1 - sink, with self-contained electric water heater.
6.   2 - 2' × 3' supply cabinets, 6' high.

Public Shelving Required—100,000 vols.

Net Area Required—8,160 sq. ft.

Total Public Seating Required—30.

Total Public Shelving Required—100,000 vols.

Total Net Area Required for Special Collections Department—10,400 sq. ft.

III. *SPECIAL USER FACILITIES*

15. PHOTODUPLICATION DEPARTMENT

Primary Function—To make photocopies of library materials at request, on the spot, for cash payment.

Secondary Functions—Microfilming, mimeographing, catalog card production, distributing Interlibrary Loan photocopies, ordering, billing, accounting.

Relationship to Other Facilities—This should be adjacent to the Periodicals Area, and in an obvious place so that all students who use that area will be aware of this facility. Also, as near to Interlibrary Loan Department as is possible, given the above requirement.

Special Requirements
Outside windows
Fluorescent lighting
Heating/Ventilation/Air
conditioning (special
heat load)
Acoustics—Specially
suppressed
Floors—carpeting
Walls—sound absorbent

Ceiling—Acoustic tile (microfilm
machine needs 8'6" clearance)
Utility services Plumbing
            Dedicated electric lines, 220 volt
            Flexible tapping of electrical outlets
            Switch to darken lights above microfilm machine
Communication Systems—Telephones

Other Design Requirements—Anything that will make life more pleasant for staff who spend 8 hours a day on their feet almost constantly.

Built-in Furniture and Equipment—Service counter and Workbar detailed below.

Movable Furniture and Equipment

1. Service bar 20' long, 2' wide, 40" high, with 4' standing room in front of it and 6' between service bar and photocopy machines.
2. 6 - photocopy machines, 4' × 4', arranged to face the service bar, with 30" passage between machines.
3. Wall-hung shelving, as much as possible on the wall at right angles to the photocopy machines, 10" nominal shelves.
4. A range of double-face shelving, as long as possible with 4' clearance between the face of shelving and the machines, using 10" nominal shelves.
5. 1 - wall-mounted work bar, 30" wide, 35" high, with cupboards for supplies underneath, as long as possible, but at least 20' long.
6. 3 - 3' × 8' tables.
7. 6 - side chairs for item 6.
8. 1 - 30" × 60" desk with typing L, near photocopy machines for supervision.
9. 2 - 30" × 60" desks with typing L, behind the range of stacks.
10. 1 - Xerox machine for catalog card production.
11. 1 - microfilm machine, 6'6" × 3'5" (has special heat load).
12. 1 - collator, 1'6" × 1'10".
13. 1 - card cutter, 3'9" × 3'3".
14. 1 - sink at end of the workbar, for washing hands, with mirror above it.
15. 1 - utility sink for washing machine parts, isolated to avoid splashing other equipment in the room.
16. 4 - vertical files.
17. 1 - supply cabinet, 2' × 3' × 6'.
18. 1 - coat hanging rack for 10.
19. Lockers for 8.

Net Area Required—1,950 sq. ft.

16. GROUP STUDY ROOMS

Primary Function—To provide rooms where groups can converse about study problems, and work them out together on a chalk board.

Relationship to Other Facilities—They must be so located, and baffled that their noise will not disturb readers.

Special Requirements
Fluorescent lighting
Heating/Ventilation/Air conditioning
Acoustics — specially suppressed
Floors—carpeting
Walls—sound absorbent

Ceiling—Acoustic tile
Separate Exhaust

Other Design Considerations—They should be paired, with a common accordion wall between them (which need not be sound absorbent) so they can open up to twice the area.

Built-in Furniture and Equipment—None.

Movable Furniture and Equipment

For each
1. 1 - 3′ × 6′ table for 6.
2. 6 - side chairs.
3. 1 - chalk board.

Public seating required—6

Net Area Required—100 sq. ft.

Identical units required—10.

Total Public Seating Required—60.

Total Net Area Required—1,000 sq. ft.

17. SMOKING LOUNGES

Primary Function—To provide a smoking area in a relaxing atmosphere.

Relationship to Other Facilities—Must be near Smoking Studies, to provide the option of both facilities.

Special Requirements
Fluorescent lighting
Heating/Ventilation/Air conditioning
Acoustics — Specially suppressed
Floors—tile

Ceiling—Acoustic tile
Separate Exhaust

Other Design Considerations—None.

Built-in Furniture and Equipment—None.

Movable Furniture and Equipment

For each
1. 20 - lounge seats.
2. Smoking urns between each pair of seats.

Public Seating Required—20

Net Area Required—500 sq. ft.

Identical units required—2.

Total Public Seating Required—40

Total Net Area Required—1,000 sq. ft.

18. SMOKING STUDIES

Primary Function—To provide a smoking area with a study atmosphere.

Relationship to Other Facilities—Must be near Smoking Lounges, to provide the option of both facilities.

Special Requirements
Fluorescent lighting
Heating/Ventilation/Air
conditioning
Acoustics—Normal
Floors—tile

Ceiling—Acoustic tile
Separate Exhaust

Other Design Considerations—None.

Built-in Furniture and Equipment—None.

Movable Furniture and Equipment

For each
1. 20 - 2' × 3' carrels with baffle and bookshelf.
2. 20 - side chairs.

Public seating required—20

Net Area Required—500 sq. ft.

Identical units required—2.

Total Public Seating Required—40.

Total Net Area Required—1,000 sq. ft.

19. TYPING ROOMS

Primary Function—To provide a room with rental typewriters, and for the use of personal typewriters, in a location where its sound will not disturb readers.

Relationship to Other Facilities—On floors of General Bookstacks, but removed and baffled from them so that it will not disturb them.

Special Requirements
    Fluorescent lighting
    Heating/Ventilation/Air
    conditioning
    Acoustics — Specially
               suppressed
    Floors—carpeting
    Walls—sound absorbent

Ceiling—Acoustic tile

Other Design Considerations—None.

Built-in Furniture and Equipment—None.

Movable Furniture and Equipment

For each
    1. 12 - 2′ × 4′ tables, typing height.
    2. 12 - secretarial chairs.

Public Seating Required—12

Net Area Required—300 sq. ft.

Identical units required—2.

Total Public Seating Required—24

Total Net Area Required—600 sq. ft.

20. HANDICAPPED USERS ROOMS

Primary Function—To provide blind users with rooms equipped with special reading machines, which they will use unaided, and a room for oral recording of printed texts or one-to-one reading.

Relationship to Other Facilities—On a main walkway for ease of access and security for the machines.

Special Requirements
    Fluorescent lighting
    Heating/Ventilation/Air
    conditioning
    Acoustics — Specially
               suppressed
    Floors—carpeting.
    Walls—sound absorbent

Ceiling—Acoustic tile

Other Design Considerations—None.

Built-in Furniture and Equipment—None.

Movable Furniture and Equipment

Reading Machine Room.
1. 2 - Kurzweil reading machines.
2. 4 - side chairs.
3. 1 - low bookcase.

Net Area Required—100 sq. ft.

Near Sighted Reading Room.
1. 2 - Visual text videotape players.
2. 4 - side chairs.

Net Area Required—100 sq. ft.

Recording Room.
1. 1 - 2' × 3' low table.
2. 2 - side chairs.

Net Area Required—75 sq. ft.

Total Net Area Required—275 sq. ft.

21.   USER INSTRUCTION ROOM

Primary Function—To instruct large and small campus classes in the use of the library (there are large requirements for media presentations).

Secondary Function—Meetings, workshops, training sessions for the library staff.

Tertiary Function—This will also be an After-Hours Study Room for the library, open all night.

Relationship to Other Facilities—Must be adjacent to Men and Women Toilets and the Snack Room, the entire group of facilities to be locked off from the rest of the library, with access from the outside without coming through the library.
Given these restrictions, it should be as available to the Reference Department as possible.

Special Requirements
Outside windows   Ceiling—Acoustic tile
Fluorescent lighting   Communication Systems Telephones
Heating/Ventilation/Air   TV
conditioning   Computer
Acoustics — Specially
              suppressed
Floors—carpeting

Other Design Considerations—Outside entrance. Separable from the rest of the library. The area must be separable into three smaller areas to accomodate 50 each by use of accordion panels, which should be as sound-inhibiting as possible.

Built-in Furniture and Equipment—None.

Movable Furniture and Equipment

Instruction Room
1. 150 - stacking, but comfortable and substantial chairs.
2. 20 - 3′ × 8′ folding tables for 6.
3. 30 - 2′ × 3′ stacking tables for 1.
4. 2 - large TV consoles.
5. 3 - ceiling-hung screens.
6. 2 - lecterns.
7. 3 - equipment carts.

Public seating required—150

Net Area Required—3,300 sq. ft.

IV. BOOKS AND READERS

22. FACULTY STUDIES

Primary Function—To provide locked rooms for long-term occupancy, for advanced research workers.

Relationship to Other Facilities—Must be removed from and baffled from reading areas, since typing will occur in them. Should be close to the general bookstacks.

Special Requirements
Outside windows   Ceiling—Acoustic tile
Fluorescent lighting
Heating/Ventilation/Air
conditioning
Acoustics — Specially
           suppressed
Floors—carpeting

Other Design Considerations—A ventilation ceiling should be considered, to provide enough air change without draft to freshen these small rooms, in which smoking will take place.

Built-in Furniture and Equipment—None.

Movable Furniture and Equipment

For each
1. 1 - 30″ × 60″ desk, with typing L and filing drawer.
2. 1 - swivel chair.
3. 1 - side chair.
4. 1 - section of wall-hung shelving behind the desk.
5. 1 - coat hook.

Public Seating Required—1

Net Area Required—48 sq. ft.

Identical units required—50

Total Public Seating Required—50

Total Net Area Required—2,400 sq. ft.

23. GENERAL SEATING

Relationship to Other Facilities—These seats should be distributed among the General Bookstacks, or near them.

Movable Furniture and Equipment

1. 100 at single carrels.
2. 101 at 2' × 3' tables.
3. 200 at 3' × 6' tables for 4.
4. 126 at 3' × 8' tables for 6.

Public Seating Required—527.

Net Area Required—13,175 sq. ft.

24. GENERAL BOOKSTACKS

Movable Furniture and Equipment

1. 4,330 sections of standard shelving to hold 541,163 volumes.

Public Shelving Required—541,163 vols.

Net Area Required—38,970 sq. ft.

V. *ADMINISTRATIVE OFFICES*

This grouping includes offices for the following:

1. Director.
2. Associate Director.
3. Assistant Directors.
4. Administrative Assistants.
5. Secretaries.
6. Machine/Supply Room.
7. Conference Room.

Primary Function—To be available to faculty, staff and students to discuss matters pertaining to the library's performance.

Secondary Function—To hold meetings with various groups.

Relationship to Other Facilities—Should be not more than one floor from Reference Department or Technical Processes Departments. The easier it is to reach from the main entrance, the more the faculty are likely to come in.

Special Requirements

Outside windows	Ceiling—Acoustic tile
Fluorescent lighting	Communication Systems Telephones
Heating/Ventilation/Air conditioning	Computer
Acoustics—Normal	
Floors—carpeting	

Other Design Considerations—This group should be designed to be pleasant, since many of the people who come here are potential benefactors of the library.

Built-in Furniture and Equipment—Wooden bookshelves, and wall-hung workbar as specified.

Movable Furniture and Equipment

25. DIRECTOR'S OFFICE
1. 1 - 3' × 6' table for workspace.
2. 1 - swivel chair without arms.
3. 1 - credenza behind item 1, containing a drawer for filing folders, some room for storing supplies and room on top for telephone.
4. 1 - typing table.
5. 6 - side chairs.
6. Wooden bookshelves behind desk.

Net Area Required—250 sq. ft.

26. ASSOCIATE DIRECTOR'S OFFICE
1. 1 - 3' × 6' table for workspace.
2. 1 - swivel chair.
3. 1 - credenza behind table, 6' long.
4. 1 - 2' × 2' end table.
5. 4 - side chairs.
6. 3 - sections of wall-hung shelving.
7. 1 - planter.
8. 1 - coat rack.

Net Area Required—250 sq. ft.

26/1. ASSISTANT DIRECTOR FOR PUBLIC SERVICES
1. 1 - 3' × 6' work table.
2. 1 - swivel chair without arms.

3. 1 - credenza behind table.
4. 4 - side chairs.
5. 1 - 2′ × 4′ table.
6. 2 - sections of wall-hung shelving.
7. 1 - coat rack.

Net Area Required—240 sq. ft.

26/2. ASSISTANT DIRECTOR FOR TECHNICAL PROCESSES
1. 1 - 30″ × 60″ desk with typing L.
2. 1 - swivel chair.
3. 1 - 3′ × 6′ table.
4. 6 - side chairs.
5. 2 - vertical files, legal size.
6. 2 - sections of wall-hung shelving.
7. 1 - coat rack.

Net Area Required—240 sq. ft.

27. ADMINISTRATIVE ASSISTANT OFFICE
1. 3 - 30″ × 60″ desks with typing L.
2. 2 - swivel chairs without arms.
3. 1 - secretarial chair.
4. 1 - 3′ × 6′ table.
5. 2 - side chairs for item 4.
6. 3 - sections of wall-hung shelving.
7. 2 - vertical files.

Net Area Required—345 sq. ft.

28. SECRETARIES AND RECEPTION OFFICES (perhaps open alcoves related to the other offices)
1. 4 - 30″ × 60″ desks with typing L.
2. 4 - secretarial chairs.
3. 1 - coffee bar, with room for storage of equipment.
4. 6 - vertical files.
5. 5 - lounge chairs.
6. 1 - 2′ × 2′ coffee table.
7. 3 - sections of wooden shelving, wall-hung.
8. 1 - combination coat closet for 10 coats and supply cabinet.
9. 1 - safe.
10. 2 - planters.
11. 1 - small Xerox machine

Net Area Required—675 sq. ft.

29. MACHINE/SUPPLY ROOM
1. A wall-hung workbar 30″ deep by 10′ long, by 36″ high, with a sink at one end, and cupboards above and below.

Net Area Required—80 sq. ft.

30. CONFERENCE ROOM (should open from secretaries office, as well as from outside)
    1. 1 - conference table for 12.
    2. 12 - side chairs.
    3. 1 - coffee bar, with room for storage.
    4. 1 - wall-hung chalk board.
    5. 1 - wall-hung tack board.

Net Area Required—200 sq. ft.

Total Net Area Required for Administrative Offices—2,280 sq. ft.

VI. *TECHNICAL PROCESSES*

The following departments are all part of the Technical Processes Division:
    1. Acquisitions Department.
    2. Catalog Department.
    3. Processing Department.
    4. Serials Department.
    5. Receiving and Shipping Department.

The operations in these departments are highly demanding detailed work requiring unusually strenuous reading tasks, of critical importance to the library's performance. The costs and efficiency of these operations are of prime concern to the library. Consequently, we stress the importance of establishing the proper relationships and flow patterns in these operations, of providing the best possible quality lighting, and of creating an environment in which it will feel pleasant to work.

These departments undergo constant change in loads, staffing, and processes and it is critically important to provide space that is flexible and as adaptable to change as is possible. A minimum of walls will be provided.

31. ACQUISITIONS DEPARTMENT

This department includes the following areas:
    1. Workroom, containing 12 sensitively interrelated activities.
    2. Bookkeeping Area.
    3. Department Head's Office.

Primary Function—To purchase, approve, and account for books for all the university library collections.

Secondary Function—To be easily available for consultation on book purchase matters to the faculty and staff.

Relationship to Other Facilities—Near Catalog Department; near a public walkway to provide easy access to faculty.

Special Requirements
Outside windows	Ceiling—Acoustic tile
Fluorescent lighting	Utility services—Dedicated electric lines
Heating/Ventilation/Air	Communication Systems Telephones
conditioning	Computer

Acoustics—Normal
Floors—carpeting in offices,
        vinyl elsewhere.

Other Design Considerations—A work flow from unit to unit will be detailed later to help the architects lay out this area workably. In an area this large, gross square footage must be allowed for main walkways.

Built-in Furniture and Equipment—None.

Movable Furniture and Equipment

Workroom (these areas should flow into each other).

Secretarial Area
1. 2 - 30″ × 60″ desks with typing L.
2. 2 - secretarial chairs.
3. 1 - 2′ × 4′ table.
4. 1 - secretarial chair.
5. 2 - vertical files.
6. 2 - supply cabinets.
7. 4 - sections of standard shelving.
8. 1 - coat rack for 12.

Net Area Required—300 sq. ft.

Order Area.
1. 1 - 3′ × 8′ table.
2. 1 - typing table.
3. 1 - Roladex address file, 2′ × 3′.

Net Area Required—165 sq. ft.

Order/Processing Equipment (between the two areas).
1. 2 - 3′ × 6′ tables.
2. 2 - 3′ × 12′ tables.
3. 8 - secretarial chairs.
4. 1 - 2′ × 4′ table.
5. 1 - secretarial chair for item 4.
6. 1 - vertical file.

Net Area Required—500 sq. ft.

Processing Supervisor.
1. 1 - 30″ × 60″ desk with typing L.
2. 1 - secretarial chair.
3. 1 - side chair.
4. 4 - sections of standard shelving.

Net Area Required—100 sq. ft.

Receiving Area.
1. 2 - 3′ × 8′ tables.
2. 1 - secretarial chair.
3. 1 - trash container, 3′ × 4′.
4. 8 - book trucks.
5. 10 - sections of standard shelving.
6. 25 - square feet of free floor space, for placing unopened cartons.

Net Area Required—500 sq. ft.

Inspection Area.
1. 1 - 30″ × 60″ desk with typing L.
2. 1 - secretarial chair.
3. 2 - 3′ × 6′ tables.
4. 2 - secretarial chairs for item 3.
5. 3 - book trucks.
6. 8 - sections of standard shelving.

Net Area Required—325 sq. ft.

L.C. Copy Area.
1. 1 - 3′ × 6′ table.
2. 1 - secretarial chair.
3. 6 - sections of standard shelving.

Net Area Required—120 sq. ft.

Searching Area (near Catalog Dept. bibliographies).
1. 10 - special 30″ × 48″ carrels, with baffles and side drawer.
2. 10 - secretarial chairs.
3. 10 - book trucks, for item 1.
4. 1 - typing stand.
5. 8 - sections of wall-hung shelving.
6. 1 - 3′ × 8′ table for item 5.
7. 4 - side chairs for item 6.
8. 3 - vertical files.
9. 1 - coat rack for 20.

Net Area Required—900 sq. ft.

Approval Area (near entrance to Acquisitions Dept., for easy access to faculty).
1. 2 - 3′ × 6′ tables.
2. 2 - secretarial chairs.
3. 3 - book trucks.
4. 8 - sections of standard shelving.
5. 6 - lounge chairs for item 4.
6. 1 - 3′ coffee table for item 4.
7. 20 - square feet of free floor space to place unopened cartons.

Net Area Required—500 sq. ft.

Holding Area.
1. 1 - 30" × 60" desk.
2. 1 - secretarial chair.
3. 2 - special carrels, 30" × 48", with baffles and side drawer.
4. 2 - secretarial chairs for item 3.
5. 6 - book trucks.
6. 64 - sections of standard shelving, to hold 8,000 vol. in process.

Net Area Required—800 sq. ft.

Gifts Area.
1. 1 - 30" × 60" desk with typing L.
2. 1 - secretarial chair.
3. 2 - 3' × 6' tables.
4. 2 - side chairs for item 3.
5. 1 - typing table.
6. 3 - book trucks.
7. 1 - vertical file.
8. 64 - sections of standard shelving.
9. 25 - square feet of free floor space to place unopened cartons.

Net Area Required—950 sq. ft.

Added Copies Area.
1. 1 - 3' × 6' table.
2. 1 - secretarial chair.
3. 2 - book trucks.
4. 12 - sections of shelving.

Net Area Required—200 sq. ft.

Bookkeeping Area.
1. 2 - 30" × 60" desks with typing L.
2. 1 - 3' × 6' desk with typing L.
3. 2 - 3' × 6' tables.
4. 5 - secretarial chairs.
5. 7 - vertical files.
6. 1 - 2' × 4' table for microfilm reader.
7. 1 - secretarial chair for item 6.
8. 6 - sections of standard shelving, 18" shelves.
9. 1 - coat rack for 8.

Net Area Required—600 sq. ft.

Bookkeeping Machine Room (must have sound suppression).
1. 1 - keypunch, 2½' × 3'.
2. 1 - verifier 2½' × 3'.
3. 1 - card sorter, 2½' × 5'.
4. 2 - secretarial chairs.

5. 1 - tub file, 3′ × 3′.
6. 4 - cabinets, 20″ × 38″.

Net Area Required—300 sq. ft.

Department Head's Office.
1. 1 - 30″ × 60″ desk, with typing L.
2. 1 - swivel chair without arms.
3. 2 - side chairs.
4. 1 - 3′ × 6′ table.
5. 4 - side chairs.
6. 4 - sections of wall-hung shelving.

Net Area Required—220 sq. ft.

Total Net Area Required for Acquisitions Department—6,500 sq. ft.

32. CATALOG DEPARTMENT

Primary Function—To catalog books and maintain bibliographic records.

Relationship to Other Facilities—Near the Acquisitions Department, and the Card Production Area of the Processing Department. As close to the main Card Catalog as is possible, under the above constrictions.

Special Requirements
Outside windows
Fluorescent lighting
Heating/Ventilation/Air conditioning
Acoustics — Normal generally; specially suppressed at cataloging
Floors — carpeting in offices, vinyl elsewhere

Ceiling—Acoustic tile
Utility services Dedicated electric lines
Electrical outlet at each desk
Communication Systems Telephones
Computer

Other Design Considerations—It would be useful to have the work stations together in one group with all their collateral stacks and equipment arranged to the side at right angles to them, to provide easy passage in and out for the catalog librarians.

This work is hard on the eyes, and the very best lighting is required.

Special attention should be paid to lending a feeling of compartmentalization to the work stations without using walls. Special attention should be paid to the feeling of this department, which should be pleasant.

Built-in Furniture and Equipment—None.

Movable Furniture and Equipment

Work Stations.
1. 17 - 30″ × 60″ desks with typing L.
2. 17 - secretarial chairs.
3. 1 - 2′ × 4′ table for microfilm reader.
4. 1 - side chair for item 3.

Net Area Required—1,330 sq. ft.

Work Shelving.
1. 36 - sections of standard shelving, near work stations.

Net Area Required—325 sq. ft.

Reference & Professional Collection.
1. 4 - sections of standard shelving.

Net Area Required—36 sq. ft.

L.C. Schedules.
1. 3 - 3′ × 12′ tables.
2. 6 - side chairs.

Net Area Required—430 sq. ft.

Shelflist/Authority File.
1. 23 - 60-drawer card catalogs (20-shelflist; 3-authority file).

Net Area Required—375 sq. ft.

Bibliographic Area (must be adjacent to the Cataloging Camera and near the Searching Area of Acquisitions Dept.).
1. 50 - sections of standard shelving @ 15′/5-shelf section.
2. 2 - 3′ × 8′ tables, 40″ high.
3. 1 - 3′ × 8′ table, for unbound issues.
4. 4 - side chairs for item 3.

Net Area Required—775 sq. ft.

Depository File (near Card Production Area of Processing, and Searching Area of Acquisitions).
1. 10 - 60-drawer card catalogs.
2. 4 - secretarial chairs.

Net Area Required—160 sq. ft.

Cataloging Camera Area (must be adjacent to Bibliographical Area).
1. Photocopy camera for LC copy.

Net Area Required—100 sq. ft.

Computer Terminal Room (must be near Acquisitions Department).

This room has the following Special Requirements

A hollow duct around the entire baseboard.
Wire-wove carpeting, grounded for static electricity.
Constant adequate humidity.

Movable Furniture and Equipment
1. 8 - 2′ × 5′ terminal tables, fitted to place the terminal screens at eye level.
2. Room beside each for a book truck.
3. 1 - 3′ × 4′ table for telephone.
4. 2 - sections of wall hung shelving.

Net Area Required—600 sq. ft.

Department Head's Office.
1. 1 - 30″ × 60″ desk, with typing L.
2. 1 - swivel chair without arms.
3. 4 - side chairs.
4. 2 - sections of wall-hung shelving.
5. 1 - vertical file.

Net Area Required—160 sq. ft.

Total Net Area Required by Catalog Department—4,290 sq. ft.

33. PROCESSING DEPARTMENT

This Department includes the following areas:
1. Card Production Area.
2. Filing Area.
3. Marking Area.
4. Binding Preparation Area.
5. Mending Room.
6. Department Head's Office.

Primary Function—To apply the terminal processes to bibliographic records, and to physical books, to make them usable in the bookstacks. To maintain the main card catalog and other bibliograpic files located outside of this department. To prepare for binding and to mend books from the stacks.

Relationship to Other Facilities—This continues work begun in the Catalog Department and the Serials Department, and must be adjacent to the first and not far from the second.

Special Requirements
Outside windows
Fluorescent lighting
Heating/Ventilation/Air conditioning
Acoustics — Specially suppressed
Floors — carpeting in office, vinyl elsewhere
Ceiling—Acoustic tile
Utility services Plumbing
Dedicated electric lines, 220 volt
Many electric outlets
Unusual electrical flexibility

Other Design Considerations—This Department requires very good quality lighting, and must be made as pleasant as possible to work in. Office landscaping should be considered for compartmentalization, without using walls, except where specified.

Built-in Furniture and Equipment—None.

Movable Furniture and Equipment

Card Production Area (near Catalog Department, Shelflist, Authority Files, Depository Files and Bibliographical Area; requires electrical outlet at each desk and table for 3 appliances).
1. 20 - 30″ × 60″ desks with typing L.
2. 20 - secretarial chairs.
3. 4 - 3′ × 5′ tables.
4. 1 - supply cabinet, 2′ × 3′.
5. 15 - sections of standard shelving.
6. 1 - coat rack for 10.

Net Area Required—2,000 sq. ft.

Filing Area.
1. 5 - 30″ × 60″ desks with typing L.
2. 5 - secretarial chairs.
3. 5 - 4′ × 10′ tables.
4. 3 - 3′ × 5′ tables.
5. 20 - side chairs for items 3 and 4.
6. 1 - vertical file.
7. 12 - sections of standard shelving.
8. 1 - coat rack for 10.

Net Area Required—1,200 sq. ft.

Marking Area (requires electrical outlet at each desk and table for 3 appliances, plus added electrical flexibility).
1. 3 - 30″ × 60″ desks with typing L.
2. 3 - 4′ × 10′ tables
3. 2 - 3′ × 4′ tables.
4. 1 - typing stand.
5. 10 - secretarial chairs.
6. 1 - Se-lin Labeler on typing stand.
7. 92 - sections of standard shelving.
8. 50 - square feet of free floor space for loaded cartons of books (2 - 25 sq. ft. areas).
9. 1 - keypunch, 3′ × 5′.
10. 20 - book trucks.
11. 2 - trash containers 3′ × 4′.
12. 1 - coat rack for 10.

Net Area Required—1,800 sq. ft.

Binding Preparation Area (near Serials and Catalog Departments).
1. 5 - 30″ × 60″ desks with typing L.
2. 5 - secretarial chairs.

3. 2 - 4′ × 12′ tables.
4. 2 - tables 3½′ × 3½′.
5. 2 - side chairs.
6. 1 - supply cabinet, 2′ × 3′.
7. 4 - book trucks.
8. 15 - sections of standard shelving.
9. 1 - coat rack for 10.
10. 1 - sink, with cupboard below and mirror above.

Net Area Required—1,150 sq. ft.

Mending Room (near Binding Preparation and Marking Areas; separate exhaust needed).
1. 3 - 30″ × 60″ desks with typing L.
2. 3 - secretarial chairs.
3. 2 - 3′ × 8′ tables, 29″ high.
4. 1 - 3′ × 8′ table, 40″ high.
5. 1 - supply cabinet, 2′ × 4′.
6. 1 - supply cabinet, 3½′ × 4′.
7. 1 - trimmer, 4′ × 6′.
8. 1 - stapler, 2½′ × 2½′.
9. 20 - square feet of free floor space for storing marble board.
10. 1 - sink with cupboard below and mirror above.
11. 14 - sections of standard shelving.
12. 1 - coat rack for 4.

Net Area Required—935 sq. ft.

Department Head's Office (close to everything).
1. 1 - 30″ × 60″ desk with typing L.
2. 1 - swivel chair.
3. 3 - side chairs.
4. 1 - 3′ × 5′ table.
5. 1 - vertical file.
6. 2 - sections of wall-hung shelving.
7. 1 - coat rack.

Net Area Required—225 sq. ft.

Total Net Area Required for Processing Department—7,300 sq. ft.

34. SERIALS DEPARTMENT

This Department includes the following areas:
1. Serials Record Area.
2. Serials Cataloging Area.
3. Department Head's Office.
4. Library Assistant/Typist.

Primary Function—To receive, record and route to their proper location all serials of the university library system. To catalog all serials.

Secondary Function—To supervise the reading area of the Periodicals Area.

Relationship to Other Facilities—Near Acquisitions, Catalog, and Processing Departments, and as close to the Periodicals Area as is possible under these constrictions.

Special Requirements

Outside windows

Fluorescent lighting

Heating/Ventilation/Air conditioning

Acoustics—Normal

Floors — carpeting in office, vinyl elsewhere

Ceiling—Acoustic tile

Communication Systems Telephones

Computer

Other Design Considerations—None.

Built-in Furniture—None.

Movable Furniture and Equipment

Serials Record Area

Supervisor
1. 2 - 30" × 60" desks with typing L.
2. 2 - secretarial chairs.
3. 2 - side chairs.
4. 1 - 3' × 6' table.
5. 1 - supply cabinet, 2' × 3', 3', 72" high.
6. 5 - sections of standard shelving.

Net Area Required—300 sq. ft.

Central Serials Record
1. 7 - custom built Kardex tables, 7' × 10'.
2. 10 - secretarial chairs.
3. 2 - tables, 3' × 10'.
4. 2 - tables 3' × 6'.
5. 3 - vertical files.
6. 1 - custom built section of 36 mail sorting bins.
7. 1 - book truck.
8. 16 - sections of standard shelving.
9. 3 - 60-drawer card catalogs.
10. 1 - coat rack for 20.
11. 20 - lockers.
12. 7 - typing stands.

Net Area Required—2,300 sq. ft.

Serials Cataloging Area
1. 4 - 30" × 60" desks with typing L.
2. 4 - secretarial chairs.

3. 4 - side chairs.
4. 1 - 3′ × 8′ table.
5. 2 - secretarial chairs for item 4.
6. 2 - 2′ × 4′ tables, for microform readers.
7. 1 - vertical file.
8. 2 - book trucks.
9. 8 - sections of standard shelving.

Net Area Required—700 sq. ft.

Department Head's Office (an enclosed room).
1. 1 - 30″ × 60″ desk.
2. 1 - secretarial chair.
3. 2 - side chairs.
4. 1 - 3′ × 6′ table.
5. 1 - vertical file.
6. 5 - sections of wall-hung shelving.

Net Area Required—280 sq. ft.

Library Assistant/Typist (just outside of Dept. Head's Office).
1. 1 - 30″ × 60″ desk with typing L.
2. 1 - typing stand.
3. 2 - secretarial chairs.
4. 2 - side chairs.
5. 1 - 3′ × 6′ table.
6. 5 - sections of standard shelving.

Net Area Required—285 sq. ft.

Total Net Area Required for SErials Department—3,850 sq. ft.

35. RECEIVING AND SHIPPING DEPARTMENT

This Department includes the following areas:
1. Receiving and Sorting Area.
2. Delivery Equipment Area.
3. Supplies Order Area.
4. Sign Production Area.
5. Supplies Storage Room.
6. Stack Storage Room.
7. Furniture Storage Room.

Primary Function—To receive shipments of all kinds and disperse them to their Proper destination throughout the university library system (including Branch Libraries). To order supplies. To produce lettered signs on demand. To store supplies and equipment for issuance as needed.

Relationship to Other Facilities—Just inside the loading dock, not far from Acquisitions and Serials Department.

Special Requirements
    Outside windows
    Fluorescent lighting
    Heating/Ventilation/Air
    conditioning
    Acoustics—Normal
    Floors—tile

    Ceiling—Acoustic tile
    Communication Systems—Telephones

Other Design Considerations—Should have a windbreak vestibule to control cold, with a 6' wide rolling overhead door, as well as a normal 3' entrance door. Should have a wide door leading into the library.

Built-in Furniture and Equipment—Shelving in the Supplies Storage Room.

Movable Furniture and Equipment

Receiving and Sorting Area
1. 4 - 3' × 12' tables, 35" high.
2. 2 - high stools.

Net Area Required—325 sq. ft.

Delivery Equipment Area.
1. 10 - sections of standard wall-hung shelving, 12" shelves, to store empty shipping boxes and supplies for wrapping.
2. 1 - 3' × 6' truck.
3. 1 - two-wheel dolly.
4. 4 - book trucks.
5. 1 - 3-wheel bicycle delivery truck.
6. 1 - bicycle.
7. 50 - square feet of floor space for stacking cartons.

Net Area Required—265 sq. ft.

Supplies Order Area.
1. 1 - 30" × 60" desk with typing L.
2. 1 - secretarial chair.
3. 2 - vertical files.
4. 1 - side chair.

Net Area Required—120 sq. ft.

Sign Production Area.
1. 2 - tables 3' × 8' for sign production machines.

Net Area Required—120 sq. ft.

Supplies Storage Room.
1. Built-in shelves 18" deep, on 6' centers, from floor to ceiling, to house supplies.

Net Area Required—1,000 sq. ft.

Stack Storage Room.
    1. An unbroken room where stack uprights can be leaned against the wall, and dismantled shelves piled up.

Net Area Required—1,000 sq. ft.

Furniture Storage Room.
    1. An unbroken space for storing furniture not currently in use, but needed for changes in processes.

Net Area Required—500 sq. ft.

Total Net Area Required for Receiving and Shipping Department—3,330 sq. ft.

VII. *MISCELLANEOUS*

36. STAFF LOUNGE

Primary Function—To provide a pleasant, relaxing area for staff coffee breaks, lunches and dinner snacks for a staff that runs from 8 am to 12 pm. It should be as attractive as possible to diminish the number of local coffee brewing emporiums.

Relationship to Other Facilities—Can be anywhere in the building, so long as it is very pleasant. There is a great deal to be said for traversing floors to get to this area, since the change is part of the refreshing experience, so long as vertical transportation is adequate in the library.

Special Requirements

Outside windows	Ceiling—Acoustic tile
Fluorescent lighting	Utility services—Plumbing
Heating/Ventilation/Air conditioning	220 volt line
Acoustics — specially suppressed	
Floors—carpeting	

Other Design Considerations—None.

Built-in Furniture and Equipment—Service counter as detailed.

Movable Furniture and Equipment

Service Area (screened by a panel from the Seating Area).
    1. 1 - service counter, 2' × 20', with cupboards above and below.
    2. 1 - 3-burner electric range.
    3. 1 - refrigerator.
    4. 1 - sink, with cupboards below and mirror above.
    5. 5 - vending machines, 2' × 4'.

Net Area Required—245 sq. ft.

Seating Area.
1.   4 - 3′ × 3′ stacking tables for 4.
2.   2 - 3′ × 8′ tables for 6.
3. 24 - lounge chairs.
4.   4 - divans for 2.
5. 28 - side chairs for items 1 and 2.
6.   2 - sections of wall-hung shelving.
7.   Large wall-hung bulletin board just outside.

Net Area Required—1,355 sq. ft.

Total Net Area Required for Staff Lounge—1,600 sq. ft.

37. STAFF TOILETS

Primary Function and Secondary Function are clear.

Relationship to Other Facilities—Near the Staff Lounge, but should not open off of it.

Special Requirements
Separate exhaust
Coat hangers on each door
Mirrors above sinks.
Shelf above sinks, 10″ wide.
Full length mirror in women's toilet.

Built-in Furniture and Equipment
1. 4 - stools, or combination of stools and urinals.
2. 2 - sinks.
3. Large container for used towels.

Required: 1 for men and 1 for women @ 200 sq. ft. each

Net Area Required—400 sq. ft.

38. PUBLIC TOILETS

Relationship to Other Facilities—On main walkways, so they can be easily found.

Special Requirements—The same as for Staff Toilets.

Built-in Furniture and Equipment
1. 4 - stools, or combination of stools and urinals.
2. 2 - sinks.
3. Large container for used towels.

Required: 3 for men and 3 for women @ 200 sq. ft. each

Net Area Required—1,200 sq. ft.

39. CUSTODIAL ROOMS

We need one large custodial room for bulk supplies and large machines for the building—300 sq. ft.
We need one custodial room on each floor @ 100 sq. ft. Shelving and plumbing for these rooms will be specified by the Plant Department.

Net Area Required—600 sq. ft.

40. PUBLIC ELEVATORS

Two will be provided side by side within clear sight of the library entrance. They will be programmed as simply as possible to respond to pushbuttons on floors.

Area included in gross square footage.

41. STAFF ELEVATORS

Two will be provided side by side, near the sorting and shelving operation in the Circulation Department. They will be key operated.

Area included in gross square footage.

42. EXHIBITION WALLS

As the floor layout develops, we will identify walls along walkways that lend themselves to exhibition of graphic works. These walls will be supplied with special lighting to display exhibitions.

No Net Area Required.

43. BOOKDROPS

As the floor layout develops, we will designate locations for two bookdrops near the main entrance of the library, in an obvious location. Each will penetrate the outside wall and lead to a depressible bookdrop inside.

No Net Area Required.

44. PHOTOCOPY MACHINES

As the floor layout develops, we will indicate logical points in general space available near strategic locations in the library as locations for coin operated photocopy machines. Each will require an electrical outlet.

No Net Area Required.

INDEX